LAW, TRUTH, AND REASON

Law and Philosophy Library

VOLUME 97

For further volumes:
http://www.springer.com/series/6210

LAW, TRUTH, AND REASON

A Treatise on Legal Argumentation

Raimo Siltala

University of Turku, Finland

Springer

Raimo Siltala
Professor in Jurisprudence
Faculty of Law
Calonianjuja 3
20014 University of Turku
raimo.siltala@utu.fi

ISSN 1572-4395
ISBN 978-94-007-1871-5 e-ISBN 978-94-007-1872-2
DOI 10.1007/978-94-007-1872-2
Springer Dordrecht Heidelberg London New York

Library of Congress Control Number: 2011931967

Printed on acid-free paper

Springer is part of Springer Science+Business Media (www.springer.com)

Acknowledgments

I wish to thank the Faculty of Law at the University of Turku for its open-minded academic atmosphere and for providing me the funding and all the facilities I needed in writing this book. Also, I wish to thank the Faculty of Law at the University of Helsinki for kindly letting me use one of their workrooms during the research process while staying in Helsinki.

I wish to thank professor Aulis Aarnio and the late professor Neil MacCormick for initiating me to the path of philosophy and jurisprudence already some years ago.

I wish to thank my friends and colleagues at the joint reading circle and researcher seminar that started in 2005 with an analysis of Neil MacCormick's impressive works on jurisprudence. The project has been active ever since. Together, we have read some of the most prominent works on jurisprudence and legal philosophy today, and we even had the privilege of hearing each of the authors in person at the concluding seminar held in Finland: Neil MacCormick (in 2006), Ronald Dworkin (in 2008), and Robert Alexy (in 2010). Now, we are reading John R. Searle's philosophical works, hoping to have him as our guest of honor in 2012. Of my many friends in the group, I would like to name the 'Four Musketeers' here, i.e. Mikko Huuskonen, Matti Kunnas, Max Oker-Blom, and Ari Wirén, without forgetting the others.

I wish to thank the Series Editors at Springer for approving my manuscript in the esteemed *Law and Philosophy Library*. I think I am very fortunate in this, since one of my main sources of inspiration here, i.e. Jerzy Wróblewski's *The Judicial Application of Law*, was published in the very same series in 1992, then hosted by Kluwer Academic Publishers. I wish to thank Neil Olivier and Diana Nijenhuijzen at Springer for their prolific mastering of the legal and administrative issues involved. Moreover, I wish to thank Anandhi Bashyam and her team in India for their very skilful editorial and technical work in the process of transforming the manuscript into a book on legal reasoning.

Finally, I wish to thank my companion Tuija for her lasting love and passion for a man who all too often vanishes into the unknown of legal philosophy and jurisprudence; our two daughters Venla and Anna for reminding me that there is life outside the university, as well; and my parents Laura and Tatu for their unconditional love, encouragement, and support in all my life.

Contents

List of Diagrams

List of Tables

Chapter 1
Introduction

1.1 The Three Ideologies of Judicial Decision-Making by Jerzy Wróblewski

In his treatise *The Judicial Application of Law*, the Polish legal philosopher Jerzy Wróblewski (1926–1990) made the distinction between the three ideologies of *bound, legal and rational*, and *free* judicial decision-making.[1]

In Wróblewski's classification, the ideology of *bound* judicial decision-making refers to a strictly systemic, formal conception of law as a closed system of enactments issued by the Parliament and the legal rules entailed in them. With reference to the totality of such rules, the judge is able to determine the outcome for an individual case by adhering to the rules of purely formal, logico-deductive reasoning. The legal rule extracted from an item of legislation will then function as the major premise in a deductive inference, while the fact-constellation of the particular case at hand will provide the minor premise for it. The only legitimate source of law under such an austere conception of law is the sum total of the formally valid enactments issued by the Parliament. As Wróblewski put it[2]:

> The ideology of bound judicial decision-making has a very simple doctrine of the "sources" of law and it can be summarised briefly: the unique primary source of law is a statute in the formal sense of the term; decisions have to be based on statutory rules.

The ideology of bound judicial decision-making effectively reiterates the ideal of a purely mechanistic judge-automaton, stripped off of any powers of genuine legal interpretation, as suggested by Baron de Montesquieu. According to him, a judge cannot legitimately claim to be more than "a mouthpiece that reads the letter of the

[1] Wróblewski, *The Judicial Application of Law*, pp. 265–314.

[2] Wróblewski, *The Judicial Application of Law*, pp. 265–314; cf. Siltala, *A Theory of Precedent*, pp. 3–6. – Cf. Wróblewski, *Contemporary Models of the Legal Sciences*, p. 88 et seq., where the author introduces the distinction between the *traditional positivist*, the *modern positivist*, the *modern antipositivist*, and the *complex "integrative"* conceptions of legal science.

DOI 10.1007/978-94-007-1872-2_1,

law", i.e. a passive organ of law-application that cannot have access to such legal discretion as is entailed in legal interpretation.[3]

Ideologically, the ideology of bound legal decision-making fosters the two ideals of *political liberalism* that aims at safeguarding the inalienable rights of the individual against any intrusions by the state or other citizens, on the one hand, and *legal positivism*, on the other, with emphasis on the formal values of legal predictability and certainty at the cost of any content-based criteria of law. Thereby, the role of arbitrariness and personal whim on part of the judge is allegedly prevented. In the continental systems of law, the ideology of bound judicial decision-making is closely connected to the birth of national codifications of law.[4] Still, any at least temporarily locked up criterion may function as the required reference for bound legal discretion.

Georg Friedrich Puchta's master idea of a highly *constructivist* legal science (*Begriffsjurisprudenz*) that focused on an allegedly closed, gapless, and internally consistent system of legal concepts and their mutual relations as its subject matter would quite effortlessly satisfy Wróblewski's criteria for the ideology of bound judicial decision-making. Puchta's highbrow legal constructivism had a profound impact on the German legal doctrine at the late nineteenth century and the beginning of the twentieth century. Similarly, the case method introduced by Christopher Columbus Langdell and his like-minded followers, like James Barr Ames and Joseph Beale, could be classified under Wróblewski's ideology of bound legal decision-making. According to Langdell's methodological agenda, the American case law was to be collected under a few general principles, as duly identified by Langdell and his school of law.[5]

Neither Hans Kelsen's *Reine Rechtslehre*, where the systemic structure of the law is defined by reference to the transcendental-logical basic norm (*Grundnorm*), nor H. L. A. Hart's analytical jurisprudence, where the boundaries of the legal system vis-à-vis the norms of political morality, religion, etiquette, or any other social phenomena are drawn with the *Queen rule* of law-identification,[6] would qualify as an

[3]"Mais, si les tribunaux ne doivent pas être fixes, les jugements doivent lětre à une telle point, quils ne soient jamais quún texte précis de la loi. (...) Mais les juges de la nation ne sont, comme nous avont dit, que la bouche qui prononce les paroles de la loi; des êtres inanimés qui n'en peuvent modérer ni la force ni la rigueur." Montesquieu, *L'esprit des lois*, pp. 399, 404. – In the critical texts by American legal realists, the notion of a judge who is stripped from all law-creating power was soon coined a *slot-machine judge*.

[4]"The ideology of bound judicial decision-making presupposes some features of the law, viz. the positivistic conception of the codified law in statutory legal systems. The law is seen as a system which is consistent and complete, a set of rules according to which one can decide any legal case without going outside the system. For the law-applying organ the system is closed and can be changed only by the law-maker. The concept of codification is extrapolated on to all of law. The completeness of legal system, often attacked by the adversaries of positivism, is linked with liberty, legal certainty and legal security." Wróblewski, *The Judicial Application of Law*, p. 278.

[5]Duxbury, *Patterns of American Jurisprudence*, pp. 14–25.

[6]I.e.: "what the Queen in Parliament enacts is law in England". Hart, *The Concept of Law* (1961), e.g. pp. 99, 104, 108, 113, 117, 142, 145.

instance of Wróblewski's ideology of bound judicial decision-making. The reason thereto has to do with the inevitable margin of free discretion reserved for the judge in the both. Though Kelsen underscored the fact that there can be no other source for the law except for the law itself,[7] he nonetheless acknowledged the idea that legal rules do leave some margin of free discretion to the judge or other law-applying official.[8] Hart, on the other hand, pointed out how legal rules, like linguistic concepts, entail a core of settled meaning, on the one hand, and a penumbra of doubt, on the other, where several interpretations of the rule are possible.[9] As a consequence, Kelsen's and Hart's analytical jurisprudence is in need of a theory of legal interpretation that neither of them provided for.

The ideology of *free* judicial decision-making in Jerzy Wróblewski's catalogue refers to a loose-edged collection of movements or schools of legal thought that share (no more than) a critical stance vis-à-vis the legal formalism of the bound ideology of legal decision-making. Unlike the bound ideology that adheres to the ideal of the *Rechtsstaat*, strictly defined, the ideology of free judicial decision-making does not entail or even imply any coherent political or legal background ideology that would be shared by all of its proponents. Rather, there is a wide range of possible social and legal prerequisites involved. What holds the various manifestations of the ideology of free judicial decision-making together is a shared critical stance towards legal formalism. In consequence, the doctrine of the sources of law is extended to cover a wide range of other kind of legal source material in addition to legislation and its internal systematics that were the only sources acknowledged by Wróblewski's ideology of bound judicial decision-making. In addition, the models of legal reasoning to be adopted include more variation than merely deductive reasoning and logico-deductive inference recognized by the ideology of bound judicial decision-making.

According to François Gény, the judge ought to have recourse to free scientific research on the law and society (*libre recherche scientifique*), and then make the legal decision accordingly.[10] Similarly, the German Free Law Movement (*Freirechtslehre*; *Freirechtsbewegung*) underscored the role of legal intuition and the sense of justice (*Rechtsgefühl*) or the sense of values (*Wertfühlen*) prevalent in the community, rejecting any striving for such a formal, systemic idea of law that had prevailed in Germany at the late nineteenth and early twentieth century. Wróblewski even classifies the quasi-legal *Führerstaat* ideology of the National Socialist Germany of the 1930s under the ideology of free judicial decision-making.[11]

---

[7] "Denn es ist eine höchts bedeutsame Eigentümlichkeit des Rechts, daß es seine eigene Erzeugung und Anwendung regelt." Kelsen, *Reine Rechtslehre* (1960), p. 73; Cf. Kelsen, *Reine Rechtslehre* (1960), p. 239: "In einem positivrechtlichen Sinn kann Quelle des Rechts nur Recht sein."

[8] Kelsen, *Reine Rechtslehre* (1960), p. 250.

[9] Hart, *The Concept of Law* (1961), pp. 124–128.

[10] On François Gény as a legal thinker, cf. Bouckaert, "Gény, François (1861–1959)"; Bergel, *Méthodologie juridique*, pp. 249–253.

[11] Wróblewski, *The Judicial Application of Law*, pp. 285, 298.

In the United States, sociological jurisprudence at the end of the nineteenth and the beginning of the twentieth century,[12] and the American realist movement since the 1920s both laid heavy emphasis on the creative role of the judge in legal adjudication. Holmes even defined the concept of law with the legal expectations of the "bad man", i.e. a potential law-breaker who is only interested in foreseeing the legal consequences of his law-defiant action by the courts of justice or other officials.[13] John Chipman Gray, in turn, pointed out that formally valid legislation is no more than a source of law, i.e. raw material that the judge may draw upon when making a legal decision. It is only the final judicial verdict that counts as the law proper for Gray[14]:

> And this is the reason why legislative acts, statutes, are to be dealt with as sources of Law, and not as part of the Law itself, why they are to be coördinated with the other sources which I have mentioned. It has been sometimes said that the Law is composed of two parts, – legislative law and judge-made law, but, in truth, all the Law is judge-made law.

The ideology of free judicial decision-making downgrades the significance of formally valid legislation and, instead, defines the law as the "law in action", i.e. the totality of decisions given by the courts of justice and other law-applying officials, social norms of various kinds, and the set of social values in the legal community.[15] Rather than the formal values of legal security and the predictability of a legal decision, as were emphasized by the ideology of bound judicial decision-making, Wróblewski's ideology of free judicial decision-making underscores the importance of case-bound reasonableness, equity, and justice on an individual basis.

The third model in Wróblewski's catalogue of judicial ideologies, the ideology of *legal and rational* judicial decision-making, is said to refer to a compromise between the bound and free ideologies of judicial decision-making. It avoids the *ultra-rationalistic* fallacy of the bound alternative, to the effect that the decision to be made by the judge is not wholly determined beforehand, and it also avoids the *irrationalistic* fallacy committed by the free alternative, to the effect that the judge's decision is not entirely unbound and free-floating, either.[16] The judge's decision is less constrained by the legal sources than under the formally bound ideology of law-application, since there now is room for the use of judicial evaluations as "a necessary element of judicial heuresis and justification".[17] But, in contrast to the ideology of free judicial decision-making, the ideology of legal and rational judicial decision-making does not approve of judge-made law, i.e. the creation of general,

---

[12]Several justices approved the ideology of sociological jurisprudence, such as Louis Brandeis, Harlan Fiske Stone, Benjamin N. Cardozo, and Felix Frankfurter, besides Oliver Wendell Holmes.

[13]Holmes, "The Path of the Law", pp. 460–461.

[14]Gray, *The Nature and Sources of the Law*, p. 125.

[15]Wróblewski, *The Judicial Application of Law*, pp. 292–293.

[16]Wróblewski, *The Judicial Application of Law*, p. 306: "Legality is ultimately treated as a formal legality which accepts the consistency of the decision with the law in force. Rationality is defined as a proper justification of decisions with good reasons."

[17]Wróblewski, *The Judicial Application of Law*, p. 310.

abstract legal rules by the courts of justice, as detached from the will-formation of the parliamentary legislator.

The ideology of legal and rational judicial decision-making is intertwined with the two seminal principles of modern Western law, i.e. *ratio* and *auctoritas*, or the *formal legality* and *rational justifiability* of a legal decision.[18] They are like the two sides of the coin, the one presupposing the existence of the other.

The *legality* of judicial decision-making refers to the idea that the judge is bound by the rule of law, having to adhere to the set of arguments derived from the mandatory sources of law in his legal decision-making. The concept of formal legality may be taken as referring to the *institutional* sources of law, such as legislation, the *travaux préparatoires*, and precedents, along with the totality of rules and principles of law that can be derived from them. Wróblewski, for one, opted for an even stricter notion of law, since he excluded precedents and other judge-made law from the concept of the legal system.[19] In the wide sense, the requirement of legality may be taken to comprise all the *institutional* and *non-institutional*, i.e. societal, sources of law acknowledged in a legal system. Such a wider notion of legality will find a better accord with the concept of law that has been defended – on separate terms – by Alf Ross and Ronald Dworkin. If the concept of law is outlined so as to entail value-laden legal principles, as well, the criterion of formal legality must be defined accordingly.

The *rationality* of judicial decision-making, in turn, is equal to the requirement that legal decisions ought to be justified with a set of *epistemic* and *axiological* reasons.[20] Though Wróblewski does not present any particular legal source doctrine in the context of his three ideologies of judicial decision-making, the requirement of the judge's recourse to such epistemic and axiological reasons may be reformulated in terms of the institutional and non-institutional sources of law and the arguments drawn from them. Instead of the axiological and epistemic reasons, one could speak of the *norm premise* and the *fact premise* of a legal decision, respectively. The legality of a judicial decision is manifested by means of the rationality conditions of judicial decision-making.

Moreover, Wróblewski introduces the distinction between internal and external justification of a legal decision. *Internal* justification refers to the relation that prevails between the outcome of a case and the normative and factual premises presented in its support, to the effect that the outcome can be derived from the combination of the said norm premise and fact premise. The norm premise is derived

---

[18] Wróblewski, *The Judicial Application of Law*, pp. 307–311. On the two requirements of *ratio* and *auctoritas* in modern law, Bergholtz, *Ratio et auctoritas. Ett komparativrättsligt bidrag till frågan om domsmotiveringens betydelse främst i tvistemål*; Aarnio, *Reason and Authority. A Treatise on the Dynamic Paradigm of Legal Dogmatics*; Siltala, *A Theory of Precedent*, pp. 179–196.

[19] "The legal system is constituted by sufficiently general and abstract rules, but does not include individual law applying decisions and inter alia judicial decisions." Wróblewski, *The Judicial Application of Law*, p. 296.

[20] Cf.: "Rationality is defined as a proper justification of decisions with good reasons. This is contrasted with the non-rational decision which is badly justified and the irrational decision which gives no reasons at all." Wróblewski, *The Judicial Application of Law*, p. 306.

from the sources of law, while the fact premise signifies the legally material facts of the case. *External* justification, in turn, refers to the justification of the epistemic and axiological premises themselves with some criteria external to the decision made.

Wróblewski explores legal reasoning with the five *levels of justification* involved. The *internal* justification of a decision, as outlined in terms of a set of epistemic and axiological reasons given for the legal outcome reached, comprises the first level of justification. The *external* justification for the said epistemic and axiological premises of the first level of justification constitutes the second level of legal justification. The third level is equal to the *logic of justification* by means of which the adequacy and appositeness of the first two levels of justification can be appraised. The fourth level of justification consists of the identification of the *presuppositions* necessary for any justification of the first three levels. The fifth, final level of justification consists of the *ultimate premises* that justify or explain the justification attained on the four preceding levels.[21] Still, the exact character of those "ultimate" premises of legal justification is left unspecified by the eminent Polish legal philosopher.[22]

Wróblewski's three categories of judicial decision-making provide a solid ground for the further analysis of legal argumentation, but as such the classification is too crude and leaves too many issues unattended. What do the criteria of *legality* and *rationality* of a judicial decision signify, to be more precise? What is it that binds the judge's legal discretion, if his discretion is constrained by factors laid down by the ideology of bound judicial decision-making? How free is the judge in his discretion, if the ideology of free judicial decision-making is preferred? Though legally unbound, is the judge still constrained by some other, non-legal factors? Wróblewski's mid-range ideology of legal and rational decision-making would seem to be the most promising for analysis, but how can the semantic values of an assertion on the construction and interpretation of law be specified, in terms of its truth-value and a specific meaning-content? The advice of just following a "legal and rational" procedure does not lead us very far here, if the underlying premises of legality and rationality are not spoken out.

1.2 The Three Situations of Legal Decision-Making by Kaarle Makkonen

In his treatise *Zur Problematik der juridischen Entscheidung. Eine strukturanalytische Studie*, Kaarle Makkonen (1923–2000) analysed the legal discretion of the judge or any other law-applying official in a manner that is highly reminiscent of Jerzy

[21] Wróblewski, *The Judicial Application of Law*, pp. 210–211. Cf. Siltala, *A Theory of Precedent*, pp. 215–216.

[22] I tackled the issue of the ultimate premises of law under Hans Kelsen's, H. L. A. Hart's, and Jerzy Wróblewski's analytical legal positivism by introducing the notion of the *infrastructures* of law in Siltala, *A Theory of Precedent*, pp. 34–39, 229–231, 255–260, 264–267.

Wróblewski's classification above.[23] Makkonen made the distinction between three different legal decision-making situations[24]:

(a) An *isomorphic* situation, where no act of legal interpretation in the proper sense of the term is required from the judge, due to the "clear and self-evident" character of the norm to be applied to the facts of the case.
(b) A *semantically vague* situation, where recourse to the semantics and methodology of legal interpretation is required from the judge due to the semantically open-ended, ambiguous character of the norm to be applied to the case at hand.
(c) A legally *unregulated* situation, where there is no legal norm available in the legal system that would have some normative bearing on the case at hand.

For the first, in an *isomorphic* situation, there is a *picture relation* between the two types of facts involved, i.e. the ones existing in the world and the ones depicted in the fact-description of some legal norm. As Makkonen put it[25]:

> For the first, we may be dealing with such a clear and patently obvious case that the applicable legal norm is immediately evident to the decision-making authority. The relation that prevails between the given facts and the facts in a legal norm is like the one between a picture and the object depicted. Of such a case, I will use the term an *isomorphic situation*.

In the case of the isomorphic situation of legal decision-making, Makkonen still introduces the classification on whether the legal norm allows only one legal consequence or whether there are several legal consequences available among which the judge may then select one. If there is only one conceivable legal consequence permitted by the norm, we are confronted with a simple case of isomorphism. Legal reasoning then follows the *syllogistic* model of logical deduction, where the enforcement of the legal consequence(s) is brought into effect by force of the existence of an isomorphic relation between the two fact-descriptions concerned and the valid rules of inference of deductive reasoning.[26]

Though legal isomorphism requires that the legal norm be entirely unequivocal and unambiguous as to its semantic meaning-content, it may still leave open a choice

---

[23]Makkonen's *Zur Problematik der juridischen Entscheidung* was published in 1965, Wróblewski's *The Judicial Application of Law* in 1992, so Makkonen was ahead of Wróblewski in time. In English the title of Makkonen's book would be: *On the Problematics of a Legal Decision-Making. A Study in Structural Analytics.*

[24]Makkonen, *Zur Problematik der juridischen Entscheidung*, p. 78 et seq. In the German original the situations of legal decision-making are as follows: *Isomorphiesituation, Auslegungssituation, ungeregelte Situation.*

[25]Makkonen, *Zur Problematik der juridischen Entscheidung*, pp. 78–79: "... kann es sich um einen so klaren und allseitig deutlich gestalteten Fall handeln, dass die anzuwendende Rechtsnorm der entscheidenden Instanz ohne weiteres sofort bekannt ist. Zwischen den gegebenen Tatsachen und den im Rechtsnormsatz dargestellten Tatsachen herrscht dann das Verhältnis des Abzubildenden zum Bilde. Wir gebrauchen für eine derartige Lage die Benennung *Isomorphiesituation*." (Italics by Makkonen; translation by the present author.)

[26]Makkonen, *Zur Problematik der juridischen Entscheidung*, pp. 79, 84–97.

within a range of feasible legal consequences for the judge. Makkonen illustrates the issue with the norms of criminal law that may leave open the choice between, say, a fine or imprisonment, and also the exact quantity of punishment to be inflicted upon the offender within the type of punishment chosen. As the court of justice needs to make a value-laden choice as to the exact legal consequences to be inflicted upon the offender from among the range of alternative legal sanctions, the model of deductive reasoning will not suffice here.

In addition, the judge may be confronted with a situation of norm conflict of two or more legal norms, both or all of which cannot be satisfied at the same time, while each norm equally stands in an isomorphic relation with respect to the facts existing in the world. That, too, is an instance of isomorphism, despite the dilemma of having to make a choice between the two or more legal norms available. The settled rules for solving a norm conflict will then be applied, such as *lex superior derogat legi inferiori*, i.e. a hierarchically superior legal norm supersedes a hierarchically lower norm,[27] *lex posterior derogat legi priori*, i.e. a subsequent legal norm supersedes a prior norm, or *lex specialis derogat legi generali*, i.e. a more specific legal norm supersedes a more general norm.[28] If the norm collision cannot be resolved by means of such formal collision norms, the judge then needs to make a value-laden choice among the two (or more) norms available.[29]

For the second, in a *semantically uncertain* or *unclear* situation of legal decision-making, recourse to the methods and canons of legal interpretation is required from the judge, since there is no isomorphic relation that could be affirmed for the case under investigation. Any would-be isomorphic relation between the two fact-constellations has become too "thin" so as to count as no more than an approximate relation of partial affinity between the two fact-situations, due to the linguistic vagueness of the norm or the lack of a corresponding state of affairs in the world. In such a case, though the judge is able to identify the norm that most likely applies to the fact-situation at hand, the application of the norm to the facts yet necessitates a semantic analysis and elucidation of the linguistic expressions entailed in the norm.[30] An act of legal interpretation is, in other words, required.

Makkonen makes a division into two different cases of where, firstly, there is only one legal norm to be applied to the facts of the case, and secondly, where the judge has to make a choice between two or more legal norms that equally apply to the facts at hand. In both situations, the judge's decision requires an act of legal interpretation in the sense of *giving*, or *ascribing*, a specific meaning-content to the particular linguistic expressions entailed in the norm formulation, instead of merely

---

[27]The meta-level conflict resolution norm *lex superior derogat legi inferiori* presupposes a settled norm hierarchy within the legal systems, as suggested by e.g. Adolf Julius Merkl and Hans Kelsen.

[28]Makkonen, *Zur Problematik der juridischen Entscheidung*, p. 95.

[29]Makkonen, *Zur Problematik der juridischen Entscheidung*, p. 95: "In der Praxis besteht also die Tätigkeit dessen, der die Entscheidung zu treffen hat, in der Widerspruchssituation hauptsächlich darin, dass er aufgrund von Gründen, die von ihm erwogen werden, die eine der beiden widersprüchlichen Bestimmungen zur Grundlage seiner Entscheidung wählt." (Italics in original.)

[30]Makkonen, *Zur Problematik der juridischen Entscheidung*, pp. 79, 97–122.

discovering the "true" meaning of the legal norm somewhere "out there" in the pre-ordered domain of legal semantics.[31] The interpretation of law, in other words, necessitates an active *act of will* on part of the institutional decision-maker entrusted with that task, exceeding the limits of a mere passive (re)cognition of the contents of the law.

As grounds for legal construction and interpretation, Makkonen refers to the well-settled arguments as commonly adopted in the legal community, such as the original intentions of the legislator and the social conditions prevalent at the time of issuing the item of legislation, with reference to the traces of *occasio legis* and *ratio legis* found in the official *travaux préparatoires* and the like documents. Makkonen also refers to the social, economic, cultural, technological, and political factors that exerted influence on the individual item of legislation concerned, reminiscent of the extra-legal considerations that had previously been recommended for the normative gap situations by Otto Brusiin in the Finnish literature on jurisprudence.[32] When the legal norm to be applied entails value-laden concepts, the choice among the alternatives is in the last resort dependent on the social preferences of the judge concerned.[33] It would seem that Makkonen does not quite exhaust the array of *institutional* and *societal* sources of law before turning to the personal preferences of the judge concerned.

For the third, in an *unregulated* situation of legal decision-making, there is no legal norm available in the legal system that could be applied to the case, and no such norm can be found even after the kind of legal construction work that is required from the judge in a semantically vague situation of legal decision-making.[34] We are thus confronted with a legal gap situation. The emergence of a normative gap in the legal system may have been induced by some unexpected breakthrough in the technological or scientific evolution or by some unforeseen change in the social settings of law, resulting in a situation where legislation (and jurisdiction) decisively lag behind the state of affairs in society. In some cases, the existence of a legally unregulated situation may be due to a deliberate legislative policy by the Parliament, with the intention of leaving some branch of social life to be covered by the settled conventional usages and practices among the professionals of the field concerned.[35]

According to the established doctrine, there is a legal gap in a legal system if some actual or merely hypothetical fact-situation is not covered by any of legal norms of the legal system concerned, with reference to the totality of norms that can be derived from the commonly acknowledged sources of law by means of

---

[31] Makkonen, *Zur Problematik der juridischen Entscheidung*, pp. 118, 131.

[32] Makkonen, *Zur Problematik der juridischen Entscheidung*, pp. 103–104.

[33] Makkonen, *Zur Problematik der juridischen Entscheidung*, p. 105.

[34] Makkonen, *Zur Problematik der juridischen Entscheidung*, pp. 79, 122–140. – Cf. Brusiin, *Tuomarin harkinta normin puuttuessa*, pp. 204–229, where Brusiin stresses the role of social scientific knowledge, if there is no legal norm that would guide the legal discretion of the judge. In English Brusiin's thesis would be: *The Discretion of the Judge in the Absence of a Legal Norm* (1938).

[35] Makkonen, *Zur Problematik der juridischen Entscheidung*, pp. 126–127.

legal reasoning. The definition of the legal system and the definition of a normative gap situation are therefore mutually interlocked. If the concept of a legal system is defined with sole reference to e.g. the institutional sources of law, the notion of a legal gap is defined accordingly. Under the notion of *law as integrity* as envisioned by Ronald Dworkin, where the totality of the legal rules and principles in a legal system constitute "a seamless web of reasons" for the judge's legal decision-making,[36] there would be no conceptual room left for normative gaps, since the normative space is in its entirety occupied by those legal principles, each with a situationist normative impact of its own.

Makkonen points out that the borderline between a semantically ambiguous situation and an unregulated situation of legal decision-making is soft-edged and open to a diversity of different interpretations.[37] In a legally unregulated situation, the judge will need to have recourse to legal *analogy* whereby the field of application of some legal norm is analogically extended so as to cover the novel case at hand as well, or, if there is no ground for such legal analogy, to the technique of *e contrario* reasoning whereby the normative impact of some would-be pertinent legal norm is rejected for the case at hand.[38] In his treatise *Tuomarin harkinta normin puuttuessa*, Otto Brusiin had effectively argued that in a situation of normative gap the judge ought to have wide recourse to the results obtained by the (other) social sciences, such as the economics, political science, and sociology, in considering the consequences of legal interpretation in society.[39] Unlike Brusiin, Makkonen does not address the social consequences of law in a normative gap situation. It seems that Makkonen follows the methodological precepts of analytical jurisprudence here, while Brusiin was more receptive to the ideas of legal phenomenology and sociological jurisprudence.

Wróblewski's and Makkonen's analysis of legal argumentation is intertwined with the issues of linguistics and semantics, as is commonplace with the texts of analytical jurisprudence. In fact, they would both seem to follow the common division of linguistic studies into the three parts of the *syntax*, *semantics*, and *pragmatics* of language. Wróblewski's ideology of *bound* judicial decision-making and Makkonen's *isomorphic* situation of legal decision-making both deal with the *syntax* of legal language. Wróblewski's ideology of *legal and rational*

---

[36] "The law may not be a seamless web; but the plaintiff is entitled to ask Hercules to treat it as if it were. (. . .) [Judge Hercules] must construct a scheme of abstract and concrete principles that provides a coherent justification for all common law precedents and, so far as these are to be justified on principle, constitutional and statutory provisions as well." Dworkin, *Taking Rights Seriously*, pp. 116–117.

[37] "It is as hard to say of the spectrum where the area of the blue ends and that of the violet begins, as it is to say of the "spectrum" of legal decision-making where the realm of legal construction ends and that of legal analogy begins." Makkonen, *Zur Problematik der juridischen Entscheidung*, p. 135. (Translation by the present author.)

[38] Makkonen, *Zur Problematik der juridischen Entscheidung*, pp. 131–132.

[39] Brusiin, *Tuomarin harkinta normin puuttuessa*, pp. 204–229, and esp. pp. 220–225 (on sociology), pp. 225–226 (on political science), and pp. 226–227 (on economics).

judicial decision-making and Makkonen's *semantically ambiguous* situation of legal decision-making are both mostly associated with issues that deal with the *semantics* of legal language. Finally, Wróblewski's *ideology of free judicial* decision-making and Makkonen's *unregulated* situation of legal decision-making are both aligned with the *pragmatics* of legal language, transcendenting the limits of linguistic analysis for social value considerations. Besides Makkonen's and Wróblewski's jurisprudence, modern semantics by Frege and Carnap constitutes the theoretical basis of the present treatise.

1.3 The Subject Matter of the Treatise: Legal Argumentation, or How to Construct and Read the Law in a Reasoned Manner

Jerzy Wróblewski's bound, legal and rational, and free ideologies of judicial decision-making and Kaarle Makkonen's isomorphic, semantically ambiguous, and unregulated situations of legal decision-making provide a solid ground for the analysis of the judge's legal discretion. Still, Wróblewski's and Makkonen's insights need to be further elaborated so as to gain a more detailed picture of the issue.

In Makkonen's theory of law, an isomorphic situation between the two fact-constellations, the one as specified in a legal rule and the other as prevalent or at least possible in the world, is given logico-conceptual priority vis-à-vis the two other situations of legal decision-making discerned, since the semantically ambiguous and the unregulated situation of judicial decision-making are defined by the *absence* of an isomorphic relation between the fact-constellations. But, to be more precise, what does it mean to say that there exists an *isomorphic* relation between the two fact-constellations? What is the relation of Wróblewski's three ideologies of judicial decision-making and Makkonen's three legal decision-making situations to the *institutional* and non-institutional, i.e. *societal*, sources of law and the social values entailed in them? As I see it, Wróblewski's and Makkonen's seminal ideas need to be read in the context of the *legal source doctrine* and the canons of *legal methodology* acknowledged in the legal community so as to gain a sharper picture of the constraints placed upon the judge's legal discretion.

In the present treatise, Wróblewski's and Makkonen's initial frame of legal analysis will be elaborated with the ten *frames of legal analysis* discerned, each with a distinct criterion, or a set of mutually converging criteria, for judging the methods and outcome of legal argumentation. In this, the philosophical *theories of truth*, like the correspondence theory, the coherence theory, and the array of pragmatist theories of truth, will provide for the initial reference for analysis, to be complemented by a set of other approaches with possibly a better grasp of the institutional characteristics of law.

After giving a general outline of the premises of legal argumentation, the scope of analysis will be tackled with the tools provided by modern semantics, i.e. Gottlob Frege's distinction of the *reference* and *sense* of a linguistic sign or expression and Rudolf Carnap's parallel method of *extension* and *intension*. The two semantic properties of a linguistic sentence are accordingly defined as the *truth-value* (reference/Frege; extension/Carnap) and specific *meaning-content* (sense/Frege; intension/Carnap) of the sentence. In the context of law we are dealing with the semantic properties of an assertion on how to construct and read the law vis-à-vis some specific fact-constellation.

At the end of the treatise, a systematic account will be given of some of the major philosophical issues of legal argumentation theory, viz. the truth-value of a legal assertion as conditional upon, and determined by, the particular frame of analysis adopted; the metaphysical "nuts and bolts" in the legal universe, as analysed under the three categories of the logical constitution, normative ontology, and structural axiology of law; and a systemic "order of things" in a set of legal rules and legal principles, as first judged in light of Carlos Alchourrón's and Eugenio Bulygin's conception of (the outcome of) legal systematics and (the process of) legal systematization and as then extended to comprise the subject matter in more general terms as a complex priority order for the rule/rule, principle/principle, and rule/principle combinations in a legal system.

The present treatise seeks to give a concise outline of the seminal issues of *how to construct and read the law* under the ten frames of legal analysis discerned, from legal isomorphism to radical decisionism in legal decision-making. The first objective of how to *construct* the law refers to the act of *identifying* the law and legal phenomena from among the phenomena in society, and *determining* their mutual relations in a complex *priority order* for the rule/rule, principle/principle, and rule/principle combinations that may emerge in a legal system. The second objective of how to *read* the law refers to the act of *ascribing* a specific meaning-content to the legal rules and legal principles so constructed vis-à-vis a specific fact-constellation, as either actually prevalent in the world or as produced by the imagination of a legal scholar. The present treatise is a contribution to the *legal argumentation theory*, approaching the issue from the point of view of *analytical jurisprudence* and drawing its major inspiration from Jerzy Wróblewski's and Kaarle Makkonen's main works. The other methodological path followed is modern semantics, as outlined by Gottlob Frege and Rudolf Carnap.

1.4 The Concept of a Frame of Legal Analysis

A frame of legal analysis is a *scheme of interpretation* that makes it possible to *identify* and *discern* the legal phenomena from among the other phenomena in society, no matter whether they are deemed to belong to the domain of political morality, economics, religion, societal etiquette, arts and crafts, sports and play, or some other field of life. A frame of legal analysis is equal in function to Hans Kelsen's and Alf Ross' seminal idea of the *scheme of interpretation* adopted for the identification and interpretation of law.[40] In specific, the frame of legal analysis

[40] In German: *Deutungschema*; in Danish: *tydningsskema*. Kelsen, *Reine Rechtslehre* (1960), s. 3 et seq.; Ross, *Om ret og retfærdighed*, pp. 56–57; Ross, *On Law and Justice*, p. 43.

as here intended provides a reference for judging the *semantic qualities* of a legal sentence or assertion, defined as its *truth-value* (reference/Frege; extension/Carnap) and specific *meaning-content* (sense/Frege; intension/Carnap). A *legal sentence* is a syntactically correctly formulated assertion on how to construct and read the law vis-à-vis some given fact-constellation x as prevalent or at least possible in the world.

Truth is a *semantic* quality, defined as a relation of correspondence, or mutual match, between a linguistic assertion and a state of affairs in the world, according to the *correspondence* theory of truth; or a quality that is applied to the mutually converging relations in a set of linguistic expressions, according to the *coherence* theory of truth; or a quality that has to do with warranted assertability, empirical testability, or expediency of an idea or conception in explaining and predicting the phenomena in the world, according to the *pragmatic* theory of truth. If the notion of truth as defined in the philosophical literature is deemed too demanding for the analysis of legal argumentation, some softened-down version of it might by adopted instead, such as the *rightness*, *adequacy*, *acceptability*, *correctness*, *appositeness*, or *warranted assertability* of the proposition in question. Without having access to *some* such frame of legal analysis and the criteria for judging the semantic qualities of the legal sentence concerned, no consistent account of legal argumentation could be given, either.

A frame of legal analysis determines a criterion, or a set of converging criteria, for judging the method and outcome of legal argumentation, as conducted by the judge or a legal scholar. There are at least ten frames of legal analysis that a theory of legal argumentation ought to account for:

(1) *Isomorphic Theory of Law*: an isomorphic, picture relation of structural similarity prevails between the two states of affairs compared, the one as given in the fact-constellation of a legal rule and the other as prevalent in the world.
(2) *Coherence Theory of Law*: mutual congruence and reciprocal support among the arguments drawn from the institutional and societal sources of law, like the notion of *legal integrity* in Ronald Dworkin's theory of law.
(3) *Societal Approval/The New Rhetoric*: approval or disapproval of the methods and outcome of legal argumentation in the intended *universal audience*, as outlined by Aristotle and Chaïm Perelman.
(4) *Philosophical Pragmatism (sensu stricto)/Social Consequentialism*: external consequences of law in society, as judged in light of the (other) human or social sciences, such as economic analysis of law.
(5) *Subjective Interpretation/Legal Exegesis*: retracing the *original intentions* of the legislator or a court of justice, as reconstructed from the law text and the *travaux préparatoires* at the back of it or the justificatory reasons given in support of a precedent.
(6) *Objective Interpretation/Analytical Legal Realism*: law as the (in past) effected and the (in future) enforceable judicial decisions, with reference to the totality of legal rights and duties that enjoy effective legal protection by courts and other legal officials.

(7) *Philosophical Conventionalism*: common *acceptance* or *recognition* of certain well-settled practices and usages in the community as having legal significance, or a set of *mutual expectations* and *cooperative dispositions* to the said effect in the community.
(8) *Legal Formalism*: the law as defined by certain logico-conceptual and systemic criteria of law, as defined by Georg Friedrich Puchta's legal constructivism in Germany and Christopher Columbus Langdell's case method in the United States.
(9) *Natural Law Philosophy*: law as a part of (absolute) social justice, as defined by the norms of religious, social, or political morality.
(10) *Radical Decisionism*: social justice on a strictly contextual, *ad hoc* basis, in denial of any meta-theory, meta-narrative, or meta-context of the law and society.

Each frame of analysis is like a lens through which the law and its key semantic qualities can be observed and critically evaluated. Without first presuming the presence of the constitutive criteria of *some* such frame of analysis, the legal phenomena could not be outlined in the first place. Each frame of analysis depicts the law in a different light, highlighting the role of some qualities and downplaying the role of others. Moreover, it is only in light of some such frame of analysis that the semantic qualities of a legal assertion, i.e. its *truth-value* and *meaning-content*, can be determined.

1.5 The Theories of Truth and Legal Analysis

In her treatise *Law without Truth*, the Italian scholar Anna Pintore puts forth the argument to the effect that the notion of truth cannot be extended to the law.[41] In that she is of course right, since her claim, so it seems, concerns the *ontology* of law, and not the *semantics* of linguistic assertions on how to construct and read the law.

The two categories of the *metaphysical* or *ontological* domain of legal norms, objects, "things", or entities, on the one hand, and the *linguistic* or *semantic* domain of assertions on how to construct and read the law, on the other, need to be distinguished from each other. The realm of law as a collection of legal rules and legal principles, and the institutional and non-institutional sources of law from which they are extracted, cannot carry the quality of being true or being false, since truth is a *semantic* quality that can only be applied to linguistic propositions or assertions, not to legal norms or other ontological entities as such. Here, the relation between law and truth is taken in the semantic sense, and not in the "metaphysical" or ontological sense adopted by Pintore. Therefore, it seems her critique will not affect my account of the semantics of legal argumentation.

[41] Pintore, *Law Without Truth*, esp. pp. 237–24.

In traditional philosophical analysis, there are three theories that predominate the truth-theoretical discourse: the *correspondence* theory, the *coherence* theory, and the *pragmatic* theories of truth.[42] In the context of law and legal analysis, the notion of *truth* may yet have to be slightly modified so as to gain a better grasp of the *institutional* character of the phenomena under consideration. That, however, will not affect my basic argument to the effect that a legal assertion on how to construct and read the law does obtain the quality of "true" or "untrue" by force of the semantic preconditions laid down by the frame of analysis adopted.

The *correspondence theory of truth* defines truth as an isomorphic relation of structural similarity between a certain linguistic expression and the corresponding phenomena or states of affairs in the world. The most noteworthy examples of such a truth-theoretical notion are Ludwig Wittgenstein's picture theory of language, as entailed in his *Tractatus Logico-Philosophicus*, and Alfred Tarski's semantic theory of truth. Wittgenstein defined the truth as a *picture relation* between language and the world. Below, I will argue that Wittgenstein's idea such a picture relation between language and the world can be applied in the legal context, as well, to the effect of shedding some bright light on the notion of an *isomorphic* relation entailed in Kaarle Makkonen's *Zur Problematik der juridischen Entscheidung*.

The *coherence theory of truth* rejects the idea of truth as an isomorphic, picture-like relation between a linguistic expression and a state of affairs in the world.[43] The reason is simple and rather easy to accept: we have no *epistemic shortcut* or a somehow privileged access to the phenomena "out there" without first having resort to the epistemic and logico-conceptual edifice that constitutes the prevalent world-view or "order of things" in the world (*épistémè*). Nor can there be any reliable knowledge of the relation that prevails between language and the world. All knowledge we may have of the phenomena in the world is conveyed to us through the conceptual categories of language. There is no escape from the prison house of language,[44] no matter how hard the advocates of the correspondence theory of truth wished for one.

To affirm the presence or absence of an isomorphic relation between a linguistic expression and the corresponding state of affairs in the world would necessitate having to step outside the domain of meaningful linguistic usage and to say what is unsayable, according to the unyielding methodological *credo* of Wittgenstein's *Tractatus Logico-Philosophicus*. Such metaphysical assertions could not satisfy the master criterion of sustaining a picture-like relation vis-à-vis some state of affairs in the world, as Wittgenstein and the logical positivists were soon to realize.

Even if the *definition* of truth were outlined by the correspondence theory, the *criteria* of truth may need to be adjusted to the requirements justified by the coherence theory. The coherence theory of truth and knowledge underscores the

---

[42]On Pintore's account of the said theories, plus the common distinction between the definition (or meaning) and the criteria of truth, Pintore, *Law without Truth*, p. 21 et seq.

[43]On the coherence theory of truth as seen from a philosophical point of view, cf. Walker, *The Coherence Theory of Truth. Realism, Anti-Realism, Idealism.*

[44]Cf. Pears, *The False Prison. A Study of the Development of Wittgenstein's Philosophy, Vols I–II.*

mutual relations of support that linguistic assertions have vis-à-vis one another. As Otto Neurath put it[45]:

> *Assertions are to be compared with assertions*, not with "experiences" or with a world, or with anything else. All of these senseless *duplications* belong in a more or less refined metaphysics and are therefore unacceptable. Each new assertion will be contrasted with the totality of those available assertions that have already been brought into harmony with each other. *An assertion is called "correct" when it can be incorporated* into this totality.

Perfectly coherent fairy-tales and other fiction tales, like the twisted reality in *Alice's Adventures in Wonderland* and *Through the Looking-Glass* or the fantasy world in J. K. Rowling's books on Harry Potter, might well satisfy even the strictest criteria of internal textual coherence, if the impact of any incoherence-inducing assertions, such as the ones produced by the natural sciences, are ruled out of consideration. The intended context of the assertions whose truth-value is to be evaluated has a crucial impact on the judgment of truth or falsity of any assertions: are we dealing with the game of *quidditch* and other oddities that twist the laws of the physics, as might take place within the stone walls of the *Hogwarts School of Witchcraft and Wizardry* in Rowling's world of imagination, or are we dealing with the more common everyday world of ours where the laws of gravity and causation have a more even grip on the phenomena?

A *pragmatic* approach to the truth covers a host of philosophical positions that all share a critique of the traditional theories of truth and knowledge. Rejecting both the correspondence theory and coherence theory of truth, the pragmatists attach the criteria of true knowledge in the approval or disapproval of any would-be true beliefs, conceptions, or assertions by the scientific or other pertinent community, on the other hand, and in the external, verifiable effects of such beliefs, on the other. Philosophical pragmatism has been a source of inspiration for a down-to-earth *consequentialist* conception of law that gives priority to the economic and other consequences of law in society. Moreover, the notion of human knowledge and argumentation based on the Aristotelian idea of *rhetoric* (and *topic*) has close affinity to the ideas of pragmatism so defined. The same goes for legal or social *conventionalism* with its emphasis on the acceptance or recognition of some societal practices and usages by the ones concerned.

Under philosophical pragmatism, the *consensus theory of truth* places the emphasis on the relation that an assertion has to a wider set of beliefs that are commonly acknowledged as true, or rather *warranted*, at the community. Thus, *warranted assertability* or similar criteria now replace the ones adopted by the correspondence or coherence theory of truth. Since it is always the scientific or other community that has the final say on the claimed truth or falsity of a belief, conception, or

---

[45] Neurath, "Soziologie im Physikalismus", p. 403 (italics by Neurath), cited in Coffa, *The Semantic Tradition from Kant to Carnap*, p. 365. Cf. Neurath, "Protocol Sentences", p. 201: "*There is no way of taking conclusively established pure protocol sentences as the starting point of the sciences*. No *tabula rasa* exists." (Italics in original.)

assertion, the correspondence and the coherence theory go equally astray in not paying attention to the community-aligned tenets inherent of all human knowledge.

Still, the scientific community as the collective subject of human knowledge may be totally mistaken as to some item of knowledge, as the transition from the earth-centred, religious world-view to the sun-centred planetary system at the beginning of the seventeenth century bears witness of. According to Galileo Galilei, the earth revolves around the sun and not the other way round, to the effect of removing earth from the centre of the universe. As is well known, the Church as assisted by the Italian and Spanish Inquisition tried hard to prevent the inevitable switch from the deeply religious mediaeval world-view to the secular, scientific conception of the world on the verge of the modern era, ultimately losing the battle over the criteria of scientific knowledge.[46]

The *new rhetoric*, based on Aristotle's philosophy of rhetorical reasoning as re-discovered in the late 1950s by Chaïm Perelman,[47] brought the notion of the *audience* of legal, moral, or political argumentation back to the focus of interest in philosophy and jurisprudence. Perelman's and thereby Aristotle's ideas of rhetoric were widely adopted in legal argumentation theory since the late-1970s by Neil MacCormick, Robert Alexy, Aleksander Peczenik, Aulis Aarnio, Jerzy Wróblewski, and by the research group *Bielefelder Kreis*.[48] The approval or disapproval of the methodology and the outcomes of legal reasoning at the universal audience has a seminal role in any rhetorical enterprise in law and legal analysis, bearing witness of the impact of philosophical pragmatism in it.

Knowledge of the world under philosophical pragmatism is defined as the *warranted assertability* of a belief or assertion. Pragmatism takes the collected *empirically observable consequences* of a scientific idea or conception as decisive vis-à-vis its truth-value. As William James insightfully put it[49]:

> Pragmatism, on the other hand, asks its usual question. "Grant an idea or belief to be true," it says, "what concrete difference will its being true make in any one's actual life? How will the truth be realized? What experiences will be different from those which would obtain if the belief were false? What, in short, is the truth's cash value in experiential terms?" – The moment pragmatism asks this question, it sees the answer: *True ideas are those that we can validate, corroborate and verify. False ideas are those that we can not.* That is the practical difference it makes to us to have true ideas; that, therefore, is the meaning of truth, for it is all that truth is known as.

---

[46] Giordano Bruno was burnt as a heretic on the Campo dei Fieri in Rome in 1600. Galileo Galilei (1564–1642), threatened by the Inquisition, was forced to deny his claim to the effect that the earth revolves round its axis and circles round the sun, and not the other way round as the Church had it.

[47] Perelman and Olbrechts-Tyteca, *Traité de l'Argumentation. La nouvelle Rhétorique*, passim.

[48] The international research group *Bielefelder Kreis* was active in the 1980s and 1990. It produced two reference works in the field of comparative legal argumentation theory: *Interpretation Statutes. A Comparative Study* (1991) and *Interpretation Precedents. A Comparative Study* (1997). In fact, Neil MacCormick, Robert Alexy, Aleksander Peczenik, Aulis Aarnio, and Jerzy Wróblewski all belonged to it, along with other high-ranking scholars associated with the analytical and rhetorical approach to the law and legal argumentation theory.

[49] James, "Pragmatism's Conception of Truth", p. 142. (Italics in original.)

The idea of *truth as verifiability*, as collected empirical evidence that can be presented in support of a scientific assertion, defines the core of philosophical pragmatism, strictly defined. The issue can also be phrased in terms of the observable consequences that are realized if the contested assertion turns out to be true. In the legal context, the gist of pragmatic philosophy has given birth to a *consequentialist* doctrine where the external effects of law in society are given prime importance. The *economic* effects of law in society have thereby gained weight. Still, the pragmatist notion of truth as warranted assertability and empirical verifiability under James' request of "what concrete difference will its being true make in any one's actual life" cannot claim title over the entire area covered by the natural sciences, as Moore and Wittgenstein have pointed out with reference to the ultimate grounds of knowledge. Besides, assertions in the field of the human and social sciences induce difficulties of their own kind in this regard, due to the inherently constructive and contested character of many of the key concepts entailed, such as democracy, the rule of law, state sovereignty, due diligence, fair trial, and equity.

Empirical observation sentences are of the type: "(I know that) the cat is on the mat", "It is snowing in the Alps now", or "The rain in Spain stays mainly in the plain". Whether they are true or not can be empirically tested, corroborated, verified, or falsified by empirical observations, i.e. the collected sense data available to us. Yet, how could we test the following propositions that patently assert something of the world, yet fail to yield to the test of such empirical observations: "I *know* that the earth existed long before my birth",[50] "I *know* that my body has never disappeared and reappeared again after an interval",[51] and "I *know* that I have never been on the moon"?[52]

According to Moore and Wittgenstein alike, such "quasi-empirical" propositions fall outside the domain of empirically testable knowledge, of reasonable doubt, and propositional truth-value, because they are – phrasing the issue in different terms – the fixed ground of the prevailing form of life, a system of pre-propositional "knowledge" (in a weak sense of the term) that is silently presupposed in all empirical propositions concerning the world, or the end points of a line of philosophical argumentation.[53] The epistemic and semantic quality of truth or untruth cannot be extended to the very grounding prerequisites of human knowledge, as Georg Henrik von Wright has pointed out.[54] They are aligned with the postulated *certainty* of the form of life, and with not any empirically falsifiable data or knowledge of the world, according to Wittgenstein.[55]

[50] Wittgenstein, *Űber Gewissheit – On Certainty*, § 84 et seq. (p. 12/12e et seq.).

[51] Wittgenstein, *Űber Gewissheit – On Certainty*, § 101 (p. 15/15e).

[52] Wittgenstein, *Űber Gewissheit – On Certainty*, § 111 (p. 17/17e).

[53] Cf. Wittgenstein, *Philosophical Investigations – Philosophische Untersuchungen*, § 217 (p. 85/85e): "If I have exhausted the justifications I have reached the bedrock, and my spade in turned. Then I am inclined to say: 'This is simply what I do.' "

[54] von Wright, "Wittgenstein varmuudesta", p. 19.

[55] Wittgenstein, *Űber Gewissheit – On Certainty*, passim.

The ultimate premises of legal validity and legal rationality, as manifested in Gunnar Berholtz' and Aulis Aarnio's notion of *reason* and *authority* in the Western legal thinking and in Jerzy Wróblewski's ideology of legal and rational judicial decision-making,[56] may be called (part of) the *infrastructures* of law and legal knowledge under such premises. They follow a similarly unyielding "non-epistemic" logic of judgment as illustrated by Moore's and Wittgenstein's examples above. Thus, the transcendental-logical *Grundnorm* in Kelsen's pure theory of law and the ultimate *rule of recognition* in Hart's *The Concept of Law* resist the act of being classified into one or the other of the two conceptual categories available, i.e. law/fact or legal validity/social effectiveness, under the premises of analytical jurisprudence. As a consequence, the ultimate premises of legal knowledge under the Western form of life cannot themselves be situated under the very same norm/fact dichotomy that is in the first place established by reference to the presumed existence of such "ultimate" criteria, without falling victim to either vicious *logical circularity* or a *never-ending regress* to ever higher premises of reasoning.[57]

Finally, the collection of philosophical theories of truth incorporates the *redundancy theory of truth*.[58] From a truth-theoretical point of view, the attribute "is true" is allegedly redundant, with no traceable effect on the truth-value of the assertion with the same propositional content. As a consequence, there is no difference in the semantic extension of the two assertions "p" and "it is true that p", or in the semantic extension of the two assertions "Venus is the morning star" and "It is true that Venus is the morning star". Both assertions express the proposition "that p" in the first example and the attribute of "the morning star" in the second example. Still, the redundancy thesis cannot plausibly be extended to sentences like: "What I am now about to tell you is true", "The first sentence on this page is true", or "I hereby swear to tell the truth, the whole truth, and nothing but the truth", without running into a grave philosophical predicament. The same goes for the redundancy theory of truth and the *Liar Paradox*. A Cretan says: "all Cretans are liars". Is the assertion true or false? Is the speaker telling the truth or is he lying? If he is telling the truth, he is lying; and if he is lying, he is telling the truth. Thus, the assertion is true, if it is false; and it is false, if it is true. In such cases, the attribute "is true" patently is not redundant or devoid of semantic content, which is contrary to the redundancy argument.

The traditional theories of truth based on the notions of the presence of correspondence, coherence, or warranted assertability in the subject matter of study all seek to provide a philosophically sound criterion, or a set of converging criteria, for judging the semantic values of a linguistic sentence, assertion, or proposition. Such theories may naturally be extended to the domain of law and legal analysis, resulting

[56] Bergholtz, *Ratio et auctoritas. Ett komparativrättsligt bidrag till frågan om domsmotiveringens betydelse främst i tvistemål*; Aarnio, *Reason and Authority. A Treatise on the Dynamic Paradigm of Legal Dogmatics*.

[57] On the notion of the infrastructures of law, cf. Siltala, *A Theory of Precedent*, pp. 197–248, 264–267.

[58] Walker, "Theories of Truth", pp. 322–325.

in different stances on how to judge the extension and intension of an assertion on how to construct and read the law. Moreover, there are other approaches to the issue that may be less philosophically rigorous but that may still reach the *institutional* premises of law. Retracing, as authentically as possible, the original historical motives of the parliamentary legislator or a court of justice vis-à-vis some item of legislation or an individual precedent, is an instance of an institutional "regime of truth" that will find a good match with a legal point of view. – Before entering the frames of legal analysis, the semantics of law needs to be briefly accounted for.

1.6 The Semantics of Law: Rudolf Carnap's Method of Extension and Intension

From the analytical point of view, linguistic analysis comprises three fields of investigation, focused on the *syntax*, *semantics*, and *pragmatics* of a linguistic expression.

The *syntax*, or syntactic dimension, of language consists of the rules that make up the either logical or descriptive *grammar* of language, with reference to the signs (the alphabet or other elementary constituents) and linguistic expressions (words or sentences) that are employed in a language. The *logical* (or formal, ideal, pure) syntax of language refers to the grammatical rules of language as seen from a logical point of view, while the descriptive syntax of language refers to the rules of grammar that are actually in use in some linguistic community.[59] Thereby, the issues dealt with by the descriptive syntax of language come rather close to linguistic pragmatism.

Semantics deals with the *reference* and *sense* a linguistic sign or expression, having to do with the convoluted relation that ties together the "words" (*les mots*), or linguistic expressions, of language and the "things" (*les choses*), or entities or phenomena or the like, in the world. The connection between the words and things is set by the prevalent order of things, or *épistémè*, as insightfully analysed by Michel Foucault in his outline of an *archaeology of knowledge* for the human sciences.[60] Finally, linguistic *pragmatics* focuses on the various uses of language in different social settings and speech act situations, along with the speaker-related or addressee-related facets of language. Such a pragmatic approach to language is illustrated by e.g. the Oxford school of linguistic philosophy. In legal argumentation on how to construct and read the law all the three facets of language gain significance but the semantic issues would seem to be the most important.

---

[59]"By the *logical syntax* of a language, we mean the formal theory of the linguistic forms of that language – the systematic statement of the formal rules which govern it together with the development of the consequences which follow from these rules." Carnap, *The Logical Syntax of Language*, p. 1. Cf. Carnap, *The Logical Syntax of Language*, pp. 1–4, 6–7.

[60]Foucault, *Les mots et les choses. Une archéologie des sciences humaines*. – The English edition of the work is titled, *The Order of Things. An Archaeology of the Human Sciences*.

The exact meaning of the two terms *syntax* and *semantics* was not entirely settled in 1934, when Rudolf Carnap published his major work *Logische Syntax der Sprache*.[61] In it, Carnap points out the affinities in linguistic usage with Hilbert who had analysed the syntax of mathematics under the term *metamathematics*, and the Polish logicians, like Jan Łukasiewicz (1878–1956), who had made use of the term *metalogic* with a similar syntactic designation. Moreover, "semantics" was used by Chwistek to denote the same object as "syntax" in Carnap's linguistic usage. Karl Bühler and his followers had used the term *sematology* for the empirical or psychological study of meanings, which in turn should be distinguished from *semasiology*, or the general study of meanings in natural languages.[62] In *Logische Syntax der Sprache*, Carnap to a great extent anticipated Alfred Tarski's later distinction between the *object language* and the *metalanguage*. For the dichotomy, Carnap uses the terms *object language* and *syntax language*.[63]

According to Carnap's demanding thesis in *The Logical Syntax of Language*[64]:

> The aim of logical syntax is to provide a system of concepts, a language, by the help of which the results of logical analysis will be easily formulable. *Philosophy is to be replaced by the logic of science* – that is to say, by the logical analysis of the concepts and sentences of the sciences, for *the logic of science is nothing other than the logical syntax of the language of science*.

Carnap's philosophical *credo* can be read as the methodological agenda for the *Wiener Kreis*, or *Logical Positivism*, that flourished in Wien from 1925 to 1935. Here, I prefer to follow the model of philosophical analysis that Carnap introduced in his later work in the 1950s, i.e. *Meaning and Necessity. A Study in Semantics and Modal Logic*. I do not undersign the young Carnap's stern methodological request that the only legitimate object of philosophical study is the logical syntax of language. In the science of law there are other scientific and philosophical commitments entailed, in addition to those comprised by the logical and linguistic elements entailed by the logical syntax of language.[65]

Ludwig Wittgenstein's philosophy was the source of inspiration for two different schools of philosophy in the twentieth century. Wittgenstein's masterwork *Tractatus*

---

[61] Carnap's *Logische Syntax der Sprache* was translated into English as *The Logical Syntax of Language* in 1937.

[62] Carnap, *The Logical Syntax of Language*, p. 9.

[63] Carnap, *The Logical Syntax of Language*, p. 4; cf. Coffa, *The Semantic Tradition from Kant to Carnap*, pp. 300–305. – Later on, even Carnap adopted the Tarskian terms of *object language* and *metalanguage*. Carnap, *Meaning and Necessity*, pp. 4–5. On how close Carnap's philosophical concerns came to those held by Alfred Tarski, cf. Coffa, *The Semantic Tradition from Kant to Carnap*, pp. 300–301, 304–305.

[64] Carnap, *The Logical Syntax of Language*, p. XIII. (Italics in original.) – Cf.: "By the *logical syntax* of a language, we mean the formal theory of the linguistic forms of that language – the systematic statement of the formal rules which govern it together with the development of the consequences which follow from these rules." Carnap, *The Logical Syntax of Language*, p. 1. (Bold in original replaced by italics here.)

[65] Siltala, *Oikeustieteen tieteenteoria*, pp. 387–460.

Logico-Philosophicus was a key source of inspiration for the *Wiener Kreis* and its austere views on science, language, and metaphysics. Wittgenstein was quick to distance his own views from any (mis)readings of his philosophical ideas by the *Wiener Kreis*. As Wittgenstein saw it, "[*Tractatus Logico-Philosophicus*] consists of two parts: the one presented here plus all that I have *not* written. And it is precisely this second part that is the important one".[66] In Wittgenstein's opinion, the adherents of the *Wiener Kreis* were completely misguided in their agenda for a scientific world-view, if it were based on Wittgenstein's *Tractatus Logico-Philosophicus*.

According to the picture theory of language, no issues of philosophical logic, metaphysics, ontology, or ethics could be meaningfully depicted by the conceptual categories of language, since they do not establish an *isomorphic* relation vis-à-vis the corresponding state of affairs in the world. The requirement of isomorphism in the language – world relation had the effect of ousting even Wittgenstein's *Tractatus* from the realm of meaningful linguistic usage, as the Austrian philosopher pointed out at the very end of the book.[67] Wittgenstein's *Tractatus Logico-Philosophicus*, like any treatise in philosophical semantics and ontology, consists of a set of linguistic assertions that cannot have a truth-value under the premises of the picture theory of language, being either *senseless* (*sinnlos*), if they are part of philosophical logic that can only be shown, not said; or downright *non-sensical* (*unsinnig*), if they are part of a philosophical metaphysics that, according to Wittgenstein, cannot even be shown. As J. Alberto Coffa has pointed out, good philosophy still ought to make the (self-defeating) effort of saying what can only be shown, i.e. the *Sinnlos*, while evading utterly nonsensical topics that cannot even be shown, i.e. the *Unsinnig*.[68]

As a contribution to linguistic philosophy, Wittgenstein's *Tractatus* deals with the logical *syntax* and *semantics* of language, leaving the issues of linguistic pragmatics out of its concern. Therefore, it cannot provide a philosophical ground of judgment for legal analysis either, except as either affirming or denying the existence of an isomorphic relation of structural similarity between the two fact-constellations, as analysed under the *isomorphic* situation of legal decision-making by Kaarle Makkonen and the *isomorphic* theory of legal argumentation based on such premises. In Wittgenstein's posthumously published works, such as *Philosophical Investigations* and *The Blue and Brown Books*, the focus of analysis was switched from the syntax and semantics of language to linguistic *pragmatics*, where the subject matter has to do with the *speaker* and *addressee*, and the particular *situation* of a linguistic expression.

---

[66]Wittgenstein in *Prototractatus*, p. 15, as cited in Coffa, *The Semantic Tradition from Kant to Carnap*, p. 142.

[67]"6.54. My propositions are elucidatory in this way: he who understand me finally recognizes them as senseless (*unsinnig*), when he has climbed out of through them, on them, over them. (He must so to speak throw away the ladder, after he has climbed up on it.) – He must surmount these propositions; then he sees the world rightly. – 7. Whereof one cannot speak, thereof one must be silent." Wittgenstein, *Tractatus Logico-Philosophicus*, p. 189.

[68]Coffa, *The Semantic Tradition from Kant to Carnap*, p. 156 (*in fine*).

The semantic constitution of a linguistic sign or expression consists of two different elements: its *reference* (Frege) or *extension* (Carnap) and *sense* (Frege) or *intension* (Carnap).[69] The *reference* of a linguistic sign or expression is equal to its coverage, or field of application, of facts, states of affairs, "things", or other entities that may dwell in the world. The *sense* of a linguistic sign or expression is equal to its specific meaning-content, as produced e.g. in contrast to the totality of all other linguistic signs or expressions in the same system of signs. On the level of linguistic sentences, the semantic categories of reference/extension and sense/intension determine the *truth-value* and specific *meaning-content* of the sentence.

The two semantic qualities of a linguistic sign or expression, *reference* and *sense* (à la Frege) or *extension* and *intension* (à la Carnap), can best be illustrated with an example provided by Frege (1848–1925). The two predicates "a morning star" and "an evening star" both have the same reference, i.e. the planet Venus, but the sense of the two attributes is very different: the predicate "a morning star" refers to a heavenly body with the inherent property of "is seen at dawn", while the predicate "an evening star" refers to a heavenly body that has the property "is seen at dusk". Yet, we are all the time speaking of one and the same object, planet Venus.[70] Similarly, the two mathematical expressions, "$2 + 1$" and "$\sqrt{9}$", both have the same reference/extension, but the sense/intension of the two expressions is different from the other.[71] Rudolf Carnap (1891–1970), another key figure in the development of formal semantics, named his system of semantics the *method of extension and intension*.[72]

At the time when Wittgenstein was writing the *Tractatus Logico-Philosophicus*, the terminology in semantics was not entirely settled, and Wittgenstein defines the sense/reference dichotomy in a manner that deviates from the conceptual usage adopted earlier by Frege (and Bertrand Russell).[73] In the present treatise, I will rather follow the linguistic usage adopted in Carnap's *method of extension and intension*, as elaborated in his mature work from the 1950s, *Meaning and Necessity. A Study in Semantics and Modal Logic.*

A linguistic expression can be a term or a sentence.[74] *Terms* may further be divided into predicates and individual terms. A *predicate* designates some quality that is attached to an entity, like "the morning star" and "the evening star" as two different attributes of the planet Venus, or "a rational being" as a definitional feature of all human kind. An *individual term* designates some individual being or

[69]Carnap, *Meaning and Necessity*, pp. 16–32.

[70]Frege, "On Sense and Reference", pp. 9–12. – On the relation between Frege's *nominatum/sense* dichotomy to Carnap's corresponding *extension/intension* dichotomy, Carnap, "On Sense and Reference", pp. 124–129.

[71]Miettinen, *Logiikka*, p. 172.

[72]Carnap, *Meaning and Necessity*, pp. 1–68.

[73]Coffa, *The Semantic Tradition from Kant to Carnap*, pp. 142–143.

[74]Niiniluoto, *Johdatus tieteenfilosofiaan*, p. 119.

subject, such as Socrates, the Greek philosopher, or James Joyce, the Irish author, as singled out by the use of the individual term. *Sentences* or *propositions* are linguistic expressions that are formulated syntactically in a correct manner and that, moreover, put forward an assertion that is either true or untrue, such as "Socrates was a talented Greek philosopher", "James Joyce is the author of *Ulysses* and *Finnegans Wake*", or "The moon is made of *Wensleydale* cheese" (according to Nick Park's great wax animation movie, *Wallace and Gromit: A Grand Day Out*), and so on.

Predicates can be divided into *one-place* predicates and *many-place* predicates. The properties of "having a red hair" or "having a high IQ" are instances of one-place predicates, and so are the two predicates of the planet Venus mentioned, i.e. "being a morning star" and "being an evening star". The relational properties of "being the child of", "being the mother of", "being taller than", and "being different from" are many-place predicates. The extension of a one-place predicate is a *class of objects*, and its intension is a certain *property*. The extension of a many-place predicate is a *relation*, and its intension is a *relational concept*.[75] According to common understanding in the literature on semantics since Frege, the extension of a sentence is equal to its *truth-value*. The intension of a sentence or proposition is equal to its (propositional) *meaning-content*.

For Carnap, the extension of a *predicate* designates a class of individuals, and the intension of a predicate designates a certain property that is attached to that class.[76] These correspond to Frege's two concepts of the reference (*Bedeutung*; *nominatum*) and sense (*Sinn*) of a linguistic expression. The extension of an *individual expression* designates a certain individual, and the intension of an individual expression is the corresponding individual concept. In Frege's systematics of semantics, there is no place for such an entity, though.[77] The extension of a *sentence* is for Frege and Carnap alike its truth-value, and the intension of a sentence is the proposition, or the "thought-content", it entails. In all, Frege's and Carnap's two systems of semantics match fairly well with each other, except for the case of individual linguistic expressions. Also, in the case of an oblique *nominatum* and oblique sense the two systems do diverge from each other, since the equations "reference equals extension" and "sense equals intension" are valid for the ordinary *nominatum* and ordinary sense only.[78] Carnap justifies his option by pointing out that, unlike Frege's model based

[75] Niiniluoto, *Johdatus tieteenfilosofiaan*, p. 120.

[76] Carnap, *Meaning and Necessity*, p. 19. – The term (general) *concept* could also be used.

[77] On the history of modern semantics and its relation to the research program of the Wiener Kreis, cf. Coffa, *The Semantic Tradition from Kant to Carnap*, where Coffa provides an excellent account of the issue.

[78] Carnap, *Meaning and Necessity*, pp. 124–129. – As examples of ordinary and oblique manner of speech one might have the sentences: "The earth revolves round the sun." (= ordinary reference and sense) and "Copernicus claimed that the earth revolves round the sun." (= oblique reference and sense). Carnap, *Meaning and Necessity*, pp. 123–124.

on the *Bedeutung* and *Sinn* of a linguistic expression, his conception of semantics is not dependent on the particular context of an expression.[79]

Summarizingly, the extension and intension of a one-place predicate, many-place predicate, an individual term, and a sentence (proposition) can be presented as follows[80]:

Table 1.1 Types of linguistic expression, and the extension and intension of each

Type of linguistic expression	Extension	Intension
One-place predicate	Class of individuals	Property, concept
Many-place predicate	Relation	Relational concept
Individual expression	Individual	Individual concept
Sentence	Truth-value	Proposition, thought-content

Frege supported his influential argument to the effect that the semantic reference of a sentence is equal to its *truth-value* by pointing out that besides the thought of a sentence we tend to attach importance to the truth or falsity of the sentence.[81] He also refers to Leibniz' interrogative argument: "what else but the truth value could be found, that belongs quite generally to every sentence if the reference of its components is relevant, and remains unchanged by substitutions of the kind in question [i.e. when a part of the sentence is replaced by an expression having the same reference]?"[82] As an unintuitive consequence thereof, all true sentences, on the one hand, and all false sentences, on the other, have the same reference, i.e. the truth or the falseness of the sentence concerned.

Carnap points out that it has become customary to use the term "extensional" for such truth-functional connections where the truth-value of the whole sentence is determined as a function of the truth-values of its components. According to him, there is a strong analogy between the truth-value of a sentence and a *predicator*, i.e. a predicative expression: it is characteristic of an *n*-degree predicator that *n* argument expressions need to be added to it in order to form a sentence. In consequence, a sentence may be taken as a predicative expression (i.e. a predicator) of zero degree,

[79] Carnap, *Meaning and Necessity*, p. 125.

[80] Carnap, *Meaning and Necessity*, pp. 1, 23–42; Niiniluoto, *Johdatus tieteenfilosofiaan*, p. 120.

[81] "The fact that we concern ourselves at all about the reference of a part of the sentence indicates that we generally recognize and expect a reference for the sentence itself. The thought loses value for us as soon as we recognize that the reference of one of its parts is missing. We are therefore justified in not being satisfied with the sense of a sentence, and in inquiring also as to its reference. But why do we want every proper name to have not only a sense, but also a reference? Why is the thought not enough for us? Because, and to the extent that, we are concerned with its truth value. (...) We are therefore driven into accepting the *truth value* of a sentence as its reference. By the truth value of a sentence I understand the circumstance that it is true or false. There are no further truth values." Frege, "On Sense and Reference", p. 10. (Italics in original.)

[82] "*Eadem sunt, quae sibi mutuo substitui possunt, salva veritate.*" Cited in: Frege, "On Sense and Reference", p. 11.

and two sentences S_1 and S_2 have the same extension, if and only if "$S_1 \equiv S_2$" is true, i.e. if and only if S_1 and S_2 are equivalent. Thus, it seems natural to define the truth-value of a sentence as its extension.[83]

Carnap's method of extension and intension is of course applicable to the semantic analysis of any linguistic expression, inclusive of legal sentences with the effect of how to construct and read the law. What is more, it may be applied to the analysis of *conventional*, i.e. institutional or societal, facts in general, once they are given a linguistic formulation. Thus, Dick W. P. Ruiter has analysed the ontological and conceptual commitments of a legal *institution* by means of the following seven categories[84]:

a) *Legal Persons*: a valid legal régime with the form of an entity that is qualified to act legally, such as the European Union.
b) *Legal Objects*: a valid legal régime with the form of an entity that can serve as the object of legal (trans)actions, such as a conveyable right of ownership.
c) *Legal Qualities*: a valid legal régime with the form of a property of a subject, such as the required majority of a legal person like a corporation.
d) *Legal Status*: a valid legal régime with the form of a property of an object, such as a listed historical monument.
e) *Personal Legal Connections*: a valid legal régime with the form of a connection between subjects, such as a personal right.
f) *Legal Configurations*: a valid legal régime with the form of a connection between objects, such as an easement (or a connection between a servient tenement and a dominant tenement).
g) *Objective Legal Connections*: a valid legal régime with the form of a connection between a subject and an object, such as the (right of) ownership of property.

When read in light of Carnap's method of extension and intension (which Ruiter does not do, since his research interest lies elsewhere), Ruiter's categories (a) and (b) designate the *extension* of a predicate, i.e. its field of application as either the subjects, or bearers, of a legal right (= point a) or as objects of a legal right (= point b), on the condition they are acknowledged in the legal system concerned. Ruiter's categories (c) and (d) designate the *intension* of such predicates, i.e. the particular properties or qualities attached to a legal subject (= point c) or an object of a legal right (= point d), as acknowledged in a legal system. The last three categories follow the logic of Carnap's method of extension and intension, too, having to do with a *two-place predicate relation* between legal subjects (= point e), between objects of legal rights (= point f), or between the combination of legal subjects and objects of legal rights (= point g).

The key question of legal analysis and legal argumentation remains unanswered, though. What is the *truth-value* of a legal sentence, i.e. a syntactically correctly

---

[83] Carnap, *Meaning and Necessity*, p. 26.

[84] Ruiter, *Legal Institutions*, pp. 96–115, and pp. 98–99 in specific.

formed assertion on *how to construct and read the law*, as judged in light of the arguments drawn from institutional and non-institutional sources of law? The answer is conditional on the *frame of legal analysis* adopted. There are nine plus one frames of legal analysis to be considered.[85]

[85]Nine plus one, and not ten, because radical, ad hoc based decisionism denies the impact of any *legally* qualified criteria in the construction and interpretation of law.

Chapter 2
An Isomorphic Theory of Law: A Relation of Structural Similarity Between the Two Fact-Constellations Compared

2.1 Kaarle Makkonen on Legal Isomorphism

Below, I will put forth and defend the argument that Kaarle Makkonen's notion of the *isomorphic* situation of legal decision-making can fruitfully be read in light of Ludwig Wittgenstein's idea that there exists an *isomorphic* relation between a meaningful linguistic expression and the corresponding fact, or a state of affairs, in the world external to language. To a great extent I will lean on Erik Stenius' (1911–1990) excellent commentary work on Wittgenstein's *Tractatus Logico-Philosophicus*, titled *Wittgenstein's* Tractatus. *A Critical Exposition of the Main Lines of Thought.*[1]

In *Tractatus Logico-Philosophicus*, Wittgenstein gives a solid philosophical account of the relation that prevails between language and the world in terms of the correspondence theory of truth, known as the *picture theory of language*. The correspondence theory of truth defines the truth of a sentence, belief, or assertion as *correspondence* or structural similarity between a linguistic expression and a state of affairs in the world. In the context of law, there is a parallel phenomenon found in an *isomorphic* relation that prevails between the fact-description of a legal norm and a corresponding state of affairs in the world. As we saw above, Kaarle Makkonen argues for such a conception in his treatise *Zur Problematik der juridischen Entscheidung. Eine strukturanalytische Studie.*

But what does it mean, to be more exact, that there exists an *isomorphic* or *picture* relation between two states of affairs? Oddly enough, Makkonen never gives a precise definition of an isomorphic relation in his major treatise, despite the fact that it is by far the most vital concept in his theory of law. He merely states on the issue[2]:

---

[1]The Finnish philosopher Erik Stenius was a student of Eino Kaila's, the Finnish adherent of the logical positivists of the *Wiener Kreis*. In his philosophical treatises, Stenius focused on symbolic logic, pre-Socratic philosophy, and the philosophy of Wittgenstein's *Tractatus Logico-Philosophicus*. His treatise, *Wittgenstein's* Tractatus. *A Critical Exposition of the Main Lines of Thought* (1960), though perhaps not widely known, is a major contribution to the topic.

[2]Makkonen, *Zur Problematik der juridischen Entscheidung*, pp. 78–79: "Erstens kann es sich um einen so klaren und allseitig deutlich gestalteten Fall handeln, dass die anzuwendende

R. Siltala, *Law, Truth, and Reason*, Law and Philosophy Library 97,
DOI 10.1007/978-94-007-1872-2_2,

> For the first, we may be dealing with such a clear and patently obvious case that the applicable legal norm is immediately evident to the decision-making authority. The relation that prevails between the given facts and the facts in a legal norm is like the one between a picture and the object depicted. Of such a case, I will use the term an *isomorphic situation.*

In an isomorphic situation of legal decision-making, there is no uncertainty as to the rule to be applied to the case, but the rule may still allow several legal outcomes, and the judge is required to make a choice among them. For instance, the norms of criminal law often leave a wide margin of discretion to the judge as concerns the type and measured quantity of punishment to be inflicted upon the offender, i.e. the choice between a fine, imprisonment, or other punishment, and the relative severity of the punishment. Even then we are dealing with an isomorphic situation, since there is no doubt as to the selection of the legal norm to be applied to the facts of the case, nor of the semantic meaning-content of the norm. The special case where there is only one legal consequence to be enforced to the facts in an isomorphic situation might be called a *simple* case of legal isomorphism. The existence of at least some discretionary leeway as to the legal outcome to be enforced is a more common situation even in the isomorphic cases of legal adjudication, though.

An isomorphic relation between the two fact-constellations may only comprise the semantically clear, *routine cases* of law-application, leaving the *hard cases* of legal adjudication totally untouched. In Makkonen's terminology, an isomorphic situation is to be distinguished from the two other decision-making situations that a judge might be confronted with when seeking to apply the law to an individual case, viz. the *semantically ambiguous* situation and the *unregulated* situation. Still, Makkonen would seem to ignore the fact that the affirmation or denial of an isomorphic relation requires an antecedent *act of interpretation* by the judge in which a *key of isomorphism* locked up for the case at hand. The presence or absence of an isomorphic relation could not be confirmed without such a judgment.

Makkonen's idea of an *isomorphic* relation between the two fact-constellations, the one as depicted in a legal norm and the other as possibly existing in the world, can be further elaborated with the *picture theory* of language, as put forth by Ludwig Wittgenstein (1889–1951) in his *Tractatus Logico-Philosophicus*. Somewhat oddly, Makkonen did not make use of Wittgenstein's *Tractatus* in his *Zur Problematik der juridischen Entscheidung*, though his philosophical stance is based on equally analytic and linguistic premises. Even the idea of a picture-like relation between the two fact-constellations concerned is common to both authors.[3]

Rechtsnorm der entscheidenden Instanz ohne weiteres sofort bekannt ist. Zwischen den gegebenen Tatsachen und den im Rechtsnormsatz dargestellten Tatsachen herrscht dann das Verhältnis des Abzubildenden zum Bilde. Wir gebrauchen für eine derartige Lage die Benennung *Isomorphiesituation*." (Italics by Makkonen; translation by the present author.)

[3] Kaarle Makkonen (1923–2000) was one of the founders of analytical jurisprudence in Finland. He was professor in jurisprudence at the University of Helsinki in 1968–1986. The absence of Ludwig Wittgenstein's *Tractatus Logico-Philosophicus* in Makkonen's analysis is all the more perplexing, since I happen to know that Wittgenstein's *Tractatus* of course belonged to Makkonen's personal library on philosophy. I know that because Makkonen was kind enough to donate the book to me at the time I was writing my own doctoral thesis on precedents in the 1990s. Of course it is possible that Makkonen regarded Wittgenstein's *Tractarian* ideas as so patently evident and widely known

2.2 The Picture Theory of Language in Ludwig Wittgenstein's *Tractatus Logico-Philosophicus*, as Read in Light of Erik Stenius' *Wittgenstein's* Tractatus. *A Critical Exposition of the Main Lines of Thought*

2.2.1 The Internal Categorial Structure and the External Configuration Structure of Reality

In *Tractatus Logico-Philosophicus*, Ludwig Wittgenstein introduced the idea of a *picture theory of language*. According to him, there exists an *isomorphic* relation between a meaningful linguistic expression and the corresponding fact or state of affairs in the world. *Reality* (*Wirklichkeit*) is the sum of the actually prevailing and merely possible *states of affairs*, and not the totality of, say, individual objects, ideas, or entities taken as such, in isolation.[4] The world (*Welt*) consists of *facts* (*Tatsachen*), i.e. the actually prevalent *states of affairs* (*Sachverhalten*) at a given moment of time.[5] A *state of affairs* consists of a combination of individual objects (entities, things), their properties and mutual relations.[6]

Wittgenstein was remarkably laconic as to what those elementary "objects", "entities", or "things" (*Gegenstände, Sachen, Dinge*) are. As J. Alberto Coffa put it: "Wittgenstein said virtually nothing directly about the character of objects. There is no example of an object in the *Tractatus* and not even a hint of what these might be."[7] Though on the level of terminology adopted Wittgenstein makes no distinction between the various kinds of "objects" (or entities, things) and

---

that no references were needed. Be that as it may, the issue can be fecundly elaborated with Ludwig Wittgenstein's philosophy.

[4]"Die Welt is die Gesamtheit der Tatsachen, nicht der Dinge." Wittgenstein, *Tractatus Logico-Philosophicus*, § 1.1 (p. 30).

[5]"Die Konfiguration der Gegenstände bildet den Sachverhalt." Wittgenstein, *Tractatus Logico-Philosophicus*, § 2.0272 (p. 36); "Die Gesamtheit der beshetenden Sachverhalte ist die Welt." Wittgenstein, *Tractatus Logico-Philosophicus*, § 2.04. (p. 36); "Das Bestehen und Nichtbestehen von Sachverhalten ist die Wirklichkeit." Wittgenstein, *Tractatus Logico-Philosophicus*, § 2.06 (p. 36). – Cf. Stenius, *Wittgenstein's* Tractatus, p. 31. Cf. Stenius, *Wittgenstein's* Tractatus, p. 31: "Thus a *Sachverhalt* is something that could *possibly* be the case, a *Tatsache* something that is *really* the case." (Italics in original.)

[6]"Der Sachverhalt is eine Verbindung von Gegenständen. (Sachen, Dingen.)" Wittgenstein, *Tractatus Logico-Philosophicus*, § 2.01 (p. 30).

[7]Cf. Coffa, *The Semantic Tradition from Kant to Carnap*, p. 150. – Cf. also Coffa, *The Semantic Tradition from Kant to Carnap*, p. 393 (note 8 to p. 150), where Coffa refers to Wittgenstein's scattered and terse remarks on the subject matter in the *Tractatus* and in Wittgenstein's later works. As examples of such objects, Wittgenstein gives the following phenomena: a point in the visual field, a patch in the visual field, the visual picture of a star, the material points of physics, and the primary colours (in Wittgenstein's *Notebooks*). In *Philosophische Bemerkungen* Wittgenstein explained, "What I once called "objects", simples, were simply what I could refer to (*bezeichnen*) without running the risk of their non-existence, i.e. that for which there is neither existence nor nonexistence." According to *Notebooks*, "relations and properties, etc. are *objects* too." The citations by Wittgenstein in Coffa, *The Semantic Tradition from Kant to Carnap*, p. 393 (note 8 to p. 150).

"predicates" that denote the qualities that may be attached to objects and the relations that might prevail between them, such a distinction is yet entailed in his idea that the "things" cannot enter the world as part of states of affairs except as bearers of certain predicates.[8] *Predicates* can be divided into *qualities* and *relations*.[9] The world is the totality of *facts*, i.e. the actually prevailing, and not merely possible, states of affairs. The facts are situated in a *logical space* where an individual state of affairs, i.e. a combination of objects and predicates, is either prevalent or not.[10]

Tractatus Logico-Philosophicus has been characterized as the *critique of pure language*,[11] since its author had the firm intention of drawing the boundaries of language and the world by means of defining the preconditions of meaningful linguistic usage.[12] When linguistic expressions are used correctly from the point of view of the logical syntax and semantics, the sentences are structurally placed in an *isomorphic* relation vis-à-vis the facts of the world or the (no more than) possible states of affairs in it, whereas any claims as to the *internal* structure of language itself are meaningless, without semantic reference. The preconditions of the logical syntax of language, or of linguistic propriety in general, cannot be captured by means of language itself.

There is a fascinating allusion to the constitutive premises of a specifically legal world-view in Wittgenstein's picture theory of language, as presented in *Tractatus Logico-Philosophicus*. Georg Henrik von Wright and Norman Malcolm, two philosophers who had a close personal acquaintance with Ludwig Wittgenstein, equally recall in their memoirs of Wittgenstein that the idea of a picture relation between the language and the world occurred to Wittgenstein while during the World War I he was reading a newspaper article of a lawsuit that had taken place in Paris in 1914. The case had dealt with a car accident, and in court the lawyers had produced a representation of the accident by means of a scaled-down model.[13] The map of the site of the accident, along with the miniature cars, horses, buildings, and human figures, the relative place and distance of each *vis-à-vis* the others,

---

[8]Stenius, *Wittgenstein's* Tractatus, p. 25: "The particular objects are perceived because this breaking-up [of a field of perception into simpler facts] is combined with a *structuring* of the simpler facts into *things* and *predicates* of things (i.e. into objects and qualities of objects and/or relations between objects). *The things and predicates* enter into the field of perception only as *elements* of facts, and that is their function." (Italics in original.) – Cf. Stenius, *Wittgenstein's* Tractatus, p. 28, 62–63, and p. 68: "... that objects and predicates enter into the world only as elements of facts, and that objects and predicates in isolation are unthinkable." – On the relation Wittgenstein's *Tractatus* bears to Carnap's semantics, Carnap, *Meaning and Necessity*, p. 9.

[9]Stenius, *Wittgenstein's* Tractatus, p. 21, note 4.

[10]"Die Tatsachen im logischer Raum sind die Welt." Wittgenstein, *Tractatus Logico-Philosophicus*, § 1.13 (p. 30).

[11]On the relationship between *Tractatus Logico-Philosophicus* and Kant's *Critique of Pure Reason*, Stenius, *Wittgenstein's* Tractatus, pp. 214–226.

[12]Wittgenstein, *Tractatus Logico-Philosophicus*, p. 26/27: "Was sich überhaupt sages lässt, lässt sich klar sagen; und wovon man nicht redden kann, darüber muss man scheigen."/"What can be said at all can be said clearly; and whereof one cannot speak thereof one must be silent."

[13]Malcolm, *Ludwig Wittgenstein. A Memoir*, p. 57; von Wright, "A Biographical Sketch", p. 8; Wittgenstein, *Notebooks 1914–1916*, p. 7/7e (*ad* 29.9.1914).

> plus other observable qualities attached to, and relations among, the objects in the model constitute the *fact-description* of a *fact-constellation*, or a *state of affairs*, that (allegedly) had taken place in Paris in 1914.
>
> The fact-constellation, as depicted by the lawyers, entailed a combination of *objects* (cars, horses, people, buildings, streets, etc.) and their *predicates* (direction of movement and velocity of each moving object, distance from other objects, etc.) at the time of the accident.[14] Similarly, a linguistic expression, if correctly formulated in light of the criteria laid down by the logical syntax of language, stands in an *isomorphic* relation, or *picture* relation, to its semantic reference, i.e. a particular fact-constellation or state of affairs. If the fact-constellation in question in fact prevails in the world, we are dealing with a *fact*; if not, we are dealing with a (merely possible) *state of affairs*, according to Wittgenstein.

According to Wittgenstein's *Tractatus*, any assertions concerning language itself are semantically empty tautologies, devoid of semantic reference except for the (possible) *analytical* truth of the concepts utilized due to their convention-based definitions. Since the relation between language and the states of affairs in the world could not be depicted by the categories of a semantically meaningful language, any linguistic assertions produced by, say, philosophical ontology, metaphysics, or linguistics are utterly meaningless, without meaningful semantic reference in the world. Thus, from a philosophical and linguistic point of view even the sentences in Wittgenstein's *Tractatus* meet a similar fate, as Wittgenstein himself pointed out at the very end of the *Tractatus*.[15]

Erik Stenius provides an excellent analysis of the ontology and semantics of Wittgenstein's *Tractatus* in his commentary work *Wittgenstein's* Tractatus. *A Critical Exposition of the Main Lines of Thought*.[16] In it, Stenius draws the distinction between the *internal* and *external* structure of a fact or state of affairs. The *internal* structure of a fact or state of affairs refers to its structural elements, i.e. objects (entities, things) and predicates (qualities, relations) the combination of which forms the elementary categorial structure of the fact or state of affairs concerned. The *external* structure of a fact, or a state of affairs, refers to the manner in which the given ontological categories have been combined so as to form a fact that actually prevails in the world.[17]

---

[14]As von Wright points out, Wittgenstein reversed the analogy and let the proposition serve as a model or picture for the corresponding state of affairs in the world. Cf. von Wright, "A Biographical Sketch", p. 8.

[15]"6.54. My propositions are elucidatory in this way: he who understand me finally recognizes them as senseless (*unsinnig*), when he has climbed out of through them, on them, over them. (He must so to speak throw away the ladder, after he has climbed up on it.) – He must surmount these propositions; then he sees the world rightly. – 7. Whereof one cannot speak, thereof one must be silent." Wittgenstein, *Tractatus Logico-Philosophicus*, p. 189.

[16]Erik Stenius (1911–1990) was professor in philosophy at the University of Helsinki in 1963–1974. *Wittgenstein's* Tractatus. *A Critical Exposition of the Main Lines of Thought* is his main contribution to the Wittgenstein studies.

[17]Stenius, *Wittgenstein's* Tractatus, p. 79: "Whereas the *external* structure of the world as a fact (or some other possible world) refers to what is *actually* the case in a given world, the *internal* structure of substance pertains only to what could *possibly* be the case in any world." (Italics in original.)

The internal structure of a state of affairs is equal to the objects, predicates and possible other elements of the *categorial structure* of merely possible ontology of the world, while the external structure of a state of affairs is equal to the *configuration structure* of the world as the facts that actually prevail in the world.[18] The *internal* structure of the world comprises the *logical syntax of language*,[19] i.e. the names given to the objects and predicates along with the logical connections required by the logical and linguistic grammar adopted, on the one hand, and the respective objects (entities, things) and predicates (qualities, relations) that form the basic categorial structure of the *elementary ontology* of the world, on the other. The combination of the logical syntax of language and the elementary ontology of the world may be called the *logical constitution of reality*.[20]

The *external* structure of the world comprises the actual configuration of the object–predicate combinations that have come into existence in the world, on the one hand, and the sum total of descriptive sentences that depict such facts, on the other. The internal *categorial* structure of reality is expressive of the logical constitution of what might be called a possible-worlds ontology, while the external *configuration* structure of the world gives effect only to such states of affairs that have been realized in the world, in the sense of providing the ground for the logical and empirical *semantics* and the philosophical *epistemology* plus the respective criteria of truth and knowledge entailed.[21]

We might say that the relation between the elementary ontology of reality and the logical syntax of language is *intensional*, to the effect that the sentences of an elementary ontology which "refer" (in a non-proper sense of the term) to the categorial structure of reality, are left without a semantic reference or truth-value in light of Wittgenstein's picture theory of language. It is only an intensional sense that may be attached to them. The relation between philosophical epistemology and the logico-empirical semantics of language, on the other hand, is *extensional*, as such linguistic expressions refer to the prevailing facts of the world, as the various configurations of objects and predicates that have come into being in the world. Such linguistic expressions carry a propositional truth-value on them, too.[22]

---

[18]The term *configuration structure* is mine, but the idea is from Stenius.

[19]The term *formal constitution of language* could also be used.

[20]The term *logical constitution* is not used by Stenius, but it is derived from Rudolf Carnap's philosophy. The term *formal constitution* could also be used.

[21]Stenius makes use of the two terms *descriptional picture theory*, with reference to the affinity between the external structure of a sentence and its semantic reference, and *ontological picture theory*, with reference to the affinity between language and the internal structure of reality. Stenius, *Wittgenstein's* Tractatus, p. 177.

[22]The intensionality and extensionality of a picture relation is based on my own interpretation and cannot be traced back to Stenius' commentary on Wittgenstein. To be precise, under the ontological and linguistic commitments of Wittgenstein's *Tractatus* a picture relation can only be extensional, since any statements concerning the internal structure of reality are without semantic reference in Wittgenstein's theory. Therefore, the term, "intensional" has been placed in brackets in the diagram below.

The states of affairs in the world and the descriptive sentences by means of which they are depicted in linguistic assertions effectively bind together the "words", or the logical and semantic categories of language, and the "things", or the constellations of objects (entities, things) and predicates (qualities, relations) in the world. In the terminology of Michel Foucault's archaeology of knowledge, we are now dealing with the *analytics of finitude* of the Western *épistémè*, in the sense of the *external* relations that exist between language and the prevailing facts in the world.[23] Summarizingly the relation of isomorphism between the language and the world on the two "levels" or dimensions discerned, viz. the *logical constitution* of reality as the internal *categorial structure* of language and reality, on the one hand, and the *analytics of finitude* as the external *configuration structure* of the "words" of language and the "things" in the world, on the other, can be depicted with the following diagram:

Language ⟵ An Isomorphic Relation ⟶ The World

a) The Logical Constitution of Reality

Internal Categorial Structure names of objects + predicates + logical connections between them (= *logical syntax of language*)	⟵⟶ (INTENSIONAL)	***Internal Categorial Structure*** objects (entities, things) + predicates (qualities, relations with several places) + combinations of objects & predicates (states of affairs) (= *elementary ontology of a 'possible-worlds' semantics*)

b) The Analytics of Finitude

External Configuration Structure description of facts, i.e. states of affairs that prevail in the world (= *logical & empirical semantics*)	⟵⟶ EXTENSIONAL	***External Configuration Structure*** facts, i.e. states of affairs that prevail in the world (= *philosophical epistemology*)

Diagram 2.1 The relation between language and the world: the logical constitution of reality and the analytics of finitude, with reference to the internal categorial structure and the external configuration structure of the world

Though two distinct states of affairs might be similar as to their internal categorial structure and external configuration structure, their substantive contents could still be different, as the following two examples of the members of a familiy and the soldiers of a military unit will show.[24]

---

[23] Foucault, *Les Mots et les choses. Une Archéologie des sciences humaines*; Siltala, *Oikeustieteen tieteenteoria*, p. 1 et seq.

[24] Stenius, *Wittgenstein's* Tractatus, p. 94.

2.2.2 A Legal Fact-Situation as an Analysed Fact-Situation

Any set of facts or states of affairs that can be analysed as different sets of combinations of objects (entities, things) and their predicates (qualities, relations) Erik Stenius calls an *articulate field*.[25] An articulate field is a fact-complex that consists of one or more facts or states of affairs, as analysed in light of some specific *key of interpretation*.[26] The terms *fact-complex*, *fact-description*, *fact-constellation*, and *fact-situation* could also be used, even though they are inclined to bring in an air of a specifically *legal* world-view that is lacking in Stenius' original analysis. Here such an allusion to the legal fact-constellations is however welcome, since it provides a link from Stenius' and Wittgenstein's philosophy to Kaarle Makkonen's philosophy of law: both share the notion of isomorphism. An *isomorphic* relation between a linguistic expression and some articulate field in the world requires that there exists a relation of correspondence, or isomorphism, within the internal *categorial* structure and the external *configuration* structure of language and reality, respectively.

Though Wittgenstein said virtually nothing in *Tractatus Logico-Philosophicus* about the true character of the "things" or objects that constitute the elementary ontology, resulting in the array of possible states of affairs in the reality and the specific facts in the world,[27] in the present *legal* context such entities may be held as equal to the elements of individual legal *fact-situations* entailed in legal norms.

The subject matter of an articulate field may comprise, for instance, the members of a five-member family, the qualities of each family member in terms of intelligence, and the parent–child relations; or the soldiers of a military unit, the personal qualities of each soldier in terms of braveness, and the relations of military authority and commandship, in the sense of a superior rank officer's authorized power to give military orders to the soldiers of an inferior rank and the corresponding duty of the inferior-rank soldiers to obey the orders given by the higher-ranking officer, in the military unit concerned. Thus, Stenius makes use of two articulate fields, or fact-situations, each comprising five objects and two predicates, i.e. one quality and one binary relation. An isomorphic relation prevails between the two fact-complexes under the criteria specified above[28]:

[25] Stenius, *Wittgenstein's* Tractatus, p. 90: "... I shall call a fact capable of being analysed in different ways a 'field'. A field so analysed that certain objects and predicates – which need not be atomic – appear as its elements I shall call an *articulate field*. To an articulate field, then, belongs (a) the fact analysed, (b) the system of elements in terms of which it is analysed. An 'articulate field' differs from an analysed 'world as a fact' only in (1) that it need not comprise more than a certain portion of the world as a fact and (2) that the elements need not be 'atomic'." Cf. also Stenius, *Wittgenstein's* Tractatus, p. 91 et seq.

[26] The term *scheme of interpretation* could also be used.

[27] Coffa, *The Semantic Tradition from Kant to Carnap*, p. 150.

[28] Stenius, *Wittgenstein's* Tractatus, pp. 70–71, 91–96.

Fact-Situation A (Articulate Field A) | **Fact-Situation B (Articulate Field B)**

	Diagram A:	**Diagram B:**
Objects:	a_1: Alan	a_2: Adams
	b_1: Brian	b_2: Barratt
	c_1: Christopher	c_2: Colman
	d_1: David	d_2: Denison
	e_1: Eric	e_2: Ellis
Qualities:	intelligence (b_1 & e_1) (=brackets)	braveness (b_2 & e_2) (=square brackets)
Binary relations:	father–son relation (=arrow)	relation of military authority (=broken arrow)

Diagram 2.2 The objects and predicates of a family and a military unit as two articulate fields

The objects of the articulate field A comprise the members of a family, a_1–e_1. The quality under inspection is the (exceptional) intelligence of a person, as depicted by a bracketed letter, and the binary relation under observation is the father–son relation, as depicted by an ordinary arrow. In the diagram, a_1 is the father of b_1 and c_1, and c_1 is the father of d_1 and e_1. Of the family members, b_1 and e_1 are (exceptionally) intelligent.

The objects of the articulate field B comprise the soldiers that belong to a certain military unit, a_2 – e_2. The quality under inspection is the (exceptional) braveness of a soldier, as depicted by a square bracketed letter, and the binary relation under observation is the relation of military authority, in the sense of being authorized to give military orders to the soldiers who are lower in military rank, as depicted by a dashed arrow. In the diagram, a_2 is in the position to give military orders to b_2 and c_2, and c_1 is in the position to give military orders to d_2 and e_2. Of the soldiers, b_2 and e_2 are (exceptionally) brave.

Though the subject matters of the two articulate fields A and B are different, there exists an isomorphic relation between the two fact-situations both as to their *internal categorial structure* and their *external configuration structure*. First of all, there exists a relation of one-to-one isomorphism between the categorial objects, qualities, and binary relations concerned: object a_1 (Alan) corresponds to object a_2 (Adams), object b_1 (Brian) corresponds to object b_2 (Barratt), and so on, with respect to each of the individual objects concerned. In a similar manner, the qualities (exceptional intelligence/braveness) and binary relations (father–son relation/superior–inferior rank of military authority) match with each other in the internal categorial structure of the articulate fields studied.

The existence of internal categorial similarity between two fact-complexes cannot yet guarantee the existence of an isomorphic relation as concerns their external configuration structure. Isomorphism would be broken in Stenius' illustration, if, say, c_1 were not the child of a_1, or if b_1 were not (exceptionally) intelligent, or if d_2 were not placed under the military authority c_2, or if e_2 were not (exceptionally) brave. In the diagram above, even the external configuration structure of the two articulate fields A and B are yet similar, to the effect that the two qualities of (exceptional) *intelligence* and (exceptional) *braveness* and the two binary relations of a *father–son relation* and *military authority* have a total match with each other.

An *isomorphic* relation prevails between two (or more) fact-complexes, each with one or several facts or states of affairs, if and only if the internal *categorial structure* and external *configuration structure* of each are similar, to the effect that the sum total of objects (things, entities) and predicates (qualities, relations) attached to them have a one-to-one *structural similarity* to one another. The presence or absence of isomorphism concerns the internal and external structure of facts, or states of affairs, only. As to their substantive content, the two articulate fields compared may still be very different, as Stenius' illustration bears witness of.

According to Stenius, isomorphism can be defined with the following four criteria[29]:

(a) Isomorphism is a relation between two (or more) *facts* or *states of affairs*, not between *things* or *predicates* as such or in isolation.
(b) Only facts that have been analysed in terms of a fixed system of *categorial elements* involved into *articulate fields* can be isomorphic vis-à-vis one another.
(c) An isomorphic relation can only prevail between two articulate fields that have the same *internal categorial structure*, and the presence of isomorphism can be ascertained only with reference to a *key of isomorphism* by means of which the similarity of the *external configuration structure* of the states of affairs can be ascertained.
(d) Isomorphism is a *symmetrical* and *transitive* relation.

An isomorphic relation may prevail between two or more facts or feasible states of affairs that can be analysed as an articulate field, not between individual objects (entities, things) or predicates (qualities, relations) as such (= point a). That is because of the ontological commitments in Wittgenstein's *Tractatus*: individual "things" may enter the world only as part of a state of affairs, and not as freestanding entities as such.[30] The objects or predicates that make up a distinct fact or a state of affairs need to be cast into a fixed model or system that constitutes an articulate

[29] Stenius, *Wittgenstein's* Tractatus, pp. 93–94. Stenius' criteria have to some extent been modified and further elaborated here. For instance, the requirement of the affinity of the external configuration structure of the two states of affairs concerned, i.e. articulate fields, is supplemented by the present author. Stenius, however, speaks of a fixed correspondence between the elements of the states of affairs concerned in light of the key on isomorphism chosen. As I see it, that criterion amounts to the affinity of the external configuration structure of the facts concerned.

[30] "...that objects and predicates enter into the world only as elements of facts, and that objects and predicates in isolation are unthinkable." Stenius, *Wittgenstein's* Tractatus, p. 25, 68. Cf.

field, since without such a fixed reference the presence of a relation of isomorphism could not be affirmed (= point b). The structural affinity or similarity of the internal and external structure of two states of affairs compared is determined by the *key of isomorphism* adopted, by means of which the objects and predicates of some fact or state of affairs, i.e. an articulate field, are locked up for the analysis. They key of isomorphism, in other words, resolves the issue as to which individual facets of the states of affairs, facts, or articulate fields under observation are deemed to be significant for the analysis of isomorphism (= point c).

The choice of a particular key of isomorphism is closely tied up with the *logical construction of reality*, i.e. the constitution of the states of affairs or fact-situations concerned and of the linguistic entities involved. In Stenius' two examples concerning the members of a family, on the one hand, and the soldiers of a military unit, on the other, there are ten objects (a_1, b_1, c_1...e_2), the two qualities of (exceptional) intelligence and braveness, as depicted above by the bracketed and square bracketed letters, and the two binary relations of the father–son and of the military superior–inferior kind, as depicted above by the ordinary and double arrows. If the qualities attached to the five objects or the relations affirmed between the objects in the articulate fields in question differ from each other in some respect, no relation of isomorphism can be ascertained vis-à-vis the fact-constellations concerned.

> The internal categorial structure of a state of affairs or fact-situation can be constructed in more than just one manner, depending on how the prevailing "order of things" in the world and the corresponding linguistic categories are constituted. An alternative categorial outline of the above example could consist of, say, 24 distinct entities: ten objects, as signified by letters with a sub-index (a_1 ... e_2), two bracketed letters (= the quality of being intelligent), two square bracketed letters (= the quality of being brave), five arrows (= father–son relation), and five broken arrows (= relation of military authority and subordination).

In Stenius' example above, an isomorphic relation is thought to prevail between the two articulate fields compared as the structural similarity of the *objects* (five members of a family/five soldiers in a military unit), *qualities* (intelligence/braveness) and *binary relations* (father–son relation/military authority) in the logical space in question. If the analysis had been focused on some other pair of qualities or relations in an articulate field "inhabited" by the said five objects, like the quality of "having a red hair" among the members of a family, or the quality of "being left-handed" among the soldiers of a military unit, or the mutual relations of affection or disgust among the persons concerned, the key of isomorphism would not have yielded an isomorphic relation between the two articulate fields concerned, unless the said properties were distributed among the members of the family or the soldiers of the military unit concerned in an identical manner to the one considered above. The same outcome holds true for any combination of objects, qualities, and relations, if the internal *categorial structure* or the external *configuration structure* (or both) of the two articulate fields compared differ from each other in some significant respect. It is only with respect to a certain key of isomorphism that the structural match of the articulate fields compared can be ascertained.

Wittgenstein, *Tractatus Logico-Philosophicus*, § 1.1.: "Die Welt ist die Gesamtheit der Tatsachen, nicht der Dinge."

The essentially symmetrical and transitive character of an isomorphic relation guarantees that the results reached in such an analysis can be extended to any other fact-situations, too, so long as the criterion of structural similarity as to their internal categorial structure and external configuration structure are satisfied (= point d). As a consequence, Stenius' illustration of the qualities and relations among the members of a family or the soldiers of a military unit may be adopted in, say, the analysis of the person who is entitled to inherit, if the twin criteria as to the internal and external structure of the articulate fields are duly met with. The Finnish Act of Inheritance (5.2.1965/40) 2:1 § decrees on the order of inheritance of the direct heirs of the deceased person as follows[31]:

> The direct heirs of the deceased person are the first to inherit. Each of the children will obtain an even share of the property in the estate. If some of the children of the deceased person has died earlier, his or her offspring will come to his or her place in the order of inheritance, and each line will obtain an equal share of the estate.

The order of inheritance in two fact-situations A and B can be depicted with the following diagram, drawn in the image of Stenius' illustration of the qualities and relations among the members of a family or a military unit:

Fact-Situation A (Articulate Field A)	**Fact-Situation B (Articulate Field B)**
Order of Inheritance under the (Finnish) Act of Inheritance *vis-à-vis* the Children of a Deceased Person	Order of Inheritance *vis-à-vis* the Children of the Deceased Person in a Hypothetical Case

	Diagram C	**Diagram D**
Objects:	A: parent (=mother or father)	a_3: Antti (=father)
	B: child (=daughter or son)	b_3: Belle (=daughter)
	C: child (=daughter or son)	c_3: Cecilia (=daughter)
	D: grandson orgrand-daughter	d_3: David (=son of a daughter)
	E: grandson or grand-daughter	e_3: Esko (=son of a daughter)
Qualities:	quality of 'being deceased' (=symbol '†' after the letter)	quality of 'being deceased' (= symbol '†' after the letter)
Binary relations:	parent–child relation (=an arrow)	parent–child relation (=an arrow)

Diagram 2.3 The order of inheritance of the children of a deceased person according to the Finnish Act of inheritance and as then realized in the world, as analysed in terms of an isomorphic relation

[31] Translation from Finnish by the present author.

According to the Finnish Act of Inheritance, the two daughters of father Antti (= a_3), viz. Belle (= b_3) and Cecilia (= c_3), are both prima facie entitled to inherit an equal share of the property left by their deceased father. In the present case, however, Belle (= b_3) had died before her father, and so all of the property will go to Cecilia (= c_3). Also one of the two sons of Cecilia, i.e. Esko (= e_3), had died before Antti (= a_3), but that has no effect on the legal order of inheritance in the case under consideration. A similar, even if more complicated analysis of an isomorphic relation between a fact-description given in the legislation and the states of affairs in the world can naturally be extended to any other legal fact-constellations. For instance, it may cover the concept of *legal ownership*, as insightfully analysed by Wesley Newcomb Hohfeld as the *jural correlatives* and *jural opposites* of such categories.[32]

2.3 The Two Requirements Placed on Legal Isomorphism

There are two essential preconditions placed on the presence of an isomorphic relation between the two fact-constellations involved. The one has to do with the *legal adequacy* of the key of the isomorphism selected, and the other with the *rule/principle* characterization of the legal norm concerned.

For the first, the *key of isomorphism* has to be adequate from a legal point of view. The requirement of *legal adequacy* refers to the idea of anchoring the isomorphic, picture relation between the two fact-constellations in the norms of the legal system in question, and not in some considerations of social, ethical, political, or religious kind that cannot draw such support from the institutional and societal sources of law in the legal system concerned. It is only on the condition that there prevails an isomorphic relation between the *internal categorial structure* and *external configuration structure* of the fact-constellation of a legal norm and the corresponding fact-description of a state of affairs in the world that the effected relation of isomorphism may properly be qualified as *legal*.

The other requirement placed on legal isomorphism has to do with the internal structure of the legal norm involved. An *isomorphic* relation between the two states of affairs, the one as defined in the fact-description of a legal norm and the other as possibly prevalent in the world, can only take place under a legal *rule*. Because of the open-ended and contextual quality of legal principles and the like legal standards, they cannot provide a fixed ground for the kind of judgment that is required for the affirmation of an isomorphic relation between the two fact-constellations in question. An isomorphic relation would be possible only if the legal principle in question were first transformed into a legal rule with clear and distinct enough semantic boundaries of application.

Kaarle Makkonen wrote that an isomorphic situation might be present even in the case of legal principles.[33] His definition of a legal principle is yet different from

[32] Hohfeld, *Fundamental Legal Conceptions as Applied in Judicial Reasoning*.

[33] Makkonen, *Zur Problematik der juridischen Entscheidung*, pp. 175–181.

the one suggested by Ronald Dworkin and then widely acknowledged in the subsequent legal literature. Makkonen can hardly be blamed for not paying attention to Dworkin's theory of law, since Makkonen's treatise *Zur Problematik der juridischen Entscheidung* was published in 1965, 2 years before Dworkin's pathbreaking article, "The Model of Rules, I", came out. In it, Dworkin presented his seminal idea of legal "principles, policies, and other sorts of standards" that exert normative influence on a judge's legal discretion in the hard cases of legal adjudication where legal rules cannot provide for conclusive guidance.[34] It is therefore easy to see why Makkonen could not know the two criteria for the analysis of legal principles that were subsequently suggested by Dworkin, i.e. sufficient *institutional support* and a *sense of approval* in the legal community.

Makkonen opts for a nominalist and conventional definition of legal principles.[35] He situates legal principles against the classical natural law tradition where legal principles are taken as a set of non-positive values and norms, endowed with the authority to delimit the legal discretion of the legislator and the courts of justice when faced with iniquity. On the other hand, Makkonen sees legal principles as part of a strictly systemic idea of law under a formalist conception of law. Moreover, legal principles are said to form an essential part of the foundational ideological premises of the law.[36] As to their role in the court's legal decision-making, Makkonen sees legal principles mainly as norms that direct the court's choice of the legal rule to be applied in a concrete case at hand or of the specific legal consequences to be inflicted under the legal rule selected.[37]

Since the principles and standards of law are, by force of their definition, open-ended vis-à-vis certain social values and collective goals acknowledged in society, and since, moreover, their field and conditions of application cannot be fully determined in advance, in isolation from a specific fact-constellation, a necessary prerequisite of legal isomorphism is missing. As a consequence, legal principles cannot serve as a ground for legal isomorphism. Contrary to what Makkonen wrote

[34]Cf. Dworkin, *Taking Rights Seriously*, p. 22: "... in those in hard cases... [the lawyers] make use of standards that do not function as rules, but operate differently as principles, policies, and other sorts of standards."

[35]"In der vorliegenden Untersuchung interessiert uns – einerlei wie die Klassifizierung und ihre Kriterien sein mögen – nur das, dass wir bestimmte Grundsätze benennen können, die wir als allgemeine Rechtsprinzipien ansehen. Da genügt zur Untersuchung ihrer Entscheidungsfunktion." Makkonen, *Zur Problematik der juridischen Entscheidung*, p. 156.

[36]Makkonen, *Zur Problematik der juridischen Entscheidung*, p. 172. Cf. Makkonen, *Zur Problematik der juridischen Entscheidung*, p. 187: "Die im Obigen vorgenommene Betrachtung zeigt, dass man aus den Grundeinstellung, die hinter den verschiedenen Gesellschaftsordnungen stehen, sog. allgemeinen Rechtsprinzipien, ideologische Grunsanschauungen herausschälen kann, die teils explicite – in geschriebenen Gesetzen – in der Rechtsordnung enthalten sind, teils implicite. Ferner haben wir gesehen, dass derartige allgemeine Rechtsgrundsätze verschiedene Aufgaben haben können; teils sind sie weitere organisatorisch-systematische Prinzipien, die auf das Normsystem selbst beziehen, teils können sie eine Entscheidungsfunktion haben, die in der juridischen Entscheidungstätigkeit hervortritt."

[37]Makkonen, *Zur Problematik der juridischen Entscheidung*, p. 188.

in his *Zur Problematik der juridischen Entscheidung*, the seminal role held by some legal principle or principles for the affirmation or denial of certain legal consequences for the facts at hand has the inevitable side-effect of ruling out the possibility of legal isomorphism.

2.4 The Transition From an Isomorphic Situation to a Situation of Semantic Ambiguity

From a legal point of view, situations in which the outcome of legal discretion is unequivocally determined by an isomorphic relation that prevails between the two fact-descriptions compared, the one as entailed in a legal rule and the other as prevailing in the world, are equal to *clear cases* of legal decision-making.[38] The prevalence of such structural similarity between the two fact-constellations is taken as a sufficient reason for giving effect to the legal outcome specified in the legal norm in question. The issues of how to construct and read the law boil down to the presence or absence of an isomorphic, picture-like relation between the two fact-constellations compared by the judge or other official.

Frequently occurring, non-problematic *routine cases* of legal decision-making ought to be distinguished from the *hard cases* of legal decision-making where there is no legal rule in the legal system that could possibly determine the outcome of the case. Using H. L. A. Hart's terminology, we might say that the routine cases of legal decision-making are situated on the settled *core of meaning* of a legal norm and the concepts entailed in it, while the hard cases of legal decision-making are situated on the more or less uncertain *penumbra of doubt* of such norms or concepts where several interpretations are possible.[39] According to Ronald Dworkin, the judge then needs to *weigh and balance* the relative impact of each of the value-laden legal principles or standards that have some bearing on the issue at hand in a hard case of legal adjudication, with reference to the set of social values and goals at the back of such principles. If there is any doubt as to the prevalence of structural similarity between the two fact-situations compared, there is no an isomorphic relation, either.

The legal significance of the relation of isomorphism is highly restricted, though. Legal principles and the like value-laden standards of legal decision-making are endowed with the twin properties of, first, due institutional support drawn from the prevalent sources of law and, second, a sense of appropriateness enjoyed among the members of the legal community, and such features break the bond of legal isomorphism. Even the kind of legal rules that require some legal discretion from the judge or other official are now left out of consideration, unless they can be recast

[38]Neil MacCormick, with good reason, prefers the term a *routine case* to that of an *easy case*, since many fields of law where routine cases frequently occur, such as tax law, parts of property law, insurance law, and so forth, are highly complex and may be far from easy from the judge's or other official's point of view. MacCormick, *Rhetoric and the Rule of Law*, p. 51.

[39]Hart, *The Concept of Law* (1961), pp. 123–124.

so as to be brought under the relation of isomorphism, pure and simple. From the point of view of a judge or a legal scholar alike, however, it is yet the *hard* cases that are most often encountered in legal analysis and stand in need of significantly more erudition and analysis, and not the routine cases that may be conveniently analysed as legal isomorphism and the Wittgensteinian picture theory of language. Even then, the choice of a key of isomorphism vis-à-vis a pair of legal fact-situations is not possible without first having constructed the two states of affairs with the help of *some* conceivable key of interpretation. In that sense, the act of interpretation always precedes the affirmation of an isomorphic situation in legal decision-making.

The pertinence of the key of isomorphism chosen may be questioned in light of the altered institutional and societal preconditions of legal decision-making, i.e. the set of social values operative at the back of the legal sources. No conception of law may effectively claim immunity or a somehow privileged standing against the subsequent changes effected in the institutional and societal background premises of law. In the course of time, some constitutive elements of the legal order, such as the human and constitutional rights lately, may make a successful claim to greater weight than their competitors. If the institutional and societal premises of law are affected by some thorough enough changes, the hard cases/routine cases dichotomy becomes altered, too. In such a situation, what used to be a routine case of legal adjudication with an isomorphic picture relation between the two states of affairs may be transformed into a genuinely hard case with no traces of structural similarity left.

> The profound legal, social, and economic changes induced by the process of European integration and the global scene of the new forms of *international*, *multinational*, and *transnational* law have to a great extent broken down the traditional bonds of legal isomorphism, turning a host of former routine cases of law into genuinely hard cases that necessitate the weighing and balancing of the value-laden principles of law entailed. Even the notion of state sovereignty has been affected. Neil MacCormick suggested the notion of a *post-sovereign* state with reference thereto.[40]

In Wittgenstein's *Tractatus Logico-Philosophicus*, an isomorphic relation between two possible states of affairs, or fact-situations, is based on the existence of structural match, similarity, or affinity between them. An isomorphic relation between a linguistic expression and a state of affairs in the world may only concern the relation between a linguistic expression and the *external configuration structure* of the state of affairs in the world, since the *internal categorial structure* of the world cannot be presented by meaningful linguistic assertions according to Wittgenstein's philosophical stance. The truth-value of a linguistic sentence can be determined by having reference to the corresponding state of affairs in the world. No question as to the truth-value of an inherently self-referential linguistic assertion, or one concerning the truth-value of a sentence without such an external reference in the world, can possibly arise.

---

[40] MacCormick, *Questioning Sovereignty*, pp. 123–136, i.e. chapter "On Sovereignty and Post-Sovereignty". Neil MacCormick's book, *Questioning Sovereignty. Law, State, and Nation in the European Commonwealth*, is a solid contribution to the changes affected in the traditional notion of a sovereign state in light of the recent European legal and social integration.

In fact, the existence of an isomorphic relation between two states of affairs or fact-situations, the one as depicted in the fact-description of a legal rule and the other as existing in the world, is conditional upon a prior act of interpretation in which the *key of isomorphism* is at least temporarily locked. Therefore, the choice of the key of isomorphism to be applied to the two sets of facts necessitates a judgment as to the external configuration structure of the two states of affairs concerned, inclusive of the *internal* categorial structure or the inherent "order of things" that is thought to prevail among the elementary objects (entities, things) and the predicates (qualities, relations) involved. The choice of the key of isomorphism to be adopted makes only one kind of isomorphic relation possible, ruling out all other types of isomorphic relations for the case at hand. The claimed existence of an isomorphic relation between the two states of affairs is thus relative to the specific key of isomorphism chosen for the task.

If the key of isomorphism is altered, the initial relation of isomorphism is broken and we may have: (a) an isomorphic situation of some other kind, if a relation of structural similarity prevails under the novel key of isomorphism, (b) no more than approximate or more-or-less inaccurate structural similarity between the two fact-situations, in the sense of a legal decision-making situation where recourse to the methodology of legal interpretation is needed in the proper sense of the term, as argued by Kaarle Makkonen, or (c) a total absence of structural similarity or even semantic match between the two fact-situations, with reference to Makkonen's idea of a unregulated situation of legal decision-making. That even the affirmation or denial of an isomorphic relation between two fact-constellations requires a prior act of interpretation seems to have gone unnoticed by Makkonen.[41]

2.5 Legal Isomorphism and Institutional Facts

An isomorphic relation between the two states of affairs, the one as given in the fact-description of a legal rule and the other as either actually or at least possibly existing in the world, is based on a *realistic* conception of language and reality. Realism in the scientific or philosophical sense is a plural notion, though. It may entail a commitment to at least seven different issues or topics: (a) *ontological* realism, (b) *semantic* realism, (c) *epistemological* realism, (d) *methodological* realism,

[41]"Bei der in der Rede stehenden Entscheidungssituation, in der zwischen den gegebenen Tatsachen und den in einer bestimmten Vorschrift geschilderten Tatsachen Isomorphie herrscht, konzentriert sich die eigentliche Entscheidungsproblematik auf die Festsetzung der Rechtsfolge. *Es ist wichtig zu beachten, dass es sich dann nicht um Auslegung der Bestimmung handelt, hinsichtlich deren Isomorphie herrscht.* Da Isomorphie gerade das bedeutet, dass die Bedeutung des Rechtsnormsatzes, der diese Bestimmung enthält, völlig klar ist, kann natürlich über diese Bedeutung keine Unklarheit entstehen. Makkonen, *Zur Problematik der juridischen Entscheidung*, p. 108. (Italics added.) The subtitle of the respective chapter in Makkonen's treatise is titled: "Die Argumentationstechnik in der Isomophiesituation", i.e. the argumentation technique in an isomorphic situation.

(e) *axiological* realism, (f) *ethical* realism, and (g) realism in *scientific concept formation* and *theory construction*.[42] It seems that the notion of isomorphism in law necessarily presupposes a commitment to at least ontological and semantic realism.

Ontological realism believes that the existence of objects, things, entities, phenomena, states of affairs, facts, or whatever are taken to "inhabit" the world is – at least, for the most part – independent from the human mind. Tables and chairs, oceans and mountains, planets and stars, or the *Eiffel* tower in Paris and the *Kheops* Pyramid in Ghiza would not cease to exist, even if they were not the object of the sense-observations of some human being or the subject of the inner reflections of some human mind at a given moment of time. The specific mode of "being in the world" of such "things", objects, facts, or entities the existence of which is dependent on a set of socio-cultural beliefs, expectations, or dispositions held by the members of the community, may yet prove problematic, when judged from the point of view of ontological realism. *Institutional facts* are prime examples of such phenomena.

The Austrian philosopher Karl Popper (1902–1994) made the distinction between the three kinds of "worlds", each with the different kinds of "things", objects, or entities entailed in it.[43] In Popper's classification, *world 1* comprises the totality of physical objects and processes of the world such as tables and chairs, stars and planets, or wombats and monotremes. Secondly, *world 2* comprises the contents of the human mind, like the sense data, observations, intentions, thoughts, dreams, and memories of an individual. Finally, *world 3* contains the totality of various kinds of societal and cultural objects, entities, or artefacts of human invention, on the condition that they have gained relative independence from the contents of any individual human mind and have thus become common property for all the human kind. Mathematical figures, scientific theories, the game of chess, the composition *Tabula Rasa* by Arvo Pärt, the European currency *euro*, and the rules and principles of some legal system all dwell in Popper's *world 3*. They also match well with the idea of socio-cultural *institutional facts* as distinguished from the "raw facts", as suggested by Elizabeth Anscombe, John L. Austin, and John R. Searle.[44]

Legal institutions, such as marriage, contract, mortgage, valid will and testament, a company with limited liability (*GmbH*), or the rule of recognition adopted in a legal system to the effect that "what the Queen in Parliament enacts is (valid) law in England", exemplify the world of such institutional facts. Both categories of facts, *raw facts* and *institutional facts*, are acknowledged by a realistic ontology, widely defined, since not even the existence of institutional facts is dependent on the contents of the mental state of any particular individual at a given moment of time. Rather, they have a relatively autonomous and, at least to some extent, established

[42] Niiniluoto, *Critical Scientific Realism*. Cf. Pihlström, *Tutkiiko tiede todellisuutta?* pp. 30–66, 72–73. The title of Pihlström's work could be translated as: *Does Science Examine the Reality?*

[43] Popper, *Objective Knowledge*, p. 106 et seq.

[44] On institutional ontology, cf. Anscombe, *Intention*; Austin, *How to Do Things with Words*; Searle, *The Construction of Social Reality*; Searle, *Speech Acts*; and on institutional legal positivism, MacCormick and Weinberger, *An Institutional Theory of Law*; MacCormick, *Institutions of Law*.

socio-cultural mode of existence, having gained independence from the mental state of any individual.[45]

Semantic realism defines the truth-value of a sentence or linguistic expression as its relation of correspondence vis-à-vis the phenomena, or states of affairs, in the world. The notion of a language – world correspondence refers to an *isomorphic* relation between the two, no matter what kind of reading is ascribed to the logical constitution of the world. Under the correspondence theory of truth, the ontology laid down in Ludwig Wittgenstein's *Tractatus Logico-Philosophicus* may serve as the ontological reference, as defined in terms of the internal *categorial structure* and the external *configuration structure* of a state of affairs in Erik Stenius' insightful analysis. In addition to ontological realism Wittgenstein's *Tractatus* is committed to a *semantic* conception of truth.

A linguistic assertion is accordingly true, if and only if it corresponds to the facts that prevail in the world external to language. In line with the basic commitments of ontological realism, the existence of a state of affairs in the world is taken as an issue that is independent from the particular contents of the sense data, flow of mental states, or specific intentions of an individual subject. As to the core issue of what it is that binds together the "words", or conceptual categories, of language and the "things", or phenomena, of the world,[46] the semantic conception of truth refers to an isomorphic relation of structural similarity between the two.

2.6 The Semantic Theory of Truth by Alfred Tarski

According to Alfred Tarski (1901–1983), the distinguished Polish logician, the truth of the assertion S may be defined as follows[47]:

> "S is true if and only if p",

where "S" is the name of a sentence and "p" is the propositional content of the sentence S. In consequence, the sentence "Snow is white" is true if and only if snow is white. Also, the sentences "Schee ist weiss" (in German), "La neige est blanche" (in French), and "Lumi on valkoista" (in Finnish) are true, if and only if snow is white. In other words, sentence is true if and only if the state of affairs depicted in its propositional content prevails in the world. Tarski's definition of truth is based on the distinction drawn between the *mention*, or name (= S), and the *use*, or propositional content (= p), of a sentence.

---

[45]Niiniluoto, too, accepts the entities that belong to Popper's world 3 into his realistic ontology. Niiniluoto, *Critical Scientific Realism*, p. 23.

[46]Cf. Foucault, *Les Mots et les choses. Une Archéologie des sciences humaines*; Foucault, *LArchéologie du savoir*.

[47]Tarski, "The Concept of Truth in Formalized Lànguages", p. 155: "(1) *a true sentence is one which says that the state of affairs is so and so, and the state of affairs indeed is so and so.*" (. . .) "(2) *x is a true sentence if and only if p.*" (Italics in original.) – Cf. Anderson, "Alfred Tarski (1901–1983), Alonzo Church (1903–1995), and Kurt Gödel (1906–1978)", p. 125.

As a consequence, legal sentence L to the effect that "A is the owner of the thing R" is true, if and only if A is the owner of the thing R. Tarski's definition of truth amounts to a formal conception of truth and truthmakers with reference to the criteria that make a sentence true or untrue. The sentence S_1 to the effect that "A is the legal owner of the thing *x*" is true, if and only if A is the legal owner of the thing *x*. Tarski's semantic theory of truth of course says nothing of the *material criteria* of legal ownership, and they need to be specified in light of the norms of the legal order. To find out whether A really is the owner of *x*, one needs adequate knowledge of the institutional and societal sources of law, along with the prevalent models of legal reasoning that have been adopted in the legal system concerned.

When analysing the truth-value of a sentence Tarski introduced the distinction between the *object language* and the *metalanguage*.[48] The emergence of self-referential linguistic paradoxes and dilemmas, like the *Liar Paradox*, is thereby evaded.[49] The Liar Paradox is a *self-referential* assertion that has proven highly problematic, when judged from a traditional philosophical point of view. By means of the Tarskian object language *vs.* metalanguage distinction, and by placing any truth-theoretical analysis on the expressions of the object language on the level of the metalanguage, the threatening self-referentiality of the Liar Paradox is avoided.

It seems that Tarski's semantic conception of truth requires having recourse to an infinite set of ever higher-order metalanguages, if the judgment of the truth-value of a linguistic sentence is extended to sentences that make up the metalanguages of an ascending order. The metalanguage $L_{(n+1)}$ is linguistically richer than the respective object language L_n because it contains the truth-defining elements peculiar to the metalanguage plus the sum total of the expressions of the object language. Yet, the idea of having an endlessly ascending order of higher-order languages for the sole purpose of determining the truth-value of linguistic expression on a lower-level language is a less than fully satisfactory philosophical precondition to maintain.

2.7 A Critical Evaluation of the Isomorphic Theory of Law

Ludwig Wittgenstein's *Tractatus Logico-Philosophicus* and the notion of ontology and linguistic semantics entailed in it provide the "missing piece" in Kaarle Makkonen's notion of a judge's legal decision-making, as outlined in terms of legal isomorphism under the picture theory of language. A legal fact-description, as laid

[48] Tarski, "The Concept of Truth in Formalized Languages". – In *Logische Syntax der Sprache*, Rudolf Carnap to a great extent anticipated Tarski's distinction between the object language and the metalanguage. Carnap used the terms *object language* and *syntax language*. Carnap, *The Logical Syntax of Language*, p. 4. On a comparison between Carnap's and Tarski's conceptions of truth, Coffa, *The Semantic Tradition from Kant to Carnap*, pp. 300–305.

[49] The *Liar Paradox* was already considered above in the Introduction. Thus, a Cretan says: "all Cretans are liars". Is the assertion true or false? Is the speaker telling the truth or is he lying? If he is telling the truth, he is lying; and if he is lying, he is telling the truth. Therefore, the assertion is true, if it is false; and it is false, if it is true.

down in a legal rule, and a specific state of affairs that exists in the world may stand in a relation of *structural similarity* under the premises of legal isomorphism, if the key of isomorphism selected matches with the contents of the legal system in question. In such a case, both the internal *categorial structure* and the external *configuration structure* of the two states of affairs concerned are in match with each other, as insightfully analysed by the late Finnish philosopher Erik Stenius.

The internal categorial structure of reality consists of the elementary "things" or objects, the specific qualities attached to them, and the relations between them, resulting in the various "things + properties" combinations that constitute the totality of the possible states of affairs. The external configuration structure of the world consists of facts only, i.e. the states of affairs that actually prevail in the world. Such a notion of language and the world, defined as the states of affairs and their linguistic descriptions, may well be placed within the semantic context of legal fact-constellations, i.e. legal fact-descriptions.

The affirmation of the presence of an isomorphic relation between the two states of affairs, the one as depicted in the (legal or other) fact-description and the other as prevailing in the world, is itself a metaphysical postulate that cannot be empirically verified. Moreover, it is something one could not even legitimately speak of, if the austere philosophical stance of Ludwig Wittgenstein's *Tractatus Logico-Philosophicus* were strictly observed in a philosophical analysis.[50] The very idea of a relation of structural similarity between the *internal categorial* structure of reality and the logical syntax of language, and the structural similarity between the *external configuration* structure of the world and the effected empirical semantics and pragmatics of language, fall outside the realm of meaningful linguistic assertions under the *Tractarian* premises. The internal structure of language and the world, along with the relation that exists between the two, can only be *shown*, whereas it cannot be *said* or described by meaningful linguistic expressions, according to Wittgenstein's *Tractatus*.[51]

As a philosophical and semantic theory on the preconditions of truth, language and knowledge, the correspondence theory of truth is well reasoned for. The same goes for its offspring in the legal context, i.e. the judgment as to the presence or absence of structural affinity between two the states of affairs compared. As was argued above, the specific ontology of Wittgenstein's *Tractatus Logico-Philosophicus*, to the effect that states of affairs are the building blocks of reality and a picture relation prevails between any meaningful linguistic expressions and the world, provides a solid definition of an isomorphic relation for Kaarle Makkonen's theory of law and legal interpretation, as well. In addition, the correspondence theory of truth can be read in light of the Tarski's semantic theory of truth. As a consequence, the sentence S to the effect that "the table is white" is true, if and only if *p*, where *p* is equal to the propositional content that the table is white" The *epistemological* and *methodological* questions of how we can possibly know

[50] Wittgenstein, *Tractatus Logico-Philosophicus*, § 6.53 – 7 (pp. 186–189).

[51] Wittgenstein, *Tractatus Logico-Philosophicus*, § 4.12 – 4.1212 (p. 78/79).

whether the table is white or not cannot be reached by such a semantic inquiry, though.

The correspondence theory of truth, as applied to the issues of how to construct and read the law, may be critically evaluated from the point of view of the other conceptions of knowledge and truth. From the point of view of the *coherence* theory, the main fault of the correspondence theory lies in the fact that it totally ignores the inherently linguistic and community-related dimensions of all human knowledge, since they cannot be captured in an isomorphic relation between a linguistic assertion and the world. Still, all human knowledge is by necessity intertwined with language, since to have *intersubjective* knowledge, and not merely a subjective intuition that cannot be conveyed to others, is to *conceptualize* phenomena in giving them a linguistic expression. In the isomorphic theory of law, issues on how to construct and read the law boil down to the one issue of the choice of the key of isomorphism, and all other issues of legal interpretation are ignored. In addition, there is no room for the impact of textual support and mutual coherence of linguistic sentences, as derived e.g. from the institutional and societal sources of law, except for the alleged structural similarity between the two kinds of fact-descriptions compared.

Judged from the point of view of a *pragmatist* notion of truth and knowledge, the notion of an alleged correspondence between language and the world bypasses the consequences and external effects that any true item of knowledge will have on the life of humans. According to the pragmatists, any true belief must pass the test of empirical *corroboration* and the judgment as to "what concrete difference will its being true make in any one's actual life" in William James' phrasing of the issue. Moreover, the correspondence theory ignores the community-aligned dimensions of knowledge, as underscored by Thomas S. Kuhn in his account of the sociology of science and the dynamics of change in it, i.e. *The Structure of Scientific Revolutions*. In the last resort, it is invariably the scientific community that has the final say on what will qualify as scientific knowledge proper and what will fail in such a test.

Viewed from the point of view of philosophical ontology and semantics, the correspondence theory is able to present a highly consistent account of the relation that is thought to prevail between a linguistic assertion and the respective state of affairs in the world. In the legal context, such an isomorphic relation deals with the fact-description entailed in a legal rule and the corresponding state of affairs in the world. The sum total of such legal fact-descriptions, as laid down by the legislator and/or enforced by the courts of justice and other officials, may neatly be read in light of such a conception of reality. The definition of truth and knowledge as an *isomorphic* relation between a linguistic fact-description and the corresponding state of affairs in the world is intuitively easy to accept in line with Alfred Tarski's semantic theory of truth.

An isomorphic approach on how to construct and read the law leaves the judge rather empty-handed, though. From the judge's point of view, legal isomorphism ignores the very issues that the judge finds the most difficult: how to apply the law in a hard case of legal adjudication where there is no isomorphic relation between the two fact-situations? In Makkonen's terminology, the situation of semantic ambiguity, where recourse to the methodology of legal interpretation is needed from the judge, and the normative gap situation where there is no legal norm that would match with the case, are both ruled out of scope of the isomorphic approach. As a consequence, the isomorphic theory of law cannot cover legal principles, since they necessitate a highly *contextual* reading of the legal precept for the case. Similarly, it fails to comprise any legal rules that are burdened with some semantic ambiguity.

Chapter 3
Coherence Theory of Law: Shared Congruence Among Arguments Drawn from the Institutional and Societal Sources of Law

3.1 Truth As Coherence Among the Sentences of a Scientific Theory

Coherence is derived from the Latin term *cohaerentia*, with reference to the quality of certain things, objects, phenomena, or entities of being *connected* or *interrelated* vis-à-vis one another. The respective verb *cohaereo* refers to the quality of being *connected* (to something), *interrelated* (with something), or *held together* (by something). Here, coherence is taken in the linguistic and philosophical, and not literary or psychological, sense of the term. Thus, coherence has to do with the *semantics*, and not with the syntax or pragmatics, of language. The *syntagmatic* and *paradigmatic* qualities of language will be addressed in detail below, since they are an integral part of any narrative structure or pattern in language.

The coherence theory of truth rejects the idea that the truth of an idea, belief, assertion, or conception could be defined as the presence of an isomorphic, picture relation between a linguistic expression and a state of affairs in the world. Instead, all knowledge we may have of the world is intertwined and interlocked with the totality of other beliefs and conceptions we consider true. Moreover, all human knowledge is ultimately conditional on the epistemic and logico-linguistic prerequisites that define the prevailing *order of things*, in the sense of the links that bind together the "words", or linguistic expressions, and the "things", or the phenomena in the world. The French philosopher Michel Foucault has suggested adopting the two terms *épistémè* and *historical* a priori of the phenomenon under consideration.[1] Contrary to what the adherents of philosophical phenomenology would have us believe, there is no *epistemic shortcut* or a somehow privileged access to the true, a priori essence of the "things", entities, or phenomena "out there", to the effect of bypassing and placing into brackets the epistemic and logico-linguistic constraints that are placed on all human knowledge by the prevalent world-view. Thus, the coherence theory of truth bypasses, ignores, or "brackets" the external reference of linguistic concepts "out there".

[1] Foucault, *Les Mots et les choses*; cf. also Foucault, *L'Archéologie du savoir*.

R. Siltala, *Law, Truth, and Reason*, Law and Philosophy Library 97,
DOI 10.1007/978-94-007-1872-2_3, © Springer Science+Business Media B.V. 2011

The philosophical predicament of truth and knowledge under such premises has to do with the lack of any external reference of linguistic propositions: how can we distinguish true assertions of the world from, say, perfectly coherent fairy-tales and other plain fiction tales? According to the critics, naïve belief in textual coherence as the ultimate criterion of the validity of an assertion resembles Ludwig Wittgenstein's argument in his *Philosophical Investigations* to the effect that buying several copies of some newspaper would guarantee the validity of some individual item of news in it.[2] Still, even if the *definition* of truth were attached to the existence of structural similarity between language and a state of affairs in the world, as suggested by the correspondence theory, the operative *criteria* for judging the truth-value of an individual assertion still need to attached to the web of sentences and beliefs that are collectively upheld by the members of the community, since all knowledge must be somehow *conceptualized* before its validity can be judged. Any intuitive beliefs or revelations that cannot be given a comprehensible linguistic formulation and be communicated to others cannot satisfy the criteria of true knowledge, either.

According to the coherence theory of truth, knowledge can only be based on an internally *coherent* set of ideas, beliefs, sentences, or assertions expressed by means of language. As a consequence, the truth-value of an individual assertion can only be judged in its relation to all the other sentences concerning that field of life. Truth is a quality *internal* to a system of beliefs that is collectively sustained by the members of the community at a certain moment of time, and not an isomorphic relation between a linguistic expression and the states of affairs in the world. We have no access to reliable knowledge of the states of affairs in the world without first having gained access to some (fairly coherent) system of linguistic concepts by means of which the phenomena, states of affairs, or the like entities in the world can be depicted.

Ordinary language is not a closed system of concepts and sentences. Since the number of concepts and meaningful linguistic sentences is unlimited, judging the truth-value of a sentence – at least in principle – necessitates having acquired an understanding of an infinitely large set of other linguistic expressions. In real life, the set of sentences under investigation is of course much more focused, in line with the epistemic needs and interests involved in the investigation. As a consequence, the frame of linguistic sense and reference may be restricted to, for instance, the set of sentences that make up the branches of theoretical physics and astronomy, if the individual assertion under scrutiny deals with the Einsteinian general and specific theory of relativity. Similarly, it might be focused on a set of sentences on how to construct and read the law, as derived from the institutional and societal sources of law in a given legal system, if the individual assertion under consideration is a legal assertion.

---

[2]Wittgenstein, *Philosophical Investigations – Philosophische Untersuchungen*, § 265 (p. 94/94e).

Otto Neurath (1882–1945), one of the key figures of logical positivism (the *Wiener Kreis*), put the philosophical and scientific credo of the coherence theory vis-à-vis knowledge and truth concisely as follows[3]:

> If a statement is made, it is to be confronted with the totality of existing statements. If it agrees with them, it is joined to them; if it does not agree, it is called "untrue" and rejected; or the existing complex of statements of science is modified so that the new statement can be incorporated; the latter decision is mostly taken with hesitation. *There can be no other concept of "truth" for science.*

He also pointed out[4]:

> *Assertions are to be compared with assertions*, not with "experiences" or with a world, or with anything else. All of these senseless *duplications* belong in a more or less refined metaphysics and are therefore unacceptable. Each new assertion will be contrasted with the totality of those available assertions that have already been brought into harmony with each other. *An assertion is called "correct" when it can be incorporated* into this totality.

In legal analysis, the coherence theory places the focus on the relation between the two kinds of sentences involved, viz. sentences on the *outcome* of interpretation, on the one hand, and sentences on *justificatory reasons* for reaching the said outcome, on the other. If the presence of an isomorphic relation between the two fact-descriptions is successfully challenged, the isomorphic theory of law will leave the judge empty-handed, with no further means of legal analysis and construction. The coherence theory of interpretation, on the contrary, provides the judge or a legal scholar with a far more flexible intellectual toolbox for legal analysis. In terms of Wróblewski's equally three-partite categories of judicial decision-making we are now dealing with *legal* and *rational* judicial decision-making. Still, the very notion of *coherence* needs to be further elaborated and, if possible, defined.

3.2 In Search for the Concept of Coherence

3.2.1 A Quantitative Approach: "The More/Longer/Greater (. . .), the More Coherent the Theory"

What does the concept of *coherence* mean, to be more precise, when applied to a scientific theory, a set of assertions on how to construct and read the law, or any other set of linguistic assertions that share a common subject matter?

---

[3]Neurath, *Philosophical Papers*, p. 53. (Italics by Neurath.) Cited in Coffa, *The Semantic Tradition from Kant to Carnap*, p. 365. – Coffa's book is an excellent account of the historical unfolding of modern semantics "from Kant to Carnap", as the title of the book has it.

[4]Neurath, "Soziologie im Physikalismus", p. 403 (italics by Neurath), as cited in Coffa, *The Semantic Tradition from Kant to Carnap*, p. 365. Cf. Quine, "Two Dogmas of Empiricism", pp. 42–43.

The concept of coherence can be divided into the two categories of *synchronic* and *diachronic* coherence. The presence or absence of *synchronic* coherence in a set of linguistic assertions can be determined *sub speciae aeternitatis*, in disregard of the constraints of time and possible change in time of the object considered. The notion of *diachronic* coherence, on the other hand, underscores the impact of tradition, history, and temporal change (or immutability) upon the subject matter. In the context of law, both the synchronic and the diachronic conceptions of coherence may gain relevance.[5] As argued above, the presence or absence of coherence in a set of linguistic expressions must be sustained without making reference to the states of affairs "out there" in the world, if a coherentist stance in philosophy is to be maintained in a consistent manner.

The definition of coherence in a standard legal dictionary makes a reference to Aleksander Peczenik's notion of *normative coherence* in the sense that "legal principles support and explain a number of legal rules and make them coherent".[6] The definition then makes a reference to Ronald Dworkin's idea of legal integrity. I will first consider Aleksander Peczenik's and Robert Alexy's notion of coherence, and I will then evaluate Ronald Dworkin's contribution to the topic.

Aleksander Peczenik and Robert Alexy define coherence as a set of qualities that have to do with the *internal sentential structure*, the *concepts* utilized, and the *subject matter* of the theory.[7] The two authors then introduce the idea of *perfect supportive structure* as the normative ideal to be pursued when judging assertions on how to construct and read the law[8]:

> The more the statements belonging to a given theory approximate a perfect supportive structure, the more coherent the theory.

According to Peczenik and Alexy, the following criteria are pertinent for the evaluation of the attainment, or failure of attainment, of a *perfect supportive structure* of a theory[9]:

1. *Number of Supportive Relations*:
   Ceteris paribus, the more statements belonging to a theory are supported, the more coherent the theory.
2. *Length of Supportive Chains*:
   Ceteris paribus, the longer the chains of reasons belonging to a theory are, the more coherent the theory.

---

[5] On the two notions of *synchronic* and *diachronic* coherence, cf. Peczenik, "Coherence", p. 124.

[6] Peczenik, "Coherence", p. 124.

[7] Peczenik, "Coherence", pp. 124–125.

[8] Peczenik, *On Law and Reason*, p. 160; Alexy and Peczenik, "The Concept of Coherence and Its Significance for Discursive Rationality", p. 131.

[9] Peczenik, *On Law and Reason*, pp. 160–177; Alexy and Peczenik, "The Concept of Coherence and Its Significance for Discursive Rationality", pp. 132–143, 144–145.

3. *Strong Support Between Statements*:
   Ceteris paribus, the more statements belonging to a theory are strongly supported by other statements, the more coherent the theory.
4. *Connections Between Supportive Chains*:

   4.1. *Ceteris paribus*, the greater the number of conclusions supported by the same premise belonging to the theory in question, the more coherent the theory.
   4.2. *Ceteris paribus*, the greater the number of independent sets of premises within the theory in question, such that the same conclusion follows from each one of these sets, the more coherent the theory.

5. *Priority Order Between Reasons*:
   If the theory in question contains principles, then, *ceteris paribus*, the greater the number of priority relations between the principles, the more coherent the theory.
6. *Reciprocal Justification of Statements*:

   6.1. *Ceteris paribus*, the greater the number of reciprocal empirical relations between statements belonging to a theory, the more coherent the theory.
   6.2. *Ceteris paribus*, the greater the number of reciprocal analytical relations between statements belonging to a theory, the more coherent the theory.
   6.3. *Ceteris paribus*, the greater the number of reciprocal normative relations between statements belonging to a theory, the more coherent the theory.

7. *Generality of Concepts and Arguments*:

   7.1. *Ceteris paribus*, the more statements without individual names a theory uses, the more coherent the theory.
   7.2. *Ceteris paribus*, the greater number of general concepts belong to a theory, and the higher their degree of generality, the more coherent the theory.
   7.3. *Ceteris paribus*, the more resemblances between concepts used within a theory, the more coherent the theory.

8. *Conceptual Cross-Connections*:

   8.1. *Ceteris paribus*, the more concepts a given theory T_1 has in common with another theory T_2, the more coherent these theories are with other.
   8.2. *Ceteris paribus*, the more concepts a given theory T_1 contains that resemble the concepts used in another theory T_2, the more coherent these theories are with each other.

9. *Number of Cases Covered*:
   Ceteris paribus, the greater number of individual cases a theory covers, the more coherent the theory.
10. *Diversity of Fields of Life Covered*:
    Ceteris paribus, the more fields of life a theory covers, the more coherent the theory.

Peczenik's and Alexy's definition of coherence is thus given in terms of attaining (or at least pursuing) *perfect supportive structure* in a theory or set of sentences. But can the concept of coherence really be defined with a set of *quantified* attributes attached to a scientific theory or other set of sentences? I think not. As I see it, the notion of coherence needs has to be defined existing in the world a set of *qualitative*, not quantitative, criteria.

In specific, the number of cases and the diversity of fields of life covered by a theory (= points 9 and 10) do not deal with the coherence or incoherence of a theory or a set of sentences at all, but rather the field of application of the theory or set of sentences, which ought to be kept apart from the criteria of internal consistency and coherence involved. Similarly, the generality of the terms utilized in a theory (= point 7) does not have with the coherence of the theory to do, but only with the scope of concepts used in it. In addition, I find several of Peczenik's and Alexy's criteria less than entirely self-evident as constituents of the concept of coherence, such as the number, rather than the intensity, of the supportive relations (= point 1), the length of the chains of reasons (= point 2),[10] the number of priority relations between principles (= point 5),[11] relation of the theory to individual and general concepts (= point 7),[12] coverage of the theory vis-à-vis individual cases and fields of life (= points 9 and 10).[13]

On the other hand, the criteria that have to do with the relative portion of strongly supported sentences (= point 3), the connections between supportive chains (= point 4), the impact of analytical, empirical, and normative relations between sentences (= point 6), and the conceptual cross-connections between concepts (= point 8) are patently significant, when judging the presence or absence of coherence in a theory or set of sentences. Still, Peczenik's and Alexy's claim of stating such criteria in quantified terms cannot be upheld.[14]

---

[10]With reference to Peczenik's points 1 and 2: an interlocking "seamless web" of a few apt reasons given in support of a certain conclusion might well be more coherent than an elaborate puzzle-work of hundreds or even thousands of wildly criss-crossing sentences, since in the latter case the internal relations between sentences are prone to become more complex and open to alternative interpretations (unless we are dealing with the fully unambiguous sentences of formal logic, artificial languages, or mathematics).

[11]Value-laden principles and other legal standards that satisfy Dworkin's twin criteria of enjoying adequate *institutional support* and *sense of approval* in the legal community cannot be locked into a fixed system of legal concepts or decision-making criteria, due to the methodology of *weighing and balancing* the value-laden principles for the case at hand. In this, legal principles are radically different from legal rules that can be placed in such a system, as exemplified by Hans Kelsen's and A. J. Merkl's idea of the norm hierarchy or norm pyramid.

[12]Why should general concepts yield more easily into parts of a theory of coherence? In fact, the issue at hand concerns the extent of the field of application of the theory in question, with general concepts providing for a larger domain of application than individual concepts, and not the coherence of the theory.

[13]In other words, the semantic reference of a theory should be distinguished from its internal structure of argumentation, while it is only the latter issue that has something to do with the concept of coherence.

[14]Peczenik answers the critique of possibly highly coherent fairy-tales by writing: "The contact with reality is provided by the criteria of coherence. Criterion 9 [number of cases covered]

It may even be the case that Peczenik and Alexy commit a *category-mistake* in the Rylean sense,[15] when they define the concept of coherence in a such purely quantified terms with reference to the common argumentation structure: "the more/longer/greater (some element of) the theory *x*, the more coherent the theory *x*". To put it bluntly, the presence or absence of coherence in a theory or a set of sentences cannot be captured by quantified formula of the type "*ceteris paribus*, the more statements belonging to a theory are supported, the more coherent the theory" (= point 1), "*ceteris paribus*, the longer the chains of reasons belonging to a theory are, the more coherent the theory" (= point 2), or "*ceteris paribus*, the greater the number of independent set of premises within the theory or the number of conclusions supported by the same premise in the theory in question, the more coherent the theory" (= points 4.1. and 4.2.), without transforming the traditional notion of law into a something like a mathematical calculation of legal theory-construction. As I see it, a totally different approach is needed here.

Moreover, the notion of coherence, too, is patently exposed to G. E. Moore's *open question argument*. The primary target of Moore's critique was the variety of theories on ethics that, according to him, all fell victim to the *naturalistic fallacy*, when they gave a definition of "good" in terms of, say, the greatest quantity of happiness brought to the greatest number as in Jeremy Bentham's utilitarian social philosophy. According to Moore, the concept of *good* is in the last resort indefinable. Any naturalistic or reductive would-be definition of "good" is invariably exposed to the open question argument: now that you have defined the notion of "good" as *x*, is *x* (genuinely) "good"?[16]

The only escape from Moore's open question argument is by acknowledging the ultimately *indefinable* character of the notion of "good", and by then having resort to the *meta-level* linguistic analysis of the concepts of "good", "right", and "just" in the different contexts or situations of ordinary language, as exemplified by the Oxford school of linguistic philosophy. Gilbert Ryle's *The Concept of Mind*, Georg Henrik von Wright's *The Varieties of Goodness*, and H. L. A. Hart's *The Concept of Law* are prime examples thereof.[17] Moore's open question argument of course affects any would-be definition of coherence, no matter whether given in quantified or qualified terms, so that route will not lead us very far out from the deadlock.

As I see it, the validity of any suggested definition of the notion of coherence can only be judged in light of its use in the legal analysis and its match with the subject

---

thus demands that a coherence theory covers a great number of 'data candidates', or 'certain statements'. Criterion 3 [strong support between statements] relates coherence to presupposed statements, which characterise a certain practice, such as legal reasoning." Peczenik, *On Law and Reason*, pp. 179–181 (the citation on p. 179). – Still, the Moorean open question argument haunts the theory: *is* such a notion in fact equal to coherence?

[15]Ryle, *The Concept of Mind*, pp. 17–19.

[16]Moore, *Principia Ethica*, pp. 58–72. " 'Good', then, if we mean by it that quality which we assert to belong to a thing, when we say that the thing is good, is incapable of any definition, in the most important sense of that word." Moore, *Principia Ethica*, p. 61. On the naturalistic fallacy and its critique, Moore, *Principia Ethica*, p. 62 et seq.

[17]von Wright, *The Varieties of Goodness*.

matter of such analysis. I think a qualitative approach fares better in that respect. As a consequence, coherence is a *relational* concept that has to do the *internal structure* of a scientific theory or set of sentences with reference to the mutual relations of the concepts, sentences, or arguments entailed vis-à-vis one another, when read in light of some key of interpretation adopted. I will return to the (re)definition of coherence after having tackled the role of legal principles in Ronald Dworkin's jurisprudence and the impact of the *Duhem-Quine Thesis*, as adopted in the philosophy of science, on Dworkin's theory of law.

3.2.2 A Qualitative Approach: "That the Law is Structured by a Coherent Set of Principles About Justice and Fairness and Procedural Due Process..."

Ronald Dworkin has defined legal coherence as *law as integrity*, i.e. as "the best constructive interpretation of past political decisions".[18] He is committed to a set of *qualitative*, not quantitative criteria, as constitutive of legal coherence. His conception of law is intertwined with the idea of legal principles with possibly no more than oblique but still legally adequate *institutional support* and *societal approval*.[19] Yet, instead of presenting a fairly precise, down-to-earth definition of legal coherence, Dworkin opts for a loose-edged collection of metaphors and analogies to corner the issue, such as the *chain novel* metaphor, where the judge is likened to the author of a novel written *seriatim*, based on a constructive reading of the prior legal and political decisions; the idea of courts as the capitals and the judges as the princes of law in the law's empire[20]; and the famous idea of the fictitious super-judge *Hercules*, "a lawyer of superhuman skill, learning, patience, and acumen",[21] who alone is allegedly capable of reaching *the best constructive interpretation of past political decisions* for a novel case at hand.[22] True, Dworkin avoids the philosophical pitfalls related to the quantification of legal coherence à la Robert Alexy and

[18] Dworkin, *Law's Empire*, p. 262. – Cf. "According to law as integrity, propositions of law are true if they figure in or follow from the principles of justice, fairness, and procedural due process that provide *the best constructive interpretation of the community's legal practice*." Dworkin, *Law's Empire*, p. 255. (Italics added.)

[19] "... in those in hard cases... [the lawyers] make use of standards that do not function as rules, but operate differently as principles, policies, and other sorts of standards." Dworkin, *Taking Rights Seriously*, p. 22.

[20] "The courts are the capitals of law's empire, and judges are its princes, but not its seers and prophets. It falls to philosophers, if they are willing, to work out law's ambitions for itself, the purer form of law within and beyond the law we have." Dworkin, *Law's Empire*, p. 407.

[21] Dworkin, "Hard Cases", p. 105; cf. Dworkin, *Law's Empire*, p. 239 et seq.

[22] Dworkin, *Law's Empire*, p. 262. – At times, Dworkin's style of argumentation is reminiscent of Lon L. Fuller's sky-soaring rhetoric, with reference to the ideals of *perfection in legality*, *legal excellence*, and *utopia in legality*, plus the appeal to *a sense of trusteeship* and *the pride of the craftsman* on part of the legislator.

Aleksander Peczenik, but his sky-soaring legal rhetoric is prone to invite trouble of another kind.

The modern conception of legal principles in guiding the judge's legal discretion is to a great extent outlined by Ronald Dworkin since the late 1960s. In his influential essay "The Model of Rules, I", Dworkin criticized the then predominant, exclusively rule-aligned notion of law that had been established in H. L. A. Hart's *The Concept of Law* in 1961. Hart had argued that in a *hard case* of legal adjudication where there is no legal rule in the legal order that could guide the judge's legal discretion and thus determine the outcome of the case,[23] the judge's role in legal discretion can be compared to that enjoyed by the legislator, free of constraints other than those imposed by the valid constitution and, in light of the subsequent legal development, international legal conventions, such as the Treaty of the European Union or the European Convention for the Protection of Human Rights and Fundamental Freedoms.

Dworkin has forcefully – and, it would seem, quite convincingly – argued that there is no area of free discretion even in a hard case of legal decision-making. Far from being totally free and unconstrained, the judge is bound by the principles of law, on the condition that they enjoy adequate institutional support and a sense of approval in the legal community. Dworkin, moreover, put forth the argument that there often is one right answer to a legal case due to the normative impact of legal principles.[24] It would seem that the role accorded to the one right answer thesis has gained too much weight in the subsequent literature, while the reservations pinpointed by Dworkin have mostly gone unnoticed by his readers and critics. First of all, Dworkin points out that there often, but not always, is one right answer to a legal problem. Secondly, the issue is looked upon from the lawyer's, and not the philosopher's, point of view.[25] What all that signifies is not easy to evaluate as concerns the legal and/or philosophical validity of Dworkin's argument.

---

[23] We are thus dealing with a normative gap situation in Makkonen's terminology, or a situation where there are two or more mutually conflicting legal rules that cannot be applied to the case at the same time.

[24] Cf. e.g. "Hard Cases" and "Can Rights Be Controversial?", both reprinted in *Taking Rights Seriously*; "Is There Really No Right Answer in Hard Cases?", in *A Matter of Principle*; and in "Appendix: A Reply to Critics", in the second, enlarged edition of *Taking Rights Seriously* in 1978.

[25] Dworkin, "Pragmatism, Right Answers, and True Banality", p. 365 where the author underscores the *pragmatic*, *anti-metaphysical* character of the one right answer thesis: "My thesis about right answers in hard cases is, as I have said, a very weak and commonsensical legal claim. It is a claim made within legal practice rather than at some supposedly removed, external, philosophical level. I ask whether, in the ordinary sense in which lawyers might say this, it is ever sound or correct or accurate to say, about some hard case, that the law, properly interpreted, is for the plaintiff (or for the defendant). I answer that, yes, some statements of that kind are sound or correct or accurate about some hard cases." – Similarly in "Can Rights Be Controversial?", p. 279: "My arguments suppose that there is *often* a single rights answer to complex questions of law and political morality." (Italics added.)

Be that as it may, in the heated debate with H. L. A. Hart Dworkin did consistently defend the idea of one right answer to a legal problem.[26] It is only in his later writings that Dworkin has changed the weight of emphasis onto the notion of *law as integrity*, with reference to "the best constructive interpretation of the community's legal practice".[27] The contested claim of the one right answer to a legal problem has given room to the analysis of legal coherence in such terms. Law as integrity entails a greater degree of inherent systematicity of law than the earlier idea of legal principles defended in "The Model of Rules, I". In that article Dworkin underscored that legal principles have only weak mandatory force on the judge's discretion[28]:

> Only rules dictate results, come what may. When a contrary result has been reached, the rule has been abandoned or changed. Principles do not work that way; they *incline a decision one way, though not conclusively*, and they survive intact when they do not prevail.

Still, Dworkin's assertion of the non-conclusive character of legal principles is in flat contradiction with the notion he defended a moment earlier in the same writing, when he commented on *Riggs v. Palmer* (115 N.Y. 506; 22 N.E. 188 (1889)). In it, the *general, fundamental maxims of the common law*, such as the principle that "no one shall be permitted to profit by his own fraud, or to take advantage of his own wrong, or to found any claim upon his own iniquity, or to acquire property by his own crime", were now enforced by the court, to the effect of overriding the valid statutory legal rule (then) in force, to the effect that the duly documented last will of the deceased person is to be enforced as such *post mortem*.[29] Contrary to Dworkin's express claim, in *Riggs v. Palmer* the general, fundamental maxims of the common law had a strong mandatory force. In fact, they had an even stronger normative impact than the statutory rule to the contrary effect. The term "mandatory force" refers to the normative impact that a legal norm or argument exerts upon the judge's or other official's legal discretion.

A legal system consists of legal norms. A *legal norm* is a combination of two states of affairs, viz. a legal *fact-situation* in the sense of some state of affairs described *in abstracto* and a set of *legal consequences* attached to those facts, as connected to one another by the *deontic operator*. The deontic operator gives the fact–legal consequences relation a legally binding quality, to the effect that legal consequences specified in the legal norm *ought* to be enforced by the judge or other

---

[26]See e.g. Dworkin, *Taking Rights Seriously*, pp. 331–338 ("Munzer and No Right Answer").

[27]"According to law as integrity, propositions of law are true if they figure in or follow from the principles of justice, fairness, and procedural due process that provide the best constructive interpretation of the community's legal practice." Dworkin, *Law's Empire*, p. 225.

[28]Dworkin, "The Model of Rules, I", p. 35. (Italics added.) – Cf. also Dworkin, "The Model of Rules, I", p. 26: "All that is meant, when we say that a particular principle is a principle of our law, is that the principle is one which officials must take into account, if it is relevant, as a consideration inclining in one direction or another."

[29]Dworkin, *Taking Rights Seriously*, p. 23: "... all laws as well as all contracts may be controlled in their operation and effect by general, fundamental maxims of the common law. No one shall be permitted to profit by his own fraud, or to take advantage of his own wrong, or to found any claim upon his own iniquity, or to acquire property by his own crime."

legal official, if the facts given in the fact-description of the legal norm are present. Following Ronald Dworkin's analysis, legal norms may be of two kinds, legal *rules* or legal *principles*.

Legal principles differ from legal rules on several accounts. In *Taking Rights Seriously*, Dworkin depicts legal principles with the following kind of criteria:

(a) *validity* and *recognition of law*: the normative impact of legal principles on the discretion of a judge is not based on their formal source of origin in legislation or individual judicial decisions to the effect of satisfying the "test of pedigree" in Dworkin's terminology, but on the *institutional support* they are able to draw from the legal source material and the *sense of approval* they enjoy in the legal community[30];
(b) *normative logic*: legal principles are applied in a *more-or-less* kind of manner, in contrast to legal rules that are applied in an *all-or-nothing*, or *either/or*, kind of manner[31];
(c) *value-ladenness*: legal principles, unlike legal rules, have a *dimension of weight* or *importance*, expressive of a *sense of appropriateness* that is attached to them in the legal community[32];
(d) *mandatory force*: the *binding effect* of legal principles is weaker than that of legal rules, as the former no more than "incline a legal decision in one

---

[30]"Yet we could not devise any formula for testing how much and what kind of institutional support is necessary to make a principle a legal principle, still less to fix its weight at a particular order of magnitude. We argue for a particular principle by grappling with a whole set shifting, developing and interacting standards (themselves principles rather than rules) bout *institutional responsibility*, *statutory interpretation*, *the persuasive force of various sorts of precedents*, the relation of all these to *contemporary moral practices*, and hosts of *other such standards*. We could not bolt all of these together into a single 'rule', even a complex one, and if we could the result would bear little relation to Hart's picture of a rule of recognition, which is the picture of a fairly stable master rule specifying 'some feature or features possession of which by a suggested rule is taken as a conclusive affirmative indication that it is a rule . . .'" Dworkin, *Taking Rights Seriously*, pp. 40–41. (Italics added.) – "But this *test of pedigree* [i.e. a rule of recognition à la Hart] will not work for the *Riggs* and *Henningsen* principles. The origin of these as legal principles lies not in a particular decision of some legislature or court, but in a *sense of appropriateness* developed in the profession and the public over time. Their continued power depends upon this sense of appropriateness being sustained." Dworkin, *Taking Rights Seriously*, p. 40. (Italics added, except in the two cases *Riggs* and *Henningsen*.)

[31]"The difference between legal principles and legal rules is a *logical* distinction. Both sets of standards point to a particular decision about legal obligation in particular circumstances, but they differ in the character of the direction they give. Rules are applicable in an *all-or-nothing* fashion. If the facts a rule stipulates are given, then either the rule is valid, in which case the answer it supplies must be accepted, or it is not, in which case it case it contributes nothing to the decision. (. . .) But this is not the way the sample principles in the quotations operate. Even those which look most like rules do not set out legal consequences that follow automatically when the conditions provided are met." Dworkin, *Taking Rights Seriously*, pp. 24, 25. (Italics added.)

[32]"Principles have a dimension that rules do not – *the dimension of weight or importance*. (. . .) it makes sense to ask how important or how weighty [a principle] is." Dworkin, *Taking Rights Seriously*, pp. 26, 27. (Italics added.)

direction or another", without being able to determine a particular outcome in the case[33]; and

(e) *method of application*: legal principles and other standards need to be *weighed and balanced* against each other, whereby the social values and goals entailed in legal principles are each weighed for the case at hand.[34]

In his subsequent writings, Dworkin has introduced the notion of *law as integrity*, with reference to the constraints placed upon the discretion of the legislator and the courts alike.[35] Integrity in adjudication is intertwined with legal coherence[36]:

> [Integrity in adjudication] requires our judges, so far as this is possible, to treat our present system of public standards as expressing and respecting a *coherent set of principles*, and, to that end, to interpret these standards to find implicit standards between and beneath the explicit ones. (...) Law as integrity asks judges to assume, so far as this is possible, that the law is structured by a *coherent set of principles* about justice and fairness and procedural due process, and it asks them to enforce these in the fresh cases that come before them, so that each person's situation is fair and just according to the same standards.

The notion of *law as integrity*, introduced in *Law's Empire*, sets the pace for Dworkin's later works, such as *Freedom's Law*, *Life's Dominion* and *Justice in Robes*. The precise content of legal integrity to some extent varies in different texts.[37] Still, the phrase *the best constructive interpretation of past political*

---

[33]"Only rules dictate results, come what may. When a contrary result has been reached, the rule has been abandoned or changed. Principles do not work that way; they incline a decision one way, though not conclusively, and they survive intact when they do not prevail." Dworkin, *Taking Rights Seriously*, p. 35. – Cf.: "Rather, [a legal principle] states a reason that argues in one direction, but does not necessitate a particular decision. (...) All that is meant, when we say that a particular principle is a principle of our law, is that the principle is one which officials must take into account, if it is relevant, *as a consideration inclining in one direction or another*." Dworkin, *Taking Rights Seriously*, p. 26. (Italics added.) – Nonetheless, in Dworkin's own classic example *Riggs v. Palmer*, however, the legal principles according to which no one may profit from his own wrong-doing was allowed to supersede the perfectly valid legal rule according to which the last will of the deceased person is to be respected.

[34]"When principles intersect (the policy of protecting automobile consumers intersecting with principles of freedom of contract, for example [in Henningsen *v.* Bloomfield Motors, Inc.]), one who must resolve the conflict has to take into account the relative weight of each. This cannot be, of course, an exact measurement, and the judgment that a particular principle or policy is more important than another will often be a controversial one." Dworkin, *Taking Rights Seriously*, p. 26. – According to Dworkin, the collision of legal rules and legal principles has to be resolved at the level of principles: "The court weights two sets of principles in deciding whether to maintain the rule ..." Dworkin, *Taking Rights Seriously*, p. 78.

[35]Dworkin, *Law's Empire*, p. 217: "I distinguished two branches or forms of integrity by listing two principles: integrity in legislation and integrity in adjudication."

[36]Dworkin, *Law's Empire*, pp. 217, 243. (Italics added.)

[37]E.g.: "According to law as integrity, propositions of law are true if they figure in or follow from the principles of justice, fairness, and procedural due process that provide *the best constructive interpretation of the community's legal practice*." Dworkin, *Law's Empire*, p. 225 (italics added); "how to make ... the best story ... from the standpoint of political morality", Dworkin, *Law's Empire*, p. 239; "Judges who accept the interpretive ideal of integrity decide hard cases by trying to

decisions would seem to capture its core fairly accurately.[38] But what is legal integrity, to be more precise?

For the first, Dworkin compares the task of the judge or other legal official to that of an author who is writing a novel *seriatim*. The judge, like the co-author of a *chain novel*, is required to continue the evolving legal narrative as found in, or rather to be reconstructed from, the sum total of prior legislative and judicial decisions, in as coherent a manner as is possible.[39] The judge, like the co-author of a chain novel, cannot resolve a hard case of adjudication in a haphazard, whimsical, or capricious manner, in disregard of the evolving legal and political narrative on how the allocation of legal rights and duties among citizens, the institution and division of decision-making authority, and the allocation of scarce material resources in society have previously been accomplished. Law as integrity equals the idea of reconstructing and carrying on the prevailing meta-narrative of law and society so that the outcome of legal discretion for the individual case under consideration and the earlier legal decisions, when read together, make up as *coherent* a narrative as is possible in light of the institutional and societal values involved.

An author of a (fictitious) novel, whether written *seriatim* or by a single author, can always bring about some unpredictable turn in the narrative. Without the possibility of such twists and turns in the evolving narrative, detective stories and other crime fiction could hardly be possible, and most other fiction would lose its edge as well if the future course of events could be fully predicted beforehand. Similarly the judge always has the possibility of overruling a precedent in favour of a totally different rule. The narrative structure of the narrative so far evolved constrains any later co-author of a chain novel, but it does so to a certain degree only.

As a consequence, a judge who is to rule on the facts of a case always has the final say on how to construct and read the law within the legal tradition, as defined by the prevailing conception of the institutional and societal sources of law and the models of legal reasoning acknowledged in the community. The judge may opt for a novel reading of the *ratio decidendi* of a prior precedent, turning the previously settled conception of *ratio/dicta* dichotomy in that case into a wholly new direction. In a chain novel effort, that would count as a fully unexpected turn in the narrative. Moreover, a judge may explicitly overrule or bluntly disregard a perfectly valid

---

find, in some coherent set of principles about people's rights and duties, *the best constructive interpretation of the political structure and legal doctrine of their community*." Dworkin, *Law's Empire*, p. 255 (italics added); "... that the grounds of law lie in integrity, in *the best constructive interpretation of past political decisions* ..." Dworkin, *Law's Empire*, p. 262 (italics added); "[Hercules] is guided instead by a sense of *constitutional integrity*; he believes that the American Constitution consists in the best available interpretation of American constitutional text and practice as a whole, and his judgment about which interpretation is best is sensitive to the great complexity of political virtues bearing on that issue." Dworkin, *Law's Empire*, pp. 397–398 (italics added); "... which interpretation, all things considered, makes the community's legal record *the best it can be from the point of view of political morality*." Dworkin, *Law's Empire*, p. 411. (Italics added).

[38] Dworkin, *Law's Empire*, p. 262.

[39] Dworkin, "How Law Is Like Literature"; Dworkin, *Law's Empire*, pp. 228–238,

precedent, which would correspond to the act of effecting a by-plot or sidetrack in the chain-novel or turning the prior course of action in the novel upside down.

For the second, the notion of integrity in law is closely intertwined with value-laden *principles* and *standards* of law that help sustain a common frame for the law and political morality in society.[40] In a hard case of legal adjudication, the normative force of legal principles on the discretion of the judge is to be duly acknowledged as pertinent criteria for legal decision-making. It seems there are three typical legal decision-making situations in which the normative impact of legal principles ought to be duly recognized: (a) a situation where the normative, guiding force of legal rules has run out or proven inadequate for the case, leaving the judge without guidance, in the sense of a normative gap or an unregulated situation in Kaarle Makkonen's terminology; (b) a situation of norm conflict between two or more legal rules which can only be solved by taking the impact of material legal principles into consideration, as are effective at the back of the rules in question[41]; and (c) a situation where the application of formally valid legal rules would yield an axiologically intolerable or totally unacceptable outcome.

For the third, Dworkin underscores the inherently *deliberative,* constructive, and self-reflective character of law and legal discretion[42]:

> Law's empire is defined by attitude, not territory of power or process. (...) It is an *interpretive, self-reflective attitude* addressed to politics in the broadest sense. It is a protestant attitude that makes each citizen responsible for imagining what his society's public commitments to principle are, and what these commitments require in new circumstances. (...) Law's attitude is *constructive*: it aims, in the interpretive spirit, to lay principle over practice to show the best route to a better future, keeping the right faith with the past. It is, finally, a fraternal attitude, an expression of how we are united in community though divided in project, interest, and conviction.

Dworkin illustrates the notion of legal integrity with the fictitious super-judge Hercules, J. whom he first introduced in the essay "Hard Cases" in 1975. In one of Dworkin's most memorable "purple passages",[43] the courts are described as the capitals and judges as the princes of the "law's empire", and Justice Hercules

---

[40]Cf.: "... in those in hard cases... [the lawyers] make use of standards that do not function as rules, but operate differently as principles, policies, and other sorts of standards." Dworkin, *Taking Rights Seriously*, p. 22.

[41]Cf. Dworkin, *Taking Rights Seriously*, pp. 77–78. "Suppose a court decides to overrule an established common law rule that there can be no legal liability for negligent misstatements, and appeals to a number of principles to justify this decision, including the principle that it is unjust that one man suffer because of another man's wrong. The court must be understood as deciding that the set of principles calling for the overruling of the established rule, including the principle of justice just mentioned, are as a group of greater weight under the circumstances that the set of principles, including the principle of stare decisis, that call for maintaining the rule as before. The court weighs two sets of principles in deciding whether to maintain the rule; it is therefore misleading to say that the court weighs the rule itself against one or the other set of these principles."

[42]Dworkin, *Law's Empire*, p. 413. (Italics added.)

[43]The term of *purple passages* was introduced by Ronald Dworkin's (now deceased) wife who referred to the highly metaphorical notions in Dworkin's text with it, as Dworkin himself mentioned during his visit in my researcher seminar in Finland in May 2008.

is depicted as "a lawyer of superhuman skill, learning, patience, and acumen".[44] Justice Hercules, and only he, may attain "the best constructive interpretation of past political decisions",[45] i.e. the most coherent reading of the legal rules and legal principles, policies, and other sorts of legal standards that can be inferred from the valid institutional and societal legal source material in the community. Though no human judge could follow Hercules in his meticulous process of such sophisticated legal construction and analysis, the former is still required to do his best to imitate Hercules' legal discretion[46]:

> The law may not be a seamless web; but the plaintiff is entitled to ask Hercules to treat it as if it were. (...) He [i.e. Hercules] must construct a scheme of abstract and concrete principles that provides a coherent justification for all common law precedents and, so far as these are to be justified on principle, constitutional and statutory provisions as well.

Hercules provides a reference for the human judges by means of which the degree of coherence attained in reading a series of precedents, other judicial decisions, or statutes may best be critically evaluated. Under such deliberative terms, even the claim of attaining one right answer to a legal problem is possible, Dworkin argues. Still, like Chaïm Perelman's notion of the *universal audience*, Dworkin's super-judge *Hercules* is a subjective thought construct only, and not something that could be subjected to some objective criteria or tests. Because of the fictitious, hypothetical character of the super-judge Hercules, any assertion on how to construct and read the law that has judge Hercules among its set of truth-constitutive premises is an *as if* kind of a claim only: if the deliberation of judge Hercules and the resulting concept of coherence is conceived in z manner, then the content of law vis-à-vis the fact-constellation x will be y.

But how could we possibly corroborate the bold claim as expressly or tacitly made by an audacious judge driven by such Herculean aspirations, to the effect that the outcome of his legal discretion truly meets up with Dworkin's standard? There is always more than one way of (re)constructing the internal coherence of law, and a host of alternative interpretative options is ruled out each time a choice for one particular outcome is made among them. It seems that belief in Dworkin's approach requires a sheer an act of faith by the legal community vis-à-vis such would-be Herculean oracles of the law, since there is no means of finding out or controlling whether the criteria of legal integrity have been met with, if the reasons given for the decision fail to fully convince the audience. Moreover, there are all too many "purple passages" of the sky-soaring, abstract metaphors, and too little of sober legal analysis, in Dworkin's account of the judge's legal deliberation.

---

[44] Dworkin, "Hard Cases", p. 105; cf. Dworkin, *Law's Empire*, p. 239 et seq.

[45] Dworkin, *Law's Empire*, p. 262.

[46] Dworkin, "Hard Cases", pp. 116–117. – *Iudex non calculat*: if the decision-making procedure of a human judge, or of super-judge Hercules, J. for that matter, could be captured in purely quantified terms, that would be equal to justice computerized and calculated. If such were the case, legal decision-making could well be entrusted to a computer. But computers rate low in the weighing and balancing of value-laden arguments.

3.3 The *Duhem-Quine Thesis*: The Inherently Holistic and Underdetermined Character of a Scientific Theory, and Its Implications for Legal Analysis

The *Duhem-Quine Thesis* as a scientific and philosophical stance is attributed to two individual thinkers, the one a physicist, Pierre-Maurice-Marie Duhem (1861–1916), and the other a philosopher, Williard Orman Van Quine (1918–2000).[47] There are two elements entailed in the *Duhem-Quine Thesis*, i.e. the *holistic* character of a scientific theory and its *underdetermined* character vis-à-vis any individual empirical observations.

For the first, judging of the truth-value of a scientific theory is a *holistic* issue, to the effect that the totality of sentences that make up a scientific explanation is considered primary vis-à-vis any individual empirical findings or, to be more exact, individual assertions based on such findings. Scientific explanation is an *all-inclusive* venture where some individual phenomenon cannot be explained except by reference to the totality of sentences that make up a scientific theory. There is no method of evaluating any individual assertion as such, or detached from the wider theoretical context or background provided by the scientific theory in question.

Science is an inherently *tradition-bound* phenomenon. Therefore, prior empirical findings and settled conceptual truths of a branch of scientific study have a strong impact on how the new empirical findings are to be treated scientifically. If the on-going tradition of a particular branch of science is abruptly broken, we are witnessing a *scientific revolution* in the Kuhnian sense of the term, or a profound *epistemic break* in the prevailing order of things that connects the "words", or linguistic expressions, and "things", or phenomena in the world, to one another.[48] In the context of law, a thorough transformation of the settled legal order would signify a social upheaval or at least a small-scale revolution. Alternatively, it could signify a return to the original position that conceptually precedes the entering into a social contract.[49]

Far more frequent than a total upheaval of the prevailing *status quo* in science is the adoption of smaller, step-by-step changes in the edifice of a scientific theory or metanarrative of law, induced by some recalcitrant empirical findings vis-à-vis a scientific theory or some novel legal or social ideas vis-à-vis the question of how to construct and read the law under some frame of legal analysis, leaving the prevailing meta-theory of science or law otherwise intact. Such *small-scale dynamics*

---

[47] Actually, the conceptions held by Duhem and Quine to a significant degree differ from each other, as is quite expectable, since the one author was a physicist and the other a philosopher. One reason for the said doctrine being commonly known as the *Duhem-Quine Thesis* is due to Quine's acknowledgment of the significance of Duhem's original ideas in the key section of his own classic article. Cf. Quine, "Two Dogmas of Empiricism", p. 41, note 17.

[48] Kuhn, *The Structure of Scientific Revolutions*; Foucault, *Les Mots et les choses. Une Archéologie des sciences humaines*.

[49] On the social contract that would be reached in the *original position* behind the *veil of ignorance* in Rawls' influential theory of social justice, Rawls, *A Theory of Justice*, pp. 136–142.

of change that may take place within the semantic confines of a scientific theory is admirably captured by Otto Neurath (1882–1945) in his metaphor of the sailors at the open sea who have to repair their ship in the midst of the ocean, never having the privilege of taking it to the dock for a total renewal and reconstruction[50]:

> *There is no way of taking conclusively established pure protocol sentences as the starting point of the sciences.* No *tabula rasa* exists. We are like sailors who must rebuild their ship on the open sea, never able to dismantle it in dry-dock and to reconstruct it there out of the best materials. Only the metaphysical elements can be allowed to vanish without trace. Vague linguist conglomerations always remain in one way or another as components of the ship. If vagueness is diminished at one point, it may well be increased at another.

The logic of scientific change, i.e. a change effected in a set of assertions that make up a *scientific explanation*, and the logic of change in *legal analysis*, i.e. a change effected in set of assertions on how to construct and read the law in light of arguments duly derived from the institutional and non-institutional sources of law, are in this respect similar. Rather than inducing a total upheaval of the meta-context of scientific or legal analysis, intellectual endeavours far more often lead to some small-scale, step-by-step adjustments in the prevailing world-view, when faced with some recalcitrant empirical findings in the natural sciences or some odd fact-constellations in the legal analysis.

For the second, and closely related to the former tenet of scientific holism, any scientific theory or set of sentences that share a common focus, common subject matter, and common context of knowledge is by necessity *underdetermined* in relation to the world of empirical observations. In the case of legal analysis, an analogical situation of underdetermination may prevail between the sentences on legal interpretation and the sentences of legal justification that are brought in their support, as drawn from the prevailing set of institutional and societal sources of law. According to the *Duhem-Quine Thesis*, a frame of scientific explanation can always be saved from the thrust of recalcitrant phenomena or empirical counter-evidence by modifying the scientific theory to such an extent as is necessary.

In the philosophy of science, the inherently *holistic* and *underdetermined* character of a scientific theory vis-à-vis any empirical evidence is known as the *Duhem-Quine Thesis*, as suggested by Pierre-Maurice-Marie Duhem and Williard Orman Van Quine. As Quine wrote[51]:

> The dogma of reductionism survives in the supposition that each statement, taken in isolation from its fellows, can admit of confirmation or infirmation at all. My countersuggestion, issuing essentially from Carnap's doctrine of the physical world in the *Aufbau*, is that our

---

[50] Neurath, "Protocol Sentences", p. 210. (Italics by Neurath). Cf. also: "The fate of being discarded may befall even a protocol sentence. No sentence enjoys the *noli me tangere* which Carnap ordains for protocol sentences." Neurath, "Protocol Sentences", p. 203.– Cf. Coffa, *The Semantic Tradition from Kant to Carnap*, p. 358: "The elements of the Protocol are 'the sentences that need no justification but serve as foundation for all of the remaining sentences of science.'" (The inner quotation from Carnap's "Die physikalische Sprache als Universalsprache der Wissenschaft", p. 438).

[51] Quine, "Two Dogmas of Empiricism", pp. 41, 43. (Italics added in the full sentence).

> statements about the world face the tribunal of sense experience not individually but only as a corporate body. (...) *Any statement can be held true come what may, if we make drastic enough adjustments elsewhere in the system.* Even a statement very close to the periphery can be held true in the face of recalcitrant experience by pleading hallucination or by amending certain statements of the kind called logical laws. Conversely, by the same token, no statement is immune to revision. Revision even of the logical law of the excluded middle has been proposed as a means of simplifying quantum mechanics; and what difference is there in principle between such a shift and the shift whereby Kepler superseded Ptolemy, or Einstein Newton, or Darwin Aristotle?

As a consequence, no individual item of empirical counter-evidence can invalidate or falsify a scientific theory, since a scientific theory can always be "saved" by making some profound enough adjustments in it. Scientific explanation is a *holistic* phenomenon that, moreover, *inconclusive* in respect to any specific body of empirical evidence.

The proper domicile of the *Duhem-Quine Thesis* is in the philosophy of science, as it deals with the relation that prevails between *empirical observations* and a *scientific theory* by means of which the empirical findings are to be explained and their future occurrence predicted. Still, the *Duhem-Quine Thesis* may be analogically extended to the relation that pertains between a *legal assertion* on how to construct and read the law vis-à-vis a given fact-constellation and the constitutive premises at the back of such assertions as defined by the *frame of legal analysis* in question. The initially scientific context of the *Duhem-Quine Thesis* ought to be kept in mind, though. As a consequence of the *Duhem-Quine Thesis*, any outcome of legal construction and interpretation, no matter how implausible it might *prima facie* seem, can always be "saved" from critique, if some radical enough changes are effected in the frame of legal analysis adopted. Once such alterations have been made to a scientific theory or a frame of legal analysis, it of course no longer is the same as it was before such alterations.

Finally, what is the relation of the *Duhem-Quine Thesis* to Ronald Dworkin's theory of legal coherence as *legal integrity* and the idea of one right answer, if the former is analogically extended to the sphere of law and legal analysis under such coherentist terms? Can Dworkin's idea of "the best constructive interpretation of the political structure and legal doctrine of their community"[52] survive the scientific and philosophical thrust of the *Duhem-Quine Thesis*? If that turns out to be the case, Dworkin's Judge Hercules could defend any legal outcome once a seamless web of legal reasons were provided in its support. Or should we rather yield to the critique presented by Duhem and Quine, to the effect that any scientific theory or legal theory is – by force of definition – underdetermined and to some extent immune to the force of any counter-evidence (in science) and counter-arguments (in law)? If that turns out to be the case, any legal outcome could be defended through making some radical enough adjustments in the frame of legal analysis adopted. Both alternatives, i.e. Dworkin's idea of legal integrity and the Quinean

[52] "According to law as integrity, propositions of law are true if they figure in or follow from the principles of justice, fairness, and procedural due process that provide *the best constructive interpretation of the community's legal practice*." Dworkin, *Law's Empire*, p. 255. (Italics added.)

thesis of the holistic and underdetermined character of any scientific theory, cannot be simultaneously sustained, or so it would seem.

The *Duhem-Quine Thesis* challenges Dworkin's coherence-aligned position on the one rights answer to a legal issue. The conflict between the two cannot be levelled in the field of law unless Dworkin's initial thesis of the one right answer to a legal problem is given up. In his later writings Dworkin has in fact softened the premises of the one right answer doctrine, though his position on the issue remains slightly ambivalent.[53] The *Duhem-Quine Thesis*, on the other hand, would seem to refute the validity of one right answer to a scientific or, analogically, legal issue, due to the holistic and underdetermined character of any scientific theory or a theory-laden conception on how to construct and read the law. To the extent that the impact of one right answer to a legal problem has been downsized in Dworkin's subsequent writings on jurisprudence, the tension between his legal philosophy and the *Duhem-Quine Thesis* is reduced. The other alternative is to lower down the level of coherence to be attained from a *total* coherence to a *partial* coherence in law, loosening the grip of the *Duhem-Quine Thesis* on legal analysis.

3.4 Towards Partial Coherence in Law

Dworkin's notion of legal integrity as the best constructive interpretation of the political structure and legal doctrine of the community, the idea of the fictitious super-judge Hercules, and the chain novel metaphor all exemplify a striving for total coherence in law. Because of the increasingly fragmented and multi-valued character of modern law, the Herculean task of attaining total coherence in law may not be a very realistic goal. Moreover, under the (alleged) post-modern condition of law, there cannot be any credible candidate for an all-encompassing meta-theory of law, with full coverage over the highly divergent, fragmented tenets of legal and social justice. Rejecting Dworkin's "noble dream" of reaching all-inclusive coherence in law,[54] we may have to content ourselves with a set of "small-scale narratives" of law, political morality, and social justice only, so as to tackle the fragmented, polycentric, and polyphonous patchwork of law.[55]

[53] Cf. Dworkin, *Justice in Robes*, p. 41: "My thesis about right answers in hard case is, as I have said, a very weak and commonsensical legal claim. It is a claim made within legal practice rather than at some supposedly removed, external, philosophical level. I ask whether, in the ordinary sense in which lawyers might say this, it is ever sound or correct or accurate to say, about some hard case, that the law, properly interpreted, is for the plaintiff (or for the defendant). I answer that, yes, some statements of that kind are sound or correct or accurate about some hard cases." Cf.: Dworkin, "Pragmatism, Right Answers, and True Banality", p. 365. – Thus, "a very weak and commonsensical legal claim (...) made within legal practice", but the more philosophical issues are not evaded thereby.

[54] On Dworkin's "noble dream", cf. Hart, "American Jurisprudence through English Eyes: The Nightmare and the Noble Dream"; Lacey, *A Life of H. L. A. Hart: The Nightmare and the Noble Dream*.

[55] On "small-scale narratives" of law and social justice, cf. Wilhelmsson, *Senmodern ansvarsrätt. Privaträtt som redskap för mikropolitik*, pp. 193–239.

Partial, small-scale coherence in law is based on the constant interplay of relative *similarity* and *difference* of some tenets in the states of affairs considered. The process of reaching a judgment in a case may accordingly be based on *analogical reasoning*, where the prior rule is now extended to cover the facts of the novel case, or fact-based *distinguishing*, where the novel case is excluded from the field of application of the prior rule. Such a model of legal reasoning has been widely adopted in the United States and Great Britain.

In the American case law on product liability for articles sold by some other instance than their original manufacturer, the two legal categories of *articles found inherently dangerous* and *articles that are dangerous only if improperly constructed* were distinguished, and the legal consequences of each category were judged differently.[56] As a consequence, a judge who is to evaluate the possible dangerousness of some novel article is facing the following question[57]:

> Taken that a loaded gun, possibly a defective gun, mislabeled poison, defective hair wash, collapsing scaffolds, a defective coffee urn, and a defective aerated bottle have been found to be articles that are *inherently dangerous*; while a defective carriage, a bursting lamp, a defective balance wheel for a circular saw, and a defective boiler have been classified as articles *dangerous only if improperly constructed*, how should e.g. a defective soldering lamp be classified in light of the two categories of articles discerned?

What is essential is the relation of relative similarity or difference that the novel facts have to the two types of categories discerned. Such a model of reasoning may be analogically extended to apply to the interpretation of statutes and possibly other sources of law, too.

A system of law based on case-to-case reasoning may quite unpredictably deviate from its sofar well-settled course, if social values or the scientific and technical environment of law go through a radical enough change. Phrasing the issue in the Wittgensteinian terms, we may say that a system of judge-made law is a *moving classification system* that is in a constant state of flux, since the rules and principles of law it entails are always subject to changes and modifications while being enforced in the context of some novel fact-situation. In the classification of "articles found inherently dangerous" *vs.* "articles dangerous only if improperly constructed" that is exactly what took place, when the New York Court of Appeals chose to take a novel stance on the possibly dangerous character of an automobile. In the case, the plaintiff had been injured because of a defective wheel of the car. In the court ruling, the well-established rule on product liability was reversed, and the former exception to the main rule was raised into a new main rule.[58] Such an inherent logic of legal

---

[56]One of the best representations of case law reasoning based on the interplay of analogy and distinguishing is given in Levi, *An Introduction to Legal Reasoning*, pp. 9–25. Cf. also Dworkin, *Justice in Robes*, pp. 66, 69; Smith, "The Redundancy of Reasoning", passim.

[57]Cf. Levi, *An Introduction to Legal Reasoning*, pp. 18–19.

[58]Levi, *An Introduction to Legal Reasoning*, pp. 20–25. The case was *MacPherson v. Buick Motor Company* (Court of Appeals of New York, 1916; 317 N.Y. 382; 111 N.E. 1050), with Benjamin Cardozo presenting the key line of argumentation in it.

argumentation may be compared Ludwig Wittgenstein's idea of a game the rules of which may – and, in fact, frequently are – altered in the course of the game.[59]

3.5 The Concept of Coherence Redefined

Above, I rejected Robert Alexy's and Aleksander Peczenik's definition of legal coherence given in *quantified* terms, i.e. "the more/longer/greater (some specific quality of) a theory, the more coherent the theory", with reference to the internal *sentential structure*, the *concepts* utilized, and the *subject matter* of the theory. Such a quantified definition of coherence yet fails to grasp the core of the issue, due to inherently *constructive* character of coherence. Ronald Dworkin, on the other hand, has opted for the *qualitative* criteria of coherence as law as integrity, or "the best constructive interpretation of past political decisions" for the novel case at hand.[60] To my mind, Dworkin succeeds better in this respect. However, he never gives a proper *definition* of coherence in the strict sense of the term, opting for a host of "purple passages" or sky-soaring metaphors instead, viz. the judge engaged in the task of writing a chain novel *seriatim*; courts as the capitals of the law's empire and judges its princes; the human judge seeking to imitate the fictitious super-judge Hercules, and so on. What we need is a far more down-to-earth definition of coherence in law.

As I see it, coherence is a relational and inherently constructive concept that has to do with the *semantic* relations that prevail among a set of assertions, sentences, concepts, or other linguistic entities that make up a scientific theory or other set of linguistic expressions. Moreover, coherence cannot be defined in quantified terms without distorting its identity. Thus, I propose the following qualitative definition, or perhaps rather a characterization, of the phenomenon of coherence, linking it to the ideas presented by structural semiotics[61]:

> Coherence is a *semantic* – and not e.g. syntactic or pragmatic – quality that is internal to the *narrative structure* or narrative pattern of a scientific theory or, in more general terms, any set of linguistic sentences, assertions, or propositions, defined as their *mutual match*, *reciprocal support*, *common alignment*, *absence of dissonance*, and/or *shared congruence*, to the effect that they collectively make sense when inserted in, and read as part of, the same narrative structure or pattern. The narrative structure or narrative pattern of a theory or a set

---

[59] Wittgenstein, *Philosophical Investigations – Philosophische Untersuchungen*, § 83 (p. 39/39e).

[60] "Law as integrity asks judges to assume, so far as this is possible, that the law is structured by *a coherent set of principles* about justice and fairness and procedural due process, and it asks them to enforce these in the fresh cases that come before them, so that each person's situation is fair and just according to the same standards. (. . .) Judges who accept the interpretive ideal of integrity decide hard cases by trying to find, in some coherent set of principles about people's rights and duties, *the best constructive interpretation of the political structure and legal doctrine of their community*." Dworkin, *Law's Empire*, pp. 243, 255. (Italics added.)

[61] The definition of coherence suggested is not very simple, but the subject matter does not seem to admit of one, either. The bunch of criteria of *mutual match*, *reciprocal support*, *common alignment*, *absence of dissonance*, and/or *shared congruence* may be taken as an approximation of the issue, with focus on different tenets involved in the notion of coherence.

of sentences, assertions, or propositions consists of a set of successive choices made in the *logico-conceptual space* or logico-conceptual universe that consists of the *syntagmatic* and *paradigmatic* dimensions of language.

Syntagmatic relations in language are based on a *sequence* or *combination* of signs, as effected in their *linear succession* in language taken as a flow of speech (*parole*). The syntagmatic axis of language follows the logic of *conjunction* ($x \wedge y$; "*x and y*"). *Paradigmatic* relations in language are based on the ever-present possibility of effecting a *selection* among the set of mutually exclusive signs, where one sign can be substituted, or replaced, by another with an equivalent or parallel value in language taken as a momentary system of signs (*langue*). The paradigmatic axis of language follows the logic of *disjunction* ($x \vee y$; "*x or y*").[62]

Roman Jakobson has called the syntagmatic dimension of language the *axis of combination*, and the paradigmatic dimension the *axis of selection*.[63] The structure of language could also be rephrased as *diachronic* positivity, as has actually come into existence in some specific discourse formation, and *synchronic* alternativity or substitutability of language, in the sense of the options open for linguistic variation, respectively.[64] The syntagmatic and paradigmatic dimensions of language can be presented with the following diagram:

Diagram 3.1 The syntagmatic and paradigmatic dimensions of language

	Syntagmatic Dimension of Language →				
Paradigmatic Dimension of Language ↓	$S_{\alpha 1}$	$S_{\alpha 2}$	$S_{\alpha 3}$	$S_{\alpha 4}$	$S_{\alpha 5}$ (…) $S_{\alpha n}$
	$S_{\beta 1}$	$S_{\beta 2}$	$S_{\beta 3}$	$S_{\beta 4}$	$S_{\beta 5}$ (…) $S_{\beta n}$
	$S_{\chi 1}$	$S_{\chi 2}$	$S_{\chi 3}$	$S_{\chi 4}$	$S_{\chi 5}$ (…) $S_{\chi n}$
	$S_{\delta 1}$	$S_{\delta 2}$	$S_{\delta 3}$	$S_{\delta 4}$	$S_{\delta 5}$ (…) $S_{\delta n}$
	$S_{\varepsilon 1}$	$S_{\varepsilon 2}$	$S_{\varepsilon 3}$	$S_{\varepsilon 4}$	$S_{\varepsilon 5}$ (…) $S_{\varepsilon n}$
	(…)				
	$S_{\nu 1}$	$S_{\nu 2}$	$S_{\nu 3}$	$S_{\nu 4}$	$S_{\nu 5}$ (…) $S_{\nu n}$

The syntagmatic and paradigmatic axes of language define a *logico-conceptual universe* or *logico-conceptual space*, within which any set of linguistic signs are situated and which makes it possible to evaluate the degree of coherence attained in the various narrative structures or narrative patterns displayed under such premises.

62 Greimas and Courtés, *Sémiotique. Dictionnaire raisonné de la théorie du langage*, pp. 266–267, 376–377 (entries on *paradigmatique*, *paradigme*, *syntagmatique*, and *syntagme*).

63 Jakobson, "Linguistics and Poetics", p. 358: "The selection is produced on the basis of equivalence, similarity and dissimilarity, synonymity and antonymity, while the combination, the build up of the sequence, is based on contiguity."

64 Cf. Foucault, *Les mots et les choses*, passim. – The notion of a *discourse formation* is based on Michel Foucault's *archaeology of knowledge* of the human sciences, as presented in his works from the late 1960s and early 1970s, viz. *Les mots et les choses*, *L'Archéologie du savoir*, and *L'Ordre du discours*, Foucault's inauguration lecture at the *Collège de France* in December 1970 (published in 1971).

The same goes for the "building blocks" of the semantic domain of law, too, such as the rules and principles of law in a legal system. In the diagram, $\mathbf{S_{xn}}$ stands for a sign, concept, sentence, or other linguistic entity.

The *syntagmatic* axis in the diagram signifies the step-by-step unfolding of linguistic entities in a narrative structure in the *diachronic*, or temporal, sense. The *paradigmatic* axis, in turn, signifies the totality of alternatives to the linguistic element chosen for the narrative pattern in a *synchronic*, non-temporal sense. The scheme of interpretation chosen for the analysis determines the narrative pattern or structure that is to be attained by means of the syntagmatic and paradigmatic dimensions of language. Different schemes of interpretation will yield divergent narrative patterns and, as a consequence, different conceptions of coherence thereby effected.

If placed in the context of the fact-constellations provided by Erik Stenius above in his reading of Wittgenstein's *Tractatus*, the values of $\mathbf{S_{xn}}$ might concern the different properties of the members of a family, stated as the (exceptional) intelligence of some of them and the existence of a parent–child relationship in the familiy; or those of a military unit, stated as the (exceptional) bravery of some of the soldiers and the existence of a relation of military authority within the unit. In such a case, an unfolding narrative of the family or the military unit would deal with the historical evolving of the said characteristics in the family or in the military unit.

The variable $\mathbf{S_{xn}}$ in the diagram may of course stand for a set of legal rules and principles, as well, like (a set of) constitutional rules, statutory rules or precedents in some branch of law. In the context of contract law there are several possible schemes of interpretation available, and each of them will yield different kinds of legal results *vis-à-vis* legal coherence. If the constitutional provisions, statutes, the *travaux préparatoires*, precedents, and possibly other kind of legal source material are read in light of protecting the legitimate expectations of the parties to a contract, the legal narrative $\mathbf{A} = [\mathbf{S_{\alpha 1}}] + [\mathbf{S_{\chi 2}}] + [\mathbf{S_{\beta 3}}] + [\mathbf{S_{\varepsilon 4}}] + [\mathbf{S_{\delta 5}}] + (\ldots) + [\mathbf{S_{\chi n}}]$ might produce the highest level of coherence. If the very same legal material is, instead, read with the purpose of reconstructing, as authentically as possible, the intentions originally held by the parties to the contract at the time of drafting it and reaching the agreement, the legal narrative $\mathbf{B} = [\mathbf{S_{\varepsilon 1}}] + [\mathbf{S_{\chi 2}}]+ [\mathbf{S_{\beta 3}}] + [\mathbf{S_{\alpha 4}}] + [\mathbf{S_{\chi 5}}] + (\ldots) + [\mathbf{S_{\alpha n}}]$ might produce the highest level of coherence.

In a diagram, the two alternatives might be presented as follows, with the choices actually made designated in bold and the options rejected designated with double strikethrough, and an arrow designating the course preferred for action.

Reading the legal material in light of the requirement of attaining *reasonableness* or equity and the balance of mutual contributions given to, and the profits drawn from, the contract would most probably produce another kind of pattern of legal rules or precedents as the highest attainable level of coherence, such as: $\mathbf{C} = [\mathbf{S_{\varepsilon 1}}] + [\mathbf{S_{\delta 2}}] + [\mathbf{S_{\alpha 3}}] + [\mathbf{S_{\alpha 4}}] + [\mathbf{S_{\beta 5}}] + (\ldots) + [\mathbf{S_{\alpha n}}]$. Finally, reading the material in light of the enhanced protection of the interests of the weaker party to the contract under a *socially sensitive* conception of private law would produce still another pattern of constructing coherence among the legal rules and principles, such as $\mathbf{D} = [\mathbf{S_{\beta 1}}] + [\mathbf{S_{\alpha 2}}] + [\mathbf{S_{\chi 3}}] + [\mathbf{S_{\delta 4}}] + [\mathbf{S_{\chi 5}}] + (\ldots) + [\mathbf{S_{\beta n}}]$. The array of feasible narratives of law and the degree of attainable legal coherence could of course be continued existing

Diagram 3.2 The syntagmatic and paradigmatic dimensions of language in the two narrative patterns A and B, with reference to two different schemes of interpretation, i.e. the legitimate expectations (= Scheme A) or original intentions (= Scheme B) of the parties to a contract

a) *Narrative Pattern A*: Legitimate Expectations of the Parties to a Private Law Contract as the Scheme of Interpretation Adopted

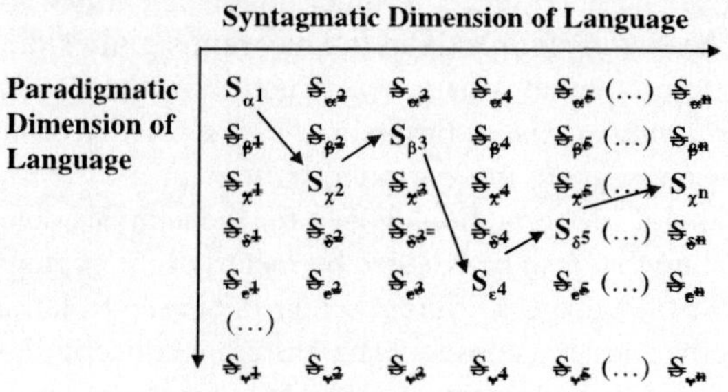

b) *Narrative Pattern B*: Original Intentions of the Parties to a Private Law Contract as the Scheme of Interpretation Adopted

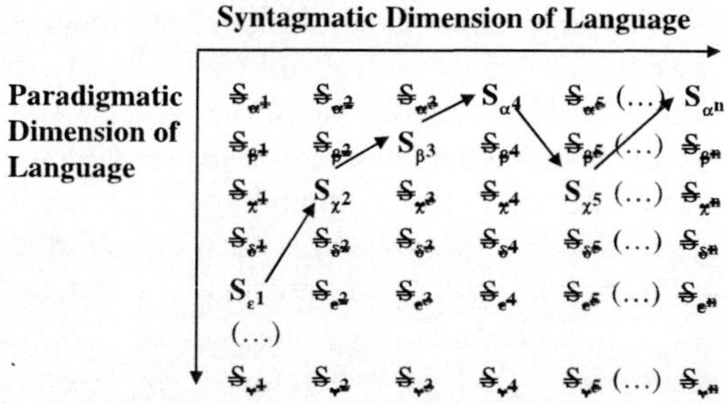

in the world any other possible scheme of interpretation to be applied to the legal material in question.

As can be seen in the diagram above, the very same legal rules or principles may be used as part of several different schemes of coherence. In the diagram, the rules or principles $\mathbf{S_{\chi 2}}$ and $\mathbf{S_{\beta 3}}$ are both able to provide support for two different narrative structures, aligned with the protection of legitimate interests of the parties to a contract, on the one hand, and the protection of the original intensions of the parties, on the other hand.

An analysis of the syntagmatic and paradigmatic dimensions of language can of course be extended to apply to any narrative pattern, no matter whether we are dealing with a scientific theory, a set of sentences of legal argumentation on how to construct and read the law, or the oddities that may take place in the fictitious world of *The Wizard of Oz*, *Alice's Adventures in the Wonderland*, or the *Hogwarts School of Wizardry and Witchcraft* in J. K. Rowling's lucid flow of imagination. The *narrative pattern*, or *narrative structure*, has a decisive role here, and it will vary according to the subject matter of the narrative. As I see it, the concept of a narrative pattern or narrative structure, plus the idea that a set of linguistic signs makes sense when read together, cannot be formalized or quantified without distorting the very issue at stake, contrary to what Alexy and Peczenik wrote above. Instead, the notion of coherence necessitates a *qualitative* approach to the issue, and the use of figurative speech cannot be wholly avoided in that task. Still, the metaphorical overload of Dworkin's approach should be avoided, if only possible.

3.6 A Critical Evaluation of the Coherence Theory of Law

There are two essential features in the coherence theory of law that need to be taken into account when compared to its alternatives among the frames of legal analysis. Firstly, the coherence theory of law acknowledges the normative impact of the various kinds of institutional and non-institutional sources of law on the legal discretion of the judge or other official, giving effect to a variety of legal sources, which is a good thing. The catalogue of legal sources acknowledged is significantly wider than under the isomorphic theory of law considered above.

Secondly, and unlike the isomorphic theory, the coherence-based approach covers the hard cases of legal adjudication, as well, where there is no isomorphic relation between the two fact-constellations. They, too, are subject to the same set of criteria of *mutual match, reciprocal support, common alignment, absence of dissonance*, and/or *shared congruence* under the *narrative pattern* adopted. In addition, the coherence theory of law may be combined with at least the key elements of legal argumentation theory under the Perelmanian new rhetoric.

The trouble with the notion of coherence in law has to do with its profoundly *constructivist* nature and the resulting lack of control as to the outcomes of legal discretion, at least if conceived in line with Dworkin's quest for all-encompassing coherence in law. The claim of one right answer, as put forth by a judge driven by the Herculean passion of attaining legal integrity as "the best constructive interpretation of past political decisions", can always be questioned by having reference to the inherently disputable, open character of law, as captured by the *Duhem-Quine Thesis* in the philosophy of science and as analogically extended to the field of law.

Moreover, the frequently voiced critique against the coherence theory of letting *coherent fairy-tales* pass the test of truth is difficult to answer in a convincing manner. The uneasy relation of the coherence theory of truth to any empirical observations can best be illustrated with an anecdote from within the *Wiener Kreis*. The mathematician Hans Hahn is said to have asked Otto Neurath for a reason why the physicists should conduct empirical experiments, if all scientific knowledge is in the last resort based on the coherence among a set of linguistic assertions, as Neurath had effectively argued.

Regrettably, Neurath's answer to Hahn's enquiry has not been preserved in the archives of the *Wiener Kreis*. According to Alberto J. Coffa, an outstanding analyst of the semantic tradition before, during, and after logical positivism, the only logical answer to Hahn's enquiry would have been that there is no reason for such experiments under Neurath's coherentist premises.[65] Still, the claimed match of

[65] Coffa, *The Semantic Tradition from Kant to Carnap*, p. 367.

Neurath's *protocol sentences*, or of any other empirical assertions of the world, are based on a relation of *correspondence* between a set of linguistic assertions and the phenomena in the world. Without the conjectured prevalence of such a language – world correspondence, there could be any *observation* sentences either, which Neurath's coherentism yet seems to totally forget.

Chapter 4
"Between the Evident and the Irrational": The New Rhetoric and Legal Argumentation Theory

4.1 The Varieties of Pragmatism and the Law

Philosophical pragmatism consists of a set of overlapping philosophical positions that all, to a greater or lesser degree, share a belief in: (a) the *instrumentalist* character of all human knowledge in the service of human action, (b) the role of the scientific or other human *community* in judging the validity of any would-be knowledge, and (c) the importance given to the *consequences* brought into effect if some belief or assertion in fact turns out to be true. Philosophical pragmatism is intertwined with the *consensus* theory of truth and knowledge. It defines the truth of a scientific theory or individual belief as being approved, accepted, or acknowledged as *warranted* in the community.

The prominent role given to the scientific community under the consensus theory of truth is neatly illustrated by Thomas S. Kuhn's sociology of science and the idea of scientific change in it. According to Kuhn's claim, it is the scientific community that has the final say on what will count as scientific knowledge and what will fail in such a test.[1] Science evolves in the sequential and, to some extent, quite unpredictable interplay of the two distinct phases of scientific progress: the usually longer periods of *normal science* are occasionally disrupted by abrupt *scientific revolutions* whereby the prevailing scientific paradigm is discarded and switched to another one. Such occasions are usually induced by some recalcitrant empirical findings, or *anomalies*, that the prevailing scientific paradigm cannot satisfactorily explain. In all this, the *scientific community* has a seminal role, since it is the scientific community that defines the notions of truth and knowledge.

[1] Kuhn's conception of science deals mostly or exclusively with knowledge in the natural sciences, and the status of the human and social sciences is left out of consideration by him. On Kuhn's conception of the theory of science and its applicability in the science of law or, in more general terms, in the human and social sciences, Siltala, *Oikeustieteen tieteenteoria*, pp. 387–460. The French philosopher Michel Foucault defended a similar kind of conception of the societal character of human knowledge in his archaeology of knowledge under the auspices of a certain *épistémè*. Foucault, *Les Mots et les choses. Une Archéologie des sciences humaines*; Foucault, *L'Archéologie du savoir*; Siltala, *Oikeustieteen tieteenteoria*, p. 1 et seq.

R. Siltala, *Law, Truth, and Reason*, Law and Philosophy Library 97,
DOI 10.1007/978-94-007-1872-2_4, © Springer Science+Business Media B.V. 2011

Still, as Kuhn openly admits, the scientific community may be collectively in error as to the scientific laws and facts of the world, which however may be discovered only much later on. The violent clash between the scholastic premises sustained by the Catholic Church and the novel, scientific, and empiricist worldview at the beginning of the seventeenth century provides a good example thereof. As is well known, Galileo Galilei was forced to publicly repudiate in front of the Italian Inquisition the validity of the scientific discoveries he had made of celestial mechanics, to the effect that the earth revolves around the sun, and not the other way round as the doctrine of the Catholic Church had it. Not even the foundations of scientific reasoning, like the laws of logic and mathematics, are totally immune to or safeguarded against such scientific revolutions or cracks in the edifice of science. In fact, several a priori conceptions of logic have been proven false, or true with respect to some specific system of logic only.

Any pragmatic account of law comprises a set of criteria that downgrade the significance of any isomorphic, picture relation that might or might not prevail between language and the world. Equally, pragmatism denies the relevance of textual coherence among the institutional and societal premises of law, as defended by the coherence theory. Under pragmatic premises, principled legal decision-making has to recede, giving room for a more down-to-earth conception of how to construct and read law.[2]

Thus, a pragmatic approach to legal argumentation underscores the kind of criteria that are based on: (a) an approval or disapproval of the methods and outcome of legal reasoning at the intended, universal audience, defined as a subjective thought construct of the speaker, according to the *new rhetoric*; (b) well-settled practices and usages in the community, defined as the presence of common acceptance or recognition of certain social phenomena as having legal significance, or a set of mutual expectations and cooperative dispositions to the said effect, among the members of the community, according to *philosophical conventionalism*; or (c) desirability of the economic or other external effects of law in society, according to *social consequentialism*. In all three types of legal pragmatism, the concept of law is closely intertwined with the linguistic and community-aligned tenets of law, at the cost of any sky-soaringly idealistic metaphysics. In addition, (d) *radical decisionism* may be taken as a fourth instance of pragmatism in law, widely defined.

Social consequentialism and ad hoc based decisionism have the most obvious connections to philosophical pragmatism pure and simple. For the new rhetoric and legal conventionalism the link to pragmatism is provided by the role that is given to the legal community in legal argumentation. – In this chapter, I will concentrate on the new rhetoric. The other variants of legal reasoning affected by philosophical pragmatism will be considered later.

---

[2]On the *principled* and *pragmatic* theories of legal reasoning, cf. Spaak, *Guidance and Constraint*, pp. 83–92. Spaak would seem to resuscitate H. L. A. Hart's famous dichotomy of the *nightmare* and the *noble dream* in jurisprudence. Cf. Hart, "American Jurisprudence through English Eyes: The Nightmare and the Noble Dream", passim.

4.2 The Universal Audience as a Subjective Thought Construct of the Speaker by Chaïm Perelman

The philosophical *corpus* of Aristotle's topics and rhetoric were rediscovered in the 1950s, when the German scholar Theodor Viehweg (1907–1988) and the Belgian philosopher Chaïm Perelman (1912–1984) both came to realize, quite independently from each other, the impact of Aristotle's writings for the analysis of legal and moral argumentation. For the subsequent evolvement of legal argumentation, the influence by Perelman (and by Lucie Olbrecht-Tyteca, the relatively unknown co-author of *Traité de l'Argumentation. La nouvelle Rhétorique*) has proven greater than Viehweg's similarly Aristotelian ideas on *topics* in practical argumentation. The theory of legal argumentation has been subsequently advanced by, for instance, Jerzy Wróblewski,[3] Neil MacCormick,[4] Aleksander Peczenik,[5] Robert Alexy,[6] Robert S. Summers,[7] and Aulis Aarnio.[8] They all belonged to the international research group *Bielefelder Kreis* that analysed the interpretation of statutory law and precedents from the point of view of comparative legal analysis and legal argumentation theory.[9]

The new rhetoric is based on Aristotle's philosophical writings on the laws of reasoning, the constitutive premises of which are not, unlike those of deductive reasoning, known to be necessarily true or necessarily untrue but are, at the most, more or less *reasonable*, *adequate*, *justified*, or *credible*, being no more than weakly "reminiscent of truth". Unlike deductive logic, rhetorical reasoning is not *truth preserving*, in the sense that the postulated truth of the premises of an inference would guarantee the truth of the outcome of the inference. Any assertions on how to construct and read the law, as derived from a combination of certain fact premises and certain norm premises, cannot claim having access to the (absolute) truth of the propositions on the content of law. Rather, they only make the more modest claim of being (no more than) *adequate*, *reasonable*, *pertinent*, or *justified* for the case at hand under the institutional and societal preconditions acknowledged in the legal community.

---

3 Wróblewski, *The Judicial Application of Law*.

4 MacCormick, *Legal Reasoning and Legal Theory*.

5 Peczenik, *The Basis of Legal Justification*; Peczenik, *On Law and Reason*; Peczenik, *Vad är rätt? Om demokrati, rättssäkerhet, etik och juridisk argumentation*.

6 Alexy, *A Theory of Legal Argumentation. The Theory of Rational Discourse as Theory of Legal Argumentation*.

7 Summers, *Essays on the Nature of Law and Legal Reasoning*; Summers, *Essays in Legal Theory*; Summers, *The Jurisprudence of Law's Form and Substance*.

8 Aarnio, *The Rational as Reasonable. A Treatise on Legal Justification*; Aarnio, *Laintulkinnan teoria*; Aarnio, *Reason and Authority. A Treatise on the Dynamic Paradigm of Legal Dogmatics*.

9 MacCormick and Summers, eds., *Interpreting Statutes. A Comparative Study*; MacCormick and Summers, eds., *Interpreting Precedents. A Comparative Study*. On precedent-based law, Siltala, *A Theory of Precedent. From Analytical Positivism to A Post-Analytical Philosophy of Law*.

> What is the audience around which argumentation is centered?" Perelman (rhetorically) asks in his *The Realm of Rhetoric*, and answers the question himself by reference to "*the gathering of those whom the speaker wants to influence by his arguments*".[10] "What is this gathering?" he then asks, and replies by saying, "It can be the speaker himself, reflecting privately about how to respond to a delicate situation. Or it may be all of humanity, or at least all those who are competent and reasonable – those whom I would call the "universal audience"...[11]

Any set of sentences that make up a scientific theory, a philosophical argument, an evaluative standpoint in ethics or in aesthetics, or a set of assertions on how to construct and read the law is always addressed at some specific *audience*. In the context of law, the *legal community* or some part of it counts as the audience for legal argumentation. The concept of a legal community can be defined in more than one way, though. It may refer to a *normative* ideal or to some community that *actually* exists. In addition, the legal community may be defined in a wide sense, with reference to all the individuals who are subject to the same legal order, or in a more restricted sense, with reference to those individuals whose legal position is somehow affected by the judicial decision made by the court of justice or the legal official in question.

The frame of argumentation on legal, social, moral, or the like issues should be defined in *general* and *universal* terms, if possible, since a dialogical, face-to-face speech situation easily turns into an irrational, persuasive stance towards the addressee of argumentation, due to the impact of contingent factors that have to do with the particular speech situation in question. Similarly, an inner monologue of the speaker with himself, as the silent debate with the inner voice of the consciousness or some other outspoken inner reflection, as exemplified by Hamlet's famous monologue in Shakespeare's play with the same title, are more likely to yield to benign *ex post facto* rationalizations of the speaker's motives than any argument presented to the universal audience.[12]

According to Perelman, the *universal audience* (*l'auditoire universel*) is a subjective *thought construct of the speaker* by means of which he seeks to align and adjust the arguments presented by him so as to convince the audience, while at the same time observing the general prerequisites of rationality.[13] Perelman's idea of

[10]"Quel est cet auditoire autour duquel est centrée l'argumentation? (...) Si l'on veut définir l'auditoire d'une façon utile pour le développement d'une théorie de l'argumentation, il faut le concevoir comme *l'ensemble de ceux sur lesquels l'orateur veut influer par son argumentation*." Perelman, *L'Empire rhétorique*, p. 27. (Italics in original.) Cf. Perelman, *The Realm of Rhetoric*, pp. 13–14.

[11]"Quel est cet ensemble? Il est fort variable, et peut aller de l'orateur lui-même, dans le cas d'une deliberation intime, quand il s'agit de prendre une decision dans une situation délicate, jusqu'à l'humanité tout entière, du moins à ceux de ses members qui sont compétents et raisonnables, et que je qualifie d'auditoire universel, en passant par une infinie variété d'auditoires particuliers." Perelman, *L'Empire rhétorique*, pp. 27–28; cf. Perelman, *The Realm of Rhetoric*, p. 14.

[12]Cf. Perelman and Olbrechts-Tyteca, *Traité de l'Argumentation*, pp. 40, 46–59.

[13]"L'auditoire présumé est toujours, pour celui qui argumente, une construction plus ou moins systématisée." Perelman and Olbrechts-Tyteca, *Traité de l'Argumentation*, p. 25 (et seq.), where the two authors reflect upon the issue under the heading, *L'auditoire comme construction de l'orateur.*

the universal audience is reminiscent of Jürgen Habermas' idea of an *ideal speech situation* (*ideale Sprechsituation*), as the both seek to rule out all kind of manipulation or other distortion from the field of rational discourse. As a consequence, Perelman made the distinction between *convincing* a universal audience by means of rational arguments and *persuading* a concrete audience in a situation where the influence of different kinds of irrational arguments is not ruled out.[14] As Perelman put it[15]:

> La distinction entre les discours qui s'adressent à quelques-uns et ceux qui seraient valable pour tous, permet de mieux faire comprendre ce qui oppose le discourse persuasive à celui qui se veut convaincant. Au lieu de considérer que la persuasion s'adresse à l'imagination, au sentiment, bref à l'automate, alors que le discours convaincant fait appel à la raison,[16] au lieu de les opposer l'une à l'autre, comme le subjectif à le objectif,[17] on peut les caractériser, d'une façon plus technique, et aussi plus exacte, en disant que le discours adressé à un auditoire particulier vise à persuader, alors que celui qui s'adresse à l'auditoire universel vise à convaincre. – Comme la distinction ainsi établie ne dépend pas du nombre de personnes que écoutent un orateur, mais des intentions de ce dernier (veut-it obtenir l'adhésion de quelques-uns ou de tout être de raison?), il se peut que l'orateur n'envisage ceux auxquels il s'adresse – meme s'il s'agit d'une délibération intime – que comme une incarnation de l'auditoire universel. Un discours convaincant est celui dont les premises et les arguments sont universalisables, c'est-à-dire acceptables, en principe, par tous les membres de l'auditoire universel. On voit immédiatement comment, dans cette perspective, l'originalité même de la philosophie, associée traditionnellement aux notions de vérité et de raison, sera le mieux comprise par sa relation avec l'auditoire universel, et la manière dont celui-ci est conçu par le philosophe.

Perelman's notion of universal audience consists of *enlightened* persons whom the speaker tries to win on his side with rational arguments. Thus, the universal audience (*l'auditoire universel*) is not an empirical phenomenon but a *subjective thought*

---

[14] Perelman and Olbrechts-Tyteca, *Traité de l'Argumentation*, pp. 34–40.

[15] Perelman, *L'Empire rhétorique*, p. 31. – "The distinction between discourses that are addressed to some individual persons and those intended to be valid for everyone allows us to better understand how persuasive discourse differs from one that aims at being convincing. Instead of thinking that persuasive discourse is addressed to the imagination, sentiments, or unthinking reactions of a person, whereas a discourse that aims at convincing someone appeals to his reason, and instead of opposing the one as essentially subjective to the other as essentially objective, we can characterize them in a more technical, and also more exact, manner by stating that the discourse addressed to a specific audience aims at persuading [its addressees], while the discourse addressed to the universal audience aims at convincing [its addressees]. – Like the distinction now established does not depend on the number of individuals who listen to a speaker but on the speaker's intentions (i.e. does he aim at the adherence of someones or of every reasonable being), it may well be that the speaker conceives of those to whom he speaks – even in the context of a private deliberation in his own mind – as a manifestation of the universal audience. A convincing discourse is one in which the premises and the arguments presented can be universalized, that is, being in principle acceptable to all the members of the universal audience. We immediately realize how in this way of looking into the issue the originality of philosophy, as traditionally associated with the notions of truth and reason, will best be understood in terms of its relation to the universal audience, and the manner in which this audience is conceived of by the philosopher." (Translation by the present author.) – Cf. Perelman and Olbrechts-Tyteca, *Traité de l'Argumentation*, p. 34 et seq.

[16] Perelman refers to Pascal's *Pensées* here.

[17] Perelman refers to Kant's *Kritik der reinen Vernunft* here.

construct of the speaker by means of which he is claimed to be able to align his line of arguments for the case at hand. In an essay where he compared Aarnio's and Perelman's notions of the intended audience of a legal sentence, Antti-Juhani Wihuri has rightly underscored the *constructive* character of Perelman's notion of universal audience[18]:

> What is essential in Perelman's concept of a universal audience is that it, too, is *a construction of the speaker who presents the arguments.* It is the speaker's own idea of what the universal audience is like. (...) According to my interpretation, the most consistent (i.e. coherent) way of conceiving the universal audience, as presented by Perelman, is to see it, indeed, as a construction of the speaker. The idea of a fictitious universal audience is simply based on the speaker's wish to argue in a universally valid manner, in the sense of giving both the arguments and the outcome reached by them a *universalized* quality.

I fully agree with Wihuri's reading of Perelman's conception of the universal audience. As a consequence, the universal audience is a subject-bound *thought construct of the speaker* by means of which he aligns and adjusts the inner rationality and argumentative force of the arguments presented by him, so as to convince his addressees of the validity of his arguments, no matter whether we are dealing with a scientific theory, a philosophical stance, an ethical point of view, a stance on aesthetics, or an assertion on how to construct and read the law.[19]

There is no *view from nowhere* to the law or to any other essentially contested object matter of human inquiry that would be totally free from the epistemic, logico-conceptual, methodological, and other commitments that constitute the prevailing "order of things", or *épistémè* in Michel Foucault's terminology.[20] The concept of rationality entailed in Perelman's notion of universal audience is, like the concept of law, a *deliberative practice* that is intertwined with the societal, linguistic, and cultural background premises of the common world-view.[21] As a consequence, there is no universally valid concept of human rationality that could be cut off from the societal and cultural frame of human knowledge and value commitments. Rather, the type of rationality ascribed to the universal audience, taken as a subjective thought construct of the speaker, is expressive of a *bounded rationality*, modified by the diverse "scenes", frames, settings, contextures, or approaches to the realm of reason and argumentation. Moreover, since the universal audience is ultimately a subject-related thought construct only, there is no universally valid audience that would be

[18]Wihuri, "Auditorion käsitteestä ja auditoriosidonnaisesta argumentaatiosta", p. 363, 364–365. (Italics by Wihuri; translation by the present author.) – Cf. Perelman and Olbrechts-Tyteca, *Traité de l'Argumentation*, pp. 25–30, with the subtitle: *L'auditoire comme construction de l'orateur.*

[19]Cf.: "... *l'accord de l'auditoire universel.* Il s'agit évidemment, dans ce cas, non pas d'un fait expérimentalement éprouvé, mais d'une universalité et d'une unanimité que se représente l'oratuer (...) *L'accord d'un auditoire universel n'est donc pas une question de fait, mais du droit.*" Perelman and Olbrechts-Tyteca, *Traité de l'Argumentation*, p. 41. (Italics in original.)

[20]The apt phase *view from nowhere* is borrowed from Thomas Nagel's book with the same title. Nagel, *The View from Nowhere*; Foucault, *Les Mots et les choses*; Siltala, *Oikeustieteen tieteenteoria*, pp. 30–32, 731–732.

[21]On the notion of a *deliberative practice*, cf. Morawetz, "Epistemology of Judging. Wittgenstein and Deliberative Practices", pp. 19–23.

common to all such diverse "scenes", frames, settings, contextures, or approaches to argumentation as conceived by the speaker.

There is an inherent, ever-present, and unresolvable tension in Perelman's notion of the universal audience, since it is stretched between the two constitutive elements of sky-soaring, subject-free *universality*, as pursued by the speaker under universal rationality, and a far more down-to-earth, speaker-bound *subjectivity*, since such rationality is in the last resort determined by the speaker's own cognitive faculties and the linguistic, cultural, and societal constraints as he conceives them.[22] As a consequence, the *solipsistic* elements of a purely subject-bound rationality and the more *universal* ones of objectivity-seeking rationality are placed in a constant, unresolvable tension in Perelman's notion of rational, convincing argumentation.

What is more, the universal audience for different types of discourse situations would seem to be potentially very different. The intended universal audience of a particular philosophical stance may be quite different from the one adopted for the evaluation of an ethical or aesthetical argument, the literary analysis of Jorge Luis Borges' imaginative short stories or other items of literature, or an assertion on how to construct and read the law in light of the prevalent sources of law. It seems that Perelman did not take this inherent, built-in tension within the concept of universal audience fully into account, when he wrote that a speaker who addresses a universal audience should be constrained only by the pertinent atemporal and absolute arguments that are quite independent of the local and historical contingencies.[23]

The prevailing *concept* of rationality will make room for a variety of different *conceptions* of rationality,[24] depending on the other constitutive ingredients of the societal, linguistic, and cultural world-view internalized by the speaker, and also on the specific interest of knowledge in the field of life concerned. The intended ideal, or universal, audience of philosophical argumentation usually implies a rather sophisticated "sense for ontology" and acquaintance with the philosophical tradition, while such knowledge often cannot be expected from an audience consisting of lawyers, theologians, physicians, or politologists.[25]

---

[22] Cf. Perelman: "L'auditoire universel est constitué par chacun à partir de ce qu'il sait de ses semblambles, de manière à transcender les quelques oppositions dont il a conscience. Ainsi chaque culture, chaque individu a sa propre conception de l'auditoire universel, et l'étude de ces variations serait fort instructive, car elle nous ferait connaître ce que les hommes ont consideré, au cours de l'histoire, comme *réel*, *vrai* et *objectivement valable*." Perelman and Olbrechts-Tyteca, *Traité de l'Argumentation*, p. 43.

[23] Perelman and Olbrechts-Tyteca, *Traité de l'Argumentation*, p. 41 *in fine*: "Une argumentation qui s'addresse à une auditoire universel doit convaincre le lecteur du caractère contraignant des raisons fournies, de leur evidence, de leur validité intemporelle et absolue, indépendante de contingences locales ou historiques."

[24] Cf.: "... one must distinguish between justifying a practice as a system of rules to be applied and enforced, and justifying a particular action which falls under these rules; utilitarian arguments are appropriate with regard to question about practices, while retributive arguments fit the application of particular rules to particular case." Rawls, "Two Concepts of Rules" (1955), in *Collected Papers*, pp. 20–46.

[25] Cf. Siltala, *Oikeustieteen tieteenteoria*, pp. 628–632.

The intended universal audience of the outcome of legal argumentation, in turn, may legitimately be expected to have gained a profound acquaintance with the institutional and societal sources of law and the models of legal argumentation adopted in the legal community. Moreover, relatively detailed knowledge of the very subject matter of legal regulation and decision-making can be required from the intended ideal, universal audience of such legal argumentation, with reference to, for instance, (a) the allocation of legal decision-making power and responsibility among the officials, (b) the allocation of effectively protected legal rights and legal duties among the citizens, and (c) the principles adopted for the allocation of the scarce resources in society. With respect to professionals in the study of history, literature, religion, or the arts and aesthetics, the situation would again be different as to the kind of knowledge required from the intended universal audience.

Moreover, not even the discursive fields of science, philosophy, or legal analysis are internally homogenous but are, instead, divided into divergent intellectual schools, branches, movements, or approaches to the issues under scrutiny, each with a different set of theoretical premises "on what there is" in the world. A scholar committed to the basic tenets of scientific and philosophical realism sees the world in a manner that is radically different from his colleague who has adopted the grounding premises of, say, phenomenology with its striving for pure knowledge, or textual hermeneutics with sensitivity towards tradition and cultural pre-understanding, or the Marxist conception of law and society where the laws of economics take priority vis-à-vis any phenomena dwelling on the ideological surface level structure of society. For the legal realist, law is a *social fact* that is brought into existence through the decisions by the courts of justice and other officials. For the other philosophical alternatives mentioned, law is conceived as the self-evident, a priori kind of a phenomenon, if legal phenomenology is opted for; a tradition-based and linguistic phenomenon, if legal hermeneutics is adopted; or an ideological surface-level reflection of the more grounding laws of economics, if a Marxist approach to the law and society is preferred.

Needless to say, the adherents of, say, American or Scandinavian legal realism, legal phenomenology, legal hermeneutics, or a Marxist conception of law and society each define the conception of law and the notion of a universal audience in highly divergent terms. Similarly, the representatives of legal positivism see the law and the criteria of legal argumentation in a manner that is very different from the one adopted in the tradition of natural law philosophy. What is common to the various readings of Perelman's universal audience under the Western *épistémè* and the resulting highly diversified conditions of valid argument is only the censure and ruling out of certain illegitimate means of influencing the audience of argumentation, such as an appeal to unfounded prejudice, the use of threat or other compulsion in argumentation, the intentional spreading out of lies and disinformation, an appeal to the formal authority of the speaker, or any other types of manipulating the audience by irrational means, as pointed out by Jürgen Habermas as the prerequisites of an ideal speech situation. Still, what will count as a legitimate step in legal argumentation before a universal audience to a great extent depends on the specific notion of rationality adopted by the speaker and the premises of the world-view adopted in the intended universal audience as the speaker conceives it.

4.3 The Realm of Rhetoric and the Quest for Value-Cognitivism

In Perelman's writings on the new rhetoric and in Aulis Aarnio's contributions to legal argumentation theory, the notion of the *audience* of argumentation gains vital importance. As concerns the audience of legal argumentation Aarnio puts forth the *regulative principle* for the legal doctrine[26]:

> Legal dogmatics ought to attempt to reach such legal interpretations that could secure the support of the majority in a rationally reasoning legal community.

Aarnio's notion of rationality in legal reasoning is defined by means of the two criteria of *legal predictability* that should guide the procedure of legal discretion and *content-based acceptability* that concerns the outcome of legal discretion.[27] But what do the key concepts of *rationality* in legal argumentation and *legal community* signify, to be more exact? Aarnio's theory of legal argumentation and the concept of legal audience are based on Perelman's idea of the new rhetoric and the notion of an ideal or universal audience entailed therein.

Aulis Aarnio bases his theory of legal argumentation on a set of theory premises, viz. Jürgen Habermas' notion of ideal speech situation (*ideale Sprechsituation*) and Chaïm Perelman's idea of an universal audience (*l'auditoire universel*)[28]; the rationality rules of legal discourse by Robert Alexy, based on Habermas' idea of communicative rationality[29]; and John Rawls' seminal idea of decision-making behind the veil of ignorance.[30] Moreover, Aarnio's theory of law is committed to Aleksander Peczenik's three-partite model of the sources of law, as now adapted to the Finnish legal system.[31]

Alexy's rationality rules of legal discourse comprise the following kinds of rules[32]:

(a) *consistency rules* prohibit the use of contradictory arguments and require that the speaker adheres to the rule of excluded middle and the general transitivity rule;
(b) *efficiency rules* prohibit the use of consciously misleading arguments based on linguistic disagreement;

---

[26] Aarnio, *The Rational as Reasonable*, p. 227.

[27] Aarnio, *The Rational as Reasonable*, p. 185 et seq.

[28] Aarnio, *The Rational as Reasonable*, pp. 202, 221–226 (on Perelman) and pp. 195–196, 224–225, 231–235 (on Habermas), Aarnio, *Reason and Authority*, pp. 202, 220–221 (on Perelman) and pp. 209, 210–211, 214–216 (on Habermas); Aarnio, *Laintulkinnan teoria*, pp. 278–279, 282 (on Perelman).

[29] Aarnio, *The Rational as Reasonable*, pp. 195–204; Aarnio, *Reason and Authority*, pp. 214–215, 222; Aarnio, *Laintulkinnan teoria*, pp. 211–216; cf. Alexy, *A Theory of Legal Argumentation*, pp. 187–206.

[30] Aarnio, *Reason and Authority*, p. 228; cf. Rawls, *A Theory of Justice*, pp. 136–142.

[31] Aarnio, *The Rational as Reasonable*, pp. 89–95; Aarnio, *Laintulkinnan teoria*, pp. 220–256; cf. Peczenik, *Vad är rätt?* pp. 209–288; Peczenik, *On Law and Reason*, pp. 319–371.

[32] Aarnio, *The Rational as Reasonable*, pp. 196–198; Alexy, *A Theory of Legal Argumentation*, pp. 187–206.

(c) *sincerity rules* require that the other party or parties to a discourse ought to be taken seriously and prohibit the use of force, deception, and prejudice vis-à-vis the other parties to a discourse;
(d) *generalization rules* prohibit the use of ad hoc and *ad hominem* arguments;
(e) *justification rules* require that each argument be backed by (other) rational arguments, if it has been challenged.

The introduction of Rawls' *veil of ignorance* in the novel context of the judge's legal discretion may invite trouble, however. In Rawls' theory of justice, the veil of ignorance was introduced as a conceptual device for framing the *original position* that is thought to conceptually precede the state of having entered a social contract.[33] By means of the veil of ignorance, Rawls could justify the adoption of the grounding rules of justice and the institutional arrangements in a society committed to the idea of *justice as fairness*. In the original position, the parties to the social contract are denied any knowledge concerning their own social position or possession of wealth, so they cannot have any specific interests to defend, either. All the knowledge they have is equal to general knowledge of the human nature and the general scarcity of resources in society.[34]

Rawls argued that the parties to the negotiations on a social contract, in which the grounding principles of social justice and the institutional arrangements in society are to be settled by rational argument, would agree upon a set of principles to the effect that each participant is given the widest sphere of personal freedom that is compatible with a similar sphere of freedom enjoyed by the others. The allocation of the scarce resources in society will be attained by reference to the principle according to which all the offices and vacancies in society are open for all to apply, on the condition that they meet up with the specific criteria demanded by the task or position concerned. Social inequality cannot be justified except by having recourse to what Rawls called the *difference principle*. Thus, improving the position of the well-off members in society is allowed only on the condition that the position of the less well-off members of society is thereby also improved.

When the veil of ignorance is detached from its initial philosophical context of drafting a social contract and placed in the context of the judge's legal decision-making process, as Aarnio suggests, the setting is radically different from the Rawlsian *tabula rasa* situation that conceptually predates the locking-up of the institutional structure of society and the principles of social justice adopted in it. The

[33]Interestingly, John Searle has argued that if there is a language in a community, it entails that the speakers have already entered a social contract (in some sense of the term), to the effect that there can be no pre-contractual original position where language would be used as a means of communication: "... to have language is already to have a rich structure of institutions. Statement making and promising are human institutions as much as property or marriage. (...) If by 'the state of nature' we mean a state in which humans live like other animals without any institutional structures, then *for language-using human beings there can be no such thing as the state of nature*." Searle, *Making the Social World*, p. 134. (Italics in original.)

[34]Rawls, *A Theory of Justice*, pp. 137–138.

judge is – *per definitionem* – placed in a decision-making situation where the institutional structure of society and the general principles of social justice have been determined *in abstracto* in legislation and/or precedents, while it is the judge's task to define their content *in concreto* for the particular case at hand. As a consequence, the Rawlsian veil of ignorance cannot be extended to the judge's legal discretion without seriously distorting its Rawlsian philosophical content. A court of justice is an *institutional fact* the existence of which necessitates the pre-existence of a set of legal rules on the court organization, judicial procedure, and the legal order in general. Thus, the idea of a veil of ignorance cannot be part of the frame that guides a judge's legal discretion, except in the rather trivial sense that the delivery of justice in a court should not pay attention to the subjective character of the persons involved in the case but only to the arguments presented by them.

Aarnio defines the audience of a legal assertion on how to construct and read the law by reference to Perelman's notion of universal audience[35]:

> The universal audience consists of *enlightened persons*, i.e. persons who are adept at using reasons. It is an *ideal* audience in the sense that no-one can possibly think of addressing the universal audience so that each and every one of its members could de facto have a stand on the issue concerned.

Aarnio makes the two further distinctions between a *concrete* and an *ideal* audience, on the one hand, and a *universal* and a *partial* audience, on the other.[36] When looked upon from the point of view of Perelman's new rhetoric, the difference between an ideal and universal audience, on the one hand, and a concrete and partial audience, on the other, is far from self-evident. Aarnio, moreover, argues that Perelman is committed to a *value-cognitivist* and *value-objectivist* position as to the definition of the universal audience[37]:

> What is important in Perelman's notion of a universal audience is that *value judgements*, too, obtain an objective character in it. Thus, Perelman makes the presumption that a value judgment is rationally justified only when each (rational) human being can accept it. Value judgments, if they successfully pass the test of approval by the universal audience, obtain a rational justification that is similar to that given to propositions concerning empirical reality. (...) If we accept the notion that in a universal audience even a *value judgment* can be justified by means of rational discretion and in such a manner that the audience will finally reach consensus, we have ended up in supporting a cognitivist theory of values. As was noted above, Perelman's treatise would seem to hint at such a possibility. This means that by increasing knowledge [on the subject of disagreement] two initially diverging standpoints, held by two distinct members of the universal audience, can be made to converge.

Aarnio's reading of Perelman might invite criticism, though, since Perelman's idea of the universal audience need not be committed to the alleged presumption of value-cognitivism or value-objectivism.

---

[35] Aarnio, *Laintulkinnan teoria*, p. 279. (Italics by Aarnio; translation by the present author.) – I make use of the original, Finnish edition of Aarnio's book here.

[36] Aarnio, *The Rational as Reasonable*, pp. 221–225; Aarnio, *Laintulkinnan teoria*, pp. 280–283.

[37] Aarnio, *Laintulkinnan teoria*, pp. 279, 282. (Italics by Aarnio; translation by the present author.)

According to Aarnio, a concrete audience can be either universal or partial. A *concrete and universal* audience comprises all the humans alive at the moment of time *t*. Such a category obviously has no field of application in legal argumentation, since the idea of having a concrete audience that would adhere to a common set of universal values is highly unrealistic. A *concrete and partial* audience consists of a restricted number of listeners, such as the attendants of a university lecture, the jury of a court, or the members of a parliamentary legislative committee in front of which arguments on legislative drafts are presented. In such a case, the sentence on legal interpretation that is put forth by the speaker either is or is not acceptable from the point of view of the listeners, while the use of manipulation, compulsion, or other kind of irrational argumentation has not been ruled out as means of influencing the audience. For Aarnio, such a conception of argumentation is not acceptable, since it pays no respect to the legitimate expectations of legal protection of the citizens.

An ideal audience, too, can be either universal or partial. An *ideal* and *universal* audience consists of all the enlightened persons, capable of taking part in rational argumentation. According to Aarnio, such a notion of the universal audience is the one introduced by Perelman. As was pointed out above, Aarnio argues that Perelman is committed to the idea of *value-cognitivism* in argumentation, while Aarnio himself opts for a relativist conception of values. Thus, in Aarnio's model there is no guarantee of an ultimate value consensus in the ideal audience, not even after a full round of argumentative turns. Finally, an *ideal* and *partial* audience consists of those persons who are committed to the rules of rational discourse, on the one hand, and who share a common *form of life* and the values entailed therein, on the other, the term "form of life" taken in the Wittgensteinian sense. The members of an ideal and partial audience all share a set of common values bound to a certain form of life, while the presumption of universal values and ultimate consensus concerning them, which Aarnio ascribes to Perelman and his notion of argumentation, need not be made.[38]

Still, the distinction between an (ideal) universal audience and concrete (partial) audience would seem to be sufficient for the present purpose. A universal audience is invariably an ideal audience if defined in the constructive and subject-aligned manner suggested above by Perelman (and Wihuri), and not in the more objectivist manner suggested by Aarnio. In consequence, the presumption of an ultimately converging consensus on values and interpretation-bound meanings can be relaxed in favour of a more permissive notion of the universal audience. When the universal audience is defined, as Perelman himself suggested, as a *subjective thought construct in the mind of the speaker* used as a reference for argumentation by him,[39] the distinction between an ideal or concrete *universal* audience gets blurred and falls down: since it is no more than a subjective thought construct of the speaker,

---

[38] Aarnio, *Laintulkinnan teoria*, pp. 282–283.

[39] Perelman and Olbrechts-Tyteca, *Traité de l'Argumentation*, pp. 25–30: *L'auditoire comme construction de l'orateur*.

the conceptual boundaries of the universal audience are for the speaker himself to define in light of the prevailing socio-cultural conception of rationality in question. And, on the other hand, since a *concrete* audience is invariably a *partial* audience as well, there is not need for the distinction between a concrete audience and a partial audience, either.

As I see it, Aarnio's argument as to the value-objectivism or value-cognitivism in Perelman's new rhetoric cannot find adequate support in the latter's writings on the issue. In fact, such a notion would be contrary to the basic philosophical premises and intentions of an Aristotelian rhetoric. The Greek philosopher's idea of rhetoric is aligned with the kind of premises, and the inferences based on them, that are *not* true or untrue by definition, unlike the tautologies and analytical truths of formal logic and mathematics of the type "a = a" or "((a → b) & (b → c)) –> (a → c)". Similarly, the claims of Aristotelian rhetoric depart from the self-evidently valid, intuitive, and a priori truths of a rationalistic or intuitive philosophy, like Descartes' famous inference *cogito, ergo sum*, and from the self-evident logico-conceptual necessities of a philosophical phenomenology or rationalistic natural law philosophy.[40] Moreover, the scope of the new rhetoric will not cover the observation sentences or protocol sentences in the sense referred to by the *Wiener Kreis*, the truth-value of which is subject to verification or falsification according to the experiential and empirical methodology of the natural sciences.

Rather, the Aristotelian rhetoric and its later Perelmanian variant deal with the kind of reasoning, the premises and conclusions of which are not known to be (necessarily) true or untrue, but are only more or less adequate, reasonable, or acceptable, as judged by audience addressed by the speaker. Instead of logical deduction and the preservation of the original truth-value of the premises of philosophical reasoning, the topics and rhetoric by Aristotle, the new rhetoric by Perelman, and the legal argumentation theory based on such premises all analyse practical reasoning and the commonly held conceptions, judgments and opinions (*opinions communes* & *sens commun*) that dwell within the realm of morals, politics, practical philosophy, and law.[41]

Within the realm of rhetoric, we are dealing with beliefs and assertions that can be argued *pro et contra* in a more or less plausible manner, to the effect of possibly convincing the intended audience, no matter whether we are dealing with a set of sentences on how to construct and read the law; the definition of good, right, and just in moral philosophy; value judgments in the study of history, literature, or aesthetics in the context of the humanities; or the interpretation of the rules of some social convention and etiquette in a social situation in the social studies. In such a discourse on what is legally or morally right and acceptable, the rigid rules of formal logic have to recede, giving way to a far more flexible conception of argumentation.

---

[40]On the self-evident truths of natural law philosophy, cf. Finnis, *Natural Law and Natural Rights*, pp. 64–65: "The good of knowledge is self-evident, obvious. It cannot be demonstrated, but equally it needs no demonstration." Cf. Finnis, *Natural Law and Natural Rights*, p. 85.

[41]Cf. Perelman, "Une théorie philosophique de l'argumentation", p. 255.

Aristotle's and Perelman's notion of the realm of rhetoric exemplifies an *ars disputationis*,[42] i.e. the skill of *reasonable disagreement* among the parties o a dispute that cannot be formalized into a set of logical syllogisms, because of the definitional uncertainty of the premises and the resulting conclusions of reasoning.

If, in fact, the process of argumentation and deliberation in front of a universal audience would ultimately lead to a converging consensus on the societal values concerned, even the process of judicial deliberation and legal argumentation would end up in an overarching consensus on the issues under scrutiny. The ideal or universal audience would then function as the ultimate reference of *consensus-seeking* legal objectivity. In ascribing the attribute of meaning-converging value-objectivism and value-cognitivism to Perelman's notion of universal audience, Aarnio's argument has the unfortunate side-effect of turning the Aristotelian idea of argumentation that takes place in terms of relative uncertainty and reasonable disagreement into one based on absolute certainty vis-à-vis the value premises entailed, since after a full round of arguments presented in front of the universal audience we would ultimately have an over-arching consensus as to the values entailed and the outcomes of legal reasoning.

The initial discord among the participants to a legal dispute would be effectively dismantled by recourse to the internal dynamics of such consensus-oriented reasoning in the universal audience, thereby turning the initial disagreement into final agreement and consensus on the values entailed. As a consequence, there would be no logical space left for the kind of *pro et contra* argumentation and, possibly, ultimate uncertainty and disagreement as to the outcome of deliberation that, however, is a distinctive mark of Aristotelian rhetoric.

The tautological, or analytical, truths of logic and mathematics; the intuitive, a priori truths of Réné Descartes' *cogito, ergo sum* and other self-evident truths of rationalistic philosophy; the logico-conceptual and metaphysical premises of phenomenological philosophy, and the equally self-evident (*per se nota*) truths concerning the human nature and human society by the natural law philosophy all claim to evade the Aristotelian idea of subjecting the conceptions, beliefs, and judgments of practical reasoning to the tribunal of a *pro et contra* argumentation, with no access to absolutely certain knowledge on the issue. Formally valid deductive logic has no need for the less-than-exact reasoning cherished by the Aristotelian or Perelmanian rhetoric[43]:

> What is evident is, at the same time, necessarily true and immediately recognizable as such. An evident proposition has no need for a proof, since such a proof would consist of a necessary deduction of something that is not evident from a set of premises that are themselves evident. – In such a system, there is no place for argumentation.

---

[42] Sampaio Ferraz, Jr., "Topique", p. 615.

[43] Perelman, "Une théorie philosophique de l'argumentation", p. 248: "Ce qui est évident est, à la fois, nécessairement vrai et immédiatement reconnaissable comme tel. La proposition évident n'a pas besoin de preuve, la preuve n'étant qu'une déduction nécessaire de ce qui n'est pas évident à partir de thèses évidents. – Dans un tel système, il n'y a nulle place pour l'argumentation." (Translation by the present author.)

Therefore, the *realm of rhetoric* occupies the logical space that extends "between the evident and the irrational".[44] It is, in other words, situated in a logico-conceptual space limited by the analytical truths of formal logic and mathematics and the self-evident truths of phenomenology and natural law theory, on the one hand, and by the irrational emotions, passions, and other phenomena that lie beyond the domain of reason, on the other. In the old and new rhetoric alike, we are dealing with what is no more than *adequate*, *justifiable*, or *reasonable* in light of the notion of a universal audience that the speaker has constructed in his mind, reflecting his idea of rationality that can be universalized for the audience at hand. Contrary to Aarnio's philosophical stance, Perelman's universal audience will have no room for the ultimately converging effect of the claimed value-consensus, value-cognitivism, or value-objectivism, due to its entailment of the uncertainty of legal argumentation and its being open to various interpretations of the social and cultural values in an *ars disputationes*. Thus, the universal audience will always leave room for the divergent, possibly dissensus-inducing arguments, instead of hosting an inducement for overarching consensus in legal or moral argumentation.

4.4 The New Rhetoric and Its Alternatives

The Aristotelian and Perelmanian approach to the issues on law provides a highly feasible alternative to the isomorphic theory and the coherence theory considered above. Like the coherence theory, the rhetorical account rejects the notion of an isomorphic relation between the specific fact-description of a legal norm and the state of affairs in fact realized in the world, as the isomorphic model of law would have it. Similarly, it turns down the idea of textual coherence among the institutional and societal sources of law under the coherentist premises or law as integrity. Now, it is the intended universal audience (*l'auditoire universel*) of legal interpretation, taken as a subject-bound, mental *thought construct* of the speaker as outlined by Chaïm Perelman and Lucie Olbrechts-Tyteca in *Traité de l'Argumentation* that will serve as the reference for legal construction or other kind of practical reasoning. The impact of the pragmatism-aligned *consensus* theory of truth can be seen here.

Perelman's new rhetoric manages to get along with a somewhat less complicated "furniture of the world", or philosophical ontology, than the isomorphic theory, since it need not adhere to the metaphysical prerequisites of the Wittgensteinian picture theory of language. Instead, a set of rationality conditions that define the characteristics of the ideal, universal audience will do. Yet, under the theoretical premises of Wittgenstein's *Tractatus Logico-Philosophicus*, the language – world relation could not itself be captured by semantically meaningful linguistic expressions, since they failed to satisfy Wittgenstein's criteria of meaningfulness.

---

[44]In French: *entre l'évident et l'irrationnel*. Perelman, "Une théorie philosophique de l'argumentation", p. 255 *in fine*.

Though the definition of truth as a language–world correspondence might be thought to best satisfy the genuinely philosophical criteria of human knowledge, turning such a definition into a workable tool of philosophical analysis will meet with grave theoretical obstacles. We cannot possibly gain knowledge of the states of affairs that prevail in the world without first having gained access to the logico-linguistic categories of the *épistémè* in Michel Foucault's sense of the term, i.e. the epistemic order of things that determines how the "words" (*les mots*) and "things" (*les choses*), or linguistic categories and the phenomena in the world, are connected to one another.[45] The chains of logic and language will not loosen their grip on us, no matter how intensely we wished for a shortcut for direct knowledge of the phenomena "out there" in the world, untouched by the possibly distorting categories of the human language and the ever-present constraints of the prevalent *épistémè*.

When the concept of truth is defined by the approval or disapproval of an ideal, universal audience, the metaphysical premises concerning the world "out there" can be loosened and a more community-based idea of human knowledge be adopted instead. The cost of such a philosophical move is paid in terms of the *constructive*, shifting rationality conditions of a universal audience, and the very conception of discourse rationality may significantly vary, depending on the particular world-view of the speaker and the context of argumentation. If the universal audience is defined, as Chaïm Perelman preferred, as a subjective *thought construct of the speaker*,[46] it can provide no more than a highly subject-related, fictitious or hypothetical reference for argumentation.

In that, Perelman's ultimate reference of legal or moral argumentation resembles Dworkin's idea of the fictitious super-judge Hercules, J. whose overwhelming capacities in legal construction and interpretation guaranteed the attainment of legal integrity. The trouble with Perelman's notion of rational argumentation has to do with the very notion of the universal audience. How could we define the universal audience as a mental construction of the speaker vis-à-vis the rationality conditions of, say, legal deliberation, while evading a down-right *solipsistic* conception of such argumentation, with no inherent links to the similar conceptions sustained by the others?

Anchoring the criteria of the truth and knowledge to the approval of an ideal or universal audience has the welcome effect of ruling out any perfectly *coherent fairy-tales* from among any set of true propositions of the world, such as the nonsensical world of the *Alice in Wonderland* or the world of witchcraft and wizardry in J. K. Rowling's books on *Harry Potter*, no matter how perfectly such an account of the (fictitional) world might meet up with the coherentist criteria laid down by the theory of literature or aesthetics.

Still, even a fully reasoned consensus on some scientific or other issue may be grounded on totally mistaken premises, like Galileo Galilei's clash with the

---

[45] Foucault, *Les Mots et les choses*; Siltala, *Oikeustieteen tieteenteoria*, p. 1 et seq.

[46] "*L'auditoire comme construction de l'orateur*", Perelman and Olbrechts-Tyteca, *Traité de l'Argumentation*, pp. 25–30.

Catholic Church and Italian Inquisition at the birth of the novel empiricist science in the seventeenth century bear ample witness of. Even the consensus theory of truth and knowledge necessitates some ontic conception of the subject matter of legal construction and of the institutional or societal premises entailed, so that the presence (or absence) of such an approval might be rightly targeted at the *legal*, and not e.g. moral, economic, or religious, phenomena. The consensus theory of truth and knowledge cannot provide the objects of legal construction by itself, but a pre-ordained conception of the world is needed.

Unlike the isomorphic theory, the coherence theory of law and the new rhetoric are able to cover the hard cases of legal discretion, too, where the judge is confronted with the interpretation of less than clear-cut rules or the weighing and balancing of legal principles, with reference to Makkonen's semantically *vague* and *unregulated* situations of legal decision-making. Perelman's theory of legal argumentation is ultimately affected by the same kind of inherent weakness as Dworkin's theory of *law as integrity*: if the universal audience is no more than a thought construct of the speaker, how can we ever be certain that the outcome of legal construction and interpretation really matches with the prevailing idea of legal justice? In Dworkin's theory, the solipsistic legal discretion of the fictitious superjudge Hercules cannot be supervised by any external means, and the same goes for the universal audience under the new rhetoric.

The coherence theory underscores the relations that prevail among arguments derived from the institutional and societal sources of law, while the new rhetoric gives priority to the reactions of the intended audience of such reasoning. The two criteria, i.e. textual coherence under the coherence theory of law and the approval or disapproval of the outcome of interpretation at the universal audience under the new rhetoric, may well lend support to one another. The justification given in support of a particular reading of the law gives indirect information of the significance accorded to the universal audience, of legal integrity, or any other criterion adopted as the reference of how to construct and read the law.

Still, the authority, or argumentative weight, of the outcome of legal reasoning cannot be extended beyond the weight or authority of the premises of the frame of analysis adopted in such legal construction. Any stance on how to construct and read the law based on the subjective thought construct of the universal audience in Perelman's new rhetoric or on the fictitious super-judge Hercules in Dworkin's theory of legal integrity is always vulnerable to G. E. Moore's *open question argument*: "now that you have defined the criterion of justice in legal argumentation as so-and-so, well, *is* that justice?" In addition, the coherence theory of law and the new rhetoric equally fail to give an account of the *external* effects of law, such as the economic consequences of law in society.

Chapter 5
Philosophical Pragmatism: Law, Judged in Light of Its Social Effects

5.1 "What, In Short, is the Truth's Cash Value in Experiential Terms?"

Philosophical pragmatism is a distinctively American phenomenon as to its origin and subsequent influence. It saw daylight in the writings of Charles S. Peirce (1839–1914), William James (1842–1910), and John Dewey (1859–1952), while Georg Herbert Mead (1863–1931) is often mentioned as the fourth representative of original pragmatism.[1] In addition, Justice Oliver Wendell Holmes, Jr. (1841–1935) may be counted as one of the early pragmatists.[2]

Still, pragmatism is not, and has never been, an internally uniform school of philosophy or intellectual movement. Rather, it consists of a set of overlapping philosophical positions that more or less share certain characteristics, as might be depicted by the term *family resemblance* by Ludwig Wittgenstein. Within the pragmatist movement, there are significant differences as to the definition of the subject matter and methodology to be adopted in philosophical research.

Of the founding figures of philosophical pragmatism, Peirce emphasized the essentially scientific characteristics of pragmatism, James its psychological tenets, and Dewey its inherent links to the idea of Western democracy.[3] What is common to all the pragmatists, though, is the idea that all human knowledge is *fallibilistic* to the effect that all true beliefs can be exposed to the trial of potential falsification in light of contrary evidence, and *instrumental* to the effect that all true ideas

---

[1] Scheffler, *Four Pragmatists. A Critical Introduction to Peirce, James, Mead, and Dewey*, p. 149 et seq.

[2] Holmes' oracle-like assertions on the law bear the impact of pragmatism. Cf.: "The life of the law has not been logic: it has been experience." Holmes, "The Common Law", p. 237; "General propositions do not decide concrete cases." Holmes, in *Lochner v. New York*, 198 U.S. 45 (1905), in Posner, ed., *The Essential Holmes*, p. 306; "The common law is not a brooding omnipresence in the sky but the articulate voice of some sovereign or quasi-sovereign that can be identified...", Holmes, "Southern Pacific Co. v. Jensen", 244 U.S. 205 (1917), as cited in Posner, ed., *The Essential Holmes*, p. 230.

[3] As Nicholas Rescher put it: "Peirce's pragmatism is scientifically élitist, James' is psychologically personalistic, Dewey's is democratically populist." Rescher, "Pragmatism", p. 712.

R. Siltala, *Law, Truth, and Reason*, Law and Philosophy Library 97,
DOI 10.1007/978-94-007-1872-2_5,

are tied up with the successful pursuance of certain human goals and objectives. Moreover, the two qualities of knowledge, i.e. being *contextual* and *workable*, have been associated with legal pragmatism.[4]

Pragmatism puts emphasis on the *utility*, *usefulness*, *successfulness*, *effectiveness*, and *verifiability* of the true ideas, no matter whether they be part of a scientific theory or just commonsensical beliefs with the help of which we structure and manage our daily life. A pragmatist point of view on the world rejects any references to some "metaphysical" or idealistic doctrines beyond the reach of human senses or the realm of the empirical. What is essential in judging the truth of some particular idea or belief is the collected, cumulated set of common experience that has been gathered of its proper functioning in the course of our daily action, no matter whether the context of judgment is a scientific theory, a philosophical stance, or just commonplace human knowledge and action. Thus, the criteria put forth by pragmatism can be applied to a variety of beliefs or ideas in the field of practical reason, like the appraisal of the good, the right, and the just in moral philosophy; the judgment of what is beautiful or aesthetically impressive in art and aesthetics; or what is legally right, acceptable, or equitable in the context of law and legal argumentation.

According to the pragmatists, there is no need for the epistemic and semantic prerequisites of an isomorphism-aligned picture theory of language and the world. Nor is there any conceptual space for the seminal preconditions of the coherence theory of truth, knowledge and legal construction, defined as internal textual coherence among the observation sentences and the theoretical sentences that make up a scientific theory or a set of sentences on how to construct and read the law. To the philosophical pragmatist, knowledge, meaning, and truth are essentially *instrumentalist* notions that are inextricably interwoven with human action, the social practices, and the successful attainment of various kinds of human endeavours: *truth is what works*.[5] Yet, in the context of law the notion of *what works* may prove to be hard to determine, because of the inherently contested character of law and because there usually is no consensus as to the values to be pursued through legal means.

Though Charles S. Peirce had tackled the issues of philosophical pragmatism as early as in the 1870s, it was William James who made pragmatist ideas widely known at the beginning of the twentieth century. *Pragmaticism*, in turn, is a neologism introduced by Peirce. With it Peirce wanted to distance his ideas from the ones presented by William James who, as Peirce saw it, had distorted the scientific grounds of pragmatism. While Peirce underlined the essentially *objective* tenets of pragmatism, James put an emphasis on the more *subjective* character of human

[4]Lind, "Pragmatist Philosophy of Law", pp. 678–679: fallibilism and the growth of knowledge, contextualism, instrumentalism, workability.

[5]Cf. James, "Pragmatism's Conception of Truth", p. 148: "We must find a theory that will *work*; and that means something extremely difficult; for our theory must mediate between all previous truths and certain new experiences. It must derange common sense and previous belief as little as possible, and it must lead to some sensible terminus or other that can be verified exactly. To "work" means both these things; and the squeeze is so tight that there is little loose play for any theory." (Italics in original.)

knowledge, in the sense of a societal belief upon which successful human action can be based.[6]

In 1907, William James outlined the pragmatist idea of truth by placing an equation between the truth of an idea or belief and the prerequisites of its verifiability in experiential terms[7]:

> Pragmatism, on the other hand, asks its usual question. "Grant an idea or belief to be true," it says, "what concrete difference will its being true make in any one's actual life? How will the truth be realized? What experiences will be different from those which would obtain if the belief were false? What, in short, is the truth's cash value in experiential terms?" – The moment pragmatism asks this question, it sees the answer: *True ideas are those that we can validate, corroborate and verify. False ideas are those that we can not.* That is the practical difference it makes to us to have true ideas; that, therefore, is the meaning of truth, for it is all that truth is known as.

Moreover, James held that the truth of an idea or belief and its *usefulness* are in all significant respects equal[8]:

> You can say of [a true idea] then either that "it is useful because it is true" or that "it is true because it is useful." Both these phrases mean exactly the same thing, namely, that here is an idea that gets fulfilled and can be verified.

At the back of James' conception of truth, there are the basic ideas of pragmatism, as presented by Charles S. Peirce as early as the 1870s:

> In order to ascertain the meaning of an intellectual conception we should consider what practical consequences might conceivably result by necessity from the truth of that conception; and the sum of these consequences will constitute the entire meaning of the conception.

The truth of a scientific or any other conception is defined by the concrete effects it will have on the course of human life: *what concrete difference will its being true make in any one's actual life?* As a consequence, the validity of a scientific idea is defined as equal with its *usefulness*, *success*, or *utility* both in structuring prior historical evidence and in predicting future human experience. What all the tenets of pragmatism have in common is the idea of *usefulness* of the true beliefs in the service of human action, no matter whether we are dealing with scientific theory and explanation, the more mundane tasks of everyday life, the virtues and vices of human conduct, or the issues of how to construct and read the law in a reasoned manner.

The success of a scientific conception or theory can be rephrased as its *testability*, *corroborativeness*, or *verifiability* in light of the criteria adopted in the community, such as the pertinent scientific community with respect to assertions produced by the natural sciences or the human and/or social sciences, and the legal community vis-à-vis the method and outcomes of legal reasoning. Truth, when defined as the usefulness or functioning of a scientific theory or some everyday conception, may be

---

[6] Rescher, "Pragmatism", p. 710.

[7] James, "Pragmatism's Conception of Truth", p. 142. (Italics in original.)

[8] James, "Pragmatism's Conception of Truth", p. 143.

combined with the consensus theory of truth and Chaïm Perelman's idea of the new rhetoric that underscores the role of the scientific or other community in judging the truth of an assertion. The later versions of a pragmatist theory of truth have in fact evolved into the direction of the consensus theory of truth.[9] Conceptions that have gained wide approval in the community have proven their usefulness as grounds for scientific explanation and everyday action, too.

Charles S. Peirce, one of the founders of modern semiotics and a key figure in the evolvement of scientific logic, approached the issues of truth and knowledge by seeking to define the criteria placed on *scientific method*. Peirce, firstly, rejected as unscientific the *method of tenacity* where a scholar stubbornly adheres to his initial beliefs and prejudices, closing his eyes at the face of any contrary evidence. Secondly, he argued that the *method of authority* does not satisfy the criteria of a scientific method, since there are no guarantees of the infallibility of the claimed authority, whether of religious, legal, or other kind. Thirdly, Peirce rejected the a priori *method* as suggested by Descartes' famous inference *cogito, ergo sum*, since it is based on the acclaimed access of human reason to the items of absolutely certain knowledge. According to Peirce, the stagnated state of philosophical metaphysics and the tough resistance of several of its age-old problems against the very best efforts of philosophical problem-solving bears witness to the inherent weaknesses of such an a priori method. Besides, many initially self-evident or a priori truths have been proven false later on.[10]

Having rejected as non-scientific the method of tenacity, the method of authority, and the a priori method, Peirce outlines the notion of a scientific method by means of the following four tenets[11]:

> (a) the properties of the subject of investigation are independent from the opinions held by the researcher; (b) scientific knowledge is brought into effect in the mutual interaction between the researcher and the subject of investigation; (c) science cannot be based on dogmas, faith, revelation, authority, or intuition but the source and criteria of knowledge in science are in the last resort grounded on experience had of the very subject of investigation; (d) it is possible to gain valid knowledge of the subject of investigation, and the scientific community can reach an agreement as to the quality of such knowledge.

Truth is the outcome of the relation that exists between a scientist and a set of empirical observations. Because being open to public disposition and critique, scientific knowledge is in the long run *self-corrective*: any mistakes made in the course of scientific investigation will ultimately tend to become corrected by the scientific community, once more and more accurate empirical evidence is provided of the subject matter of investigation.[12] It is therefore possible, at least in principle, to ultimately reach a consensus on the validity of some particular belief or item of knowledge.

---

[9] Rescher, "Pragmatism", p. 710.

[10] Peirce, *Pragmatism and Pragmaticism*, pp. 233–242.

[11] Peirce, *Pragmatism and Pragmaticism*, pp. 242–244; Niiniluoto, *Johdatus tieteenfilosofiaan. Käsitteen- ja teorianmuodostus*, p. 83.

[12] Niiniluoto, *Johdatus tieteenfilosofiaan. Käsitteen- ja teorianmuodostus*, pp. 83–84.

Peirce's idea of knowledge is *fallibilistic*: each intellectual stance or belief can be challenged and, possibly, proven erroneous by some novel experiential evidence. There are no self-evident truths whose validity would be wholly immune to, or effectively resistant to, scientific testing. For Peirce, truth is an *absolute* quality attached to an idea or belief. In a situation where all the conceivable empirical evidence concerning some phenomenon has been gathered, the conceptions held by the scientific community will *converge*, ultimately leading to a reasoned consensus in it. The scientific community and the criteria of verifiability adopted in it gain a key role in how the set of true beliefs and conceptions is to be defined.

Of the founders of American pragmatist movement in philosophy, John Dewey strongly underscored the psychological and testable properties of knowledge. He introduced the novel term *warranted assertability* as the justifiability or verifiability of certain belief or conception. Dewey regarded scientific knowledge and laws as no more than *working hypotheses* that need to be tested by empirical evidence. Therefore, scientific reasoning is "a logic relative to consequences rather than to antecedents, a logic of prediction of probabilities rather than one of deduction of certainties."[13] At the back lies Dewey's instrumentalist notion of human knowledge, which makes it possible to predict the course of future events and, in more general terms, to accomplish various kinds of human activities.

Similarly, for William James truth is not some static, constant, or eternal property of a belief or conception *sub specie aeternitatis*. Rather, it is "something that happens" to an idea when it is (empirically) verified. For James, truth is a verb rather than a noun, as Morris Dickstein has insightfully pointed out.[14]

A pragmatic conception of science and knowledge matches well with Thomas S. Kuhn's seminal idea of the dynamics of change in a scientific community, as presented in his breakthrough work, *The Structure of Scientific Revolutions*. For Kuhn, science is an essentially *collective* enterprise, based on the commonly held beliefs in the scientific community. Moreover, scientific knowledge is *fallibilistic* so that it is subject to be falsified when encountered with strong enough empirical evidence to the contrary effect.[15] According to Peirce and Kuhn, it is the *scientific community* that has the final say on what will count as science proper, as judged in light of the testability, verifiability, or utility of the theory or some individual assertion, and what will fail such a test. The *scientific community* may be defined as the group of individuals who have a university degree in and/or have gained expertise knowledge in, say, theoretical physics, chemistry, medicine, mathematics, or law. There is no higher religious or political authority or a scientific "court of

---

[13] As cited in Mendell, "Dewey, John (1859–1952)", p. 204.

[14] "The truth of an idea is not a stagnant property inherent in it. Truth *happens* to an idea. It *becomes* true, is *made* true by events. Its verity *is* in fact an event, a process, the process, namely, of its verifying itself, its veri-*fication*. Its validity is the process of its valid-*ation*." James, "Pragmatism's Conception of Truth", p. 142 (all italics and formattings in original). – Cf. Dickstein, "Introduction: Pragmatism Then and Now", p. 7: "James insists that truth or meaning is a process, an action leading to a pay-off, a verb rather than a noun."

[15] Kuhn, *The Structure of Scientific Revolutions*.

appeal" that could settle some scientific issue by declaring what is to be held as true vis-à-vis some contested issue at hand.[16]

Modern philosophical pragmatism is represented by for instance Richard Rorty, Thomas C. Gray, Richard Posner, and Stanley Fish.[17]

5.2 The Lure of Pragmatism and the Law

The urge for pragmatism has had several implications for the study of law. For the first, Justice Holmes and the young Karl Llewellyn forcefully argued for the *prediction theory of law*, to the effect that the law be defined by reference to foreseeing the future course of legal decisions at the courts and other officials. As Llewellyn put it[18]:

> This doing of something about disputes, this doing of it reasonably, is the business of law. And the people who have the doing in charge, whether they be judges or sheriffs or clerks or jailers or lawyers, are officials of the law. *What these officials do about disputes is, to my mind, the law itself.* (...) It will be [the judges'] *action* and the available means of influencing their action or of arranging your affairs with reference to their action which make up the "law" you have to study. And *rules*, in all of this, are important to you so far as they help you see or predict what judges will do or so far as they help you get judges do something. That is their importance. That is all their importance, except as pretty playthings.

Yet, even Llewellyn admitted that it is in light of the legal rules of the legal system concerned that the prediction of future court decisions and any efforts of influencing them are possible. Even before Llewellyn, Justice Holmes had insisted on looking upon the law from the point of view of the "bad man" who is only interested in forecasting the likely legal consequences to be inflicted upon him, if he breaks the law[19]:

---

[16]The Catholic Church had such a privileged position as a kind of court of last instance concerning scientific truth at the beginning of the modern era. Giordano Bruno was burnt as a heretic on the square of the *Campo dei Fieri* in Rome in 1600. Galileo Galilei (1564–1642), after having been threatened with the instruments of the Inquisition, had to deny his heretical doctrine to the effect that that the earth revolves around its axis and around the sun, while allegedly muttering to himself: "E pur si muove." (And yet it [the earth] moves, i.e. revolves around the sun.) – In the Soviet Union of the Stalinist era, even scientific truths were approved or disapproved by the Communist Party. Any scientific theories that were deemed ideologically suspect were declared false. On the other hand, the biologist Lysenko's erroneous doctrine concerning the inheritance of some acquired properties was declared to be valid science by the Communist Party because of ideological reasons.

[17]Dickstein, ed., *The Revival of Pragmatism*. Cf. Rorty, *Consequences of Pragmatism. (Essays: 1972–1980)*; Fish, *Doing What Comes Naturally. Change, Rhetorics, and the Practice of Theory in Literary and Legal Studies*.

[18]Llewellyn, *The Bramble Bush*, pp. 3, 5. (Italics in original.) – Later on, Llewellyn tried to distance himself from the sternness of that stance, now claiming that: "They are, however, unhappy words when not more fully developed, and they are plainly at best a very partial statement of the whole truth." Llewellyn, *The Bramble Bush*, p. X.

[19]Holmes, "The Path of the Law", pp. 460–461. (Italics added.)

> Take the fundamental question, What constitutes the law? You will find some text writers telling you that it is something different from what is decided by the courts of Massachusetts or England, that it is a system of reason, that it is a deduction from principles of ethics or admitted axioms or what not, which may or may not coincide with the decisions. But if we take the view of our friend the *bad man* we shall find that he does not care two straws for the axioms or deductions, but that he does want to know what the Massachusetts or English courts are likely to do in fact. I am much of his mind. *The prophecies of what the courts will do in fact*, and nothing more pretentious, *are what I mean by the law*.

Still, even for Holmes the effected decisions by the courts and other officials served as a pertinent source of law or, as he put it, *sibylline leaves* from which a legal scholar could make predictions as to the course of law at the courts and other officials.[20]

Holmes' cynical figure of the bad man, only interested in the consequences likely to be inflicted upon him if he chooses not to observe the law, is – perhaps a bit surprisingly – lurking even in the background premises of Aulis Aarnio's and Aleksander Peczenik's theory of legal argumentation which in other respects leans on very different philosophical premises. According to Aarnio and Peczenik, the binding character of law is in the last resort based on the *sanctions* that are likely to be inflicted upon a stubborn, dissenting judge who refuses to comply with the legal norms entailed in legislation and other strongly binding sources of law. As a consequence, a charge for misconduct in office may be inflicted upon a judge who stubbornly refuses to comply with the mandatory sources of law, such as the constitution, legislation, and customary law (in Finland).[21]

The place reserved for the bad man, or the potential law-breaker, in Holmes' cynical prediction theory of law is now occupied by the obstinate, dissenting judge whose idea of the rule of recognition to a significant degree deviates from the one adopted by his peers and the legal profession at large.[22] As to the weakly binding sources of law, such as the *travaux préparatoires* and precedents, an unofficial sanction may entail professional reproach from the other judges and lawyers, according to Aarnio.

For the second, legal pragmatism entails the idea that the merits and dismerits of a legal decision are to be judged primarily, if not even exclusively, by the social

---

[20] "The object of our study, then, is prediction, the prediction of the incidence of the public force through the instrumentality of the courts. – The means of the study are a body of reports, of treatises, and of statutes, in this country and in England, extending back for 600 years, and now increasing annually by hundreds. In these sibyllian leaves are gathered the scattered prophesies of the past upon which the axe will fall. These are what properly have been called the oracles of the law." Holmes, "The Path of the Law", p. 457.

[21] Aarnio, *The Rational as Reasonable*, pp. 89–90; Aarnio, *Laintulkinnan teoria*, p. 220; Peczenik, *Vad är rätt?* p. 214. – As to the binding character of customary law, there is even a statutory stipulation to that effect in the Finnish Act of Judicial Procedure.

[22] The prominent role of legal sanctions is of course one of the key characteristics in John Austin's and Hans Kelsen's analytical legal positivism, as well.

consequences thereby brought into effect. Walter Wheeler Cook's reflection on the judge's method of interpretation in 1927 gives a good account thereof[23]:

> The logical situation confronting the judge in a new case being what it is, it is obvious that he must legislate, whether he will or no. By this is meant that since he is free so far as compelling logical reasons are concerned to choose which way to decide the case, his choice will turn out upon analysis to be based upon considerations of social or economic policy. An intelligent choice can be made only by estimating as far as this is possible the consequences of a decision one way or the other. To do this, however, the judge will need to know two things: (1) *what social consequences or results are to be aimed at*; and (2) *how a decision one way or other will affect the attainment of those results*. This knowledge he will as a rule not have; to acquire it he will need to call upon the other social sciences, such as economics. (...) Underlying any scientific study of the law, it is submitted, will lie one fundamental postulate, viz., that human laws are devices, tools which society uses as one of its methods to regulate human conduct and to promote those types of it which are regarded as desirable.

Cook argues for an *instrumentalist* and *consequentialist* notion of law where the social consequences of law are the primary criterion in legal decision-making. The truth or, rather, the justifiability, usefulness, equity, or warranted character of sentences on how to construct and read the law can thus be evaluated in light of the economic, social, or other consequences brought into effect by law in society. The impact of a thoroughly consequentialist analysis of law and society endorsed by Cook boils down to the two questions italicized in the text extract above: (1) what social consequences or results are to be aimed at; and (2) how a decision one way or other will affect the attainment of those social goals.

For the third, Cook's view of a judge leans on an idea of future legal science that was presented by O. W. Holmes at the end of the nineteenth century[24]:

> For the rational study of the law the black-letter man may be the man of the present, but the man of the future is *the man of statistics* and *the master of economics*. (...) I look forward to a time when the part played by history in the explanation of dogma shall be very small, and instead of ingenious research we shall spend our energy on a study of the ends sought to be attained and the reasons for desiring them. As a step toward that ideal it seems to me that every lawyer ought to seek an understanding of economics. The present divorce between the schools of political economy and law seems to me an evidence of how much progress in philosophical study still remains to be made.

Holmes' insight on the profile of the future lawyer to a great extent anticipates the emergence of the empirical human and social sciences in the twentieth century, with coverage of a variety of the fields of social research, such as economic analysis of

[23] Cook, "Scientific Method and the Law", p. 249. (Italics added.) – Cook emphasizes how it is not a judge's task to find some pre-existing, concealed meanings in the legal rules in force but, instead, to give them a meaning content for the case at hand. Cook, "Scientific Method and the Law", pp. 248–249: "His [the judge's] task is not to find the preexisting but previously hidden meanings of the terms in these rules; it is to give them a meaning." Cf. similarly in Makkonen, *Zur Problematik der juridischen Entscheidung*, pp. 111, 118.

[24] Holmes, "The Path of the Law", pp. 469, 474. (Italics added.)

law, legal statistics and the mathematics of social risk analysis, legal anthropology, and legal psychology.[25]

As I see it, Holmes' bold prophecy has proven both true and false at the same time, viz. true in the sense that the diversified perspective of the human and social sciences on law has gained significant ground amongst the scientific community; but false in that such a social scientific view law has not been able to replace the traditional task of the "black-letter law" in legal doctrine. As I see it, it will never succeed in ousting it from the family of legal research, either. Each of the various branches of the human and social sciences with focus on the legal phenomena has a specific research interest and "intellectual toolbox" of its own.[26] Legal doctrine (*Rechtsdogmatik*) or technical legal analysis as a study on how to construct and read the law vis-à-vis some either actual or merely hypothetical fact-constellation in society has a legitimate research interest that finds ample support in society, and there are no hints in the modern (or postmodern) society that might disqualify the said core task of legal doctrine in the foreseeable future. Seeking to give a reasoned answer to the seminal question of legal doctrinal analysis, i.e. *how should a given fact-constellation x be legally judged?,* will remain the core task for legal science in future, as well.

Finally, a pragmatist view on law is characterized by the *contextual* criteria for legal decision-making. It therefore strikes a far better chord with legal principles and other context-sensitive, openly value-laden standards of law than with legal rules, valid by force of their formal source of origin and – at least if Hans Kelsen's stern quest for methodological purity is approved – totally blind to the social consequences thereby brought into effect. Legal pragmatism is in essence *anti-formalist*, and formalism is a typical of legal rules, not of legal principles.[27] In contrast to what has been argued by the representatives of legal formalism, legal argumentation can never take place in a social or ideological void, detached from the constitutive value premises operative in the various legal instruments.

---

[25] Naturally, the emergence of the empirical social sciences in the field of law did not take place overnight or without dead ends in search for a working conception of enquiry. Cf. Schlegel, *American Legal Realism and Empirical Social Science*, where an account is given of the early pathfinders of modern empiricist social sciences.

[26] Here, I will not wish to enter the discussion on whether the human and social sciences count as "genuine" science in the strict sense of the term. Certainly they do not, if by "science" is meant a commitment to an empiricist and/or experiential methodology and a research interest aligned with the explanation and prediction of the phenomena. The human and social sciences have a different agenda, and they, too, qualify as scientific inquiry, if – and only if – the commitments that constitute the matrix of scientific research, i.e. the *ontological*, *epistemological*, *methodological*, *logico-conceptual* and *axiological* premises of inquiry, are duly satisfied in them. Cf. Siltala, *Oikeustieteen tieteenteoria*, passim.

[27] On legal formalism, see e.g. Summers, "Form and Substance in Legal Reasoning"; Summers, "The Formal Character of Law"; Summers, "Theory, Formality and Practical Legal Criticism"; Summers, "How Law is Formal and Why it Matters"; Cf. Siltala, *A Theory of Precedent*, pp. 41–63, where a parallel reading is given of Robert S. Summers' idea of legal formalism and Ronald Dworkin's idea of legal principles, and the claim of the affinity of the two doctrines is argued for.

The urge for realism in jurisprudence may yet be of a somewhat older origin than what the standard learning has it, dating its birth in the writings by Holmes, Pound and sociological jurisprudence at the beginning of the twentieth century. Recently Brian Z. Tamanaha has convincingly argued that the legal realists of the 1920s and 1930s were not the precursors or forerunners of the realist trend in the legal studies but, rather, the "end tail" or culmination point of a tradition that goes back in time for at least a century.[28] Still, the thrust of the realist and pragmatist trend in jurisprudence has found its strongest manifestation in the modern economic analysis of law since the 1960s.

5.3 "These Doctrines Form a System for Inducing People to Behave Efficiently..."

Modern *economic analysis* of law is centred at the University of Chicago. Its starting point was R. H. Coase's essay "The Problem of Social Cost" in 1960. In it, Coase tackled the issue of the *external effects* of legal regulation. He argued that in a situation where the transaction costs are zero and where there is no external regulation that would have a distorting effect on the decision-making situation, scarce resources would be allocated in a manner that is most efficient.[29]

A year later, in 1961, Guido Calabresi published the highly influential essay, "Some Thoughts on Risk Distribution and the Law of Torts".[30] That article plus the author's later subsequent writings on law and economics, such as *The Costs of Accidents* in 1970 and "Property Rules, Liability Rules, and Inalienability: One View from the Cathedral", co-authored by Calabresi and A. Douglas Melamed, in 1972, looked upon the law of property and tort from the point of view of economic analysis of law. The authors introduced a set of concepts like *economic efficiency* and *distributional goals* that were, at least in the legal context, novel. In "Prices and Sanctions", Robert Cooter drew a parallel between the legal sanctions and the economic prices set on a certain type of behaviour.[31] The first edition of Richard A. Posner's influential book, *Economic Analysis of Law*, saw the daylight in 1973. In it, Posner gives a concise view of law seen from the point of view of economics.

---

[28] Tamanaha, *Beyond the Formalist-Realist Divide*, p. 107: "Viewed in this longer frame, it appears more accurate to situate the "legal realist" at the *tail end* of about a half-century of a continuous steam of candid realism about law and judging. (...) What especially stands out about expressions of skeptical realism is the similarity of the arguments across time. Rantoul in 1836, Hammond in 1881, the legal realists in the 1920s and 1930s, and Critical Legal Studies in the 1970s and 1980s (and others along the way) all argued in interchangeable terms that judges have the freedom to decide cases in accordance with their political views and to cover these decisions with legal justifications."

[29] Coase, "The Problem of Social Cost".

[30] Calabresi, "Some Thoughts on Risk Distribution and the Law of Torts". – On the birth of the economic analysis of law, Posner, *Economic Analysis of Law*, pp. 23–24.

[31] Cooter, "Prices and Sanctions".

What all variants of the economic analysis of law have in common is the weight placed on *economic* criteria as the prime reference of legal analysis, no matter whether specified in line with the *Chicago School of Economics*, as in Posner's voluminous writings on various topics of law and economics; the more legally tinted view of *neo-institutionalism*, as suggested by Douglas C. North; the *public choice theory* with emphasis on resource allocation on the public sector; or some other alternative centred on economic issues. As a consequence, the key concepts of analysis are given in terms of economic efficiency and the optimality of the allocation of scarce resources in society, both in legislation and in jurisdiction.

According to Posner's thesis, the legal rules, principles, and doctrines that make up the American common law to a significant degree follow an inherent logic that can be rephrased in economic terms, i.e. the pursuit of economic efficiency. Posner argues for the inherent economic logic of the common law[32]:

> The common law is to most lawyers a collection of disparate fields, each with its own history, vocabulary, and bewildering profusion of rules and doctrines; indeed, each field may itself seem a collection of only tenuously related doctrines. Yet we have seen that the law of property (including intellectual property), of contracts and commercial law, of restitution and unjust enrichment, of criminal and family law, and of admiralty law *all can be restated in economic terms* that explain the principal doctrines, both substantive and remedial, in the fields of (largely) judge-made law. *These doctrines form a system for inducing people to behave efficiently*, not only in explicit markets but across the whole range of social interactions. In settings in which the cost of voluntary transactions is low, common law doctrines create incentives for people to channel their transactions through the market (whether implicit – the marriage market for example – or explicit). They do this by creating property rights (broadly defined) and protecting them through remedies designed to prevent coerced transfers – remedies such as injunctions, restitution, punitive damages, and criminal punishment. In settings in which the cost of allocating resources by voluntary transactions is prohibitively high, making the market an infeasible method of allocating resources, the common law prices behavior in such a way as to mimic the market.

Posner's claim of the implicit economic logic of the common law can be read in a descriptive or a normative sense. According to a *descriptive* account of the issue, the evolvement of American common law is based on premises that have had the effect of enhancing economic efficiency and the goal of wealth maximization in society.[33] According to the parallel *normative* claim, that is how things ought to be, as well: economic efficiency and the criteria that foster economic prosperity ought to guide the course of the American law in future, too.[34] In the context of legislation and other institutional legal source material, that gives effect to the conception that the economic consequences of law should have priority over other kinds of considerations in the construction and reading of law.[35]

---

[32] Posner, *Economic Analysis of Law*, pp. 249–250. (Italics added.)

[33] Posner, *Economic Analysis of Law*, pp. 249–250.

[34] On a similarly *descriptive/prescriptive* reading of Posner's pragmatism, cf. Tamanaha, *Law as a Means to an End*, pp. 118–119.

[35] On the notion of *legisprudentia*, or jurisprudential analysis of the process of legislation, cf. Wintgens, "Creation and Application of Law from A Legisprudential Perspective. Some Observations on the Point of View of the Judge and the Legislator".

Posner points out that his thesis on the implicit logic of common law, to the effect of striving for optimal cost efficiency in society through judicial decisions, cannot be taken as an all-embracing model that would categorically rule out the impact of any alternative readings of the common law. Instead, it is at the most an *approximation* of the laws of social reality within the common law where the ideals of economic rationality are complied with more or less imperfectly only. The reason why the decision-making process of the judge or other official may deviate from the ideal of economic efficiency is mostly due to the *conventional* patterns of decision-making adopted by the judiciary, and to the in-built resistance against any profound changes in the legal tradition. Still, Posner argues that the economic point of view will provide the best explanation for the court decisions and the decisions given by other law-applying officials.[36]

But if the non-contested fact that the "law in action", as enforced by the courts of justice and other law-applying officials, tends to lag behind the ever-changing social and economic conditions in society were for a moment set aside, and the evolving story of the common law were be read in light of a more-or-less all-encompassing economic rationality, the economic explanation of law and society can be stretched like an elastic rubber band to cover all legal issues that may surface, no matter how close or how far they are situated from the economic base of society. Any empirical counter-evidence to Posner's thesis will leave his final conclusions untouched, since the no-more-than approximate nature of his claim will always leave room for any such exceptions. As a consequence, Posner's thesis of the implicit economic logic of the common law is a non-refutable *postulate* of legal analysis, and not an initial hypothesis that could be empirically corroborated and possibly refuted in the course of the study.

5.4 "Why Efficiency?" and "Is Wealth a Value?" – A Critical Evaluation of the Economic Analysis of Law, with Brief Comments on the Marxist Theory of Law

In Europe, jurisprudential discourse on an economic analysis of law has for the most part been focused on the relatively general and theoretical issues of law, such as *de*

---

[36]Posner, *Economic Analysis of Law*, pp. 252–253: "Despite all of the above, not every common law doctrine has an economic rationale. (...) Some of the discrepancies between law and economics may be the result of simply of lags explicable in economic terms, the phenomenon economists call "path dependence". Because the law for good economic reasons places heavy weight on continuity, law tends to lag behind changing social and economic conditions. Nevertheless, economic efficiency does not provide a complete positive theory of the common law. But it does provide a uniform vocabulary and conceptual scheme to aid in making the common law understandable as a coherent whole, and thus to balance the heavily particularistic emphasis of traditional legal education and reasoning." – The term "logico-conceptual toolbox" is mine, but the idea is Posner's.

lege ferenda analysis of future legislation.[37] The critique of bypassing or forgetting the institutional frame of legal adjudication even applies to the proficient Italian scholar Ugo Mattei and his highly challenging *Comparative Law and Economics* in 1997. Despite his whole-hearted commitment to the basic theses of American legal realist movement, Mattei still ignores the impact of any institutional constraints placed upon a judge or other law-applying official when he analyses the subject matter by the novel combination of comparative law and economics.[38]

Pragmatism-aligned legal consequentialism gives precedence to the social effects of law, and especially the economic consequences of law have a key position there. The *institutional* sources of law, along with the legal rules and legal principles that can be derived from them by means of legal reasoning, now have to recede, giving room for a more straightforward appraisal of the economic effects of legislation and judicial adjudication. In the branches of law that have an inherent bond with the issues of trade and commerce, marketing, financing and monetary transactions, economic effects of law are, so to say, built in the very subject matter of legal regulation. Therefore, the economic consequences of law may gain significantly more normative, binding force in such fields of law than what the standard doctrine of the sources of law, like the one by Aarnio and Peczenik, would allow. For Aarnio and Peczenik, the economic effects of law are ranked as merely permissive arguments in the legal discretion of the judge.

There are limits to what can be attained by use of the intellectual tools provided by the economic analysis of law, though. As Posner himself admits, economics-based argumentation cannot be extended to become an all-inclusive legal reason, without at the same time cutting off the judge's discretion from the institutional premises of law, such as the constitution, statutes, precedents, and the *travaux préparatoires* at the back of legislation, if any. The exceptions to the extent of economic analysis in law that Posner was willing to concede to were due to the collective thought patterns prevalent among the judiciary and the inherent resistance of the legal tradition toward external change. Yet, restrictions on the use of economic arguments in the context of law could more plausibly be justified by reference to the institutional sources of law and the entailed value premises that comprise a diversity of social values besides those of economic kind.

Thus, the greater than merely permissive impact of economics-based arguments in law is restricted to the branches of law that have an inherent connection to the

[37] A notable exception to the absence of a judicial perspective within the law and economics movement is of course Justice Richard Posner whose argumentation is deeply rooted in the soil of the judge-made *common law* tradition in the United States. Posner, *Economic Analysis of Law*, pp. 249–250.

[38] Mattei, *Comparative Law and Economics*, pp. 69–146 and esp. pp. 101–121, where the author deals with the sources of law of legislation under the subtitle *The Competitive Relationship among Sources of Law* and makes use of the seminal texts of such heavy-weight American legal realists as Jerome Frank and John Chipman Gray but, at the same time, ignores the judge's or other official's view as to the law. In addition, with the term "sources of law" Mattei refers to the source material that is available to the legislator, while established linguistic usage relates the said notion rather to a judge's or other legal official's view as to the constitutive premises of law.

economic structures and economic activities, such as the production of goods and services, finance, insurance, marketing, and trade and commerce in general. The stance advocated by Posner and his followers in the law and economic movement is far better suited to the analysis of the law of property and transactions than any other branches of law. When applied to the law of the European Union and the respective national regulation of the EU Member States on issues that have to do with the regulation of internal market, commercial law, the law of investment, banking, financial instruments, transferable bonds and securities, and economic transactions, the *intellectual toolbox* provided by the economic analysis of law will yield far more reasonable results than in the field of marriage, adoption, euthanasia, care for the children, the elderly and the handicapped, human rights law, and social security issues in general. In the latter, other value considerations than those of purely economic or financial kind are given priority.

Similarly, in scientific research, literature, music, and other arts and crafts, the economic aspect is usually not the only or the primary driving force for human motivation. Reduction of such human endeavour to the economics of financing, production and (sometimes) transaction of cultural artefacts would hardly meet with the professional vocation and self-understanding of the artists or scientists themselves.

Economic analysis of law has a somewhat ambivalent relation to the Marxist conception of law and society. Like law and economics, the Marxist notion is focused on the relation that prevails between the law and economy, and the institutional structures and forces of production have a major role in both. What distinguishes the two from each other has to do with a very different conception of the "metaphysics" of society, in the sense of the relation that prevails between the law and economy in society. For a Marxist scholar, the deep-structure level *economic* phenomena determine the shape and course of the surface-structure level *ideological* phenomena in society. In the economic analysis of law, in turn, the institutional modes of legal regulation and judicial decision-making are taken to be constitutive as to the institutional structures of economy, or any other institutional structures for that matter.[39] The Marxist theory of law and society entails a thoroughly *metaphysical* doctrine of

[39] On the forces and relations of production in society and on the capital as the "transcendental-logical" subject in society, endowed with an inherent capacity of autonomous self-production, cf. Hänninen, *Aika, paikka, politiikka*. – Hänninen's Marxist reading of Georg Lukács' theory of society, to the effect of discerning the three levels of society, each with a distinctive kind of subjects in it: (a) individual subjects with individually ascribable intentions, (b) collective subjects with a distinct class-consciousness, and (c) the capital as the "transcendental-logical" subject that observes the laws of its own self-reproduction in society, provided the original inspiration for Kaarlo Tuori's three-layered model of law and society. In Tuori's *Critical Legal Positivism*, the Marxist frame of analysis is to some extent downgraded, making room to a more openly positivist account to the law, now outlined with reference to Hans Kelsen's and H. L. A. Hart's theories of law. Yet, contrary to what the author argues, Tuori's idea of the multi-levelled structure of law, where the deeper levels of law are able to resist any abrupt efforts towards legal change on part of the legislator and the courts of justice, cannot be reconciled with a truly *positivist* notion of law, as advocated by Kelsen, Hart, and the other main representatives of analytical legal positivism. – I will consider the issue at more depth in Section 6.5. The Unresolvable Dilemma of Kaarlo Tuori's Critical Legal Positivism.

the relations that are thought to prevail between the law, economy, and society, and a lot depends on how in more specific terms such metaphysics is conceived. The economic analysis of law, in turn, is committed to a highly *instrumentalist* notion of the law, economy, and society, leaning on the liberalist tradition in social philosophy and a pragmatist idea of social engineering.

Politically, the economic analysis of law and a Marxist conception of law and society are at the two opposite ends of the line. A Marxist notion of law and society defines the notions of social justice in terms of a leftist ideology and the interests of the working class; while an economic analysis of law most often underscores the adverse political ideology of economic efficiency, market rationality, free competition, and the most efficient allocation of the scarce resources in society. However, there is no inherent obstacle to utilizing the outcomes gained by an economic analysis of law for the benefit of, say, moderate welfare social politics and social law for the attainment of optimal (re)allocation of scarce material resources and risk positions in society, in line with the Scandinavian welfare state model in this respect.

The core issue of law and economics still remains unanswered: *why* should the enhancement of economic prosperity, enrichment, and economic efficiency be given decisive priority over other values in society? The set of values acknowledged in legislation and other institutional sources of law may quite drastically differ from the ones preferred by those involved in economic transactions. In the intellectual debate with Richard Posner and Guido Calabresi, Ronald Dworkin (re)phrased the issue in the titles of his two articles as "Why Efficiency?" and "Is Wealth a Value?"[40] Dworkin's answer was firmly in the negative: the pursuit of economic prosperity and economic welfare as such do not qualify as an adequate value basis for the law and society, and a striving for economic efficiency cannot deplace the protection of the inalienable rights of individuals.

Dworkin's own idea of social justice through law is based on the primacy of *arguments of principle* that safeguard the rights of individuals in society over *arguments of policy* that promote some collective goals of, say, the welfare state. According to Dworkin, rights of individuals and arguments of principle "trump" over collective goals and arguments of policy.[41] Still, the question why *social justice* is given the status of a trump in the judge's legal decision-making, while *economic justice* is not given such a standing, is left unanswered by Dworkin. The locked-up priority order in-between the two is a *postulate* in Dworkin's theory of law, and not an argument with sufficient backing, to the detriment of the values of a welfare state or libertanianism alike.

In "Why Efficiency?", Dworkin approvingly cites John Rawls' ingenious idea of the *original position* with the help of which Rawls outlined the preconditions for

[40]Dworkin, "Is Wealth a Value?"; Dworkin, "Why Efficiency?". – Both articles are reprinted in Dworkin's *A Matter of Principle*. In the former, Dworkin evaluates Richard Posner's classic account of the issue in *Economic Analysis of Law*; and in the latter, he estimates Guido Calabresi's similarly influential work *The Costs of Accidents*.

[41]Dworkin, "Hard Cases", pp. 82–84; Dworkin, "A Reply to Critics", pp. 364–366; Dworkin, *Law's Empire*, passim.

individual liberty and social equality in the social contract. Here, I will not enter the discussion on Rawls' influential theory or its relation to Dworkin's notion of law.[42] Still, Dworkin's idea of law as integrity, unlike Posner's or Calabresi's economic analysis of law, makes room for the *institutional* sources of law and the rules and principles of law extracted from them. Though not without inherent dilemmas of its own, Dworkin's coherentist approach better guarantees the *legality* and *rationality* of the outcome of legal deliberation.

[42]Dworkin, "Why Efficiency?", p 279. – On Rawls' methodology as a model for Dworkin, cf. Dworkin, *Justice in Robes*, pp. 241–261. When visiting my post-graduate seminar (in Finland) in May 2008 and asked about the relation of his theory of law vis-à-vis John Rawls' theory of social justice, Dworkin admitted that there are no doubt similarities in the *methodology*, though not in content, in Rawls' seminal idea of a deliberative equilibrium and his own idea of legal deliberation in terms of the law as integrity.

Chapter 6
Analytical Legal Positivism: Retracing the Original Intentions of the Legislator Under Legal Exegesis

6.1 Scientific Positivism Defined

Legal exegesis is based on a *positivist* conception of law. The term "positivism" is yet ambiguous, since it may denote at least two different things: *scientific positivism*, based on a positivist conception of science, and *legal positivism*, based on a voluntarist conception of law.

Scientific positivism, or positivism in the context of *philosophy of science*, refers to the philosophical stance to the effect that scientific knowledge can only be based on empirical observations, as then shaped into the form of causal laws, explanations, and predictions in the natural sciences. No traits of metaphysical speculation; nor intuitive, self-evidently valid or a priori assertions outside the safe realm of empirical observations and experiential knowledge; nor any personal values or subjective ideological preferences of a scientist may have legitimate footing in science, so conceived.

The term "positivism" was originally introduced in the 1830s by Auguste Comte (1798–1857) as part of his methodological agenda for a mature science, free from all religious or metaphysical predisposition, bias, and prejudice that had plagued Western science in the past. In the full-grown, positivist phase of human knowledge, *empirical* science based on scientific observations and experiments would displace any misguided references to the allegedly self-evident principles of man and the world as provided by theology and philosophical metaphysics. Similarly, John Stuart Mill (1806–1873) underscored the role of empirical observations as the true source of all scientific knowledge.

In the 1920s and 1930s, the *Vienna Circle* (*Wiener Kreis*) pushed the positivist *credo* of science to the utmost limits. The specific stance in the philosophy of science, as propounded by the *Wiener Kreis*, was to be known as *logical positivism* [1] To be more precise, the two intellectual movements of *logical positivism* and *logical*

[1] Niiniluoto and Koskinen, eds., *Wienin piiri*; esp. Manninen, "Uuden filosofisen liikkeen ja sen manifesti synty", pp. 27–128.

R. Siltala, *Law, Truth, and Reason*, Law and Philosophy Library 97,
DOI 10.1007/978-94-007-1872-2_6,

empiricism need to be distinguished from each other, even though they are often mistakenly identified with each other.[2]

Logical positivism, as represented by Rudolf Carnap, Friedrich Waismann, Otto Neurath, Kurt Gödel, and Moritz Schlick, among others, counts as an influential stance vis-à-vis the philosophy of science in the 1920s. A major philosophical argument put forth by the logical positivists was to the effect of reducing the realm of meaningful linguistic propositions (in the terminology suggested by Rudolf Carnap and Otto Neurath) into *protocol sentences*, or sentences that are empirically verifiable, ruthlessly expelling from the domain of science all metaphysical speculation and the meaningless, nonsensical expressions that did not satisfy the criterion of empirical verifiability. Wittgenstein's *Tractatus* served as the source of inspiration for the logical positivist, even though in a manner that Wittgenstein himself did not fully endorse. Still, *Tractatus* was now read as a methodological program for a positivist science, based on empirical observation sentences and the logic of truth conditions applied to them. The name *Wiener Kreis*, or the *Vienna Circle*, refers to the logical positivists.

Logical empiricism, on the other hand, as represented by e.g. Hans Reichenbach and Carl Hempel, is a later intellectual movement the influence of which on science and the philosophy of science continued to prevail even at the second half of the twentieth century. Instead of Vienna, Austria, its geographic centre was Berlin, Germany. Carnap, Feigl, and Hempel first started as logical positivists but later switched over to logical empiricism.[3]

There are several common features in the two intellectual movements, though, which may explain the common confusion of them into single school of thought in the philosophy of science. Logical positivism and logical empiricism were both initiated as a reaction to the post-Kantian, idealistic philosophy of science at the end of the nineteenth century. They both underscored the significance of empirical knowledge and modern logic in the service of science. Equally, they both looked upon the methodology of the natural sciences as the model and reference for all scientific research. Both emphatically rejected idealistic, speculative metaphysics of all kind. Logical empiricists took a partly critical stance as to the philosophical commitments and ideas related to the theory of science that had been upheld by their predecessors, the logical positivists. The philosophical impact of logical positivism had come to an end before the 1950s, whereas the influence of logical empiricism continued until the latter half of the twentieth century. Of the philosophers who started as adherents of logical positivism, Rudolf Carnap, Herbert Feigl, and Carl Hempel changed over to contribute to logical empiricism.[4]

Georg Henrik von Wright (1916–2003) defined scientific positivism with the following three tenets in his *Explanation and Understanding*[5]:

---

[2]Salmon, "Logical Empiricism", p. 233.

[3]Ray, "Logical Positivism", pp. 243–251; Salmon, "Logical Empiricism", pp. 233–242.

[4]Salmon, "Logical Empiricism", p. 234.

[5]von Wright, *Explanation and Understanding*, p. 4.

(a) *methodological monism*, or the idea that there can be only one valid scientific method;
(b) the idea that exact natural sciences, and *mathematical physics* in specific, set a methodological ideal or standard for all the other kinds of science, with the humanities included, and
(c) the idea of adopting *causal explanation* in science instead of teleological or intentional explanations.

Kyösti Raunio, a Finnish social scientist, has concisely defined the positivist conception of science for the human and social sciences by means of the following five rules[6]:

(a) the rule of *phenomenalism*, to the effect that only immediate sense experience can offer a reliable ground for scientifically grounded knowledge of reality;
(b) the rule of *nominalism*, to the effect that abstract scientific concepts are to be derived from sense experience and, in turn, theoretical terms ought to be translatable to the language of empirical observations;
(c) a *non-cognitivist stance towards values and norms*, to the effect of separating the facts that make up the "world of *Is*" (*Sein*) from the values and norms that make up the "world of *Ought*" (*Sollen*), while denying the status of scientific knowledge from any value statements and normative assertions, since they amount to no more than mere expressions of emotion or the will of the speaker concerned;
(d) the rule of *methodological naturalism* or *methodological naturalist monism*, to the effect that the methodology of the natural sciences is to be applied in the field of the human and social sciences, as well; and
(e) the *nomothetic* rule, to the effect that the goal for science is to state general laws, or statements that consist of general law-like assertions, of reality.

Frequently the term *positivism* is however adopted in a more loose-edged manner even in the philosophy of science, with reference to any research that only deals with facts that can be observed by reference to some objective criteria, without making any commitment to some value-laden considerations as to the nature of reality. A "cheerful positivist", as Michel Foucault (1926–1984) described his agenda of an archaeology of knowledge for the human sciences,[7] is fully satisfied with just describing, as objectively as possible, the subject matter of research, refraining from all normative, critical evaluations of his own. Such a scientific methodology

[6] Raunio, *Positivismi ja ihmistiede*, pp. 112–115.

[7] "Analyser une formation discursive, c'est donc traiter un ensemble de performance verbales, au niveau des énoncés et de la forme de positivité qui les caractérise; ou plus brièvement, c'est définir le type de positivité d'un discours. Si, en substituant l'analyse de la rareté à la recherche des totalités, la description des rapports d'extériorité au thème du fondement transcendantal, l'analyse des cumuls à la quête de l'origine, on est un positiviste, eh bien *je suis un positiviste heureux*, j'en tombe facilement d'accord." Foucault, *L'Archéologie du savoir*, pp. 164–165. (Italics added.)

resembles the one suggested by Leopold von Ranke (1795–1886), whose idea of legitimate historical research was confined to finding out "what in fact had taken place" (*wie es eigentlich gewesen*) in some historical occasion.[8]

What often goes unnoticed by the positivists themselves is that even a positivist stance in science entails a set of value commitments built in the methodology adopted: the philosophical stance of excluding any value considerations from the domain of science is itself a value-laden position. Under Michel Foucault's or Leopond von Ranke's expressly positivist premises of doing research, one need not adhere to the austere methodological theses of the logical positivists or the logical empiricists, but a less strictly defined stance vis-à-vis the subject matter and methodology of science will do, especially in the context of the humanities or the social sciences.

6.2 What Is Analytical Philosophy?

Analytical philosophy is not a uniform "school, doctrine, or body of accepted propositions" of philosophy, as the standard definition in a standard dictionary of philosophy has it.[9] It is not an intellectual movement that would be drawn together by some shared collection of philosophical theses or other fixed foundation, even if the privileged status given to Ludwig Wittgenstein's *Tractatus Logico-Philosophicus* in the analytical circles of the *Wiener Kreis* comes close to having such a standing. Rather, the analytical movement in philosophy refers to a certain kind of approach, style, or mentality of "doing philosophy" that is most often associated with the works of Gottlob Frege (1848–1925), Bertrand Russell (1872–1970), G. E. Moore (1873–1958) and, in specific, Ludwig Wittgenstein (1889–1951). The four philosophers and their intellectual followers make up the four cornerstones of the analytical and linguistic movement in philosophy.

Wittgenstein's *Tractatus* provided the main source of inspiration for the adherents of *logical positivism*, such as Moritz Schlick (1882–1936), Otto Neurath (1882–1945) and Rudolf Carnap (1891–1970). Wittgenstein's later, posthumous works, such as *Philosophical Investigations*, *The Blue and Brown Books*, and *On Certainty*, provided a very different insight into the relation of language and the world, manifested in the *Oxford school of linguistic philosophy*, as exemplified by the works of Elizabeth Anscombe (1919–2001), John L. Austin (1911–1960), Gilbert Ryle (1900–1976), and H. L. A. Hart (1907–1992).[10] According to the

[8]"Man hat der Historie das Amt, die Vergangenheit zu richten, die Mitwelt zum Nutzen zu künftiger Jahre zu belehren, beigemessen; so hoher Ämter unterwindet sich gegenwärtiger Versuch nicht: er will bloss zeigen, *wie es eigentlich gewesen*." Cited in: Kalela, *Historiantutkimus ja historia*, p. 50. (Italics added.)

[9]Heil, "Analytic Philosophy", p. 22.

[10]A good introduction to the thematics of analytical philosophy is provided in the two books edited by A.P. Martinich and Ernest Sosa, *A Companion to Analytic Philosophy* and *Analytic Philosophy. An Anthology*. Similarly, the essay collection, *The Linguistic Turn. Essays in Philosophical*

methodological *credo* of analytical philosophy, the only legitimate task for philosophy is *linguistic analysis*, i.e. the logical syntax of language, as in Wittgenstein's *Tractatus Logico-Philosophicus* and Carnap's *Logische Syntax der Sprache*, or, alternatively, an analysis of the common linguistic practices and usages in the community, as in John L. Austin's *How To Do Things with Words*, Gilbert Ryle's *The Concept of Mind*, and H. L. A. Hart's *The Concept of Law*.[11]

Analytical philosophy rejects all notoriously metaphysical, idealistic, or speculative ways of "doing philosophy", as endorsed by the Marxist and the Heideggerian approaches to philosophy in specific. According to the unyielding methodological *credo* of analytical philosophy, logico-conceptual precision is to be pursued in science, and all deceptive references to metaphysical idealism, philosophical introspection, self-evidently valid or a priori truths, or other philosophical speculation that cannot produce scientific, empirically verifiable propositions concerning the facts of the world are to be avoided.[12] The existential claims of Martin Heidegger's (1889–1976) fundamental ontology provided an easy target for the vehement critique of the *Wiener Kreis*. As Heidegger himself wrote[13]:

> What is to be investigated is being only and – *nothing* else; being alone and further – *nothing*; solely being, and beyond being – *nothing. What about this Nothing? ... Does the Nothing exist only because the Not, i.e. the Negation, exists?* Or is it the other way around? *Does Negation and the Not exist only because the Nothing exists?* ... We assert: *The Nothing is prior to the Not and the Negation*.... Where do we seek the Nothing? How do we find the Nothing?... We know the Nothing... *Anxiety reveals the Nothing*.... That for which and because of which we were anxious, was "really" – nothing. Indeed: the Nothing itself – as such – was present.... *What about this Nothing? – The Nothing itself nothings.*

Such metaphysical and, according to the logical positivists, utterly senseless, meaningless assertions were to be sternly rejected from the field of sober philosophy and science, to the effect of rephrasing the Heideggerian question in terms of a meta-level linguistic analysis as follows: "What is it that you mean, to be more precise, when you say that 'The nothing nothings itself'?" Rejecting the lure of any futile metaphysics, analytical and linguistic philosophy focuses on the semantic *truth-conditions* of a linguistic assertion: how can we possibly know whether Heidegger's key claim of the essence of "Being-in-the-World" as care, concern,

---

Method, gives a balanced account of the endeavours of the linguistic movement in philosophy. Cf. Soames, *Philosophical Analysis in the Twentieth Century, Vols. 1–2*.

[11]The title of Ryle's *The Concept of Mind* served as a model for Hart's *The Concept of Law*.

[12]The fate of e.g. psychoanalysis was similar, since its assertions of the unconsciousness could be neither verified nor falsified.

[13]Heidegger in his "Was ist Metaphysik?", as cited in Carnap, "The Elimination of Metaphysics Through Logical Analysis of Language", p. 69. (Italics in original.) – On the key phrase "Das Nichts nichtet", cf. also Waismann, *The Principles of Linguistic Philosophy*, p. 334. – The German verb "vernichten" from which Heidegger's "nichten" is derived signifies the (act of) obliterating, annihilating, or destroying (something). There is no similar connotation entailed in the English expression adopted in the translation, viz. "nothing" used as a verb. A more accurate translation of Heidegger's metaphysics might be: "nothingness annihilates (itself)".

or anxiety (*Dasein als Sorge*), or of the annihilating character of *nothing* is true, or – which amounts to the same question – how could we possibly *corroborate* any such assertions? The answer provided by analytical philosophy was firmly in the negative: metaphysical assertions are *senseless*, devoid of any reference outside of language and, therefore, without truth-value or sensible meaning. Besides Heideggerian metaphysics, analytical and linguistic philosophy focused its most severe critique on the Marxist philosophy or any other fields of human enquiry, like psychoanalysis and theology, in which the assertions could neither be verified nor falsified with reference to certain empirical observations in the world.

Even though it rejected the pursuit of a scientific world-view, the Oxford school of ordinary language is built on the premises initially laid down by Ludwig Wittgenstein's *Tractatus Logico-Philosophicus* and the logical positivists. A.M. Quinton gives a concise summary of the relation between the methodology adopted by the Oxford school of linguistic philosophy, on the one hand, and the one adopted by Wittgenstein and the logical positivists, on the other[14]:

> In general terms, then, the method of the Oxford philosophers lay somewhere in between the professed method of Wittgenstein and the methods of the logical positivists of the 1930s. With the positivists and against Wittgenstein they believed that the job of philosophy was to set out the logical properties and relations of the various forms of discourse in a systematic way. But with Wittgenstein and against the positivists they rejected the ideal of linguistic perfection suggested by formal logic, concerning themselves with the description of language as it actually is rather than with the extrication of some ideal essence from it or with the proposal of a logically superior conceptual system as an alternative to it.

The Oxford school of linguistic philosophy thus carried on the Wittgensteinian agenda of defining the relation between language and the world.

6.3 Legal Positivism Defined

Legal positivism is to be distinguished from logical positivism. According to the Italian legal philosopher Norberto Bobbio (1909–2004), *legal positivism* can be defined existing in the world the following seven characteristics[15]:

(1) Concerning the *subject matter of enquiry*: law is to be taken as a social fact and not as a value, to the effect that legal phenomena, since they are analogical to the phenomena studied by the natural sciences, can be studied by a similar method as adopted in the natural sciences. A legal scholar is required to refrain from taking any evaluative stance on the moral qualities or the goodness or evilness of the law. Finally, a theory of legal validity can be derived from the above in line with legal formalism.

---

[14] Quinton, "Contemporary British Philosophy", p. 546 – in O'Connor, D.J., ed. *A Critical History of Western Philosophy*. Hampshire & London: MacMillan Publishing, 1964, pp. 530–555.

[15] Bobbio, *Il Positivismo Giuridico*, pp. 151–154 (*I punti fondamentali della dottrina giuspositivistica*).

(2) Concerning the *definition of law*: the concept of law is defined as its coerciveness in a society, in line with the notion of law as a social fact.
(3) Concerning the *sources of law*: legislation is regarded as the primary source of law, and a complex theory is then developed as to its relation to the other sources of law, such as customary law and judicial decisions.
(4) Concerning the *theory of a legal norm*: a legal norm is defined as a command or an imperative [issued by the sovereign];[16] and, as a consequence, permissive norms and the addressee of such legal commands may induce theoretical difficulties to legal positivism.
(5) Concerning the *theory of a legal order*: the legal order is defined as internally coherent and complete, to the effect that:

   (a) the co-existence of antinomical, i.e. contradictory or mutually contrary norms is ruled out by the presumed *coherence* of the legal order, and
   (b) the existence of normative gaps is ruled out by the presumed *completeness* of the legal order.

(6) Concerning the *method of legal science*: legal interpretation is defined in terms of purely formal, mechanistic jurisprudence, to the effect of denying any genuinely norm-creating discretion of the judge.
(7) Concerning the *theory of absolute obedience to the law*: the law ought to be obeyed because it is valid law, irrespective of its substantive content (*ein Gesetz is ein Gesetz*).

Bobbio's points (1)–(4) are essentially in match with the common idea of legal positivism today, even if he gives more weight to the sanction-based tenets of law than e.g. H. L. A. Hart. However, Bobbio's extremely formalistic idea of a legal system (= Bobbio's point 5) and of legal interpretation (= Bobbio's point 6), and the idea of absolute obedience to the law, irrespective of its content (= Bobbio's point 7), is too constricted to comprise the complexity of modern law. Therefore, I will use John Austin's, Hans Kelsen's, H. L. A. Hart's, and Jerzy Wróblewski's conceptions of law as the primary source of inspiration here.

In line with Bobbio's definition above, legal positivism refers to a *voluntarist* stance to the effect that the law in force is defined as a compound of the acts of volition and individual, subsequently retraceable decisions issued by the sovereign ruler, as John Austin (1790–1859) thought in the 1820s. The "sovereign" may refer to the various *institutional* decision-making organs of a legal order, endowed with either *legislative* or *judicial* powers,[17] if a wider and more modern notion of law

[16] I.e. commands, issued by the sovereign ruler, as in John Austin's theory of law, or some other state institution, like the Parliament. Bobbio, however, leaves the definition of a sovereign untouched.

[17] The *legislator* is in fact a plural noun, since it may refer to a host of institutionally qualified law-giving authorities, such as the Parliament, the President of the Republic at the State Council, the Ministries, and other administrative bodies that are endowed with the power to issue legal norms. In addition, the legislative organs of the European Union need to be added thereto, i.e. the European

and sovereignty is opted for. The use of the attribute "valid" in the legal context is restricted to legal enactments, precedents, and other court decisions that can (only) be initially created, subsequently altered, legally enforced, and ultimately annulled by an act of will by the legislator, a court of justice or other legal official. Modern law is *positive law* (*ius positivum*), and not something that dwells in the divine order of things or something that can be discovered by the faculties of the human reason.

Modern *analytical* legal positivism is based on the idea of drawing a sharp distinction between the formal validity of law and its moral merit or dismerit. An evil law is still valid law, if it has been correctly enacted. As John Austin admirably put it[18]:

> The existence of law is one thing; its merit or demerit is another. Whether it be or be not is one enquiry; whether it be or be not conformable to an assumed standard, is a different enquiry. A law, which actually exists, is a law, though we happen to dislike it, or though it vary from the from the text, by which we regulate our approbation and disapprobation.

Austin focused his critique on Sir William Blackstone's conception of law where the two issues were irredeemably intertwined, as they are in all theories of law based on natural law philosophy.[19] The subject matter of legal research for a legal positivist consists of the valid rules of some legal order only, i.e. the sum total of norms laid down by the sovereign ruler. Any judgments concerning the actual contents of law falls outside of the legitimate sphere of study for the legal positivist.

Legal positivism has an uneasy relation to the norms of *customary law*, since the binding character of customary law cannot be traced back to an express act of will by the sovereign ruler, i.e. the Parliament or other ultimate lawgiver. If the law is defined as the outcome of will-formation of a sovereign ruler, customary law falls outside the concept of law, strictly defined. Similarly, legal positivism commonly ignores the impact on the judge's discretion of value-laden principles of law and other legal standards that cannot be identified by sole reference to their source of origin, as captured by the notion of the *rule of recognition* by H. L. A. Hart.[20] The binding force of legal principles is instead based on (possibly oblique but still legally adequate) *institutional support* and content-based *sense of approval* that they draw from the various institutional and non-institutional sources of law in society.[21] Under a positivist notion of law, individual legal subjects are even able, when acting in line with the power-inducing legal norms, to alter their legal relations vis-à-vis other legal subjects by making a valid contract, a will, or some other private law instrument.

Parliament, Council, and Commission. – Similarly, the term "court" should be use with coverage of other officials endowed with law-applying powers, as well.

[18] Austin, *The Province of Jurisprudence Determined*, pp. 157–159. – For a critique of Ronald Dworkin for not observing the said distinction and returning to a "pre-Benthamite" conception of law, cf. Neil MacCormick's sharp essay "Dworkin as Pre-Benthamite".

[19] Austin, *The Province of Jurisprudence Determined*, pp. 157–159.

[20] Hart, *The Concept of Law* (1961), pp. 97–107.

[21] Dworkin, *Taking Rights Seriously*.

Like Austin, the Austrian legal philosopher Hans Kelsen (1881–1973) defined the legitimate sphere of legal analysis by reference to what the law in a given society *is*, not what it *ought to be* when judged from the point of view of natural law philosophy or critical political morality in general.[22] The price for such austere methodological purity was paid in the restrictions placed on legal science: a legal scholar was not allowed to present any priority order among the semantically possible outcomes for the case in hand, being under obligation to refrain from taking any evaluative or preferential stance on the issue at hand.[23]

The traditional idea of the legal doctrine or legal dogmatics (*Rechtsdogmatik*) as an enquiry into the *systematization* and *interpretation* of the legal norms of some legal order vis-à-vis a variety of fact-constellations was excluded from legitimate research, since it failed in Kelsen's test of scientificity. The methodology to be adopted in legal science was restricted to what Kelsen called *eine wertfreie Beschreibung ihres Gegenstandes*,[24] i.e. a value-free description of its subject matter, the valid norms of a legal order. Questions concerning the content of law could not be reached by a scientifically valid methodology, except in the trivial sense of presenting a set of technical meta-level collision norms, such as *lex superior derogat (legi) inferiori* and *lex specialis derogat (legi) generali* for a legal system.

Intellectual confusion has been induced by the fact that the *subject matter* of a legal positivist research may have been defined more or less in line with the descriptive and empiricist criteria of scientific positivism, focusing on the social facts only and leaving the personal values and ideological preferences of the scholar out of the scope of study; while the *methodology* of such research may have fallen short of the prerequisites of a positivist approach of science as defined by the *Wiener Kreis*. Alf Ross, for one, was perhaps all too quick to place an equation mark between the two categories of legal positivism and scientific positivism[25]:

> Considering how the term "positivism" is used in general philosophy, it seems to me reasonable to take the term "legal positivism" in a broad sense to mean an attitude or approach to the problems of legal philosophy and jurisprudence, an approach *based on the principles of an empiricist, antimetaphysical philosophy*.

Natural law philosophy, as a major alternative and logical counterpart to Ross's account of legal positivism, is characterized with reference to "... the belief that the law cannot be exhaustively described or understood in terms of empiricist principles, but requires metaphysical interpretation, that is, interpretation in light of the rational

---

[22] "Sie [die reine Rechtslehre] versucht, die Frage zu beantworten, was und wie das Recht ist, nicht aber die Frage, wie es sein oder gemacht werden soll. Sie ist Rechtswissenschaft, nicht aber Rechtspolitik." Kelsen, *Reine Rechtslehre* (1960), p. 1.

[23] "Rechtswissenschaftliche Interpretation kann nichts anderes als die möglichen Bedeutungen einer Rechtsnorm herausstellen.", Kelsen, *Reine Rechtslehre* (1960), p. 353.

[24] Kelsen, *Reine Rechtslehre* (1960), p. 84.

[25] Ross, "Validity and the Conflict between Positivism and Natural Law", p. 148. (Italics added.)

or divine nature of man, a priori principles and ideas transcending the world of the senses."[26]

Ross, moreover, defines the "kernel" of an empiricist approach to the law by means of the two theses.[27] Firstly – though Ross would seem to be moving in a logical circle here, begging the question – the belief in the existence of natural law is erroneous, since all law is, by definition, positive law. That, however, is a mere stipulation, not a philosophical argument.

Secondly, the existence of positive law can be established in purely factual, empirical terms, "based on the observation and interpretation of social facts (human behaviour and attitudes)".[28] Ross' very terminology, i.e. observation *and interpretation* of social facts, yet reveals that no straightforwardly empiricist approach alone, detached from the methodological elements of constructive interpretation, can cover the subject matter of legal science, even though in the preface to the English edition of his *Om ret og retfærdighed* Ross boldly claims "to carry, in the field of law, the empirical principles to their ultimate conclusions".[29] In Ross' jurisprudence, the *normative ideology internalized by the judges*,[30] when employed as a scheme of interpretation in qualifying certain social facts as legal phenomena,[31] signifies the intrusion of an inherently constructive, interpretation-laden element into the field of analysis reserved for purely empiricist observation by Ross.

What is common to all the variants of legal positivism and legal realism alike is the idea that law is a *social fact*, and not some social ideal irredeemably beyond the reach of human endeavours. The key difference between legal positivism, on the one hand, and legal realism and sociological jurisprudence, on the other, is that the former defines the law with reference to the general, abstract rules issued by the legislator, while the latter opt for the individual judicial decisions as laid down by the courts of justice and other legal officials. In the latter, the empiricist "law in action" will take over from the more idealist "law in the books".

---

[26] Ross, "Validity and the Conflict between Positivism and Natural Law", p. 148.

[27] Ross, "Validity and the Conflict between Positivism and Natural Law", pp. 148–149.

[28] Ross, "Validity and the Conflict between Positivism and Natural Law", p. 149.

[29] Ross, *On Law and Justice*, p. IX: "The leading idea of this work is to carry, in the field of law, the empirical principles to their ultimate conclusions. From this idea springs the methodological demand that the study of law must follow the traditional patterns of observation and verification which animate all modern empirical science; and the analytical demand that the fundamental legal notions must be interpreted as conceptions of social reality, the behaviour of man in society, and as nothing else.'" – As the Finnish scholar Markku Helin has convincingly argued, there is a *hermeneutical* element entailed in Ross' *Om ret og retfærdighed*, though Ross would not seem to have been entirely conscious of its impact. Helin, *Lainoppi ja metafysiikka*, pp. 159–169.

[30] In Danish.: *den normative ideologi der besjæler dommeren*. Ross, *Om ret og retfærdighed*, p. 56. Cf. Ross, *On Law and Justice*, p. 43.

[31] In German: *Deutungschema*; in Danish: *tydningsskema*. Cf. Ross, *Om ret og retfærdighed*, p. 41; Kelsen, *Reine Rechtslehre* (1960), p. 3 et seq. – Ross' early work *Theorie der Rechtsquellen. Ein Beitrag zur Theorie des Positiven Rechts auf Grundlage dogmenhistorischer Untersuchungen* was deeply influenced by Kelsen's *Reine Rechtslehre*. It may be that the similarity in thought vis-à-vis the scheme of interpretation dates from that period in Ross' legal thinking.

Thomas Morawetz made the following acute observation as to choice of subject matter of legal positivism and its alternatives in the field of jurisprudence[32]:

> Accordingly, positivists distinguish sharply between analytical legal theory and normative legal doctrine. The first involves the analysis of the nature of legal rules, legal validity, institutional structure, and so on, but not normative questions such as what rights should be part of the system and how those rights are to be understood. Critical theorists, like positivists, characteristically distinguish between questions about the nature of law (e.g. as legitimating ideology) and the particular merits, demerits, and uses of normative responses to legal issues. On the other hand, natural law theorists often address these issues in ways that bridge analytical and normative questions.

What the legal positivists share with the scientific positivists is a denial of mixing facts with values in scientific enquiry.

As a consequence, the concept of law under legal positivism may be defined so that the law is based on an *act of will* of the (sovereign) legislator or some other institutional lawgiver, and it is – at least *prima facie* – arbitrary in content, or free from any content-bound criteria derived from religion or political morality. Thus, Neil MacCormick defined legal positivism with the following two criteria[33]:

(i) The existence of laws is not dependent on their satisfying any particular moral values of universal application to all legal systems,
(ii) The existence of laws depends upon their being established through decisions of human beings in society.

There is a variety of intellectual currents under the heading "legal positivism", though. *Analytical legal positivism* stresses the volition-based character of law, having reference to the will-formation of the legislator, while *institutional legal positivism* underscores the linguistic and institutional elements involved in the creation, enforcement, alteration, and derogation of law. Common to them both is the emphasis laid on the *acts of will* of a legally competent decision-making body, such as the legislator or a court of justice. Below, I will consider analytical and institutional legal positivism, before entering the (historically older) semantic realm of *legal exegesis* under the French and Belgian *exegetical school of law* (*École de l'Exégèse*) in the nineteenth century.[34] Moreover, in the recent jurisprudential writings on legal positivism the distinction between *exclusive legal positivism* and *inclusive legal positivism* has been made. The division between the two is based on whether the distinct social values that are entailed in the rule of recognition of a given legal order are part of valid law or not.

Below, I will tackle *analytical* and *institutional* legal positivism, along with the *exclusive* and *inclusive* subcategories of the former. Kaarlo Tuori's *critical* legal

---

[32] Morawetz, "Law as Experience: The Internal Aspect of Law", p. 215, note 74.

[33] MacCormick and Weinberger, *An Institutional Theory of Law*, pp. 128–129.

[34] On analytical legal positivism, Siltala, *A Theory of Precedent*, pp. 17–21; Siltala, *Oikeustieteen tieteenteoria*, pp. 32–40, 876–877; on institutional legal positivism, Siltala, *Oikeustieteen tieteenteoria*, pp. 43–45.

positivism will be considered, as well, though it seems to miss some of the very definitional qualities of legal positivism, strictly defined. – The saga of modern legal positivism begins with H. L. A. Hart's *The Concept of Law*.

6.4 The Saga of Modern Legal Positivism

6.4.1 Analytical Legal Positivism

Analytical legal positivism has drawn inspiration from analytical and linguistic philosophy. As an intellectual "school" of legal thought it is yet older than its counterpart in general philosophy or the philosophy of science. Both intellectual movements share a whole-hearted striving for conceptual precision and a similar aversion toward any sky-soaring, "puffy" metaphysics that cannot withstand the test of empirical corroboration and validation. In jurisprudence the impact of the analytical and linguistic approach can be seen in H. L. A. Hart's writings since the 1950s and 1960s.

The roots of an analytical approach to law and language can be traced back to the writings by William of Ockham (1285–1347), a Fransiscan friar and a nominalist philosopher in the Middle Ages. In the heated theological (and philosophical) debate with the Pope John XXII on the nature of the property rights of donations received by the Franciscan order, William of Ockham wrote the thesis *Opus nonaginta dierum*, defending a highly sophisticated conception of legal ownership that predates the one that was put forth by analytical jurisprudence several centuries later. *Ockham's razor*, i.e. the law of parsimony in philosophical explanation, is commonly attributed to William of Ockham.[35] As a consequence, any postulated entities in a philosophical ontology or the grounds of philosophical explanation are not to be multiplied beyond what is absolutely necessary. According to Ockham, *less is more* in ontology and philosophical explanation.

According to analytical legal positivism, the concept of law can be defined by the following four criteria.

Firstly, modern law is by definition *positive* law (*ius positivum*), based on an *act of will* of the sovereign legislator in Austin's theory of law or some other decision-making body with an institutionally acknowledged standing, such as the Parliament, the Council of State, or a court of justice, in Kelsen's and Hart's jurisprudence. The law-making power of the legislator is at least in principle unconstrained by any moral, content-bound criteria that could logically and conceptually precede an act of will by the legislator, and the same goes for the courts' judicial discretion. Being itself the outcome of such institutional decision-making, the law of a state or some international community, like the European Union, cannot be subject to some

[35] There is no one authoritative formulation of Ockham's razor. It has been given a host of different formulations, such as: *entia non sunt multiplicanda praeter necessitatem* or *entia non sunt multiplicanda sine necessitate* or *frustra fit per plura quod potest fieri per pauciora* or *pluralitas non est ponenda sine necessitate*.

standards of an eternal, immutable, and supra-positive natural law, the positivists claim.

Secondly, and closely related to the previous tenet, valid rules of law are to be identified by their formal *source of origin* in legislation or judicial decisions. With reference to such a *test of pedigree*, as Dworkin a bit sardonically put it, legal rules are distinguished from the norms of political morality, religion, sports and play, and societal etiquette in all of which the substantive content of a norm has more bearing than its formal source of origin. Legal enactments and administrative regulations, on the other hand, are binding because of their source of origin, not because of their substantive content. Yet, even Hart ultimately had to alleviate that methodological and epistemic demand with the *minimum content of natural law* in *The Concept of Law*.[36]

Thirdly, the validity or normatively binding character of law is ultimately based on *coercion*, since the threat of *official sanction* in the case of non-compliance with some valid legal rule is one of the definitional characteristics of legal positivism.[37] In Kelsen's *Reine Rechtslehre*, the mandatory character of a legal rule is ultimately based on the threat of a legal sanction that will be inflicted upon a disobedient judge who refuses to apply a valid legal norm.[38] The secondary rules of change and adjudication in Hart's *The Concept of Law* and, from the ontological point of view, the rather problematic rule of recognition as part of it, are a notable exception to the inherently sanction-based notion of law in Hart's version of legal positivism.

Fourthly and finally, analytical legal positivism is committed to a *rule-based* conception of law, ruling out from the sphere of law the impact of value-laden principles and standards of law with adequate institutional support and societal approval.

Still, analytical legal positivism notably fails to provide a satisfactory account of the judge's act of legal interpretation. In the writings by the major figures of the movement, i.e. John Austin, Hans Kelsen, H. L. A. Hart, and Jerzy Wróblewski, the issues of legal interpretation and legal argumentation are treated in the passing only, and the focus of analysis is placed on other topics, such as the definitional characteristics of positive law as a command by the sovereign ruler, backed by the threat of force in the form of a sanction and distinguished from the precepts of natural law or social morals (Austin), the internal structure of law along with the methodological purity of the science of law (Kelsen), or the rule-aligned concept

[36] Hart, *The Concept of Law* (1961), pp. 189–195.

[37] In a similar manner Max Weber, one of the founders of modern sociology of law, defined the law by means of the state's monopoly as to the use of coercion in Weber, *Wirtschaft und Gesellschaft*, pp. 29–30, 821–824. – Cf. also Ross, *Om ret og retfærdighed*, pp. 41–47 (Chapter 7: "'Dansk ret' er regler om monopoliseret udøvelse af fysisk tvang ved offentlig myndighed").

[38] Kelsen, *Reine Rechtslehre* (1960), pp. 51–55. – The idea of law being based on sanctions is repeated in Aulis Aarnio's and Aleksander Peczenik's theory of legal sources where the binding force of legislation (and customary law) is justified by reference to the possible infliction of a sanction upon a disobedient judge.

of law and its relation to morality (Hart).[39] In Neil MacCormick's institutional theory of law, the issues of legal interpretation are dealt with more erudition, but he would seem to belong to the later *institutional* variant of legal positivism, and not the more "orthodox" analytical trend by Austin, Kelsen, and Hart. Moreover, there are elements drawn from the new rhetoric or even non-analytical theory of law in Neil MacCormick jurisprudence, so it is not an instance of positivism, pure and simple.[40]

The founder of analytical legal positivism, John Austin, distinguished general *laws or rules* from *occasional or particular commands*.[41] As an example of the latter, i.e. occasional or particular commands, Austin referred to individual judicial decisions.[42] Hart renamed Austin's sanction-based notion of law as the *gunman situation writ large*, since the bank-robber, like the legislator in Austin's theory of law, uses the threat of force to have his will complied with. To Hart's mind, Austin's idea of positive law was in essence a set of *orders backed by threats*, as issued by the lawgiver.[43] Hart, however, failed to take notice of the fact that for Austin the law consists of general rules as issued by the sovereign legislator, and occasional or particular commands were explicitly ruled out of the realm of law. Yet, since Austin's focus of interest is on the definition of the concept of law and its autonomy vis-à-vis social morality, he does not properly address issues of legal interpretation in the book.

Hans Kelsen's *Reine Rechtslehre* is a highly ambitious theory of the *science of law*, carefully "purified" from all non-legal elements no matter whether they deal with the impact of, say, religion, politics, moral philosophy, sociology, economics, or societal etiquette vis-à-vis the law. Yet, even Kelsen mostly bypasses the question of legal interpretation. In the first edition of *Reine Rechtslehre*, the question of interpretation is totally ignored. It is only at the end of the second edition of *Reine Rechtslehre*, written almost as a kind of postscript to the book, Kelsen introduces the distinction between the *authentic* and *inauthentic* acts of interpretation. Authentic interpretation refers to the *norm-creating* act by a judge or other legal authority whereby a legal norm is created. Inauthentic interpretation, in turn, refers

---

[39] Summarizingly (and critically) on the idea of legal interpretation in analytical legal positivism, see Fuller, *The Morality of Law*, pp. 224–227.

[40] Neil MacCormick's institutional theory of legal interpretation will be considered at more depth in Section 12.3.1. "Neil MacCormick's Theory of the Three C's in Legal Reasoning: from Consistency and Coherence to the Consequences of Law" below.

[41] "Commands are of two species. Some are *laws* or *rules*. The others have not acquired an appropriate name, nor does language afford an expression which will mark them briefly and precisely. I must, therefore, note them as well as I can by the ambiguous and inexpressive name of '*occasional* or *particular* commands'." Austin, *The Province of Jurisprudence Determined*, p. 25.

[42] Austin, *The Province of Jurisprudence Determined*, p. 27: "To conclude with an example which best illustrates the distinction, and which shows the importance of the distinction most conspicuously, *judicial commands* are commonly occasional or particular, although the commands which they are calculated to enforce are commonly laws or rules."

[43] Hart, *The Concept of Law* (1961), pp. 18–25.

to the act of interpretation by a legal scholar or ordinary citizen, devoid of any such law-creating power.[44]

The outcome of an *authentic* act of legal interpretation is a valid legal norm, either a *general* norm issued by the legislator or an *individual* norm tailored for the case at hand by a court of justice or other legal official.[45] An act of interpretation by the parliament has to do with the semantics of the constitution; while an act of interpretation by a judge or other official deals with the semantics of (mostly) legislative enactments and administrative regulations of various kind. According to Kelsen, the difference between general norms, as created by the legislator, and individual norms, as laid down by the courts of justice or other law-applying officials, is one of degree only, and not a qualitative one. The general norms issued in legislation are step-by-step specified and concretized in the course of legal adjudication through the individual acts of interpretation by judges and other legal authorities.

The outcomes of legal science only count as instances of inauthentic legal interpretation, since such an act of interpretation is devoid of any norm-creating, norm-altering, norm-enforcing, or norm-derogating force. In terms of John L. Austin's and John Searle's later speech act theory, one might say that an act of interpretation by a legal scholar by definition lacks the kind of *perlocutionary* force that the act of interpretation by the legislator, a court of justice, or legal authority is endowed with.

According to Kelsen, the legitimate task of legal science, if it wishes retain its status as science and not be reduced to mere politics, can only be *eine wertfreie Beschreibung ihres Gegenstandes*,[46] in the sense of a value-free *description* of the valid legal norms of a legal order and of the hierarchical, pyramid-like totality they constitute. A legal scholar is not allowed to present a preference order of any kind among the semantically possible readings of the valid legal norms. If the content of the law is semantically ambiguous, lending support to more than just one interpretation, as is the case if we are not dealing with an *isomorphic* situation of legal decision-making (à la Makkonen), then all a legal scholar may legitimately do is to present the semantically possible alternatives of interpretation while refraining from giving any kind of preference order of them.

From the judge's *committed* point of view as well as from a legal scholar's more *detached* point of view to the law, the intellectual cost of Kelsen's purification of legal science from all value-laden, interpretation-aligned elements is all too high: the most pertinent issues tackled by traditional legal analysis and legal doctrine – i.e. what is the content of law vis-à-vis some state of affairs *x* in light of the institutional and non-institutional sources of law and the canons of legal methodology

---

[44]On conflict-resolution norms, Kelsen, *Reine Rechtslehre* (1960) pp. 210–212, 275; on authentic and inauthentic interpretation, Kelsen, *Reine Rechtslehre* (1960) pp. 346–354 and especially pp. 351–352. Cf. Alf Ross'notions of legal science and legal politics, Ross, *Om ret og retfærdighed*, p. 385 et seq.

[45]"Die Interpretation durch das rechtsanwendende Organ ist stets authentisch. Sie schafft Recht (...) authentisch, daß heiβt rechtsschaffend", Kelsen, *Reine Rechtslehre* (1960), p. 351, 352.

[46]Kelsen, *Reine Rechtslehre* (1960), p. 84.

adopted – are ruled out of consideration as inherently unscientific. The issue of legal interpretation has proven to be the *Achilleus' heel* of legal positivism in general.

Hart's notion of law entails a well-known theory of legal semantics based on the insights of Ludwig Wittgenstein's later philosophy and the Oxford school of ordinary language philosophy. According to Hart, linguistic concepts, and legal rules that incorporate such concepts, have a *core of certainty*, where the semantic meaning content is clear and unambiguous, and a *penumbra of doubt*, where several readings of the concept or rule are equally possible.[47] Following Thomas Morawetz' terminology, we might say that the notion of law as a *deliberative practice* that is always open to novel reinterpretations is entirely located in the penumbral area of Hart's two-fold semantics.[48] Yet, even Hart mostly ignores the thorny issues of legal interpretation, as he sees them as (no more than) part of a wider semantic theory of the core and the penumbra, as now applied to a legal context. When dealing with the interpretation-bound semantic realm of the penumbra of rules, the judge's legal discretion is compared to the discretion enjoyed by the legislator, only restrained by the valid constitution and, though Hart did not foresee the issue, the rules, principles, and standards of law that can be derived from the duly ratified international conventions, such as the European Convention of Human Rights.[49]

The absence of a credible theory of legal interpretation and the lack of societal elements in Hart's concept of law has not gone unnoticed by the less benign commentators and critics of his legal thinking. True, Hart's essentially semantic notion of law and legal interpretation would seem to ignore the legal community at which the outcome of interpretation is yet directed, as pointed out by Chaïm Perelman and the school of new rhetoric since the late 1950s. Similarly, Lon L. Fuller, the prominent American natural law philosopher, held Hart's notion of law as seriously inadequate, since it fails to give effect to the inherently goal-oriented, purpose-directed, and community-aligned nature of law.[50]

The most influential of Hart's many critics is no doubt Ronald Dworkin who has relentlessly blamed Hart for not taking the inherently *constructive* tenets of law duly

[47]Hart, *The Concept of Law* (1961), pp. 123–124.

[48]Morawetz, "Epistemology of Judging. Wittgenstein and Deliberative Practices". Cf. Siltala, *Oikeustieteen tieteenteoria*, pp. 25–32, 895.

[49]Hart, *The Concept of Law* (1961), pp. 121–132, 200–201. – Hart makes remarkably little use of any supranational human rights instruments in his argumentation on legal interpretation, though Britain of course is one of the founding members of the European Convention of Human Rights in 1950 and one of the first states to ratify it.

[50]Fuller, *The Morality of Law*, pp. 224–227 et seq., where Fuller criticizes the notion of legal interpretation upheld by H. L. A. Hart, Hans Kelsen, John Austin and John Chipman Gray: "These diverse ways of confronting a shared predicament suggest that there is something fundamentally wrong with the premises that serve to define the problem. I suggest that the difficulty arises because all of the writers whose views have just been summarized [i.e. Hart, Austin, Kelsen, Gray] start with the assumption that law must be regarded as *one-way projection of authority*, instead of being conceived as a *collaborative enterprise*. Fuller, *The Morality of Law*, p. 227. (Italics added.)

into account.[51] Contrary to what the Hart and other advocates of analytical jurisprudence would have us believe, judges are not allowed to have resort to freewheeling discretion of a "small-scale legislator" in the *hard cases* of legal adjudication in which there are no legal rules that would apply to the facts of the case or, alternatively, the rules that are available for the judge contradict each other. Hence they cannot provide a satisfactory answer to the legal issue at hand. According to Dworkin, in such cases the judges make frequent use of "principles, policies, and other sorts of standards" of law.[52]

And to Dworkin's mind, that's how things ought to be as well: the *rights* of an individual or group of individuals, based on such legal principles or standards with institutional support and societal approval, should be the ultimate ground of legal argumentation. Though Hart did not respond to Dworkin's critique in his lifetime, there are some scattered notes on the issue in the postscript to the second edition of Hart's *The Concept of Law*, as posthumously published in 1994.[53] I will consider those arguments in the section on inclusive legal positivism below.

Of the key representatives of analytical legal positivism in the twentieth century, there is still one figure that should be mentioned, viz. the Polish legal philosopher Jerzy Wróblewski (1926–1990). Like Austin before him, Wróblewski ruled individual judicial decisions outside of the concept of a legal system in his major treatise *The Judicial Application of Law*[54]:

> The legal system is constituted by sufficiently general and abstract rules, but does not include individual law applying decisions and inter alia judicial decisions.

As individual court rulings were left out of Wróblewski's notion of a legal system, it is no wonder that he did not present a theory of legal interpretation. Rather, he chose to deal with the more general issue of the different judicial ideologies, distinguishing the three categories of *bound*, *free*, and *legal and rational* judicial ideology.[55] The same goes for Kaarle Makkonen, the Finnish legal philosopher, who introduced a similar list of the judge's decision-making situations of an isomorphic, semantically ambiguous, or entirely unregulated kind.[56]

---

[51] Dworkin succeeded Hart in the Oxford chair of jurisprudence in 1968, very much to Hart's own approval.

[52] Cf. Dworkin, *Taking Rights Seriously*, p. 22: "... in those in hard cases... [the lawyers] make use of standards that do not function as rules, but operate differently as principles, policies, and other sorts of standards."

[53] Hart, *The Concept of Law* (1994), pp. 238–276 and 244–268.

[54] Wróblewski, *The Judicial Application of Law*, p. 296.

[55] Wróblewski, *The Judicial Application of Law*, pp. 265–314; cf. Siltala, *A Theory of Precedent*, pp. 3–6.

[56] Makkonen, *Zur Problematik der juridischen Entscheidung*, p. 78 et seq.

6.4.2 Institutional Legal Positivism

Institutional legal positivism, as elaborated by Neil MacCormick (1941–2009) and Ota Weinberger (1919–2009), has further modified Austin's, Kelsen's, and Hart's analytical legal positivism. An institutional approach to the law sees the law and legal phenomena as *institutional facts* that can (only) be initially created, subsequently altered in content, legally enforced, and ultimately derogated by *speech acts*, as successfully performed by the legislator, a court of justice, or other official.[57] The theory entails a specific conception of language, the world, and the relation between the two, as defined in the form of *speech acts* and *institutional facts*. An institutional theory of law is based on the linguistic philosophy of Elizabeth Anscombe, John L. Austin, and John Searle.[58]

According to the institutional theory of language and the world, reality consists of two kinds of facts, viz. *brute facts* and *institutional facts*. Brute facts are "raw", empirically observable phenomena the existence of which is not conditional on the prevailing linguistic, societal, or cultural conventions upheld by the members of the community concerned.[59] Institutional facts, on the other hand, rely on a set of societal, linguistic, or cultural conventions for their very existence, in the sense of some "brute" facts read in the light of specific rules of either legal or social kind. In institutional facts, empirical facts and normative rules of legal or social kind are thus inextricably intertwined with each other.[60] MacCormick's and Weinberger's institutional legal positivism is committed to a *realistic* ontology, and it acknowledges the existence of conventional, rule-bound facts, in addition to raw facts.

Legal phenomena, such as the national constitution, various kinds of private law contracts and agreements, wills, property rights, legislative acts passed by the Parliament, and a request for a preliminary ruling made to the Court of the European Union, are examples of rule-bound, institutional facts whose existence is conditional on a set of legal rules and principles. Such an idea of there being a conceptual link between some phenomena in society and a set of legal rules or principles is not a total novelty, however. In fact, Hans Kelsen pointed out in the 1920s that the semantic reference of the concept of a *state* is co-existent with a set of formally valid legal

---

[57] MacCormick and Weinberger, *An Institutional Theory of Law. New Approaches to Legal Positivism*, passim; Weinberger, *Law, Institution and Legal Politics*, esp. pp. 3–29, 148–185.

[58] Anscombe, "On Brute Facts"; Anscombe, *Intention*; Austin, *How to Do Things with Words*; Searle, *Speech Acts. An Essay in the Philosophy of Language*.

[59] Tables and chairs, waterfalls and mountains, black holes (i.e. collapsed stars), galaxies, and dark matter are all brute facts that will continue to exist irrespective of human beliefs and conventions. On raw facts and institutional facts, cf. Anscombe, "On Brute Facts", passim.

[60] Institutional ontology is usually stated in terms of facts (or prevailing states of affairs), rather than individual objects, entities, or "things". That may be related to the issue that institutional facts are *per definitionem* intertwined with societal rules and thus come, so to say, already equipped with certain properties. The Wittgensteinian ontology sketched above in the context of the correspondence theory and the related idea of isomorphism is therefore suited to institutional facts, as well, if the other preconditions of isomorphism are duly satisfied.

rules. In other words, a state is a shorthand description for the totality of legal norms in the field of e.g. constitutional law, administrative law, financial law, criminal law, procedural law, and international law of some legal order. Contrary to what some legal philosophers had claimed prior to Kelsen, a state does not have any "organic" or sociological mode of existence outside of the normative realm defined by such legal norms.[61]

According to MacCormick and Weinberger, a *legal institution* consists of three kinds of rules: (a) *institutive* rules that define the conditions for the coming into existence of an institution, (b) *consequentialist* rules that define the legal consequences brought into effect by a legal institution, and (c) *terminative* rules that define the terms of derogation of a legal institution.[62]

Issues of legal interpretation have not been at the focus of interest by institutional legal positivism, either. Instead, the research efforts of the "institutionalists" have been on the *ontological* project of the preconditions for the initial *creation*, subsequent *modification* in content, due *enforcement* at the courts of justice and other officials, and ultimately *derogation* of legal norms through the institutional speech acts by the legislator, courts of justice, or other legal authorities. Neil MacCormick, for sure, introduced a challenging theory of how to construct and read the law in his breakthrough work *Legal Reasoning and Legal Theory*. That fine item of legal scholarship, however, would still seem to rely on the constitutive premises of the new rhetoric and analytical argumentation theory, and not those of an institutional theory of law. In fact, MacCormick's linguistic turn to the institutional theory took place in *An Institutional Theory of Law. New Approaches to Legal Positivism*, coauthored with Ota Weinberger and published in 1986.

Under legal positivism, widely defined, the thorny issues of legal interpretation have been tackled mainly by the French and Belgian *exegetical school of law* (*École de l'Exégèse*) in the nineteenth century. Before turning into questions of legal exegesis, I will consider the most recent variants of analytical legal positivism, viz. *exclusive* and *inclusive* legal positivism, and the highly challenging notion of collective *intentionality*. The reader should note that the chronological order is not preserved here, since exclusive and inclusive legal positivism is a phenomenon of the late twentieth and the twenty-first century, while the exegetical school of law had its heyday at the nineteenth century.

---

61 Kelsen, *Der Soziologische und der juristische Staatsbegriff. Kritische Untersuchung des Verhältnisses von Staat und Recht*, passim, where Kelsen argues *contra* e.g. Jellinek's notion of a state.

62 MacCormick and Weinberger, *An Institutional Theory of Law*, pp. 52–53; MacCormick, *Institutions of Law*, pp. 49–50.

6.4.3 Exclusive and Inclusive Legal Positivism

In recent literature on jurisprudence and legal philosophy, the relation of legal positivism to natural law philosophy has been analysed with the two concepts of *exclusive*, or *strong*, legal positivism and *inclusive*, or *soft* or *incorporatist*, legal positivism. The key issue is how the concept of law is defined vis-à-vis the norms of prevalent social or political morality.[63]

Exclusive legal positivism defines the notion of legal validity with reference to purely conventional criteria, i.e. the formal *source of origin* of a legal norm. Hans Kelsen's pure theory of law seeks to provide a theory of legal science the subject matter of which is defined in strictly legal terms, as carefully "purified" from all non-legal elements, no matter whether they of social, political, economic, moral, or religious kind. As a consequence, the norms that make up the prevalent or critical political morality in society could not have any bearing on the systemic validity of an individual legal norm. Under such premises, the law is defined by reference to the will of the sovereign legislator or a legally competent court of justice, and no external or moral criteria can be imposed upon the law.[64] Thus, Kelsen's theory of law fulfils the criteria of exclusive legal positivism with flying colours.

Exclusive legal positivism seeks to satisfy John Austin's methodological request of enforcing a clear-cut division between the validity of law and its substantive, content-bound qualities.[65] John Chipman Gray, an early American legal realist who to a certain extent followed Austin's ideas, reached a similar conclusion in his *The Nature and Sources of the Law*[66]:

> The great gain in its fundamental conceptions which Jurisprudence made during the last century [i.e. 19th century] was the recognition of the truth that the Law of a State or other organized body is not an ideal, but something which actually exists. It is not that which is in accordance with religion, or nature, or morality; it is not that which ought to be, but that which is.

Ronald Dworkin has adopted the (perhaps slightly ironic) term *test of pedigree*[67] for such a formal, source-oriented criterion by means of which valid rules are to

[63] Summarizingly, Marmor, "Exclusive Legal Positivism"; Himma, "Inclusive Legal Positivism". – As representatives of exclusive legal positivism, Himma counts Joseph Raz, Scott Shapiro and Andrei Marmor; and as representatives of inclusive legal positivism, H. L. A. Hart, Jules Coleman, W.J. Waluchow and Matthew Kramer. Hans Kelsen with his pure theory of law would qualify as a key figure in the school of exclusive legal positivism as well. Himma, "Inclusive Legal Positivism", p. 125.

[64] Kelsen, *General Theory of Law and State*, p. 113; Kelsen, *Reine Rechtslehre* (1960), p. 201.

[65] Austin, *The Province of Jurisprudence Determined*, p. 157. Cf. Hart, "Positivism and the Separation of Law from Morals"; Fuller, "Positivism and Fidelity to Law – A Reply to Professor Hart".

[66] Gray, *The Nature and Sources of the Law*, p. 94. – Cf. Hart, *The Concept of Law* (1961), p. 203 (i.e. "the great battle-cries of legal positivism"). Hart's page reference to Gray's *The Nature and Sources of the Law* is would seem to be erroneous, however.

[67] Dworkin, *Taking Rights Seriously*, p. 40.

be identified and distinguished from the norms of political morality under Hart's analytical legal positivism. The impact of legal principles and other value-laden legal standards is thereby rejected, as Dworkin has pointed out.

Inclusive legal positivism, on the other hand, is committed to the idea that the rule of recognition that is commonly acknowledged in a legal system may well entail a reference to some inherently content-oriented criteria, but such a reference is not a necessary but merely contingent facet of the law. To the extent that the rule of recognition does in fact entail some moral criteria, the judge may, or perhaps is even obliged, to have recourse to such moral criteria in the identification of valid law. In the standard commentary work, Kenneth Einar Himma uses Hart's *The Concept of Law* as a prime example of inclusive legal positivism.[68]

Contrary to what Ronald Dworkin has argued, the ultimate rule of recognition in Hart's theory of law may entail a reference to some content-bound criteria, which clearly matches with the core ideas of inclusive legal positivism. In the chapter titled "Law and Morals" in *The Concept of Law*, Hart addresses the issue in quite open terms[69]:

> In some systems, as in the United States, the ultimate criteria of legal validity explicitly incorporate principles of justice or substantive moral values; in other systems, as in England, where there are no formal restrictions on the competence of the supreme legislature, its legislation may yet no less scrupulously conform to justice or morality.

Moreover, Hart comments on the relation of legal positivism vis-à-vis natural law theory were essentially in line with inclusive legal positivism[70]:

> Here we shall take Legal Positivism to mean the simple contention that it is in no sense a *necessary* truth that laws reproduce or satisfy certain demands of morality, though in fact they have often done so.

And in the posthumous postscript to the second edition of *The Concept of Law* Hart replies to Ronald Dworkin:

> This [Dworkin's criticism] is doubly mistaken. First, it ignores my explicit acknowledgèment that the rule of recognition may incorporate as criteria of legal validity conformity with moral principles or substantive values; so my doctrine is what has been called "soft positivism" and not as in Dworkin's version of it "plain-fact positivism". Secondly, there is nothing in my book [*The Concept of Law*] to suggest that the plain-fact criteria provided by the rule of recognition must be solely matters of pedigree; they may instead be substantive constraints on the content of legislation such as the Sixteenth or Nineteenth Amendment to the United States Constitution respecting the establishment of religion or abridgements of the right to vote.

Though Hart's ideas of law in *The Concept of Law* clearly contribute to the tradition of inclusive legal positivism, the contingent but nonetheless prevalent relation between the law and morality that is acknowledged in, e.g., the constitution of the United States is not duly acknowledged in the original, 1961 edition of Hart's *The*

[68] Himma, "Inclusive Legal Positivism", pp. 125, 139, 141–143.

[69] Hart, *The Concept of Law* (1961), p. 199.

[70] Hart, *The Concept of Law* (1961), pp. 180–181. (Italics added.)

Concept of Law. Notwithstanding the brief reflections on the issue in Chapter on "Law and Morals", the rule of recognition is treated as a source-oriented criterion only in the said book. Indeed, Hart's own prime example of the ultimate rule of recognition for the English legal system is given in the *Queen rule*, i.e. what the Queen in Parliament enacts is (valid) law in England.[71] Hart fails to deepen his analysis in this respect so as to comprise the morals-impregnated clauses of the American constitution, though he does touch upon the issue in the passing. Since Hart's self-pronounced goal in *The Concept of Law* was to provide a *general* theory of law, one might have expected him to give a more thorough analysis of the relation that may prevail between the three key elements of his legal theory, viz. law, morality, and the rule of recognition that provides for the transition from the world of facts to the world of norms.

Nor in his other writings on jurisprudence did Hart devote much attention to the said commitments to an inclusive, or "soft", legal positivism, and to what might follow thereof as to the concept of law and the idea of legal interpretation. In the heated debate with the American natural law philosopher Lon L. Fuller (1902–1978), Hart was quick to point out that although there was no *logical* obstacle for the rule of recognition to entail even some principles of morality and justice, the disregard of which would lead to the invalidity of a legal norm, constitutions do not generally "invite trouble" by taking that kind of form.[72]

In discussing the shape of the rule of recognition in the modern Western legal systems, Hart refers to the written constitution, "ordinary" legislation, and precedents.[73] Fully unfolded, the rule of recognition would of course comprise a reference to all the *institutional* and *societal* sources of law whose normative impact on the judge's legal discretion is acknowledged in the legal system concerned.

As concerns legal interpretation, *exclusive* legal positivism will not bring about much of a change to what was mentioned above in the context of Austin's and Kelsen's theories of law. Kelsen put forth the argument that the act of legal interpretation by a judge's is *authentic* in character, since it creates a binding legal norm for the case at hand; while legal interpretation by a legal scholar is no more than *inauthentic* in character, since it lacks any legally enforceable effects.[74] Knowledge of the authenticity of a judge's or other legal official's act of legal interpretation cannot provide much guidance for the judge on *how* he should construct and read legal rules, any more than a corresponding knowledge of the inauthenticity of the act of interpretation by a legal scholar can provide such guidance for the latter. Moreover, Kelsen's austere conception of the legitimate task for legal science will not admit of

[71] Hart, *The Concept of Law* (1961), e.g. on pp. 99, 104, 108, 113, 117, 142, 145.

[72] Hart, "Lon L. Fuller: *The Morality of Law*", p. 361.

[73] Hart, *The Concept of Law* (1961), p. 98.

[74] Kelsen, *Reine Rechtslehre* (1960), pp. 350–354. – "Die Interpretation durch das rechtsanwendende Organ ist stets authentisch. Sie schafft Recht. (...) Von der Interpretation durch ein rechtsanwendendes Organ unterscheidet sich jede andere Interpretation dadurch, daβ sie nicht authentisch ist, das heiβt: daß sie kein Recht schafft." Kelsen, *Reine Rechtslehre* (1960), p. 351, 352.

any recommendations as to the mutual preference order of the semantically possible outcomes of interpretation.[75]

The same scarcity as to the criteria of legal interpretation would seem to hold true even for Hart's theory of law. According to Hart, the act of interpretation by a judge or a scholar is defined by the two-geared semantics of the *core of settled meaning* and the *penumbra of doubt* that determines the elucidation of any legal rule that entails linguistic concepts.[76] In a *hard case* of legal decision-making, the legal discretion enjoyed by the judge is then compared to that of a "small-scale legislator", only constrained by the valid constitution and, in light of the subsequent legal development, by the international treaties and conventions that have an effect on domestic law, such as the Treaty of the European Union or the European Convention on Human Rights.

As a consequence, the soft, incorporated, or inclusive character of Hart's legal positivism, as acknowledged by Hart himself in the postscript to *The Concept of Law*, would not seem to have left any significant imprint on his notion of legal interpretation in the said book or in Hart's other key contributions to analytical jurisprudence. If consistently applied, inclusive legal positivism would seem – at least to some extent – to open legal discretion to ideas entailed in the political or social morality, as underscored by Ronald Dworkin vis-à-vis legal principles.

What is common to the various strands of legal positivism is the *voluntarist* idea to the effect that the boundaries of law can be determined by reference to the will-formation of the (sovereign) legislator, courts of justice and other legal officials. The theoretical foundations of such will-formation were drawn "in the thin air" by the key representatives of analytical legal positivism. There is yet one tenet of legal positivism in the wide sense of the term that has devoted major attention to the issue of legal interpretation, viz. the *Exegetical School of Law* in France and Belgium in the nineteenth century. As the school of legal exegesis predates most of the writings that were classified as analytical legal positivism above, it cannot be classified as an instance of modern legal positivism *sensu stricto*. Still, it shares with it the key element of seeing the law as the product of intentional will-formation by the lawgiver, which entitles the use of the term "positivism" here. In addition, the notion of *collective intentionality*, as ascribed to the parliamentary legislator or a court of justice with several members, needs to be elucidated. First, however, one would-be variant of modern legal positivism still needs to be considered.

---

[75] "Rechtswissenschaftliche Interpretation kann nichts anderes als die möglichen Bedeutungen einer Rechtsnorm herausstellen." Kelsen, *Reine Rechtslehre* (1960), p. 353.

[76] Hart, *The Concept of Law* (1961), pp. 124–128.

6.5 The Unresolvable Dilemma of Kaarlo Tuori's Critical Legal Positivism

Despite the author's several express allusions to Hans Kelsen's and H. L. A. Hart's analytical legal positivism as the theory reference of his conception of law,[77] Kaarlo Tuori's *critical legal positivism* fails to qualify as an instance of legal positivism, strictly defined. In his major treatise *Critical Legal Positivism*, Tuori criticizes Kelsen's and Hart's "traditional", i.e. analytical, legal positivism for failing to attain the two main objectives of modern jurisprudence: to define the *boundaries* of law in a clear-cut manner vis-à-vis the other phenomena in society, such as the norms of religion or political morality, and to provide for a content-based critique of law so as to judge the *legitimacy* of law.[78] Tuori's own *critical* variant of positivism allegedly succeeds better in those two tasks. In it, Tuori combines an extensive array of theory-laden fragments into a complex synthesis of law, drawn from Sakari Hänninen's novel reading of Georg Lukács' Marxist theory of law and society, representing the oldest theoretical layer in Tuori's conception of law,[79] and from the writings by Max Weber, Jürgen Habermas, Michel Foucault, François Ewald, Fernand Braudel, Pierre Bourdieu, Ronald Dworkin, John L. Austin, and John R. Searle.[80]

According to Tuori, modern law is a historically evolving entity that consists of three different layers or sediments: the *deep-structure* level, the level of the *legal culture*, and the *surface-structure* level of law.[81] The phenomena that dwell at the *deep-structure level* of law, such as the basic concepts of law and the most grounding principles of law, are the least malleable and the most resistant to the efforts of legal change by the legislator and the courts of justice. The phenomena at the *level of legal culture*, such as the general principles and general doctrines of law, are relatively more malleable while showing resistance to the efforts of legal change by the parliamentary legislator and the courts of justice. It is only the phenomena that dwell on the "stormy" or "turbulent" *surface-structure level* of law, such as individual legal enactments and individual judicial decisions, that are entirely malleable at will by the legislator and the courts of justice, showing no resistance to efforts of legal change.

By embedding the quasi-autonomous phenomena at the deep-structure level of law and the level of legal culture in the allegedly positivist frame of analysis Tuori

[77] Tuori, *Critical Legal Positivism*. p. 8.

[78] Tuori, *Critical Legal Positivism*. p. 8: "Traditional legal positivism is not able to answer certain fundamental questions about the law which gain importance under the conditions of modern law, culture and society. These are the questions of the *limits* and the *criteria of the legitimacy* of the law." (Italics in original.) – Tuori speaks of the limits of the law. I use the term boundaries in the same sense here.

[79] Cf. Hänninen, *Aika, paikka, politiikka. Marxilaisen valtioteorian konstituutiosta ja metodista*.

[80] Tuori, *Critical Legal Positivism*, p. 121 et seq.

[81] On the three levels of law in Tuori's conception of law, cf. Tuori, *Critical Legal Positivism*, p. 147 et seq.

strikes a patent discord with the constitutive premises of Kelsen's and Hart's analytical jurisprudence, since Kelsen and Hart were both committed to a consistently *voluntarist* conception of law, with no "levels" or sediments of law that would be out of reach of the will of the sovereign legislator, the courts, or other officials.[82] In this, Tuori's conception of law has far more affinity with a *phenomenological* and, indeed, a *Marxist* account of the law and society, to the effect that the *economic* deep-structure level phenomena of society determine the manifestations of the phenomena at the *ideological* surface-structure level of society under the Marxist premises. There is more from Karl Marx and Georg Lukács, than from Hans Kelsen and H. L. A. Hart, in Tuori's multi-layered conception of law.

Tuori confidently puts forth the claim of simultaneously attaining the two divergent goals set for a *positivist* and for a *critical* theory of law, respectively, as even reflected in the title of his treatise, *Critical Legal Positivism*. Thus, he seeks to defend a *voluntarist* conception of law in line with Kelsen's and Hart's analytical legal positivism; while at the same time making room for a content-based *critique* of law in line with Dworkin's seminal idea of value-laden legal principles. As I see it, Tuori's effort of combining the two mutually contradictory elements is bound to fail, for logico-conceptual reasons. A genuinely voluntarist conception of law with sharply drawn boundaries (à la Kelsen and Hart), which at the same time would make room for content-based critique of law (à la Dworkin), is a *chimaera*, or something that for logico-conceptual reasons cannot exist.

A positivist, *voluntarist* conception of law draws the boundaries of law vis-à-vis political morality, religion, or any other normative phenomena in society in a clear-cut manner, as illustrated by Kelsen's transcendental-logical *Grundnorm* and Hart's ultimate rule of recognition as the criteria of legal validity in a legal system. The impact of value-laden principles and standards of law is, however, excluded from the domain of law by Kelsen and (probably) by Hart,[83] since they do not satisfy the master criterion of having a formal source of origin, or "pedigree" as Dworkin put it, in some individual decision issued by the sovereign legislator or given by a court of justice. If, on the other hand, the legal system is defined so as to make room for the value-laden principles and standards of law in Dworkin's sense of the term, the boundaries of the law become blurred vis-à-vis the political morality in society. *Porous legality*, or legality punctured by the impact of the openly value-laden principles and standards of law, will then occupy the place of Kelsen's methodological purity and Hart's judge-oriented rule of recognition.

---

[82]Even Hart's notion of the minimum concept of natural law fully accords with a voluntarist notion of law, as we are dealing with certain contingent, and not necessary or a priori, constraints on the legislator's discretion.

[83]Hart's philosophical position is slightly ambivalent here, since in the posthumously published *Postscript* to *The Concept of Law* (1994) he made some concessions to the stance known as inclusive legal positivism in this respect, to the effect of allowing a larger role for legal principles than the adherents of exclusive legal positivism, like Kelsen.

The two goals Tuori set for himself, i.e. a *voluntarist*, positivist conception of law (à la Kelsen and Hart) that would also make room for a content-based critique of law, as derived from the *political morality* in the community (à la Dworkin), cannot both be attained at the same time, but the one or the other has to yield so as to make room for the other. The end result is a zero-sum game between those two ingredients of modern jurisprudence, necessitating a choice between Kelsen's and Hart's formal, *rule*-based conception of law and Dworkin's openly value-laden, *principle*-oriented conception of law.

6.6 One Step (or Two) Back in History: The Exegetical School of Law (*École de l'Exégèse*) in France and Belgium in the Nineteenth Century

The *Exegetical School of Law*, i.e. *École de l'Exégèse*, was dominant in France and Belgium in the nineteenth century.[84] It sought to severely restrict the legal source material available for the judge in his legal decision-making. According to the exegetical notion of law, legislation is the primary, if not the only, source of law that the judge may legitimately have resort to in his legal discretion.[85] The law was defined as equal to the will of the sovereign legislator, as found in legislation and the *travaux préparatoires*.

The heyday of the exegetical school was in 1830–1880. The years from 1804 to 1830 were the years of its formation, and the years from 1880 to 1900 were the years of its disintegration.[86]

Though the representatives of the exegetical school approved the key ideas of a non-positive natural law, such ideas were regarded as too vague to guide the legal discretion of the judge. Rather, it was assumed that the fundamental principles of natural law had now been given an indisputable expression in the form of written law. Enacted law was once again seen as *ratio scripta*, i.e. "reason expressed in a written form", as the master collection of Roman law texts, *Corpus Iuris Civilis*, had been for the mediaeval lawyers.[87] As Boudwijn Bouckaert has convincingly

[84]The most comprehensive account of the exegetical school of law is Bouckaert, *De exegetische school. Een kritische studie van de rechtsbronnen- en interpretatieleer bij de 19de eeuwse commentatoren van de Code Civil*. – Cf. also Halpérin, "Exégèse (École)", passim.

[85]Bouckaert, "Exegetical School", pp. 276–278. – "The theory of legal sources of the exegetical school was dominated by the conviction that the written law was by far the most important source of the law. (...) The written law was also regarded as the nearly exclusive source of the law." Bouckaert, "Exegetical School", p. 277.

[86]Bouckaert, "Exegetical School", p. 277.

[87]"All authors of the exegetical school expressed their faith in a suprapositive natural law, to which the legislator owed full respect. The philosophical origin of their natural law views varied greatly: some were of a Christian thomistic inspiration, others were lockean, still others were hegelian. Their allegiance to natural law, however, did not alter their unconditional recognition of the written law as the decisive source of positive law. The natural law was considered to be too vague to serve

argued, the exegetical school provided the link between rationalistic natural law thinking dating from the time of the French revolution and the school of modern legal positivism in the twentieth century.

The school of *analytical jurisprudence* in England, outlined by John Austin in the 1830s, and the extremely formal, conceptualist, and constructive notion of law under the German school of *Begriffsjurisprudenz* are parallel phenomena to the French and Belgian exegetical school of law. The German *Begriffsjurisprudenz* gradually evolved from the historicist, "organic" notion of law that had been suggested by Friedrich Carl von Savigny earlier in the nineteenth century.

The emergence of the would-be all-inclusive national law codifications at the turn of the eighteenth and nineteenth century is a key precondition for the emergence and breakthrough of the exegetical school of law. Of the law codifications, the French civil code (*Code civil*) in 1804 is deservedly the best known. The codification movement had its swansong in the completion of the highly influential German civil law book (*Bürgerliches Gesetzbuch*) that came into force in 1900. Since the early nineteenth century von Savigny and the other adherents of the historical school had strongly underscored the role of the "organic", free-evolving societal customs in a legal community as the primary source of law. In a more sophisticated legal system, like the one in the Germany of the nineteenth century, the legal profession was thought to occupy a privileged position as the most authentic interpreter of the *Volksgeist*, or the "spirit of the nation", that according to von Savigny defined the very essence of the law.

The fierce intellectual debate between the historicist approach, as defended by von Savigny, and the uprising positivist approach, as represented by Thibaut and the codification movement, ended at the turn of the nineteenth and twentieth century in an almost total defeat of the historicists and almost as complete a victory of the codification ideology of the legal positivists.[88] Ever since, the role of customary law has been in steady decline in the Western world. As the legislation-oriented model of law, proliferated by Thibaut and the codification movement, ultimately won the upper hand, a major demand was created for the kind of methodology on how to construct and read legislative enactments, which the exegetical school of law could provide.

The call of the French and Belgian exegetical school was for *authenticity* in legal interpretation in retracing – as authentically as possible – the original intentions and motives behind an act of legislation. The authoritative text of an enactment and the

as a criterion for the practical decision of the judge. Natural law principles needed to be specified by the positive legislation. As most authors of the school thought that most natural law principles were elaborated in the civil code, positive law was nearly completely identified with natural law." Bouckaert, "Exegetical School", p. 277.

[88]Friedrich Carl von Savigny's "Vom Beruf unserer Zeit für Gesetzgebung und Rechtswissenschaft" and Anton Friedrich Justus Thibaut's "Über die Nothwendigkeit eines allgemeinen Bürgerlichen Rechts für Deutschland" were the battle-cries of the two intellectual movements. Both texts are included in Hans Hattenhauer's compilation of essays, *Thibaut und Savigny. Ihre Programmatische Schriften*.

travaux préparatoires at the back of it were the primary, if not the only, legitimate source in retracing the legislator's original intentions. Logical and linguistic methods of interpretation were utilized, as well, such as inferences of the *e contrario* and *a fortiori* kind, plus analogical reasoning the importance of which increased towards the end of the nineteenth century.[89]

At the end of the nineteenth and the beginning of the twentieth century, the exegetical school with its constrained legal source doctrine had to recede even in the French-speaking countries, at least partly due to the impact of various kinds of *empirical*, *sociological*, and *realist* approaches to law. In France, the polymorphic and eclectic approach to law by François Gény, with its emphasis upon the "scientific" and historic character of legal analysis, took the lead for a moment. The gist of Gény's ingenious methodological program was grasped by the loose catch-phrase *libre recherche scientifique*, or the pursuit of free scientific research in law, with recourse to a variety of (mostly) empirical and historical tools in legal analysis.[90] Another approach that attacked the idealistic and formalist premises of the exegetical school was the *Free Law Movement* (*Freirechtslehre*; *Freirechtsbewegung*), by Eugen Ehrlich among others.[91] The school of *Interessenjurisprudence*, as envisioned by Rudolf von Jhering, underscored the goal-oriented, interest-laden tenets of law at the end of the nineteenth century, even though the outcomes of such purposeful orientation in law were to a great extent modified by the social and political compromises that are frequently reached during the legislative process.[92]

In line with von Jhering's methodological *credo*, and in fact partly due to the original inspiration drawn from it, *sociological jurisprudence* in the United States looked upon the law as a case of social engineering, i.e. as an effective tool for the attainment of certain social goals.[93] In the French legal culture, the dominant traits of legal formalism, such as the predominant recourse to highly legalistic reasons and the essentially terse, magisterial style of judicial decisions bear witness to the impact of the exegetical school even today.[94]

Contrary to the thesis of the exegetical school, parliamentary legislation is not the only legitimate source of law in any Western legal system anymore. Rather, an array of institutional and societal sources, both of national and transnational kind, now provide for the criteria of legal discretion. The idea of giving impact to the will-formation of the parliamentary legislator is yet a major institutional premise in all Western societies, as given effect in the constitution, legislative enactments

---

[89]Bouckaert, "Exegetical School", pp. 277–278.

[90]On Gény's "libre recherche scientifique", cf. Bergel, *Méthodologie juridique*, pp. 249–253.

[91]Ehrlich, "Frei Rechtsfindung und freie Rechtswissenschaft", passim.

[92]von Jhering, *Der Zweck im Recht*, p. I: "Der Zweck ist der Schöpfer des ganzen Rechts", i.e. [social] purpose is the creator of all law, as von Jhering claimed in the motto of the book.

[93]Pound, *Social Control through Law*; Pound, "Law in Books and Law in Action".

[94]MacCormick and Summers, eds., *Interpreting Statutes*, pp. 171–212, 500–508 (and p. 502 in specific); MacCormick and Summers, eds., *Interpreting Precedents*, pp. 103–140. Cf. de Lasser, *Judicial Deliberations*, pp. 27–61, 166–202.

and the *travaux préparatoires*, if any. Such an ideology is expressive of the Western *rule of law* ideology in which the will of the legislator looms large.[95] Recently, Pekka Hallberg has presented an analysis of the notion of a rule of law ideology by means of the following four elements: (a) legality in social decision-making, (b) proper balance among the stately powers, (c) respect for the constitutional rights and human rights of individuals, and (d) the functioning of the legal and social system in general.

Today, the impact of the French and Belgian exegetical school in law can be seen in at least three different phenomena. Firstly, the French legal culture has retained many formalistic tenets initially advocated by the exegetical school. Since the French Cour de Cassation served as the model for the European Court of Justice (now: Court of the European Union), the style of reasoning of the latter court, too, bears the impact of high legal formality. That can be seen in, for instance, the fact that the Justices of European Court are not allowed to write a dissenting opinion to its rulings.

Secondly, the *travaux préparatoires* are acknowledged as an important source of law in most Western legal systems, as they provide authorized information of the original legislative intentions and motives of the legislator. In Sweden and Finland, legislative drafting material such as committee reports, memoranda, bills, and the like documents are often quite profound, highly professional, and detailed,[96] even though the enormous volume of the current national and EU-based legislation has, perhaps rather understandably, lowered the standard of meticulousness. And thirdly, the idea of retracing the original intentions of the prior court still looms large in the system of precedents in the United Kingdom.[97]

6.7 A Critical Evaluation of Legal Exegesis

Legal interpretation is the Achilleus' heel of legal positivism. All the variations of legal positivism discerned, i.e. *analytical*, *institutional*, *exclusive*, and *inclusive* legal positivism, equally fail to present a philosophically satisfactory account of the "nuts and bolts" of how to construct and read the law in the substantive, content-oriented sense of term, and not in the sense of merely presenting some structural

[95]Hallberg, *The Rule of Law*, pp. 70–91; Hallberg, *Prospects of the Rule of Law*, p. 146. – On the rule of law ideology in general and in legal comparative perspective, cf. Costa and Zolo, eds., *The Rule of Law. History, Theory and Criticism*.

[96]On the *travaux préparatoires* and the historical will of the legislator, Peczenik, *Vad är rätt?* pp. 241–259. – According to Article 64 of the Internal Rules of Procedure of the Finnish Parliament (1999/40), the line of reasoning presented in support of some legislative bill in the respective Parliamentary Committee Report are held to have been authoritatively accepted, unless the Parliament expressly decides otherwise. Thereby, significant authority is conferred on such reasons.

[97]MacCormick and Summers, eds., *Interpreting Precedents*, pp. 315–354; Siltala, *A Theory of Precedent*, pp. 84–90.

typology or classification of the different legal decision-making situations.[98] In John Austin's, Hans Kelsen's, H. L. A. Hart's, and Jerzy Wróblewski's analytical writings on jurisprudence, the focus of interest has been elsewhere, viz. on the concept and internal structure of law, and the separation of law from morality. As to the operative criteria of legal construction and interpretation, analytical and institutional legal positivism leaves the judge rather empty-handed.

The closest *methodological* parallel to legal exegesis can be found in traditional theological studies where the will of the Almighty God has been retraced or reconstructed, as authentically as possible, in the corpus of holy writings. In the context of law, more secular institutional authorities, like the Parliament and courts of justice, now occupy the privileged position in how to construct and read the law. Within the jurisprudential tradition, the *exegetical school of law* (*École de l'Exégèse*) made the most significant contributions to the construction and interpretation of law. It anchored such criteria to the will of the legislator, giving effect to the law text and the official *travaux préparatoires* at the back of an item of legislation. Respect for the institutional will-formation of the Parliament has been an integral part of the modern *rule of law* ideology. There are other elements entailed in it, as well, like an effective protection of the human and constitutional rights of an individual.

The claimed authenticity of legal interpretation is yet difficult to judge. How can the legal community be convinced that the outcome of legal (re)construction truly matches with the original intentions of the parliamentary legislator or the court of justice that issued a particular precedent? The situation is like the one facing the judge or a legal scholar under Ronald Dworkin's idea legal integrity as "the best constructive interpretation of past political decisions in the legal community".[99] For the hard cases of legal adjudication where the original intentions of the legislator are often hard to find, recourse to the *hypothetical will* of the legislator has been suggested as a way out of the dilemma. As a consequence, the judge or legal scholar ought to reason how the legislator would have reacted to the facts of the current case, had it made such a judgment. Yet, retracing the hypothetical will of the legislator is no more than a wild guess of something that cannot be ascertained.

It is one of the strengths of the positivist and exegetical approach that it gives full credit to the *institutional* premises of law. Its inherent weaknesses have to do with the historical, backward-looking orientation of legal analysis under legal exegesis, which to a great extent diminishes its utility as a tool of legal analysis in times

[98]Nor does Kaarlo Tuori's *critical legal positivism* address the substantive issues of legal interpretation and argumentation. The focus in Tuori's theory of law is on the issues of legal *ontology*, seeking to find an answer to the question of "what is law". Tuori answers to that question by means of the three levels (i.e. surface level, level of legal culture, and deep-structure level of law) and the two dimensions of law (i.e. legal norms and legal practices). Tuori, *Critical Legal Positivism*, pp. 121–216.

[99]Dworkin, *Law's Empire*, p. 262. – Cf. "According to law as integrity, propositions of law are true if they figure in or follow from the principles of justice, fairness, and procedural due process that provide the best constructive interpretation of the community's legal practice." Dworkin, *Law's Empire*, p. 255.

of social change or upheaval. If the institutional and societal values at the back of legislation are in a state of being transformed, there is perhaps not much sense in seeking to enforce the historical will of the legislator or some outdated values acknowledged in the historical archives of precedent-based law.

Chapter 7
Legal Realism: The Law in Action, Not the Law in Books, As the Subject Matter of Legal Analysis

7.1 Philosophical Realism Defined

Philosophical or scientific *realism* is a plural notion, i.e. a *cluster concept* with a multitude of references (extensions) and senses (intensions). According to Ilkka Niiniluoto and Sami Pihlström, it may refer to at least the following seven types of phenomena[1]:

1) *ontological* realism: there exist mind-independent reality, i.e. reality is (at least for the most part) independent of the human mind,
2) *semantic* realism: truth is a semantic relation between language and reality, as depicted in, for instance, Alfred Tarski's correspondence theory of truth,
3) *epistemological* realism: reliable knowledge of the world can be attained,
4) realism in *scientific theory construction* and *concept formation*: properties of truth and falsity are applicable to the outcomes reached by scientific research language, such as descriptions, laws, and scientific theories,
5) *methodological* realism: there exist the best methods for pursuing knowledge,
6) *axiological* realism: truth is one of the aims of philosophical or scientific enquiry, and
7) *ethical* realism: moral values exist in reality.

The varieties of scientific realism would seem to some extent overlap with each other. Yet, all types of scientific realism presume a common, shared commitment to the grounding premises of *ontological* realism: without the presumed existence of a mind-independent reality there could not be realism of a semantic, epistemological, scientific, methodological, axiological, or ethical kind, either.

A) *Ontological realism* defines reality – at least for the most part – as independent from the contents of any individual human mind. The existence of the phenomena in the world is not contingent on whether they are the subject matter of

[1] On the varieties of philosophical realism, Niiniluoto, *Critical Scientific Realism*, pp. 2–13. Cf. Pihlström, *Tutkiiko tiede todellisuutta?*, pp. 30–66, 72–73.

R. Siltala, *Law, Truth, and Reason*, Law and Philosophy Library 97,
DOI 10.1007/978-94-007-1872-2_7,

the human consciousness, i.e. the sense data, recollections, or some other mental states of mind of someone, at a given moment of time. Tables and chairs, forks and knives, rocks and stones are trivial examples of the common, domestic entities acknowledged by a realistic ontology. Similarly, the planets, stars, galaxies, pulsars, white dwarfs, black holes, magnetic fields, radioactive radiation, and the like phenomena make up the "furniture of the world" in the field of macro-scale astronomy and physics. *Institutional* facts are far more enigmatic in this regard, since their existence depends on the presence of certain conventions in the community, defined as the shared expectations (Lewis), "we-intentionality" in the sense of collective acceptance or recognition of certain phenomena (Searle), mutual expectations (Lagerspetz), or the combination of mutual expectations and cooperative dispositions (den Hartogh) among the members of the community vis-à-vis certain phenomena.

Similarly, the idea of there being commonly shared things, entities, or artefacts that have been initiated by an individual human mind but have subsequently been "objectified" in the sense of having gained independence from the contents of any human mind belong to the realm of conventional facts. They dwell in what the Austrian philosopher Karl Popper (1902–1994) called the *Third World* as part of his three-partite ontological scheme. According to Popper, the *Third World* of objectified ideas and cultural artefacts is to be distinguished both from the *First World* of physical objects or physical states and from the *Second World* of mental states or states of individual human consciousness.[2] The entities of the *Third World* entail, for instance, mathematical figures, scientific theories and symbols (Newton's theory of gravity, Einstein's general theory of relativity, Heisenberg's indeterminacy principle, the formula $E = mc^2$), works of art (Leonardo da Vinci's *Mona Lisa*, Michelangelo's *David*, Arvo Pärt's *Tabula Rasa*), monetary currencies, and legal institutions (marriages; contracts; valid wills; mortgages; the national constitution; the original Rome Treaty, as later modified by the Maastricht, Amsterdam, Nice, and Lisbon Treaties). The entities that dwell in Popper's *Third World* need not be ruled out of the domain of a realist ontology, though. Ilkka Niiniluoto, for one, has endorsed the existence of institutional, convention-bound facts as part of his realist conception of ontology.

B) *Semantic realism* defines the truth of a linguistic sentence or proposition as a relation of *correspondence* between the proposition and a phenomenon or state of affairs in the world external to language. Under the Tarskian premises, the sentence or proposition S_X, to the effect that "it is raining", is true if and only if it is raining. Similarly, the sentence or proposition S_Y, to the effect that "legal norm *n* is valid in the legal community LC", is true if and only if legal norm *n* is valid in the legal community LC. Under the Tarskian premises, the truth-value of a sentence or proposition is determined by comparing its propositional content to the corresponding state of affairs that either prevails or not in the reality,

[2] Popper, *Objective Knowledge*, p. 106 et seq.

i.e. whether it is raining and whether legal norm *n* is valid in the legal community LC in the two examples above.[3] Tarski's semantic realism of course rules out the alternatives to the correspondence theory of truth, such as the coherence theory and the pragmatist theories of truth.

C) *Epistemological realism* signifies the idea that reliable knowledge can be attained of reality by scientific means. A *critical* epistemological realist can be distinguished from a *naïve* one, in that the first, but not the second, acknowledges the fact that all human knowledge is conditional on the conceptual frame adopted and, as a consequence, can never be absolutely true or absolutely false but only true or false under the premises defined by the said frame.[4] In the context of law, the frame of analysis defines the logico-conceptual and epistemic preconditions of legal analysis. The criteria that define epistemological realism match well with those of ontological realism, realism in scientific theory construction and concept formation, and semantic realism as endorsed by the Tarskian correspondence theory of truth. As a consequence, epistemological realism ought to be kept apart from epistemological idealism, phenomenology, philosophical scepticism, and philosophical pragmatism, all of which deny the possibility of obtaining reliable knowledge of an objective, subject-independent reality.[5] Epistemological realism is compatible with scientific *fallibilism*, or the inherent self-corrective capacity of science.[6]

D) Realism in *scientific theory construction* and *concept formation* extends the quality of being true or false into scientific theories and the concepts entailed. As a consequence, theoretical concepts, such as positrons, quarks, and the spin-value of elementary particles in quantum physics, refer to actually existing "things", entities, or phenomena in reality, and so do their inherent properties and mutual relations that prevail among them. Scientific laws and generalizations, like Isaac Newton's classic theory of gravity and Albert Einstein's theory of relativity, are accordingly either true or false. Equally, realism in scientific theory construction renounces all *instrumentalist* criteria for the evaluation of truth in a scientific theory, to the effect that that the utility, success, or approval of a conception by the scientific community might serve as the criterion of its truth or validity. Also, it rejects scientific *descriptivism* to the effect that theoretical terms in science could be returned to or translated into terms of an empirical observation language. Under a realist notion of scientific theory construction and concept formation, a scientific theory is true, if and only if the laws and concepts it entails refer to the phenomena that actually exist in the reality; not if the theory is claimed to be efficient, economical, functional, or successful in

[3] On Tarski's theory of truth, Tarski, "The Concept of Truth in Formalized Languages"; Niiniluoto, *Critical Scientific Realism*, pp. 55–64; Pihlström, *Tutkiiko tiede todellisuutta?*, pp. 45–52.

[4] Pihlström, *Tutkiiko tiede todellisuutta?*, pp. 34–35.

[5] Pihlström, *Tutkiiko tiede todellisuutta?*, p. 35.

[6] According to Charles S. Peirce, the scientific method entails an element of *public justifiability* and *self-correctiveness*. Niiniluoto, *Johdatus tieteenfilosofiaan*, pp. 81–85; Peirce, *Johdatus tieteen logiikkaan ja muita kirjoituksia*, pp. 137–150; Siltala, *Oikeustieteen tieteenteoria*, pp. 469–471.

instrumentalist sense, nor if the theoretical terms it contains could be turned into empirical observation terms.

E) *Methodological realism* validates the best methods for attaining true insights of reality, in line with the grounding premises of ontological and epistemological realism, and realism in scientific theory construction and concept formation. The variations of methodological anti-realism, on the other hand, share a denial of such truth-aligned qualities of scientific theories, opting for other criteria for the evaluation of a scientific theory or methodology, such as the empirical adequacy of a theory by van Fraassen; the common acceptance of a scientific theory in the scientific community by Thomas S. Kuhn; or the pragmatic usefulness and effectiveness of a theory in the service of practical life by William James.[7]

F) *Axiological realism* in science puts forth the thesis that the pursuit of truth, or some notion analogical to truth, is the ultimate goal of all scientific research, at the cost of various kinds of instrumentalist or pragmatist goals.

G) Finally, *ethical realism* is committed to the idea that values have objective existence in reality, and not only as the contents of the human consciousness. Its inherent links to the theory of science are thinner than those of methodological or axiological realism.

7.2 Legal Realism, American and Scandinavian

Scientific realism can be defined by means of an overlapping set of criteria that define the qualities of an ontological, epistemological, semantic, methodological, axiological, and ethical realism, plus realism in scientific theory construction and concept formation. *Legal* realism, in turn, refers to a variety of approaches to the law that share certain "realistic" qualities, such as the *sociological school of law* in Europe and *sociological jurisprudence* in the United States, *American legal realism*, and *Scandinavian legal realism*. The various realist approaches to law share two tenets only: a *critique of legal formalism* and the idea of *law as a social fact*, and not a social or moral ideal.

Sociological jurisprudence, as advocated by Oliver Wendell Holmes, Jr. (1841–1935), Roscoe Pound (1870–1964), and John Chipman Gray (1839–1915) at the turn of the 20th century, to a great extent paved the way for the American realist movement. The methodological *credo* of the sociological movement boiled down to Pound's demand of replacing the barren *law in the books* of the traditional legal doctrine and the "Landellian orthodoxy" by the *law in action*, as found in the decisions given by the courts and other officials. *American legal realism* had its heyday in the mid-1920s to mid-1930s, with Jerome Frank (1889–1957), Karl N. Llewellyn (1893–1962), Walter Wheeler Cook (1873–1943), and Felix S. Cohen (1907–1953) as its key proponents. In the Nordic countries, *Scandinavian*

[7] Pihlström, *Tutkiiko tiede todellisuutta?*, pp. 57–58; Niiniluoto, *Critical Scientific Realism*, p. 160 et seq.

legal realism was a parallel realist and sociological phenomenon, as represented by Karl Olivecrona (1897–1980), Vilhelm Lundstedt (1882–1955), Per Olof Ekelöf (1906–1990), Torstein Eckhoff (1916–1993), and Alf Ross (1899–1979).[8]

Robert S. Summers has suggested the concise term *pragmatic instrumentalism* for the three intellectual movements of philosophical pragmatism, sociological jurisprudence, and legal realism in America,[9] but the term has not rooted in literature on jurisprudence.

As with the mutual relation of scientific positivism and legal positivism, the various facets of *legal realism* need not be committed to the basic tenets of fully-fledged *scientific realism*. What the diverse branches of legal realism have in common is a critical, detached stance as to all the schools and approaches to law with a non-realistic bent, viz. legal idealism as proffered by the natural law philosophy; analytical legal positivism with its emphasis on the historical will of the sovereign and the original intentions of the legislator under legal exegesis; and the excesses of legal formalism under the German or American constructivism.

The American schools of sociological jurisprudence and legal realism were heavily influenced by philosophical pragmatism, as embodied in the writings by Charles S. Peirce, William James, and John Dewey.[10] Scandinavian legal realism had a very different taste for philosophy, placing its focus on the theory of legal science, and not philosophical pragmatism. One of the key ideas cherished the Scandinavian realists was the effort of "saving" the legal science from the fierce attacks made by the famous Swedish philosopher Axel Hägerström (1868–1939). Idealistic metaphysics in all its manifestations, with the legal doctrine included, had been the main target of Hägerström's relentless, nihilistic critique directed at the philosophy of science. To Hägerström's mind, lawyers' belief in the existence of legal rights and duties was childish, or a sign of immaturity, since such assertions lacked semantic reference outside the wild imagination of the legal profession. According to Hägerström, assertions on, say, the legal right of ownership were to be rejected as instances of a totally senseless metaphysics.[11]

---

[8]A kind of legal realist program was pursued by the German Free Law movement, too, as represented by Oscar Bülow, Eugen Ehrlich, Hermann Kantorowicz, and Hermann Isay. Larenz, *Methodenlehre der Rechtswissenschaft*, pp. 59–62; Wieacker, *Privatrechtsgeschichte der Neuzeit*, pp. 579–581.

[9]Summers, *Instrumentalism and American Legal Theory*, pp. 19–26 (and pp. 22–23 in specific); Horwitz, *The Transformation of American Law 1870–1960*, p. 169 et seq.; Summers, ed., *American Legal Theory*; Golding, "Jurisprudence and Legal Philosophy in the Twentieth-Century America – Major Themes and Developments". Cf. also Tamanaha, *Beyond the Formalist–Realist Divide*, in which the ingenuity of the realist movement is strongly undermined.

[10]Summers, *Instrumentalism and American Legal Theory*; cf. Summers, ed., *American Legal Theory*; de Been, *Legal Realism Regained*, p. 177 et seq.

[11]On Scandinavian legal realism, Helin, *Lainoppi ja metafysiikka*, pp. 11–260. – *Praeterea censeo metaphysicam esse delendam* (i.e. "Besides, I think that metaphysics ought to be deleted"), as Hägerström's own nihilistic slogan sounded. Helin, *Lainoppi ja metafysiikka*, p. 32.

Analytical legal realism, as manifested by Alf Ross, looks upon the law and legal phenomena as a collection of social facts, and not social ideals. The *normative ideology* collectively and more-or-less uniformly internalized by the judges holds a key position in Ross' theory of law: it is by means of such knowledge that the constitutive premises of the judges' future legal decisions can – "with reasonable accuracy", as Ross put it – be predicted by the legal science.[12] The truth-value of any legal predictions is *approximate* and *probable* in kind only, and never absolutely certain, categorically true, or even in principle verifiable. If the judicial ideology goes through a change in content, all predictions made of the future course of adjudication need to be altered accordingly, but the judges seldom give any pre-warning of such intentions as they might have.

Ross' notion of the constitutive premises of legal science, when viewed in light of the *ontological*, *epistemological*, *semantic*, *methodological*, and *axiological* commitments of such research, plus the ones that define the elements of *scientific theory construction* and *concept formation*, would seem to seamlessly match with the philosophical commitments endorsed by scientific realism. The effected law in action at the courts and other legal officials provides legal science with a fixed reference against which its legal assertions can be evaluated. The idea of law as a social fact, and not a social ideal, corresponds to the ontic commitments of a realist philosophy of science, if institutional facts, too, are acknowledged in it.

Methodologically, legal realism has often entailed an empiricist or sociological approach to the law, where priority is given to the effected court practice, rather than any intentions originally held the legislator or the outcomes of legal analysis as produced by legal science.[13] The law in action is allowed to displace any law in the books,[14] whether conceived as ideal law, perfectly just law, formally valid law, or the law that was historically intended by the legislator but that may still lack any means of effective enforcement at the courts and other officials.

The qualities that constitute a realistic stance in *scientific theory construction* and *concept formation* are more difficult to classify vis-à-vis scientific realism *vs.* instrumentalism in Ross' theory, since the theoretical concepts involved, like the normative ideology collectively internalized by the judges, may be taken to refer to the phenomena that exist "out there", in line with scientific and philosophical *realism*, or as useful instruments of scientific (re)presentation and prediction only, in line with scientific and philosophical *instrumentalism*. In the former case, scientific concepts do obtain a specific truth-value according to the criteria laid down by

---

[12]In Danish: *den normative ideologi der besjæler dommeren*. Ross, *Om ret og retfærdighed*, p. 56. The term "judges" comprises all kinds of law-applying officials in Ross' theory of law.

[13]Ross refers to the idea of an empiricist approach in the preface to the English edition of *Om ret og retfærdighed*. Such an empiricist approach is not equal to scientific realism, though. Ross, *On Law and Justice*, p. IX. – Of the representatives of Scandinavian legal realism, Theodor Geiger had the strongest inclination towards a fully-fledged sociological approach to the law. Geiger, *Vorstudien zu einer Soziologie des Rechts*.

[14]The terms *law in the books* and *law in action* were coined by Roscoe Pound. Cf. Pound, "Law in Books and Law in Action", pp. 12–36.

the correspondence theory of truth. In the latter case, it is the utility and success of such theoretical concepts in the service of, say, predicting the future outcomes of legal adjudication that determine their worth in the science of law. The analytical and realist tradition in practical legal analysis in the Nordic countries greatly underscored the *functional* role of scientific concepts, inclining the analysis towards the instrumentalist tradition.

Ethical realism may perhaps be bypassed in the present context, except as having reference to such values in society that are able to draw institutional support in the court decisions and decisions given by other officials. In such a case we are dealing with the kinds of social values that have gained adequate ground in the institutional premises of law.

7.3 The Legacy of American Legal Realism

The most uncompromising of the American realists, Jerome Frank (1889–1957) was acquainted with, and inspired by, the use of psychology and psychoanalysis in explaining the legal discretion of the judge. He was a rule-sceptic, denying the existence of legal rules in advance of an individual judicial decision. The only thing that a legal scholar could have access to in predicting the outcome of any future judicial decisions was a set of prior judicial decisions in which the judges had reacted, in a certain manner, to the facts presented to them, along with the individual motives, ideological preferences and aversions, and psychological denials in the mind of the judge concerned. According to Frank's psychological and psychoanalytical insight, the lawyers' quest for absolute legal certainty and belief in the judge's infallibility inevitably bore witness of intellectual immaturity and a child-like yearning for fatherly authority.[15]

Yet, far more common among the realists than Frank's openly avowed rule-scepticism and even nihilism as to the existence of legal rules prior to a judicial decision was the tendency to highlight the inherently vague and underdetermined character of the law. The vehement critique by the realists against "mechanistic jurisprudence" was directed against Christopher Columbus Langdell's (1826–1906) and Joseph Beale's (1861–1943) highly formalist case method that had gained predominance in legal science and education during the latter part of the nineteenth century, carrying its impact over to the twentieth century.

The intellectual legacy of the sociological jurisprudence and the legal realist movement has left an imprint on at least the following tenets in subsequent jurisprudence.

For the first, Holmes' oracle-like prophecy of the future of legal science, to the effect that the future of legal analysis was reserved for "the man of statistics and the

[15] Frank, *Law and the Modern Mind*, pp. 259–269. – For a good account of the legal realists and their agenda, cf. Tamanaha, *Law as a Means to an End*, pp. 60–76. Cf. also Summers, *Instrumentalism and American Legal Theory*; Summers, ed., *American Legal Theory*.

master of economics",[16] would seem to have become true in the breakthrough of an *economic analysis of law* and similar strands of empirical legal research that leans methodologically on the social sciences in the twentieth century.[17] Novel fields of socio-legal enquiry have emerged, like the sociology of law, economic analysis of law, legal anthropology, legal statistics and the mathematics of social risk analysis. Such fields of socio-legal analysis bypass the research interest of technical legal analysis in the sense of *legal doctrine* (*Rechtsdogmatik*). Instead, they focus on the external effects and consequences of law in society (= legal sociology); economic efficiency and wealth maximization attained by legal regulation and effectiveness of the resulting recourse allocation in society (= economic analysis of law); or the analysis of law, social risks, and other legal phenomena by means of statistical and mathematical analysis (= legal statistics and social risk analysis).

The ever-persistent rumours concerning the death of traditional legal doctrine would seem to be premature, however, since there is, and will continue to be, a constant demand for the kind of knowledge in society that traditional legal doctrine is able to provide in terms of technical legal construction and analysis. No sociological or economic analysis of law will be able to answer the question of how to construct and read the law, even though the results obtained in sociological and economic analysis may well be utilized in legal doctrinal analysis.

For the second, Myres S. McDougal's (1906–1998) and Harold D. Lasswell's (1902–1979) idea of policy-oriented *configurative jurisprudence* would seem to bear the imprint of the realist tradition in legal analysis.[18] What is characteristic of McDougal's and Lasswell's model of legal research is the adoption of a *phase analysis* of the legal decision-making situation and its social context, representing the situation on a level of abstraction that best matches it and the social values and goals entailed.[19] Like the legal realists, McDougal and Lasswell sought for an alternative to legal formalism, bending the analysis towards philosophical pragmatism and instrumentalism. Also, the emphasis placed on law as a viable instrument of *social engineering* and the *de lege ferenda* reflections in the legal doctrine are in line with the realists' stance towards the law and society.

---

[16]Holmes, "The Path of the Law", p. 469. – According to Golding, the famous opening line in Holmes' *The Common Law*, to the effect that "The life of the law has not been logic; it has been experience." was openly targeted at Langdell. Golding, "Jurisprudence and Legal Philosophy in the Twentieth-Century America – Major Themes and Developments", p. 442; Holmes even coined Langdell "the greatest living legal theologian" of the time. Tamanaha, *Law as a Means to an End*, p. 64, note 24, citing Holmes' Book Review of the Second Edition of Langdell's Casebook, in 14 *American Law Review* (1880).

[17]Schlegel, *American Legal Realism and Empirical Social Science*.

[18]The terms *jurisprudence of the policy sciences*, *policy-oriented jurisprudence*, *contemporary legal realism* and *the New Haven school* or *approach* have also been used of the said intellectual movement. Cf. Nagan and Willard, "Lasswell/McDougal Collaboration: Configurative Philosophy of Law", p. 481. The basic text of *configurative jurisprudence* is Lasswell and McDougal, *Jurisprudence for a Free Society. Studies in Law, Science and Policy*.

[19]Nagan and Willard, "Lasswell/McDougal Collaboration: Configurative Philosophy of Law", p. 482.

For the third, though the issue is far from uncontested, the *Critical Legal Studies* movement with its emphasis on the social and political commitments of the law, legal science, and legal education has carried on the agenda of the realists. In the 1970s and 1980s, the *Crits* launched a fierce critique of the traditional conception of the law. The *Crits* sought to bring law back its true political premises, stripping the law bare from any false validity ground outside the realm of the political. They greatly underscored the inherently vague character of all law, denying in open terms the Dworkinian or other pretensions of having access to a one right answer to a legal dispute. In their crusade against legal formalism, the *Crits* would seem to have taken up the torch lit up by the most cynical of the realists, Jerome Frank, the famous rule-sceptic, and the young Karl Llewellyn, for whom legal rules were nothing more than pretty playthings for those childish enough. Denying the political character of the law was the gravest of the many errors committed by traditional legal science. Roberto Mangabeira Unger's *False Necessity* is a good example of the CLS endeavours in which the law is seen as part of politics pure and simple[20]:

> *False Necessity* (. . .) carries to extremes the thesis that everything in society is politics, mere politics, and then draws out of this seemingly negativistic and paradoxical idea a detailed understanding of social life.

In all this, the *Crits* no doubt provide a "nightmarish" account of law for the standards legal positivists, such as H. L. A. Hart.[21] From a methodological point of view, the CLS approach is (or perhaps: was) characterized by its all-embracing syncretism, internal fragmentation into ever-smaller pockets as preferred approaches to the law, and the opting for sheer methodological anarchism and eclecticism in legal analysis. Duncan Kennedy's methodological reflection in his *A Critique of Adjudication* is a good example thereof[22]:

> This book is methodologically eclectic. It uses concepts, techniques, and models of performance drawn from technical legal analysis, jurisprudence, neo-Marxism, Weberian sociology, semiotics and structuralism, psychoanalysis, historicist narration, Lewinian field theory, phenomenology, modernist fiction, and deconstruction.

---

[20]Unger, *False Necessity*, p. 1. – Cf. Thomas Morawetz' use of Duncan Kennedy's happy phrase, to the effect that the law is steeped with *politics all the way down*. Morawetz, "Law as Experience: The Internal Aspect of Law", p. 218. Cf. also Kennedy, "Freedom and Constraint in Adjudication: A Critical Phenomenology", passim. Kennedy makes use of the acronymic expression HIWTCO, or "how-I-want-to-come-out", with reference to the essentially idiosyncratic, non-legal motives and strategies guiding the judge's or other legal official's legal decision-making. Kennedy, "Freedom and Constraint in Adjudication: A Critical Phenomenology", p. 548 et seq. Cf. Kennedy, *A Critique of Adjudication*, passim; Kairys, ed., *The Politics of Law. A Progressive Critique*, passim. – Martti Koskenniemi's fine book, *From Apology to Utopia. The Structure of International Legal Argument*, applies a thoroughly CLS-spirited methodological (but not necessarily very Derridean) conception of deconstruction to the structures of argumentation in international law.

[21]Cf. Hart, *Essays in Jurisprudence and Philosophy*, pp. 123–144 ("American Jurisprudence through English Eyes: The Nightmare and the Noble Dream"). Hart, however, did not deal with the nihilistic agenda of the *Crits* in his essay. For Hart, the nightmare vision of law was represented by the American legal realists who yet were more moderate than the *Crits* in their critique of law.

[22]Kennedy, *A Critique of Adjudication*, p. 15.

Kennedy's methodological stance leads to obstinate philosophical dilemmas so soon as the theoretical consequences of the divergent and at least partly conflicting philosophical premises are fully unfolded. Moreover, despite any incantations to the contrary effect by the realists or the *Crits*, traditional legal analysis and doctrine is still "alive and kicking", as the (other) human and social sciences have not been able to oust it from the realm of scientific enquiry.

The like-minded, mutually converging nature of the two intellectual movements, the realists and the *Crits*, is far from non-contested, though. Wouter de Been has forcefully and, as far I can see, quire convincingly argued against the common conception that the overly nihilistic agenda of the *Crits* could be seen as a follow-up of the realists' sceptical stance towards the law and legal science.[23] To put it concisely: the realists put their faith in pragmatic instrumentalism and social engineering through the law; whereas the *Crits* believed in (almost) nothing and looked upon the law as part of the problem and not as a solution to the pertinent social issues. The legal realists endorsed a realist ontology, manifesting a rather commonsensical view of the law and society; while the *Crits* were committed to a free-wheeling constructivist option as to the issues of social ontology in line with the Marxists, the structuralists, or some other European school of philosophy as to the issues of social ontology. Finally, the basically optimistic, functionalist stance of the realists as to the attainment of social progress and the New Deal through the law has had to recede in the writings by the *Crits*, giving room for a pessimistic, defeatist conception of law as a radically autonomous, self-determined phenomenon that follows a logic of its own under the Marxist, the structuralist, the feminist, or other constitutive premises freely and eclectically borrowed from the Continental philosophical tradition.[24]

7.4 The Concept of A Judicial Ideology by Alf Ross, and the Rule of Recognition by H. L. A. Hart

Though H. L. A. Hart is commonly known as a key representative of analytical legal positivism in the footsteps of Hans Kelsen, Hart's definition of the rule of recognition as a collective, more or less uniformly shared commitment among the judges and other officials to a similar set of institutional and non-institutional legal sources draws his theory of law rather close to Alf Ross' analytical legal realism.[25] Concerning the rule of recognition in a modern legal system Hart writes as follows[26]:

[23] de Been, *Legal Realism Regained.*

[24] A good comparison of the legal realists and the *Crits* is found in de Been, *Legal Realism Regained*, p. 177.

[25] There is, however, the much criticized and, so it seems, mostly unwarranted reference to the methodology of descriptive sociology in the Preface to Hart's book. Hart, *The Concept of Law* (1961), p. V.

[26] Hart, *The Concept of Law* (1961), p. 98.

> In a modern legal system where there are a variety of "sources" of law, the rule of recognition is correspondingly more complex: the criteria for identifying the law are multiple and commonly include a written constitution, enactment by a legislature, and judicial precedents. In most cases, provision is made for possible conflict by ranking these criteria in an order of relative subordination and primacy.

In a legal system the boundaries of which are drawn by reference to the rule of recognition, the judges and private citizens alike are able to identify the valid rules of law and draw them apart from all that is not law. According to the legal realists, a legal order may comprise various kinds of legal norms, such as legal rules and legal principles, on the condition that they are entailed in the *normative ideology collectively internalized by the judiciary* (Ross)[27] or are identified by the *rule of recognition* collectively adopted by the judges and other law-applying officials (Hart).[28]

Ross' judicial ideology entails the institutional and societal sources of law, along with the criteria of legal decision-making that may be inferred from them through legal argumentation.[29] According to Ross, the range of legal source material available to the judge varies from fully complete, "hard-and-fast" legal rules that can be applied to a case in a straightforward manner to the various kinds of incomplete, "yet-to-be-formed" legal arguments that only provide some general guidelines for the judge's legal discretion, so that the judge will then need to formulate an exact rule of law for the case at hand by drawing on such less-than-complete material.[30]

In Ronald Dworkin's later terminology one could speak of legal *rules*, identified by their formal source of origin in legislation or jurisdiction, on the one hand, and legal *principles*, policies and other sorts of standards that enjoy possibly only oblique but still legally adequate institutional support and sense of approval in the legal community, on the other.[31] What they have in common is the normative pressure they exert upon the judge's or other official's legal discretion. Unlike Dworkin's coherence-seeking conception of law under the law in integrity, neither Ross nor Hart make any claims as to seeking to enforce a highly coherent legal narrative in the course of the judge's legal decision-making.[32] Rather, case-to-case bound reasoning will do, if it stays in line with the prevalent judicial ideology or rule of

---

[27] Ross, *Om ret og retfærdighed*, p. 56: "Retsvidenskaben beskæftiger sig med den normative ideologi der besjæler dommeren."

[28] On H. L. A. Hart's legal philosophy, Hart, *The Concept of Law* (1961); Lacey, *A Life of H. L. A. Hart: The Nightmare and the Noble Dream*.

[29] "... at man ved retskilderne forstår indbegrebet af de faktorer der øver indflydelse på dommerens formulering af den regel hvorpå han baserar sin afgørelse", Ross, *Om ret og retfærdighed*, p. 56.

[30] "... fra sådanne tilfælde, i hvilke kilden præsterer dommeren en fuldt færdig retsregel der blot overtages af dommeren til sådanne tilfælde, i hvilke kilden ikke byder dommeren andet og mere ond visse inspirerende ideer ud fra hvilke han selv formulerer den regel han har brug for." Ross, *Om ret og retfærdighed*, p. 56.

[31] "... in those hard cases ... [lawyers] make use of standards that do not function as rules, but operate differently as principles, policies and other sorts of standards." Dworkin, *Taking Rights Seriously*, p. 22.

[32] "Law as integrity ask judges to assume, so far as this is possible, that the law is structured by a *coherent set of principles* about justice and fairness and procedural due process, and it asks them

recognition adopted by the judiciary. If the prevalent judicial ideology (à la Ross) or the rule of recognition (à la Hart) is taken to entail such systemic elements, as well, the situation is of course different.

In light of Robert S. Summers' conception of legal formality, we may speak of the different levels of legal *formality* that is manifested by legal rules and legal principles, respectively. Legal rules are inherently *formal* legal arguments, detached and at least nominally cut off from the social values they were deemed to exemplify and promote in society at the time when they were enacted by the legislator or enforced by a court or other official. Legal principles, in turn, are no more than *weakly formal* legal arguments that, by force of their definition, have retained their intertwinement with the particular values they exemplify and seek to promote in society.[33]

According to Ross, any legal assertions on how to construct and read the law are *predictions* of future court decisions, based on the legal source material available for the legal scholar. As such, legal predictions can never be absolutely certain or absolutely true but more or less probable only as to their epistemic status.[34] The common judicial ideology among the judges provides a reference with which such legal predictions can first of all be made and then be critically evaluated. If the constitutive premises of the prevalent judicial ideology are not altered in an unexpected manner, a legal scholar may produce legal sentences that, according to Ross, are "with considerable certainty" true[35]:

---

to enforce these in the fresh cases that come before them, so that each person's situation is fair and just according to the same standards." Dworkin, *Law's Empire*, p. 243. (Italics added).

[33]Despite the differences in terminology, i.e. legal rules and principles in Dworkin and the different levels of legal formality in Summers, the subject matter is more or less the same in the both, even though Dworkin and Summers do not have any cross-references to the other scholar's theory of law. A parallel reading of Dworkin and Summers can be found in Siltala, *A Theory of Precedent*, pp. 49–54.

[34]"Når den retsvidenskabelige påstand om, at en vis regel er gældende dansk ret, som påvist efter sit realindhold er en forudsigelse om reglens anveldelse i fremtidige retsafgørelser, følger heraf, at sådanne påstande aldrig kan gøre krav på absolut sikkerhed, men kun kan hævdes med *større eller mindre sandsynlighed*, alt efter styrken af de holdepunkter, fremtidskalkulationerne hviler på. Sandsyndlighedsværdien kan variere over hele feltet lige fra praktisk vished og ned til værdier omkring 0,5. Der kommer herved en relativitet ind i retsvidenskabelige sætninger, som det er vigtigt at have for øje, men som altfor ofte overses. (...) I virkeligheden er påstanden om, at en regel er gældende ret, noget højst relativt. Om man vil, kan man også sige, at en *regel kan være gældende ret i højere eller mindre grad varierende med den grad af sandsynlighed, hvormed det kan forudsiges, at den vil finde anvendelse*." Ross, *Om ret og retfærdighed*, s. 58. (Italics in original.)

[35]"Retsvidenskaben beskæftiger sig med *den normative ideologi der besjæler dommeren.* Kendskab til denne ideologi (og dens tolkning) sætter os derfor i stand til *med betydelig sikkerhed* at forudberegne det retsgrundlag, hvorpå visse fremtidige afgørelser vil blive truffet, og som altså vill figurere i domspræmisserne." Ross, *Om ret og retfærdighed*, pp. 56–57. (Italics added; translation by the present author.) – On the inherently collective character of the judges' normative ideology, cf.: "Det er i det foregående talt snart om "dommeren", snart om "domstolene". Forudsætningen for, at man kan operere med begrebet "dansk ret" som et for det hele retssamfund fælles, identisk system er, at de individuelt forskellige dommere besjæles af en fælles,

> Legal science deals with the *normative ideology internalized by the judge*. Knowledge of that ideology (and its interpretation) places us in a position to predict, *with considerable certainty*, the legal grounds upon which certain future [court] decisions will be based, and which will be part of the normative premises of those decisions.

Ross' notion of the *normative ideology internalized by the judge* may comprise both legal rules and legal principles, on the condition that they are part of the normative ideology adopted by the judges and other officials. As such, the concept of a judicial ideology is entirely neutral as to the content it may have in a legal system.

H. L. A. Hart, in turn, defines the concept of law with reference to the ultimate *rule of recognition* in the legal system, in the sense of a set of institutional and non-institutional, or societal, sources of law generally acknowledged by the judges and other officials in their task of identifying the valid legal rules. In Hart's *The Concept of Law*, legal principles are at least *prima facie* excluded from the domain of law, since they cannot be identified by reference to their formal source of origin only, as is required in Hart's jurisprudence.[36]

The question whether the norms of *legal methodology*, i.e. the meta-level rules and principles of legal argumentation that guide the judge's and legal scholar's process of legal construction and interpretation, is part of Ross' judicial ideology and Hart's rule of recognition, cannot be answered by a simple yes or no. It seems that Ross' idea of the prevalent judicial ideology could be read so as to comprise the meta-level norms of legal reasoning, too. According to Ross, it is the task given to the legal science to predict the course of future court decisions "with considerable accuracy", as he put it, by having recourse to the judicial ideology among the judges and other legal officials. Without such knowledge, the success of legal predictions would be very low, which would seem to strike the balance in favour of a more permissive reading of Ross' theory, even though Ross did not address the issue directly.

In comparison, Hart's rule of recognition is more closely tied up with the issues of an institutional epistemology of law, as distinguished from the issues of legal

---

overindividuel ideologi, og at det derfor kommer ud på et, om man refererer til "dommeren" eller til "domstolene". Retten er et socialt, d.v.s. overindividuelt fænomen. I det omfang, den enkelte dommer motiveres af særegen ideosynkrasi, henregnes denne ikke til "dansk ret" – selv om den naturligvis ligefuldt er en faktor der må tages i betragtning af den der er interesseret i at forudkalkulere en konkret retsafgørelse." Ross, *Om ret og retfærdighed*, pp. 48–49.

[36]Nonetheless, Hart does make a reference to the case where the rule of recognition may indeed include content-bound elements, in addition to purely formal criteria, related to the source of origin of a legal source or argument. The possibility of such content-bound elements has the effect of turning his theory of law into one of *inclusive*, or *soft*, legal positivism. "In some systems, as in the United States, the ultimate criteria of legal validity explicitly incorporate principles of justice or substantive moral values; in other systems, as in England, where there are no formal restrictions on the competence of the supreme legislature, its legislation may yet no less scrupulously conform to justice or morality." Hart, *The Concept of Law* (1961), p. 199. If such is the case, there is no obstacle – at least "in principle" – of taking legal principles in Hart's rule of recognition as well. Cf. Hart, *The Concept of Law* (1994), p. 250, where Hart's reply to Dworkin's criticism of his rule-bound theory is posthumously presented.

methodology, since the rule of recognition would not seem to have any significant impact on the methods to be adopted in legal reasoning. In general, issues of legal interpretation are touched upon only in the passing in Hart's *The Concept of Law*[37]; whereas Ross devotes far more concern to the topics of methodology under the prediction theory of law. Still, even Hart's theory of law presupposes the presence of relative uniformity of the court praxis vis-à-vis the commonly acknowledged sources of law in the legal community, brought into effect by the judges' shared commitment to a similar rule of recognition. If there were not a relatively common conception of the models of legal reasoning among the judges, there could be no uniformity in legal praxis, either. As a consequence, it seems that Hart's rule of recognition, too, has to comprise some elements of legal reasoning, even if Hart did not directly address the issue himself.

Thus, it seems that Ross' notion of judicial ideology and Hart's master rule of recognition can both be read so as to comprise the norms of judicial *methodology*, too, in addition to the legal source material that constitutes the institutional *epistemology* of law. In Ross' theory, those methodological elements would entail both legal rules and legal principles, though Ross in 1953, when the first edition of *Om ret og retfærdighed* came out, of course could not make use of Dworkin's much later terminology of the "principles, policies and other sorts of standards"[38] that have a normative impact on the judge's legal decision-making. In Hart's theory, the few allusions made to the methodology of legal argumentation encompass legal rules only, since value-laden principles and standards of law do not satisfy the formal criteria laid down by the rule of recognition.

Issues concerning (the outcome of) legal systematics and (the process of) legal systematization are left quite untouched both by Ross' normative ideology of the judges and Hart's master rule of recognition, which is yet quite understandable. Rarely, if ever, do the judges aim at producing a specific outcome in terms of pure legal systematics, as detached from the issues of legal interpretation. The issues of legal systematics and legal systematization rather belong to the domain of legal science and legal analysis, and not that of judicial decision-making, even though legal interpretation entails an at least tacit conception of legal systematics in the sense of a complex priority order among the *rule/rule*, *principle/principle*, and *rule/principle* combinations in a legal system.

Alf Ross and H. L. A. Hart both make the assumption of an essentially *collective* and, at the same time, more or less *uniform* character of the master criterion used for the identification of law. By means of the judges' normative ideology (Ross) or the rule of recognition (Hart), the valid norms of a legal system can be identified and distinguished from all that is not law, such as the norms of social or political

[37] Cf. Hart, *The Concept of Law* (1961), pp. 120–132. There, Hart outlines the semantics of legal interpretation with reference to the *core of settled meanings*, on the one hand, where the meaning-content of law is unambiguous, and the *core of penumbra*, on the other, where several interpretation outcomes are equally possible. Cf. Hart, *The Concept of Law* (1961), pp. 200–201, where Hart briefly touches upon the issues of legal interpretation.

[38] Dworkin, *Taking Rights Seriously*, p. 22.

morality, societal etiquette, sports and play, arts and crafts, and religion.[39] Such a presupposition is not entirely unproblematic, but on a general level is seems to hold true: judges very rarely dispute as to whether an individual item of legislation or a precedent really counts as valid law. Thus, the criteria adopted for rule-identification would seem to a great extent converge among the judiciary. Hart points out that the question of whether some legal rule is valid law in the legal community is very rarely posited in express terms by the judges. According to Hart, that incontestable fact lends support to the stance that the rule of recognition actually fulfils its prime function as an operative criterion in unifying the methods of legal adjudication.[40] Like Ross, also Hart refers to the logico-conceptual truism that speaking of a legal system presupposes the essentially collective character of the criteria of recognition involved, since otherwise there could be no legal system in the first place.[41]

Alf Ross' idea that it is the task for legal science to produce legal predictions of future court decisions on the basis of the *normative ideology* internalized by the judges deviates from the more straightforwardly *behaviouristic* prediction theory that was advocated by the proponents of American legal realism and sociological jurisprudence. Thus, Oliver Wendell Holmes and the young Karl Llewellyn saw the issue in terms of "what the courts will do in fact", when faced with a certain kind of fact-situation. In Holmes-inspired American jurisprudence, the "black-letter" analysis of law was to recede, giving room for a variety of the novel human and social sciences of law. For Ross, it is not only the legal response of the judges to certain kind of behaviour or the psychological, statistical, or sociological laws investigated by the social sciences that shed light on the legal phenomena. Rather, it is a compound of the judges' *behaviour* in the context of the prior cases or precedents, to be studied by empirical means as provided by the social sciences, on the one hand,

---

[39]"... the rule of recognition exists only as *a complex, but normally concordant, practice of the courts, officials, and private persons in identifying the law by reference to certain criteria.* Its existence is a matter of fact." Hart, *The Concept of Law* (1961), p. 107. (Italics added.) – Cf. Hart, *The Concept of Law* (1961), p. 111 (italics added): "Here what is crucial is that there should be a *unified or shared official acceptance* of the rule of recognition containing the system's criteria of validity." – On Alf Ross' reflection on the collective nature of law and judicial ideology: "Det er i det foregående talt snart om "dommeren", snart om "domstolene". Forudsætningen for, at man kan operere med begrebet "dansk ret" som et for det hele retssamfund fælles, identisk system er, at de individuelt forskellige dommere besjæles af en fælles, *overindividuel ideologi*, og at det derfor kommer ud på et, om man refererer til "dommeren" eller til "domstolene". Retten er et *socialt*, d.v.s. *overindividuelt fænomen.* I det omfang, den enkelte dommer motiveres af særegen ideosynkrasi, henregnes denne ikke til "dansk ret" – selv om den naturligvis ligefuldt er en faktor der må tages i betragtning af den der er interesseret i at forudkalkulere en konkret retsafgørelse." Ross, *Om ret og retfærdighed*, pp. 48–49. (Italics added.)

[40]The question whether the judge's normative ideology or the rule of recognition, which draws the borderline between the law and the not-law, is itself *inside* or *outside* of the law cannot be answered by a straightforward yes or no. I have reflected on the ontological status of Kelsen's basic norm and Hart's rule of recognition in Siltala, *A Theory of Precedent*, pp. 221–229; Siltala, *Oikeustieteen tieteenteoria*, pp. 711–730. The argument of course applies *mutatis mutandis* to Ross' idea of the ultimate premises of the judicial ideology.

[41]Hart, *The Concept of Law* (1961), pp. 112–113.

and the judicial *ideology* that consists of more traditional legal material such as the sources of law, on the other, that are the essentials for Ross' theory of law.[42]

7.5 The Formal Validity and Efficient Enforcement of Law

Legal realism entails a realist epistemology of law, seeing the law and legal phenomena as empirically observable social facts, and not as a social or moral ideal. What is perhaps slightly disturbing is that legal realism is based on theoretical premises that cannot be justified with philosophical criteria provided by philosophical realism itself. When trying to answer the question of what will count as a legally qualified legislator, a court of justice, or other institutional authority endowed with the power to create, modify, enforce, or derogate the rules of law will necessitate having recourse to a set of valid rules in the field of constitutional law and the law of court organization and judicial procedure. They, in other words, cannot be identified by mere reference to Justice Holmes' dictum of "what the courts will do in fact". Rather, the Parliament, a court of justice, or a legal official is an *institutional fact*, the existence of which by necessity requires the formal validity – and not merely realism-aligned effectiveness – of a set of legal norms that define the legal constitution of the institution in question and the procedure to be followed in the parliament's act of law-making or, respectively, a set of legal norms that define the court structure and judicial procedure to be followed in the enforcement of law in courts.

Without first assuming the existence of such a normative frame of analysis, no judgment could be made concerning the validity of an item of legislation, a judicial precedent, or an administrative decision given by an administrative body in the legal system concerned.[43] Therefore, a realistic definition of law needs to be modified in a manner that entails a set of normative, constitutive qualities of law, as well:

> The law is the sum total of arguments, or reasons for judgment, that exert normative impact on the legal discretion of a judge or other official, as derived from the institutional and non-institutional, or societal, sources of law that can be identified with reference to the judicial ideology collectively and more or less uniformly internalized by the judiciary (Ross) or the rule of recognition commonly adopted by the judges and other legal officials (Hart). In addition, the concept of a legal system necessitates the validity of the rules of constitutional law and the law of court organization and judicial procedure, as defined by legal positivism (Kelsen) and not by analytical legal realism.

As a consequence, there are two kinds of constitutive elements, intertwined with each other even in the realism-aligned concept of law now under consideration, viz. the constitutive premises of *legal realism* that define the effected "law in action"

---

[42] Ross, *Om ret og retfærdighed*, pp. 41–66.

[43] Ross, *Towards a Realistic Jurisprudence*, pp. 61–62. Cf. Helin, *Lainoppi ja metafysiikka*, p. 143: "Like the concepts of a 'state', '[legally] competent organ', and 'sovereign', similarly a 'court of justice' and 'judge' are legally qualified concepts. (. . .) The law cannot be defined in an exhaustive manner by reference to the judge's behavior, since we already need to know something of the legal order so as to find out who is a judge." (Translation by the present author.)

of court decisions, as suggested by Alf Ross and H. L. A. Hart, and the constitutive premises of *legal positivism* that lay down the criteria for the validity of the norms of constitutional law and the law of court organization and court procedure, among others, as suggested by Hans Kelsen. A mere reference to the law in action of the effected court practice will leave the *legally qualified* status of the parliament, courts of justice and other law-applying officials unexplained. Taken individually, neither of the two is able to provide a satisfactory definition of law.

Without the effectiveness of the "law in action" at the courts of justice and other officials, as provided for by analytical legal realism, legal positivism would fall victim to the critique of upholding the validity of mere "paper rules" which, though valid in the formal sense, might lack the quality of being effectively enforced by the courts and other authorities. Even Kelsen with his urge toward methodological purity in legal science ultimately had to make such a concession, by making room for the overall effectiveness of the legal system (*im grossen und ganzen wirksam).*[44] But neither can analytical legal realism alone provide for an overarching definition of law, without at the same time presupposing the formal validity of constitutional law and that of the court organization and judicial procedure.

Summarizing, the interlocking character of law under the twin premises of (analytical) legal positivism and (analytical) legal realism can be presented as follows:

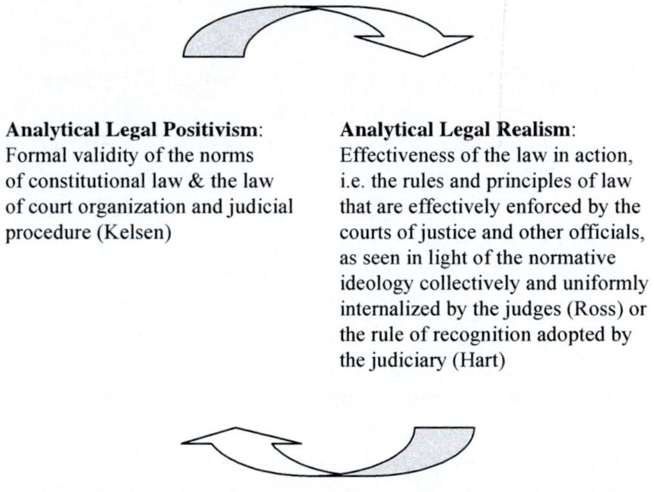

Diagram 7.1 Mutually interlocking relation of the formal validity of law under legal positivism and the effectiveness of the law in action under legal realism

[44] Kelsen, *Reine Rechtslehre* (1960), p. 219: "Eine Rechtsordnung wird als gültig angesehen, wenn ihre Normen *im grossen und ganzen* wirksam sind, das heiβt tatsächligt befolgt und angewendet werden. Und auch eine einzelne Rechtsnorm verliert ihrte Geltung nicht, wenn sie nur in einzelnen Fällen nicht wirksam ist, das heiβt nicht befolgt oder angewendet wird, obgleich sie befolgt und angewendet werden soll." Kelsen, *Reine Rechtslehre* (1960), p. 219. (Italics in original.) – Kelsen thereby rules out of consideration such individual *desuetude* cases in which a formally valid legal norm is not, for some reason or another, applied in the court practice.

In fact, Kelsen's legal normativism and Ross' analytical legal realism would each seek to provide an answer to a different kind of scientific enquiry. Kelsen's pure theory of law defines the constitutive criteria of what will count as law, and the line of reasoning is backward-looking and historical, in line the constitutive premises of law: how can the normative character or binding nature of the law be justified? The answer is anchored in the historically first constitution of a legal system with an unbroken tradition of legal constitutions, as supported by the transcendental-logical presupposition of the *Grundnorm*. Ross, on the other hand, delineates the issues of legal validity and legal interpretation with reference to the normative ideology internalized by the judges, and the line of reasoning is *forward-looking*, future-oriented, in line with the prediction theory of law: how can the semantic meaning-content of legal rules and other standards of law be determined for the cases to come?

Both scholars define the criteria of legal validity and the identification of the valid norms of a legal system, Kelsen with the transcendental-logical *Grundnorm* and Ross with the judicial ideology collectively adopted by the judiciary and other legal officials. Still, the question of legal interpretation is never properly tackled by Kelsen, who was happy to devote just a few pages to the issue, as a kind of *post scriptum*, at the very end of the second, 1960 edition of the *Reine Rechtslehre*. For Ross, on the other hand, the issues of how to construct and read the law are expressly tackled by means of the judge's normative ideology.

7.6 A Critical Evaluation of Analytical Legal Realism

Analytical legal realism defines law as the sum total of the rules and principles of law, along with the corresponding legal rights and duties allocated to individual legal subjects, that are *effectively enforced* by the courts of justice and other legal officials and that, because of the normative ideology collectively internalized by the judges (à la Ross) or the rule of recognition collectively adopted by the judiciary (à la Hart), will most probably continue to be so enforced in the near future, as well. The *law in action* as enforced by the courts of justice and other officials (à la Pound) now has priority over the law in the books, i.e. the law as originally intended by the legislator or subsequently "glossed" by the legal science.

Since individual court decisions are the fixed reference on how to construct and read the law under the Rossian premises, no *internal* critique of law is possible, except by having recourse to the claimed inherent integrity, well-settled nature, or presumed continuity of the court practice, when judged in light of the legal source doctrine and the models of legal construction and interpretation as commonly adopted by the courts and other officials. An *external* critique of law, on the other hand, is of course possible by reference to the criteria presented by the political morality in society or the natural law philosophy in general. One advantage of both analytical legal realism (à la Ross) and analytical legal positivism (à la Kelsen), when combined in the manner suggested above, is the achievement of conceptual clarity of the concept of law vis-à-vis anything that is not law, such as norms of political morality, religion, or societal etiquette. Another advantage of analytical legal positivism and analytical legal realism alike, when compared to social pragmatism or natural law philosophy, is that the *institutional* dimension of law is now duly taken into account.

Analytical legal realism is committed to a *realistic* ontology and epistemology. As a consequence, the law is defined as the totality of phenomena that dwell in the *world of facts* (*Sein*), i.e. individual legal decisions issued by the courts and other law-applying officials, rather than the totality of phenomena that inhabit the *world of ought* (*Sollen*), such as norms. Under such premises, the metaphysical "furniture of the world" is outlined so as to match with an empiricist frame of analysis. Here, the interlocking premises of analytical legal realism, on the one hand, and analytical legal positivism, on the other hand, vis-à-vis the definition of law ought to be kept in mind, though.

Under analytical legal realism, judicial decision-making power is vested at the courts of justice and other law-applying authorities. The courts of justice are no more than the "tip of the iceberg" in the field of jurisdiction, in the sense that they are not the only authorities that have power to shape the course and content of the law. In specific, there is a variety of *ombudsmen*, *arbitration boards*, and other authorities involved, such as (in Finland) the Parliamentary Ombudsman, the Chancellor of Justice, the Ombudsman of Minority Rights Protection, the Gender Equality Ombudsman, the Ombudsman of the Bankruptcy Issues, and the Data Protection Ombudsman, plus a host of official and semi-official arbitration boards and the like. All those officials are involved in the administration of justice, though each with a different legal or quasi-legal agenda. The normative impact of such decisions and resolutions to a great extent varies, too, ranging from mere recommendations to binding precepts of law. Moreover, their temporal directionality may vary, in the sense of whether they are taken as an evaluation of the past decisions only or as normative guidance for the future conduct of officials, too.[45]

[45]In Finland, Jaakko Jonkka, currently the Chancellor of Justice, has stressed that the decisions given by Chancellor of Justice, even if given as a response to a complaint made by an individual whose legal rights allegedly have been violated by some state official, are frequently "forward-looking" in character as well, endowed with the intention of guiding the future conduct of officials. Jonkka, "A Model for the Weighing and Balancing of Interest in the Prosecutor's Legal Discretion".

Chapter 8
Legal Conventionalism: Law as an Expression of Collective Intentionality

8.1 Brute Facts and Institutional Facts

A *convention* refers to a well-settled societal practice or usage that is commonly observed by the members of a community and utilized as a criterion of normative judgment, because it is *accepted* or *recognized* as having such a status by them. David Lewis (1941–2001) laid down the philosophical grounds of conventionalism in his treatise *Convention. A Philosophical Study* in 1969.[1] Conventions are expressive of *collective intentionality*, i.e. common acceptance or recognition in a community to the effect that certain social phenomena are endowed with legal significance or, alternatively, there exist mutual expectations to the said effect in the community. That "A knows that B knows that A knows that B knows that A knows (and so on, *ad infinitum*) that *x*", where *x* is some contingent belief or conception, accounts for the structure and configuration of collective intentionality under philosophical conventionalism. Conventions entail common beliefs concerning e.g. the value and use of the common currency (euro, dollar, yen) in economic transactions; international agreements made on the time-zones and calendar; customs related to various kinds of social events, situations and festivities; the norms of customary law, like the *lex mercatoria*; and so on.

The "things", or states of affairs, that philosophical conventionalism deals with can be divided into two categories: *brute facts* and *institutional facts*.[2] Brute facts are facts, or states of affairs,[3] the existence of which is not dependent on the human mind, human community, human language, or human culture. Brute facts consist of various kinds of physical or mental facts. They include such incontestable truths as the fact that the distance between the sun and the earth is (according to John Searle) ca. 93 million miles, that water (H_2O) freezes at the temperature of 0°C and boils at

[1]Lewis' book to a great extent leans on the insights of mathematical game theory.

[2]On brute facts and institutional facts, Searle, *Speech Acts. An Essay in the Philosophy of Language*, pp. 50–53; Searle, *The Construction of Social Reality*, pp. 27–29; Anscombe, "On Brute Facts".

[3]Following Ludwig Wittgenstein's linguistic usage, facts are actually prevalent states of affairs in the world, while states of affairs are merely possible configurations of various objects, their qualities and mutual relations.

R. Siltala, *Law, Truth, and Reason*, Law and Philosophy Library 97,
DOI 10.1007/978-94-007-1872-2_8,

100°C at the sea level air pressure, and that the gravity of a heavenly body can be defined in proportion to its mass and in inverse proportion to its distance from the point of observation.

The units of measurement in Searle's example, *Celsius* and *mile*, are based on institutional, not brute facts. An account given in sole terms of brute facts would only delineate there being an undefined, relatively long distance between the sun and the earth or the phenomenon that water freezes in some cold circumstances and boils in some relatively hot circumstances.

> What happened in the world of brute facts and the world of institutional facts, respectively, when the c. 2.500 scientists gathered for the *International Astronomical Union* (IAU) meeting in Prague in 2006 reached the resolution that Pluto would no longer qualify as a planet? *Being a planet* is an institutional qualification of a "thing", defined by the following three criteria: it must be in orbit around the Sun; it must be large enough that it takes on a nearly round shape; and it has cleared its orbit of other objects.[4] Pluto was disqualified as a planet because its elliptical orbit overlaps with that of Neptune. While the world of *brute facts* was not affected by the astronomers' decision, the rock called Pluto still revolving the sun out there; the world of *institutional facts* is decisively different ever since. Without Pluto, the number of planets that circulate the sun is now eight, not nine as it used to be with Pluto among the planets.

Since brute facts do not lean on the workings of the human mind for their being in the world, they would not cease to exist, if no one believed in their existence, if no one ever devoted her thoughts or unshared attention at them, and if no one ever presented an argument in favour of their existence. The existence of planets and stars, magnetic fields and forces of gravity, and black holes, white dwarfs and red giants as objects of astronomy, or the existence of more common household items, such as tables and chairs or forks and knives, refers to such brute facts that are quite independent from the intentions of individual human will or socio-cultural conventions.[5] The same goes for the inexistence of unicorns, dragons, the Ministry of Magic, and the *Hogwarts School of Witchcraft and Wizardry* outside of the world of fiction by J. K. Rowling.

Institutional facts are facts, or states of affairs, the existence of which is conditional on the fulfilment of certain preconditions of societal, cultural, linguistic, or legal kind. Institutional facts comprise a wide array of phenomena in society, such as the fact that full house defeats flush and straight flush defeats four of a kind in the game of poker; that the rook moves orthogonally and the bishop diagonally in the game of chess; that according to Chapter 10, Article 1 of the Finnish Act of Inheritance, a valid will requires the signature of two qualified witnesses who were both present at the occasion of making the will; and that the Court of the European

[4]"Pluto loses status as a planet", http://news.bbc.co.uk/2/hi/5282440.stm; broadcast on 24th Aug., 2006; visited on 27th Nov., 2006.

[5]Of course, the *naming* of planets, stars, and so on, as e.g. Jupiter, Saturn, or Betelgeuze is based on linguistic and scientific conventions in the community of astronomers, but that will not affect the argument made.

Union has the legal power to give a preliminary ruling on the validity and interpretation of EU law according to Article 234 of the EU Treaty, when such a request has been submitted to the Court by some national court of an EU Member State.[6]

> Linguistic and social philosophers commonly speak of institutional *facts*, and not of institutional "things", objects, or other metaphysical entities in the world – but why? Such a manner of speech is not very intuitive or self-evident, and the "man in the Clapham omnibus" or some other coinage of an average person would find such a linguistic usage odd. The reason for the fact-based manner of speech may have something to do with Ludwig Wittgenstein's ontological stance in *Tractatus Logico-Philosophicus*. For Wittgenstein, the (actually existing) facts in the world and the (merely possible) states of affairs in the reality were the basic constitutive elements of ontology. Individual "things", objects, or the like entities may enter the world only as part of a possible state of affairs, and not as freestanding entities as such, taken in isolation.[7] Similarly, the combination of "objects", their inherent properties and mutual relations into states of affairs seems to be the basic ontological category for institutional or conventional philosophy.

Institutional facts can be divided into the two categories of general and abstract *institutions*, such as the institutions of marriage, contract, and last will and testament under the norms of some legal order; and individual and particular *instances* of the former, such as the marriage between A and B, a particular contract reached by X and Y, or the last will and testament made by Z.[8] The institutions/instances dichotomy corresponds to the *type/token* distinction in linguistic philosophy. It also matches with John Rawls' original distinction between the *concept* and different *conceptions* of some social phenomenon, like democracy, justice, or the rule of law ideology.[9]

The terminology adopted by John R. Searle is slightly different from the one adopted here. Searle draws the distinction between the *constitutive rules* of e.g. the

---

[6]When the legislator makes use of some brute facts in an enactment or when a court of justice makes use of brute facts in a legal judgment, are we thereafter dealing with brute or institutional facts, when reference is made to the enactment or legal judgment concerned? Tables and chairs in someone's house and "tables" and "chairs" in legislation or legal judgment need not be the same thing.

[7]"... that objects and predicates enter into the world only as elements of facts, and that objects and predicates in isolation are unthinkable." Stenius, *Wittgenstein's* Tractatus, p. 25, 68. Cf. Wittgenstein, *Tractatus Logico-Philosophicus*, § 1.1.: "Die Welt ist die Gesamtheit der Tatsachen, nicht der Dinge."

[8]On the institutional character of law, MacCormick, *Rhetoric and the Rule of Law*, 63–68; MacCormick, *Institutions of Law*.

[9]Rawls wrote in "Two Concepts of Rules": "In this paper I want to show the importance of the distinction between justifying a practice and justifying a particular action falling under it. (...) one must distinguish between justifying a practice as a system of rules to be applied and enforced, and justifying a particular action which falls under these rules; utilitarian arguments are appropriate wrtih regard to to question about practices, while retributive arguments fit the application of particular rules to particular case." Rawls, *Collected Papers*, pp. 20, 22. – Rawls used the practice or institution of punishment as an example here. With the term "practice", he refers to "any sort of activity specified by a system of rules which defines offices, roles, moves, penalties, defenses, and so on, and which give the activity its structure". As examples thereof Rawls refers to games and rituals, trials, and parliaments. Rawls, "Two Concepts of Rules", p. 20, n. 1.

game of chess and the (mere) *conventions* of the game.[10] The constitutive rules of chess are, as the very term implies, constitutive of the game, defining its identity among the field of two-player games. The constitutive rules of chess incorporate e.g. the rule that the game ends in a checkmate or a draw. Moreover, the constitutive rules of chess qualify certain moves as legitimate in chess and certain pieces of the game as the king, the queen, a bishop, a rook, a knight, and a pawn, to be drawn apart from the legitimate moves and pieces of any other game, such as the checkers, mah jong, go, or the game of *quidditch* in Rowling's Harry Potter books. The conventions of chess, in turn, entail e.g. the fact that the king is usually larger in size than the pawn. Conventions are *arbitrary* in kind, whereas constitutive rules cannot be arbitrarily changed.[11] Regrettably Searle does not elaborate any further the distinction between the constitutive rules of a social practice and mere conventions in it.

Yet, the constitutive rules of chess or of any other game are or, at least, were at the time they were formed just as arbitrary and contingent in their substantive content as the mere conventions (in the sense suggested by Searle) of chess or of any other game are. The distinction between the constitutive rules and conventions of the game is therefore not watertight or intuitive as such. What is it that makes chess the game of chess? Would we still speak of the game of chess if it were played without the queen?, as Ludwig Wittgenstein notably pondered in his *Philosophical Investigations*. The idea of such logico-conceptual bonds that link social phenomena with certain constitutive rules is not entirely novel, though. In the 1920s, Hans Kelsen wrote that the concept of a *state* cannot be defined except by reference to the norms of (mainly) constitutional, administrative, and international law. The "state" is just a shorthand description for a set of legal norms, and there is no "organic" or otherwise "pre-existing" state outside the sphere of legal norms.[12]

A social *convention* can be defined as the outcome of an institutional fact and, in specific, the constitutive rules entailed in it. Social conventions are *institutional facts* defined by constitutive rules. According to Searle, the common form of an institutional fact is: "X counts as Y in context C".[13] Such constitutive rules define a *scheme* (or *frame*) of interpretation on how to construct and read certain social phenomena

---

[10] Alf Ross, too, made use of chess as an example of community-shared rules and the judge's internal point of view as to the law under the premises of Ross' analytical legal realism. Ross, *Om ret og retfærdighed*, pp. 22–28.

[11] "It is perhaps important to emphasize that I am discussing of *rules* and not *conventions*. It is a rule of chess that we win the game by checkmating the king. It is a *convention* of chess that the king is larger than a pawn. "Convention" implies arbitrariness, but constitutive rules in general are not in that sense arbitrary." Searle, *The Construction of Social Reality*, p. 28. (Italics in original.)

[12] Kelsen, *Der Soziologische und der juristische Staatsbegriff. Kritische Untersuchung des Verhältnisses von Staat und Recht.*

[13] Searle, *Speech Acts*, pp. 51–52: "[Institutional facts] are indeed facts; but their existence, unlike the existence of brute facts, presupposes the existence of certain human institutions. It is only given the institution of marriage that certain forms of behavior constitute Mr. Smith marrying Miss Jones. (...) These 'institutions' are systems of constitutive rules. Every institutional facts is underlain by (a system of) rule(s) of the form 'X counts as Y in context C'". – Cf. Searle, *The Construction of Social Reality*, pp. 28, 43–51. Cf. also Lagerspetz, *A Conventionalist Theory of Institutions*, p. 13; den Hartogh, *Mutual Expectations. A Conventionalist Theory of Law.*

in a certain social setting. It is only in light of *some* such frame of interpretation that some brute facts can be ascribed the status of an institutional fact. Thus, it is only with reference to the Finnish constitution taken as a scheme of interpretation that the speeches given and the votes cast from the moment of time (t_1) to (t_2) in the Plenary Session Hall of the Parliament of Finland can be given the status of an institutional fact: the Finnish Parliament assembled for the reading of a legislative bill. The norms of the (Finnish) constitution function as the frame of interpretation here. In addition, some institutional fact may be qualified anew by another legal act, yielding a novel reading of the original institutional fact in question. Such is the case when the legal composition of some institution is redefined or requalified in either legislation or jurisdiction, giving it a novel legal meaning.

8.2 The Definitional Characteristics of Institutional Facts by John R. Searle, with Special Concern for Self-Referentiality

In his *The Construction of Social Reality*, John R. Searle depicts institutional facts with the following six tenets[14]:

(1) many, but not all, social concepts are *self-referential*;
(2) institutional facts are often, but not always, created by explicit *performative utterances*, i.e. *speech acts*;
(3) *brute facts* are logically primary vis-à-vis institutional facts;
(4) institutional facts cannot exist in isolation but are always *interrelated*, i.e. part of a larger systemic whole;
(5) social *acts* and *processes* have logical priority over social objects and products; and
(6) there is a *linguistic* component in many, but not all, institutional facts.
Moreover, I would still add:
(7) institutional facts are based on *constitutive rules*.

Most of Searle's points are fairly obvious, if the conventionalist premises of analysis are taken at their face value in configuring language and the world. Searle, moreover, makes use of the distinction between the *types* and *tokens*, or *institutions* and *instances*, where the former refers to the general idea of some institutional fact, such as money, marriage, or right of ownership *in abstracto*; while the latter refers to some particular example of an institutional fact *in concreto*, such as the 10 euro note in my wallet at present or the marriage of A and B.[15]

[14] Searle, *The Construction of Social Reality*, pp. 32–37 et seq.

[15] On the *type/token* distinction with reference to money as a general social institution (= *type*) and money as individual bank notes and coins (= *token*), cf. Searle, *The Construction of Social Reality*, pp. 32–34, 53.

I will first consider Searle's points 2–6, and then point 1. Though Searle speaks of institutional facts in more general terms, I will use legal phenomena as prime examples of institutional facts here.

Institutional facts both in the sense of institutions *in abstracto* and their instances *in concreto* can be *created*, *altered* in content, and *abolished* by institutional speech acts endowed with *perlocutionary* force (= Searle's point 2).

As Searle points out, the presence of an express linguistic utterance is not the only, or even a necessary, precondition for the creation of an institutional fact.[16] In the context of law, the *institutional* sources of law do follow the logic of such linguistic perlocutionary utterances, as expressed by the legislator, courts of justice, other legal authorities, or legal subjects in the context of private law transactions; while the array of *societal* sources of law, such as customary law and the standards of professional legal ethics, do not need to be so expressed in order to have legal bearing. Tacit consent will do for the rules and principles of a customary origin. Even some convention-bound gesture may produce legal or social effects.[17]

Institutional facts logico-conceptually presuppose the existence of brute facts (= Searle's point 3), due to their inherently socio-cultural and linguistic character. The world of institutional facts is a kind of ontological upper-layer that is built upon the world of brute facts. Institutional facts dwell in Karl Popper's *Third World*, or the world of socio-cultural objects, as differentiated from the physical and mental phenomena of Popper's *First World* and the *Second World*, respectively.

According to Searle, an institutional fact cannot exist in isolation but only in co-existence with other facts (= Searle's point 4), being part of a larger systemic whole. It seems that at least part of those other facts need to be institutional, as well. For instance, the social institution of money requires a system of commerce for the exchange of goods and services in monetary terms, which in turn requires a system (or, rather, a notion) of property and legal ownership. Similarly, marriage as an institutional fact signifies an interlocking system of contractual relations, promises, and obligations among the married couple.

Searle's institutional ontology underscores the significance of social *processes* and social *acts*, and downgrades the impact of social *things* and social *products* as outcomes of such social acts or processes (= Searle's point 5). In the legal context, priority is thus given to the *power-conferring* norms and the use of legal *power* at the cost of the duty-imposing norms and the resulting fact of norm-observance or norm-breaking by the members of the community. The *dynamic* element of norm-creation and of legal power in general is stressed at the cost of the *static* elements of law, i.e. the resulting legal rights and duties brought into effect by the acts of legal will-formation. Still, as underscored by Hans Kelsen in his *Pure Theory of Law*, the

16 "... a very large number, though by no means all of [institutional facts], can be created by explicit performative utterances." Searle, *The Construction of Social Reality*, p. 34.

17 In the Roman Empire, the act of raising or lowering of the Emperor's thumb sealed the fate of a gladiator who had lost the fight in the arena. Such a gesture may be taken as a kind of institutional speech-act, as well, though there is no express linguistic utterance involved, but only the thumb gesture.

static and the dynamic approaches to the legal system are two equally legitimate points of view in legal analysis.

The inherently linguistic dimension of institutional facts (= Searle's point 6) is effortlessly incorporated in any conception of the legal institutions.[18]

It is only the *self-referential* character of social concepts and of institutional facts (= Searle's point 1) that is somewhat problematic in Searle's catalogue. By "self-referentiality" he refers to the fact that e.g. money as an institutional fact is based on the widely shared belief that certain objects, such as bank notes, coins, or their electronic substitutes, are commonly *believed to be,* or *used as,* or *regarded as* money by the members of the community.[19] A radical decrease in the common belief in the value of money, as in the hyperinflation in the Weimar Republic in the 1920s, would ultimately lead to the collapse of the whole monetary system and the withering away of the institutional character of bank notes and coins.[20] That is no doubt true, but I think we are not dealing with the phenomenon of self-referentiality now. Rather, the issue can better be explained as a set of *mutual expectations* among the members of the community vis-à-vis the monetary system and its specific manifestations.

In fact, Searle would seem to use the term *self-referentiality* in more or less the same sense as Eerik Lagerspetz uses the term *mutual expectations* and Govert den Hartogh the terms *mutual expectations* and *cooperative dispositions*.[21] At the back, there lies David Lewis' conventionalist philosophy.[22]

Viewed in light of Hans Kelsen's analytical jurisprudence, the notion of self-referentiality will find a more plausible field of application, but that will take us off the beaten track of Searle's philosophical conventionalism. As Kelsen wrote of the *self-constituting* character of modern positive law[23]:

---

[18]Merely tacit contractual or other arrangements are an exception thereto.

[19]"Logically speaking, the statement "A certain type of substance, x, is money" implies an indefinite inclusive disjunction of the form "x is used as money or x is regarded as money or x is believed to be money, etc." But that seems to have the consequence that the concept of money, the very definition of the word "money", is *self-referential*, because in order that a type of thing should satisfy the definition, in order that it should fall under the concept of money, it must be believed to be, or used as, or regarded as, etc., satisfying the definition." Searle, *The Construction of Social Reality*, p. 32. (Italics added.) – Cf. Lagerspetz, *A Conventionalist Theory of Institutions*, pp. 45–51.

[20]"If everybody stops believing it is money, it ceases to function as money, and eventually ceases to be money. (. . .) And what goes for money goes for elections, private property, wars, voting, promises, marriages, buying and selling, political offices, and so on." Searle, *The Construction of Social Reality*, p. 32.

[21]Lagerspetz, *A Conventionalist Theory of Institutions*; Lagerspetz, *The Opposite Mirrors. An Essay on the Conventionalist Theory of Institutions*; den Hartogh, *Mutual Expectations. A Conventionalist Theory of Law.*

[22]Lewis, *Convention*, passim.

[23]Kelsen, *Pure Theory of Law*, p. 71. – Cf.: "Denn es ist eine höchts bedeutsame Eigentümlichkeit des Rechts, daß es seine eigene Erzeugung und Anwendung regelt. Die Erzeugung der generellen Rechtsnormen, das ist das Verfahren der Gesetzgebung, ist durch die Verfassung geregelt, und formale oder Prozessgesetze regeln die Anwendung der materiellen Gesetze durch die Gerichte und Verwaltungsbehörden. Daher die den Rechtsprozess darstellenden Akte der Rechtserzeugung und Rechtsanwendung (die, wie wir gesehen werden, selbst auch Rechtserzeugung ist) für die

> For it is a most significant peculiarity of law that it regulates its own creation and application. The creation of the general legal norms – the process of legislation – is regulated by the constitution; the formal or procedural statutes regulate the application of the material statutes by the courts and administrative authorities. Therefore, the acts of law creation and law application that constitute the legal process are considered by legal cognition only to the extent that they form the content of legal norms – that they are determined by legal norms; hence the dynamic theory of law is also directed toward legal norms, namely toward those that regulate the creation and application of the law.

According to Kelsen, the basic norm (*Grundnorm*) is the necessary transcendental-logical precondition for identifying the norms of valid law and for distinguishing them from anything that is not law, whether it be the norms of religion, etiquette, or political morality in society.[24]

Niklas Luhmann (1927–1998) and Gunther Teubner have insightfully analysed the self-constitution of modern law with the notion of legal *autopoiesis*.[25] An autopoietic theory of law approves Kelsen's notion of legal self-constitution but refuses to acknowledge the basic norm as the ultimate ground of legal validity. According to Luhmann and Teubner, modern law is indeed *self-referential*, i.e. reflexive and autopoietic in character: the law exerts normatively binding force on the judge or other official, because it is an inherently *self-constituting, self-defining*, *self-regulating*, *self-legitimating*, and *self-justifying* phenomenon. The dilemma affecting Kelsen's pure theory of law and Luhmann's and Teubner's autopoietic conception of law alike is the one met with by Baron von Münchhausen in the German folktale: having fallen deep into the swamp, von Münchhausen lifted himself back onto the solid ground by pulling from his own hair. The critique of a *vicious circle* strikes with equal force any consistent account of legal positivism, if the validity of law is justified by reference to the criteria found in that legal system itself.

Since there is no external reference that could provide for the ultimate validity ground of law under analytical legal positivism, the analysis of the ultimate premises of law ends up either in a *logico-conceptual circle* ("constitution C_n is normatively binding, since it is legally valid") or, alternatively, in an *endless regress* to ever higher grounds of justification ("constitution C_n is normatively binding, since it derives its validity from the historically prior constitution $C_{(n-1)}$, and so on, *ad infinitum*"), i.e. the two options that Kelsen sought to evade by means of the basic

Rechtserkenntnis nur insofern in Betracht kommen, als sie den Inhalt von Rechtsnormen bilden, durch Rechtsnormen bestimmt sind; so daß auch die dynamische Rechtstheorie auf Rechtsnormen gerichtet is, und zwar auf jene, die die Erzeugung und Anwendung des Rechts regeln." Kelsen, *Reine Rechtslehre* (1960), p. 73.

[24]The idea of the legal *Stufenbau*, or the hierarchical structure of law, was initially suggested by Adolf Julius Merkl and then adopted by Kelsen. Cf. Merkl, "Das Recht im Lichte seiner Anwendung"; Merkl, "Das doppelte Rechtsanlitz. Eine Betrachtung aus der Erkenntnistheorie des Rechtes"; Merkl, "Prolegomena einer Theorie des rechtlichen Stufenbaues".

[25]Luhmann, *Das Recht der Gesellschaft*, p. 188 et seq.; Teubner, *Law as an Autopoietic System*, pp. 13–46; Teubner, "How the Law Thinks: Towards a Constructivist Epistemology in Law", passim.

norm[26] The price for such a move is paid in the *undefinability* of the basic norm itself on the *norm/fact* axis, and the same goes for Hart's rule of recognition or any other final reference of legal validity under self-referential, closed prerequisites of legal analysis.[27]

Nonetheless, legal conventionalism need not make a commitment to the criteria of semantic closure, self-referentiality, or self-constitution of social concepts and institutional facts, but mere common acceptance or recognition of certain social phenomena as legally significant will do. The issue is different as concerns the very *ultimate* criteria of such a closed, autonomous system of norms, values, or items of knowledge. The idea of law and social ethics based on the *a priori*, self-evident *basic values*, as argued by John Finnis in his *Natural Law and Natural Rights*,[28] need to be defined as closed vis-à-vis any external criteria of judgment, if they are taken as the ultimate reference for ethical or legal judgment. Similarly, a system of would-be knowledge in which epistemic uncertainty is ruled out by means of the postulated infallibility of some scientific or, say, religious authority may well fulfil the terms of systemic closure and inner consistency. The status of the ultimate premises of such a system of knowledge or values cannot be effectively questioned without falling victim to the two-horned dilemma of a vicious circle or endless regress (or both).

If the claimed self-referentiality of social concepts and institutional facts is left out of concern here, the other criteria specified by Searle would seem to suit well to the task.

8.3 Conventions as Mutual Expectations of the Members of a Community

The idea of conventions as a set of *mutual expectations* among the members of a community is grounded on David Lewis' widely influential book *Convention. A Philosophical Study*, published in 1969. In it, Lewis defined a convention as follows[29]:

> A regularity *R* in the behaviour of members of a population *P* when they are agents in a recurrent situation *S* is a *convention* if and only if it is true that, and it is common knowledge in *P* that, in almost any instance of *S* among members of *P*,
>
> (1) almost everyone conforms to *R*;
> (2) almost everyone expects almost everyone else to conform to *R*;
> (3) almost everyone has approximately the same preferences regarding all possible combinations of actions;

---

[26] Cf. Siltala, *A Theory of Precedent*, pp. 213–214.

[27] On the problematic ontology of the ultimate premises of law under (analytical) legal positivism, Siltala, *A Theory of Precedent*, pp. 229–231.

[28] Finnis, *Natural Law and Natural Rights*.

[29] Lewis, *Convention*, p. 78. That is the final definition of a convention. Preliminary versions are presented earlier in the book.

(4) almost everyone prefers that any one more conform to R, on condition that almost everyone conform to R;
(5) almost everyone would prefer that any one more conform to R', on condition that almost everyone conform to R',

where R' is some possible regularity in the behaviour of member of P in S, such that almost no one in almost any instance of S among members of P could conform both to R' and to R.

Lewis' idea of a convention set the pace for subsequent enquiries into the subject matter. In his treatise, Lewis contrasted the notion of convention with that of an agreement, social contracts, norms, rules, conformative behaviours, and mutual imitation. Lewis' approach is based on a *game-theoretical* model where the expectations of the other participants will affect the choices made by the one from whose point of view the issue is evaluated.

Later on, Eerik Lagerspetz has elaborated the concept of an institutional fact in explicit terms as a set of *mutual expectations* among the members of a community. In line with Searle's and Lewis' analysis above, he treats money, political legitimacy, and law as examples of conventional, institutional facts. According to Lagerspetz, the general form of mutual expectations or beliefs (= MB) is as follows[30]:

(MB′) It is mutually believed in a population S that *p* iff [i.e. if and only if]
(1) everyone in S believes that *p*;
(2) everyone in S believes that everyone in S believes that *p*; and so on *i* times, when *i* is the number of reiterations needed to describe the beliefs of the members in S ($2 \leq i < \infty$);
(i + 1) everyone in S believes that no one in S has any such beliefs of a higher order (> *i*) about the beliefs of the members of S which would have an effect on the behaviour of any member.

According to Lagerspetz, the general form of an institutional or conventional fact (= CF) is as follows[31]:

(CF) "*a* is *F*" expresses a conventional fact iff it is a necessary and a sufficient condition for *a*'s being *F* that
(1) it is a mutual belief in the relevant population S that *a* is *F*, and
(2) in the situations of the relevant type, (1) is at least partial reason for the members of S to perform actions which are meaningful because *a* is *F*.

[30] Lagerspetz, *A Conventionalist Theory of Institutions*, p. 18. (Italics added.)
[31] Lagerspetz, *A Conventionalist Theory of Institutions*, p. 19. (Italics added.)

The general form of a regulative rule (= R) is as follows[32]:

(R) R is a regulative rule in S if
(1) the members of S generally comply with R;
(2) there is a mutual belief in S that R is a regulative rule in S, and
(3) [point] (2) is at least a partial reason for [point] (1).

According to Lagerspetz, the general form of a definition rule (= DR) is as follows[33]:

(DR) R is a definition rule in S if
(1) the members of S generally count *a*'s as *F*'s;
(2) it is a mutual belief in S that there is a definition rule R in S which defines *a*'s as *F*'s, and
(3) [point] (2) is at least a partial reason for [point] (1).

Instead of a definition rule, one might use the more familiar term *constitutive* rule.

In addition, Lagerspetz gives the following rule of inference or rule of reasoning (= RR)[34]:

(RR) R is a rule in S if there is a rule R′ in S which defines R as a rule in S."

The three rules (R), (DR), and (RR), taken together, are a *necessary* and *sufficient condition* for the existence – or, perhaps rather, validity – of a rule in S. The term "exists" (or, again, "is valid") in S is, however, ambiguous in the legal context, since the existence (or validity) of a legal rule is a contested issue. There is, in other words, a host of mutually exclusive theories of legal validity, based on the *systemic validity* of a norm under legal positivism, *empirical efficacy* of the "law in action" under legal realism, and *axiological justice* of any would-be legal norms under natural law philosophy.[35] For Lagerspetz, social institutions are systems of existing, interlocked rules.[36]

Like Lagerspetz but adopting a less formal frame of analysis, the Dutch scholar Govert den Hartogh has defined conventionalism by the two intertwined criteria of *mutual expectations* and *cooperative dispositions* among the members of a community. Adding the element of cooperative dispositions to the notion of conventionalism would seem to have the effect of excluding from the realm of law the

---

[32]Lagerspetz, *A Conventionalist Theory of Institutions*, p. 22.

[33]Lagerspetz, *A Conventionalist Theory of Institutions*, p. 23. (Italics added.)

[34]Lagerspetz, *A Conventionalist Theory of Institutions*, p. 23.

[35]Wróblewski, *The Judicial Application of Law*, pp. 75–85; Aarnio, *The Rational as Reasonable*, pp. 33–46.

[36]Lagerspetz, *A Conventionalist Theory of Institutions*, p. 23.

disinterested "bad man" under Holmes' prediction theory of law. Holmes' potential law-breaker might well share a set of mutual expectations with the judges as to the contents of the law in force, but he certainly is not committed to the same cooperative dispositions with the judges. Quite on the contrary, the bad man resolutely breaks down any illusions of abiding by the law, which deviates from the idea of cooperative dispositions.

According to den Hartogh, the two ingredients of social conventions lean on and presuppose each other[37]:

> The conventionalist theory of obligatory norms I propose has two main components: patterns of *mutual expectations*, and *cooperative dispositions*. (...) I will argue that they have an internal reference to each other. Cooperative dispositions consist in being prepared to honour each other's justified expectations, and those expectations are justified by the existence of the dispositions. An important corollary of this fact is that the mutual expectations of the people participating in a social norm cannot have developed independently of any pre-existing expectations. Only if the pattern of expectations already exists in a general way, is it possible to form concrete expectations of behaviour in any particular case. (...) If this corollary is accepted, it follows that the conventionalist theory can only explain the maintenance of either conventions or norms, not their emergence.

Some of the conventions analysed by den Hartogh are *formal*, such as statutes and judicial decisions, and some are *informal*, such as customary law and legal principles. He then defines a system of law with the following four tenets[38]:

(a) a system of conventions, i.e. transparent patterns of *mutual expectations* of higher and lower orders, governing a significant part of the interactions of a group of people;
(b) a mutually known commitment to the *avoidance of* certain specific *suboptimal outcomes* as the mutually recognized point of the system;
(c) mutually ascribed *cooperative dispositions*; and
(d) the existence of one or more *formal conventions*: the mutual recognition of the authority to specify what the system requires (legislative and adjudicating authority).

Legal conventionalism requires a link to the institutional and non-institutional sources of law, as now read in light of their common acceptance or recognition in the community or the presence of a set of mutual expectations and cooperative dispositions to the said effect. The weight of emphasis is therefore on the non-institutional, societal tenets of law.

---

[37] den Hartogh, *Mutual Expectations*, p. 20. (Italics added.)

[38] den Hartogh, *Mutual Expectations*, pp. 220–221. (Italics added.)

8.4 Nominalism *vs.* Realism: Are Intentions Attributable to a Collective Agent as a Whole or to Its Individual Members Only?

Based on John R. Searle's linguistic philosophy, Dick Ruiter has criticized Eerik Lagerspetz' idea of reducing the collective intentionality of a community to the intentions held by the individual members of the community.[39] Ruiter and, quite independently of him, John Searle have defended the argument that a complete reduction of collective intentionality to the plurality of individual intentionalities involved cannot capture the truly *collective* character of the will-formation in an assembly or other collection of individuals. The collective intentionality of a soccer team or a symphony orchestra is claimed to be something more than, and different from, the sum total of the individual intentions held by the members of the group concerned.[40] The reasons given by Searle in support of his argument are not entirely convincing, though. In his mind, individual intentions, or *I intentionality* as Searle puts it, cannot be transformed into a *We intentionality* of a genuinely collective kind. Therefore, no reductive model of intentionality can truly grasp collective intentionality[41]:

> In my view all these efforts to reduce collective intentionality to individual intentionality fail. Collective intentionality is a biologically primitive phenomenon that cannot be reduced to or eliminated in favor of something else. Every attempt at reducing "We intentionality" to "I intentionality" that I have seen is subject to counterexamples. – There is a deep reason why collective intentionality cannot be reduced to individual intentionality. The problem with [me] believing that you believe that I believe, etc., and you believing that I believe that you believe, etc., is that it does not add up to a sense of *collectivity*. No set of "I Consciousness", even supplemented with beliefs, adds up to a "We Consciousness". The crucial element in collective intentionality is a sense of doing (wanting, believing, etc.) something together, and the individual intentionality that each person has is derived *from* the collective intentionality that they share.

The question whether to define intentionality in *individualist* or *collective* terms is ultimately based on a choice between *nominalist* and *realist* ontology. For the nominalist, the intentions held by the individuals who make up a symphony orchestra, a football team, a parliament, or a multi-membered court of justice is all there is in the world. As a consequence, there is no such thing as the collective intentionality of a symphony orchestra, a football team, a parliament, or a court of justice with several justices, but the intentions to be taken into account are equal to the sum total of the individual intentions of the subjects involved. For the realist, in turn, there exist

---

[39]Ruiter, *Legal Institutions*, p. 22.

[40]Ruiter, *Legal Institutions*, p. 22; Searle, *The Construction of Social Reality*, p. 24.

[41]Searle, *The Construction of Social Reality*, pp. 24–25. (Italics in original.) – Cf. also Tuomela, *The Philosophy of Social Practices. A Collective Acceptance View*; Tuomela, "Collective Acceptance, Social Institutions, and Social Reality"; Tuomela, "Collective Intentionality and Social Agents"; Tuomela, *The Philosophy of Sociality. The Shared Point of View*.

genuinely collective agents with a will-formation that surpasses that of its individual members.

However, Searle's argument as to the missing notion of *We intentionality* in the nominalist accounts of ontology is not entirely convincing. Being an ontological realist, Searle in effect *presupposes* and *postulates* the existence of collective intentionality, and denounces the nominalists for not doing so, while it is the very existence or non-existence of the said phenomenon that is at stake here. Searle's above characterization of collective intentionality as a "biologically primitive phenomenon that cannot be reduced to or eliminated in favour of something else" will not settle the issue without falling victim to a mistake of a *non sequitur* kind.

> But how could an assertion on philosophical ontology be tested, validated, corroborated, or proven true or false? Is the constitution of the world such as depicted by the nominalists or by the realists? As I see it, there is no legitimate way of testing an ontological assertion without committing a logical fallacy – for the simple reason (as the Argentinian author Jorge Luis Borges once pointed out) that we have no access to the reality "out there", without the intrusion of a host of logico-conceptual, epistemic, and other prerequisites that make up the prevalent world-view, with a certain conception of ontology entailed. Each assertion on the constitution of reality by necessity entails some (pre)ontological stance on "what there is" in the world. In other words, each ontological assertion begins with a tacit presupposition: "If we presuppose the validity of a realist, idealist, institutional (etc.) ontology, things are so-and-so in the world" or "On the condition that a realist, idealist, institutional (etc.) ontology is presumed, things are so-and-so in the world." The only criterion that can be applied to a system of ontology is its *internal consistency* or some meta-level criterion of philosophical parsimony, or the like standard.

The grounding choice between nominalism *vs.* realism cannot be resolved by recourse to some higher master criterion that would settle the issue once and for all. Rather, the issue necessitates a choice between two (or more) different grounding premises of philosophical analysis and configurations of a world-view. According to Ludwig Wittgenstein's philosophical stance in his *On Certainty*, any assertions on the ultimate constitution of reality or the ultimate prerequisites of knowledge fall outside the domain of human knowledge, reasonable doubt, and propositional truth-value, since they constitute the ultimate ground of a form of life, a system of pre-propositional "knowledge" that is silently presupposed in all assertions concerning the world, or the ultimate end points of philosophical argumentation.[42] As a consequence, the attributes of (being) true or false cannot be extended to such pre-propositional prerequisites of human knowledge. The concept of knowledge cannot be extended to the prerequisites of knowledge itself, as Georg Henrik von Wright pointed out.[43]

[42]Cf. Wittgenstein, *Philosophical Investigations – Philosophische Untersuchungen*, § 217 (p. 85/85e): "If I have exhausted the justifications I have reached the bedrock, and my spade in turned. Then I am inclined to say: 'This is simply what I do.'" – In *On Certainty*, Wittgenstein to a great extent followed the philosophical lead of G. E. Moore's line of argumentation.

[43]von Wright, "Wittgenstein varmuudesta", p. 19.

Still, there is a meta-level philosophical argument that lends indirect support to the nominalist position in ontology, viz. the *Ockham's razor* or the principle of parsimony in philosophical and scientific explanation. Reliance on Ockham's razor would seem to turn the scales in favour of nominalism, to the effect of giving philosophical priority to the option with fewer metaphysical commitments or postulates as to the "furniture of the world".

The contrary position in ontology may be backed by the *linguistic* argument that the idea of institutional authorities with collective will-formation frequently surfaces in the legal speech, and the lawyers seldom express any specific difficulties in participating in such discourse. Lawyers in other words commonly present arguments concerning the historically authentic intentions of the parliamentary legislator, as retraced in the text of an enactment and the *travaux préparatoires*, if any; judicial intentions held by a court of justice in the context of issuing a precedent or line of precedents; the corporate will-formation of a joint-stock company, as determined by the board of directors or similar organ; the will of an undistributed estate of a deceased person; and so on. The idea of such collective will-formation would seem to draw major support from the professional self-understanding and common manner of speech of the legal profession so that the intentions of the Parliament or a court of justice, as are traced in the respective legal source material, are detached from opinions held by the individual members of the parliament or by individual justices.

8.5 The Institutionally Qualified Character of Legal Conventions

Legal conventions may be either *formal* and *institutional* or *informal* and *customary* in character. Formal legal conventions have an institutional character, such as state treaties, the constitution, legislation, administrative regulations, precedents and other court decisions.[44] Informal conventions are of customary origin, such as *lex mercatoria*, the law of the Internet, and other norms of *transnational* origin; decisions given by private and semi-official arbitration boards in society; and the guidelines entailed in professional legal ethics and acknowledged standards of good legal practice among the legal profession.

Noel B. Reynolds and Thomas J. Lowery have divided legal conventions into *social conventions* and *customary practices*, depending on whether the members of a community consciously acknowledge some conduct as having conventional force, or whether they just tacitly accept it in their social practices.[45] Social conventions are consciously acknowledged in the community.[46] Customary practices, in turn, are based on a historically evolving tradition the conventional character of

[44]On formal legal conventions, den Hartogh, *Mutual Expectations*, pp. 113–116, 150–153.

[45]Reynolds and Lowery, "Convention and Custom", pp. 161–162.

[46]On the two concepts of "law as unconscious conventional custom" and "law as a conscious conventional creation of social norms, (...) deriving from all the people in particular society", Reynolds and Lowery, "Convention and Custom", p. 162.

which need not be consciously reflected in the community. Rather, such practices are based on a *tacit knowledge* that guides the conduct through silently adopted models. Tacit knowledge on law "is learned by doing (...) rather than by acquiring rules for doing it", according to Michael Polanyi.[47] Consciously adopted legal conventions à la Reynolds and Lowery are more or less equal to *formal* and *institutional* conventions, while tacit conventions are more or less the same as *informal* and *customary* conventions. Here, the focus is mostly on informal conventions, since formal conventions were treated above under analytical legal positivism.

Legal conventionalism differs from natural law philosophy in that the content of law is now seen as *contingent*, and not necessary, *a priori*, or prepostulated as in natural law philosophy. Whether motor vehicles are prescribed to use the right-hand or the left-hand side of the road in the road traffic legislation, and whether the First of May or the Ascension Day are national holidays or not – these are morally neutral issues settled by explicit legal conventions, and the content of such conventions is quite arbitrary.

Formal legal conventions might be turned into informal ones, though. Such is the case if, for instance, Hart's ultimate rule of recognition, taken as a commonly shared commitment among the judges and other officials to some criteria of legal rule-recognition, is deemed to exist because of a widely shared acceptance or recognition to the said effect among the judges, establishing a set of mutual expectations and cooperative dispositions towards convergent behaviour in their judicial decision-making.[48] Neil MacCormick's reading of Hart's master rule would seem to lend support to such a reading[49]:

> Since only a madman would frame and adopt such a standard [i.e. rule of recognition] without conscious animadversion to the standards he sees and understands others in a like position of responsibility to be using, there are strong reasons to expect a high degree of agreement and conformity among the judiciary in this matter – so that it is indeed not uncommon for the observer to be able to specify with reasonable accuracy the rule of recognition as it "exists" at a given time. (What is more, conformity tends to reproduce itself because of the pressure which it generates upon potential "mavericks", or indeed, to be cynical about it, because of the strong prudential reasons which those who run a system have for keeping it running on an agreed basis.)

Nonetheless, a fully consistent conventionalist reading of the legal phenomena fails to give a satisfactorily account of the *institutional* premises of modern law. In any Western legal system, arguments extracted from the institutional sources of law are

[47] Kuhn, *The Structure of Scientific Revolutions*, p. 191: "To borrow once more Michael Polanyi's useful phrase, what results from this process [of following paradigms as shared examples] is "tacit knowledge" which is learned by doing science rather than by acquiring rules for doing it."

[48] Hart, *The Concept of Law* (1961), p. 107: "... the rule of recognition exists only as a complex, but normally concordant, practice of the courts, officials, and private persons in identifying the law by reference to certain criteria. Its existence is a matter of fact."; Cf.: "The question whether a rule of recognition exists and what its content is, i.e. what the criteria of validity in any given legal system are, is regarded throughout this book as an empirical, though complex, question of fact." Hart, *The Concept of Law* (1961), p. 245 (note to p. 97).

[49] MacCormick, *Legal Reasoning and Legal Theory*, p. 241. – Cf. also MacCormick, *Institutions of Law*, pp. 56–57.

deemed as legally binding vis-à-vis the legal discretion of the judge, not because of a set of prevailing mutual expectations among the judiciary to the said effect, but because such arguments are seen to satisfy with the criteria of rule-identification with reference to the constitution, parliamentary legislation, precedents, and the *travaux préparatoires* in the legal system concerned. The institutional character of law is the primary reason for its legal validity, while the fact of the common criteria of rule-recognition (à la Hart) or a collective judicial ideology (à la Ross) is a derivative issue therefrom.

A mere reference to an existing collective acceptance or recognition of certain social facts among the judiciary or the legal profession will not qualify them as legal, if the *institutional* premises of law are not there to support such a claim. Hart's and Ross' moderately realist premises need to be supplemented by the ones derived from Kelsen's analytical jurisprudence so as to better grasp the institutional nature of law, as argued above.

Let us consider an example to illustrate the institutional linkage of conventional facts in the domain of law.

John F. Nash was awarded the Nobel Prize in economics in 1994 (together with John C. Harsanyi and Reinhard Selten) for his achievements in mathematical game theory already in the 1950s. Nash fell seriously ill for schizophrenia later in the 1950s and 1960s. During an early phase of his mental illness, when his ailing condition had not been diagnosed, nor was widely known among his peers at the University of Princeton, he was offered a professor's tenure in mathematics at the University of Chicago. The offer was considered genuinely attractive. To everyone's astonishment Nash turned down the offer, explaining that he had just been invited to become the Emperor of the Antarctic. At Princeton he also made the odd claim that in the cover of a recent *Life* magazine, where Pope John XIII was presented, it was in fact Nash who was being depicted. The reasons he gave for his conclusion failed to convince his listeners, though, when Nash explained his stance: unlike Pope John XIII, for whom "John" was the papal name attached to the high office, "John" was the true birthname of his. Besides, 23 had always been Nash's personal favourite among the primes. Therefore, the picture in the cover of the *Life* magazine entailed a coded message to Nash that only he could properly decipher.

If the Nash' delusions had in fact been acknowledged as valid by the community of mathematicians and scientists at the University of Princeton, satisfying the conventionalist criteria of there being common acceptance, recognition, or a set of mutual expectations to the said effect, would that fact have made Nash the Emperor of Antarctic? Absolutely not, unless the *institutional* preconditions for his claim were satisfied, as well. Without adequate institutional support found in the international state treaties on the legal status of the Antarctic, Nash' self-description would count as an instance of grand delusion only, irrespective of how widely his claims were in fact acknowledged or disproved among the members of the scientific community at Princeton. Thus, a mere reference to a set of mutual expectations existing in the community is not enough to guarantee the legal character of some social phenomenon, if the *institutional* premises at the back of the conception are not there to support the claim.

Thus, the term *institutional* obtains a slightly different meaning in general philosophy and in jurisprudence. In philosophy, an institutional fact refers to the presence of collective intentionality as common *acceptance* or *recognition* of certain social phenomena as having conventional significance. The terms *mutual expectations* and (possibly) *cooperative dispositions* can also be used, resulting in the line of reasoning: "A knows that B knows that A knows that B knows that A knows (and so on, *ad infinitum*) that *x*", where *x* is a contingent, collectively held belief or conception. In legal argumentation, an institutional fact refers (mainly) to formal conventions, in the sense of the social phenomena that are officially acknowledged as having legal force in the community, such as the constitution, legislation, the *travaux préparatoires*, precedents, and so on. The emphasis laid on such institutional sources of law at the cost of the non-institutional, or societal, ones in modern legal thinking understandably diminishes the use of conventionalist premises in legal analysis. Therefore, the roots of legal conventionalism need to be looked for in the writings by the historical school of law in the nineteenth century.

8.6 Shared Legal Convictions as an Expression of the *Volksgeist*, or the Spirit of the Nation, by Friedrich Carl von Savigny

The primacy of community-based customary law over formally valid enactments can be traced back to Friedrich Carl von Savigny (1779–1861), whose writings gave birth to the *historical school of law* in Germany. The origins of law were to be found in the organically evolving *spirit of the nation* (*Volksgeist*), and the *common legal consciousness* of the people (*die gemeinsame Rechtsüberzeugung des Volkes*) would guide the "organic" path of the law without any whimsical, capricious intrusions on part of the legislator. Savingy's notion of law was outlined in 1814 when his influential essay, "Vom Beruf unserer Zeit für Gesetzgebung und Rechtswissenschaft", came out. In it, Savigny fiercely criticized the legal codification ideology that had been influential in Austria and France.

According to Savigny, the French and Austrian idea of drafting would-be all-inclusive codifications in the various branches of law was grounded on false, mistaken premises as to the true nature of law. Instead of legal codifications, primacy was to be given to the authentic *legal convictions* that were prevalent among the members of the community concerned. Savigny's bold (re)definition of the concept of law had a profound impact on legal thinking in Germany at the nineteenth century, effectively challenging modern legal voluntarism at the back of the codification movement.[50] Now, Savigny set out on a mission to resist any demands for legal codification. His chief opponent in the intellectual strife concerning legal

[50] "Diese Konzeption musste in der Augenblick eine tiefgehende Veränderung erfahren, in dem Savigny – zuerst in der Schrift über "Beruf unserer Zeit" – nicht mehr das Gesetz, sondern die gemeinsame Rechtsüberzeugung des Volkes, den "Volksgeist", als die ursprüngliche Quelle allen Rechtes ansah." Larenz, *Methodenlehre der Rechtswissenschaft*, p. 13.

codification was Anton Friedrich Justus Thibaut (1774–1840). Thibaut had urged the codification of even the German law, so as to meet with the criteria that had been set up earlier in Austria and France.[51]

According to Savigny, the concept of law was to be attached to the *shared legal convictions* among the members of the legal community, as given expression in the well-settled usages of *customary law* in traditional legal systems and in the *lawyers' law* (*Juristenrecht*) or *law professors' law* (*Professorenrecht*) in the more sophisticated legal systems, i.e. law as conceived by the legal profession and the professors of law in specific.[52] It was the task of legal science to provide an analysis of the *common legal consciousness* in the legal community, given *in terms of legal institutes* (*Rechtsinstitute*) or *legal relations* (*Rechtsverhältnisse*) and the *organic systemic unity* (*organische Zusammenhang*) that was thought to prevail among such elements of law.[53] Moreover, a legal institute was deemed to be primary vis-à-vis any individual legal norms. Savigny's idea of the inner systemic unity of law and the primacy of legal institutes vis-à-vis any individual legal rules paved the way for Georg Friedrich Puchta's conceptualist notion of law at the latter half of the nineteenth century.[54]

8.7 The Transformations of Customary Law in Modern Society

For Friedrich Carl von Savigny, shared legal convictions in a legal community cover a wide range of material from customary law usages among lay persons to the instances of more specific *Juristenrecht* or *Professorenrecht* among the legal profession or some fraction of it. In modern law, emphasis is placed on the profession-bound tenets of law, at the cost of the legal conceptions held by ordinary people. *Customary law* comprises all well-established practices, habits, usages, and customs that are collectively deemed to have legal impact on some issue by the legal community at large or some branch of it.[55] It need not be consciously acknowledged to have such a position by the members of the legal community. Tacit acceptance

[51] On the intellectual strife on codification by Thibaut and Savigny, cf. *Thibaut und Savigny. Ihre Programmatische Schriften*. The book entails Thibaut's opening essay, "Über die Nothwendigkeit eines allgemeinen Bürgerlichen Rechts für Deutschland", and Savigny's response, "Vom Beruf unserer Zeit für Gesetzgebung und Rechtswissenschaft", along with other basic writing by the two prominent authors of the said intellectual strife.

[52] On Savigny's concept of law, Wieacker, *Privatrechtsgeschichte der Neuzeit*, pp. 381–399; Larenz, *Methodenlehre der Rechtswissenschaft*, pp. 11–18; Reimann, "Savigny, Friedrich Carl von (1779–1861)", pp. 772–773. – On Savigny's *Juristenrecht*, Larenz, *Methodenlehre der Rechtswissenschaft*, p. 392. – Savigny's first name is seen written with either *c* or *k* in different sources. Of the major commentators, Karl Larenz uses the form Friedrich Karl von Savigny, while Franz Wieacker uses the form Friedrich Carl von Savigny.

[53] On legal institutes and legal relations in Savigny, Wieacker, *Privatrechtsgeschichte der Neuzeit*, p. 398; Larenz, *Methodenlehre der Rechtswissenschaft*, pp. 14–15, 18.

[54] Larenz, *Methodenlehre der Rechtswissenschaft*, p. 15.

[55] Cf. Klami, "Tapaoikeus", pp. 1135–1137.

will do, but the legislator may have given express recognition to some such practices in the formally valid legislation.[56]

Sometimes the legislator quite deliberately leaves the more detailed regulation of some legal issue to be specified through the self-regulation of the group of individuals or institutions concerned, with reference to the "organically" evolving professional practices and semi-autonomous criteria entailed in the professional standards adopted. The settled norms, practices, and usages that guide the professional standard of *due diligence* in book keeping, accounting, and stock exchange are examples of professional self-regulation that is formally recognized in legislation. Since the breakthrough of modern codifications of law at the late eighteenth and early nineteenth century, the role of customary law has been in constant retreat in the Western world, however, providing no more than a supplementary source of law in cases where there is no legislation or settled precedent on the issue.

Due to the rapid pace of change in modern society, legislation tends to lag behind the needs of legal intervention. As a consequence, there will be gaps in the coverage of future cases by the statutes and precedents. Moreover, the normative impact of legislation may be evaded by the adoption of *arbitration clauses* of either substantive or procedural (or both) kind in the private law transactions. Arbitration clauses are favoured in business-to-business transactions because of their claimed advantages in terms of the swiftness, higher professional quality, and better confidentiality of the decisions thereby rendered, on the one hand, and because of the corresponding disadvantages of the normal judicial process, on the other, i.e. the non-predictable and non-expertise character of the ordinary courts when dealing with highly complicated issues in commercial transactions.

As to their normative function, customary norms are more affiliated to value-laden principles and standards of law than to clear-cut legal rules on three grounds. Firstly, the norms of customary origin cannot be initially created, subsequently altered in content, or ultimately derogated by an act of will of the legislator or a court of justice. Secondly, and related to the first point, customary norms cannot be identified by some formal criteria only, as exemplified by Hart's rule of recognition. As with legal principles, the criterion of enjoying (some kind of) institutional support and content-based sense of approval in the legal community in question is enough, to the effect that such conventional practices cannot be formalized or locked in a rule-like criterion without distorting the issue. Finally, customary law often cannot be captured in the form of a single, authentic, and authoritative linguistic formulation. Rather, the exact linguistic formulation of a legal custom may vary from one context of application to another.

[56]The normative impact of customary law is expressly acknowledged in Article 11 of Chapter 1 of the Finnish Act of Judicial Procedure: "The judge shall carefully consider the right grounds and purpose of the law and give the verdict accordingly, but not against it or according to his own mind. The customs of the land shall also be his guide in giving the verdict, if there is no legislation on the issue." (Translation by the present author.) The said article of the (Swedish and) Finnish law dates back to year 1734.

8.8 Legal Conventionalism and Legal Argumentation Theory

Legal conventionalism, as defined here with reference to the common acceptance or recognition of certain social phenomena as having legal significance or as a set of mutual expectations and cooperative dispositions among the members of the community, is primarily based on the role of *non-institutional*, societal, and community-aligned sources of law. Thus, it gives effect to customary law, such as *lex mercatoria*, and the *profession-specific* standards of good practice and due diligence in the various branches of law. The (semi-)autonomous self-regulation by some profession, such as the ethical guidelines of good professional practice adopted by the attorneys-at-law, book-keepers, auditors, and stock brokers, may have been officially acknowledged in legislation.

Rephrasing the issue in William James' philosophical pragmatism: what difference does it make as to our methods of constructing and reading the law, if the premises of philosophical conventionalism were fully extended to the field of law? According to Govert den Hartogh, conventionalist legal arguments entail[57]:

(1) the argument from the meaning of the legislative statement,
(2) the argument from subjective legislative intention,
(3) the argument from substantive values,
(4) the argument from principles,
(5) the argument from substantial conventions,
(6) the argument from analogy,
(7) the argument from precedent.

As such, they do not differ much from the types of argument that are recognized and given legal effect in the standard legal doctrine. In fact, a conventionalist approach to the law will not to any significant degree alter the method or the resulting outcomes of legal analysis, when compared to the conclusions attained by the *Bielefelder Kreis*, based on a combination of the premises of analytical legal positivism and the new rhetoric, as den Hartogh openly admits.[58] If the constitutive criteria of law, such as the rule of recognition in Hart's analytical jurisprudence, are read in a conventionalist manner, a conventionalist approach to the law may be taken as a subcategory of Hartian legal positivism with a dint of the new rhetoric à la Perelman and the *Bielefelder Kreis*.

The priority given to the non-institutional, societal, and community-created sources of law over the institutional ones under legal conventionalism, strictly defined, may prove hard to justify in a modern legal system. A set of institutional

[57] den Hartogh, *Mutual Expectations*, pp. 221–230.

[58] "This study [by the *Bielefelder Kreis*] resulted in a list very closely resembling the one I developed in this chapter. I take this to be a corroboration of the conventionalist account. Conventionalism can go beyond the mere enumeration of forms of legal argumentation, and provide an explanation of their use." den Hartogh, *Mutual Expectations*, p. 230. – Cf. MacCormick and Summers, eds., *Interpreting Statutes. A Comparative Study*, pp. 512–525.

premises in law, such as ratified state treaties, national constitution, statutes, administrative regulations, and precedents, are commonly identified as having primacy in a modern conception of law. Any other arguments or sources of law that fail to show such an institutional backing are taken as *supplementary* sources only, to be adopted if there is no legislation (*sensu largo*) or precedents available on the issue. Still, the impact of non-institutional sources of law has survived, despite the vast volume of legislation and precedents. The reasons are fairly obvious: the legislator or a precedent-issuing court of justice can never hope to gain complete coverage of the diversified, highly complex fact-constellations in the modern society by means of *ex ante* enactments. Therefore, other legal or quasi-legal instruments are needed, too.

Moreover, the key role given to the value-laden principles of law in the decisions by the Court of the European Union and the European Court of Human Rights have boosted the impact of principle-oriented legal argumentation at the cost of formally valid legal rules in the legal systems within the reach of the two European courts. The ideas promoted by philosophical conventionalism fit in that picture fairly well, or at least better than analytical legal positivism as conceived by John Austin, Hans Kelsen, and H. L. A. Hart.

Chapter 9
"Die Rechtssätze in ihrem systematischen Zusammenhang zu erkennen" – The Thrust of Legal Formalism

9.1 A Genealogy of Legal Concepts by Georg Friedrich Puchta

The *Historical School of Law*, founded by Friedrich Carl von Savigny (1779–1861) at the early nineteenth century, underscored the historical essence and roots of law. It highlighted the role of the *Volksgeist*, i.e. the historically evolving "spirit of the nation" on the evolvement of the law. The *Volksgeist* of a nation found its paramount expression in the *customary law* and, in the more sophisticated legal systems, in the legal conceptions and doctrinal constructions created by the *legal profession* (*Juristenrecht*, *Professorenrecht*). Towards the end of the nineteenth century, the historicist notion of law became transformed into full-fledged *conceptualist jurisprudence* in Germany. A hierarchical system of legal concepts, as created by the legal science so as to deal with the legal issues, was placed at the centre of legal analysis. Among the German conceptualists there were Georg Friedrich Puchta (1798–1846), Bernhard Windscheid (1817–1892), and the young Rudolf von Jhering (1818–1892), who later turned into a vehement opponent and critic of legal formalism under the *Interessenjurisprudence*, or jurisprudence based on the analysis of social interests in law.[1] It was Philipp Heck, himself a proponent of the *Interessenjurisprudenz*, who introduced the openly pejorative term *Begriffsjurisprudenz* for the German conceptualists.[2]

According to the *Begriffsjurisprudenz*, there is an immutable logico-conceptual element in law "frozen' in the *legal concepts* and their mutual *systemic relations*. Even earlier, the historical school of law had found the immutable element of law in the community-centred legal concepts, like the *spirit of the nation* (*Volksgeist*) and the "organically" evolving *legal consciousness* of its people. Concisely: von Savigny underscored the role of historically evolving legal institutes as the subject matter of legal analysis; while Puchta attached legal analysis to the legal concepts (*Rechtsbegriffe*), legal sentences (*Rechtssätze*), and the set of logico-conceptual, or logico-deductive, conclusions derived from the former.[3]

---

[1] Larenz, *Methodenlehre der Rechtswissenschaft*, p. 49.

[2] Larenz, *Methodenlehre der Rechtswissenschaft*, p. 49.

[3] On conceptualist jurisprudence and Puchta's legal thinking in specific, Larenz, *Methodenlehre der Rechtswissenschaft*, pp. 19–24; Wieacker, *Privatrechtsgeschichte der Neuzeit*, pp. 399–402;

R. Siltala, *Law, Truth, and Reason*, Law and Philosophy Library 97,

DOI 10.1007/978-94-007-1872-2_9,

Puchta introduced the notion of a *genealogy of legal concepts* (*Genealogie der Begriffe*), with reference to the systemic relations that are thought to prevail among legal concepts in a closed, gapless system of such concepts. It was the task of legal science to construct such a systemic totality of law, and then place individual legal problems in it, so as to derive sentences on legal construction and interpretation under highly conceptualist and systemic premises. Before Puchta, von Savigny, too, had underscored the need for a "philosophical", i.e. systematic, method of interpretation on side with a historical, i.e. exegetical-hermeneutical, one.[4] Puchta illustrated the genealogy of legal concepts with a *pyramid of legal concepts* (*Begriffspyramide*): legal concepts were presented as part of a logico-systemic, hierarchical, internally consistent, and gapless whole. In Puchta's pyramid of legal concepts, the field of application of a legal concept is the wider, and its substantive content is the narrower, the higher the legal concept is placed in the systemic hierarchy of legal concepts. In contrast, the field of application of a legal concept is the narrower, and its substantive content is the wider, the lower the legal concept is situated in the pyramid of legal concepts.[5] Puchta's methodology was strictly *logico-deductive*.[6]

On the top of Puchta's *Begriffspyramide*, there are the abstract and general legal concepts with the help of which an overall view can be attained of the legal system concerned. At the same time, their information value and value of use in guiding the judge's legal discretion is rather low. As we proceed towards the lower levels of the *Begriffspyramide*, the substantive elements of law gain more weight, as the concepts become more and more content-bound. At the same time, their field of application becomes narrower, and the idea of gaining an overall view of the legal system is increasingly compromised. At the top of the pyramid of legal concepts in the field of private law, Puchta, like Bernhard Windscheid after him, placed the notion of a *subjective right*.[7]

In Puchta's legal formalism, concepts other than the strictly legal ones were to be purged out of the realm of law and legal science. In that, Puchta to a great extent anticipated the logico-conceptual purity of Hans Kelsen's *Pure Theory of Law* in the twentieth century. According to Puchta's methodological agenda for legal science, the social context of law and legal adjudication could – and, in fact, even ought to – be ignored in the course of enforcing the inherent "logic" of legal concepts and their systemic relations. For instance, a right to establish and use a pathway

---

Bydlinski, *Juristische Methodenlehre und Rechtsbegriff*, pp. 109–113; Ogorek, *Richterkönig oder Subsumtionsautomat?*, pp. 198–211.

[4]Larenz, *Methodenlehre der Rechtswissenschaft*, pp. 17–18, Wieacker, *Privatrechtsgeschichte der Neuzeit*, pp. 397–398.

[5]Larenz, *Methodenlehre der Rechtswissenschaft*, pp. 20–21.

[6]Wieacker, *Privatrechtsgeschichte der Neuzeit*, p. 400: "Da Puchta die 'organischen Rechtsverhältnisse' und 'Institutionen' Savignys in der Sache aufgegeben hat, ist die Hierarchie der Begriffe von den Axiomen aus abwärts lückenlos hergestellt und die Deduktion der einzelnen Rechtssätze und Entscheidungen erst in Strenge möglich geworden."

[7]Larenz, *Methodenlehre der Rechtswissenschaft*, p. 30.

on land owned by someone else (*Wegeservitut*) was defined as the right to use such property,[8] without there being any need to ponder upon the wider social or economic implications of allowing, or not allowing, such third party use of land property.

There is one element in Puchta's model that yet stands in stark contrast to Adolf Julius Merkl's and Hans Kelsen's later notion of formal norm hierarchy, where a legal norm invariably derives its validity from another, higher-level norm and, ultimately, from the presumed, transcendental-logical basic norm. In Puchta's idea of the genealogy of legal concepts, the constitutive elements of law bear impact on the substantive content, and not only as to the formal structure, of law.[9] Thus, the concepts of a (legal) *person*, *responsibility*, and *imputability* in the context of criminal law (*Person*, *Verantwortlichkeit*, *Zurechnungsfähigkeit*) are linked to the questions of social ethics in Puchta's key writings on the issue. The concept of a *legal subject* (*Rechtssubjekt*) was not yet developed into such a formal and relational concept as it was to become in Kelsen's pure theory of law, carefully "purified" of all content-oriented implications.[10]

9.2 A Jurisprudence, Based on Legal Concepts and Their Systemic Relations

For the proponents of legal conceptualism, all legal knowledge is *constructive*, *systemic* and *logico-conceptual* in kind. It was no longer historically evolving knowledge of the societal practices that reflect the "organically" developing inner logic of the "spirit of the nation", the *Volksgeist*, as had been argued by Friedrich Carl von Savigny.[11] But nor could it be derived from the allegedly self-evident ideas of a religious or secular justice, as argued by natural law philosophy. At the basis of Puchta's legal formalism, one can see echoes of the rationalistic natural law philosophy from the eighteenth century and, in specific, Christian Wolff's ideas on the systemic structure of law and the deductive model adopted in its analysis. In Puchta's model, however, such systemic elements were to be derived from the

---

[8] Larenz, *Methodenlehre der Rechtswissenschaft*, p. 21.

[9] Yet, even in Kelsen's pure theory of law, conflict norms such as *lex superior derogat legi inferiori* and *lex posterior derogat legi priori* were allowed to guide legal interpretation.

[10] Larenz, *Methodenlehre der Rechtswissenschaft*, p. 23.

[11] On Savigny's conception of law, Wieacker, *Privatrechtsgeschichte der Neuzeit*, pp. 381–399; Larenz, *Methodenlehre der Rechtswissenschaft*, pp. 11–18. – As to Savigny's doctrine of the sources of law, Larenz points out the following: "Savigny – mostly in his writing 'Beruf unserer Zeit' – regarded not only legislation but also the common legal conviction of the nation, the *Volksgeist*, as the most original source of all law. The method by means of which one can reach such a conviction of the law is obviously not by logical deduction but by direct experience and vision." (Translation by the present author.) Cf.: "Savigny – zuerst in der Schrift über 'Beruf unserer Zeit' – nicht mehr das Gesetz, sondern die gemeinsame Rechtsüberzeugung des Volkes, den 'Volksgeist', als die ursprüngliche Quelle allen Rechtes ansah. Die Form, in der sich eine solche Überzeugung allein bilden kann, ist offenbar nicht die einer logischen Deduktion, sondern die der unmittelbaren Empfindung und Ansschauung." Larenz, *Methodenlehre der Rechtswissenschaft*, pp. 13–14.

German *Pandektenrecht*,[12] not from the general idea of justice and the immutable nature of man as in Wolff's writings.[13]

The path to Puchta's legal formalism was paved by von Savigny's writings on the historically evolving character of law. Notably, Savigny had cherished the idea that in a modern, sophisticated legal system, as the one in Germany, it is the *legal profession* that has privileged access to the true spirit of the *Volksgeist*, making it possible for the legal profession to attain an authentic reconstruction of the law of the nation. Such a scholarly conception of the law, defined as a *Juristenrecht* or a *Professorenrecht* by von Savigny, denotes an obvious shift from customary law to a scientifically constructed, scholarly conception of the law:[14]

> It is the task of legal science *to observe legal sentences in their systemic context*, i.e. as legal sentences that are dependent on and derivable from each others, so as to be able to present the *genealogy* of individual legal sentences from the general principles until their outermost sprouts. In this, even the kind of legal sentences will be brought into consciousness and further cultivated that entail the *spirit of national law* in a concealed manner and, since they have not become part of the common legal conviction of the community in its transactions, nor been the very subject matter of any acts of legislation, are now for the first time presented as *products of scientific deduction*. Thereby the science of law steps forward as a third source of law, on side of the already existing two sources of law. The law so conceived is *scientific law* or, when it is brought into open daylight by the endeavours of the lawyers, the *lawyers' law*.

Puchta's highbrow legal conceptualism enhanced a scientific conception of law as the *lawyers' law* (*Juristenrecht*) or the *law professors' law* (*Professorenrecht*),

---

[12]The term *Pandektenrecht* refers to the norms of Roman law adopted in the Germany that was split into a mosaic of tiny principalities until its stately unification in 1871. The highly impressive German civil law codification, *Bürgerliches Gesetzbuch* (BGB), did not come into force until 1900.

[13]Larenz, *Methodenlehre der Rechtswissenschaft*, p. 23; Wieacker, *Privatrechtsgeschichte der Neuzeit*, pp. 373–374.

[14]"Es ist nun die Aufgabe der Wissenschaft, *die Rechtssätze in ihrem systematischen Zusammenhang*, als einander bedingende und voneinander abstammende, *zu erkennen*, um die *Genealogie* der einzelnen bis zu ihrem Prinzip hinauf verfolgen und ebenso von den Prinzipien bis zu ihren äussersten Sprossen herabsteigen zu können. Bei diesem Geschäft werden Rechtssätze zum Bewuβtsein gebracht und zutage gefördert werden, die in dem *Geist des nationellen Rechts* verborgen, weder in der unmittelbaren Überzeugung der Volksglieder und ihren Handlungen noch in den Aussprüchen des Gesetzgebers zur Erscheinung gekommen sind, die also erst *als Produkt einer wissenschaftlichen Deduktion* sichtbar entstehen. So tritt die Wissenschaft als dritte Rechtsquelle zu den ersten beiden; das Recht, welches durch sie entsteht, ist *Recht der Wissenschaft*, oder, da es durch die Tätigkeit der Juristen ans Licht gebracht wird, *Juristenrecht*." Puchta, *Cursus der Institutionen, I*, p. 36, as cited in: Larenz, *Methodenlehre der Rechtswissenschaft*, p. 21. (Italics added; translation by the present author.) – Cf. Wieacker, *Privatrechtsgeschichte der Neuzeit*, pp. 400–401; cf. Wieacker, *Privatrechtsgeschichte der Neuzeit*, p. 399: "Puchta's *Gewohnheitsrecht* (I 1828; II 1837) takes the road of the *Pandektenwissenschaft* consequently from the spirit of the nation to the inevitable end of the monopoly of lawyers" (translation by the present author); cf.: "Puchtas *Gewohnheitsrecht* (I 1828; II 1837) geht den für die Pandektenwissenschaft unvermeidlichen Weg von Volksgeist zum Juristenmonopol konsequent zu Ende."

on side with legislation and customary law.[15] From the point of view of legal construction, legal conceptualism entailed a strict commitment to legal *formalism* that banned all openly value-laden considerations from the sphere of law and the judge's legal discretion, no matter whether they be of social, economic, or other kind. Legal phenomena were now to be situated in a systemic grid that consists of legal concepts or legal sentences, and the logical consequences of law were to be drawn from it. As an eminent German scholar in legal history, Franz Wieacker, put it:[16]

> A given legal order is invariably a closed system of institutions and legal sentences and, indeed, independent from the social reality of the conditions of human life that are regulated by the institutions and legal sentences. Under such preconditions, it is yet in principle possible to correctly resolve all the legal cases that may emerge by means of a mere logical operation, by subsuming the case under a hypothetical judgment that is entailed in a general legal dogmatic sentence produced by the legal science (which is also tacitly entailed in the legal concepts produced by the legal science).

Puchta's formalism redefined the judge's act of legal decision-making as subject to a closed, gapless *logico-conceptual calculus* in which axiomatic-deductive logic and the formal modes of reasoning determine the final outcome.

In light of Jerzy Wróblewski's three ideologies of judicial decision-making discerned above,[17] the German conceptualists (mostly) aimed at following the ideology of *bound* legal decision-making,[18] accompanied by the idea of *one right answer* to a legal case and the stern request made by de Montesquieu that the judge be no more than "the mouth that reads the letter of the law", without any powers of genuine legal interpretation.[19] The judge was regarded as a merely passive *subsumtion automaton*, stripped of any rights of legal discretion so as to evaluate the social context of a legal sentence or legal concept.[20] Witty American critics of legal formalism were quick to coin such a notion of judicial decision-making the doctrine of the *slot-machine*

---

[15] Ogorek, *Richterkönig oder Subsumtionsautomat?*, p. 199.

[16] "Eine gegebene Rechtsordnung is stets ein geschlossenes System von Institutionen und Rechtssätzen, und zwar unabhängig von der sozialen Realität der durch die Institutionen und Rechtssätze geregelten Lebensverhältnisse. Unter dieser Voraussätzung ist es aber prinzipiellt möglich, alle anstehenden Rechtssätze allein durch eine logischer Operation richtig zu entscheiden, welche den Fall unter das hypotetische Urteil subsumiert, das in einem allgemeinen dogmatischen Lehrsatz (und implicite auch in der rechtswissenschaftlichen Begriffen) enthalten ist." Wieacker, *Privatrechtsgeschichte der Neuzeit*, p. 433. (Translation by the present author.)

[17] Wróblewski, *The Judicial Application of Law*, pp. 265–314.

[18] Mostly, because, as will be argued below, the German conceptualists did approve of the use of legal analogy under certain conditions, somewhat loosening the requirement of only applying strict logical deduction in law.

[19] "Mais, si les tribunaux ne doivent pas être fixes, les jugements doivent l'être à une telle point, qu'ils ne soient jamais qu'un texte précis de la loi. (. . .) Mais les juges de la nation ne sont, comme nous avont dit, que la bouche qui prononce les paroles de la loi; des êtres inanimés qui n'en peuvent modérer ni la force ni la rigueur." Montesquieu, *L'esprit des lois*, pp. 399–404.

[20] Larenz, *Methodenlehre der Rechtswissenschaft*, p. 22.

judge. As a consequence, the science of law became more and more alienated from the social, political, and moral context of law and legal adjudication.[21]

Still, even the scholars who advocated the ideas of a conceptualist jurisprudence quite openly acknowledged the possibility of cases for which the legal sentences or legal concepts, as produced by the legal science, could not provide a satisfactory answer and where, as a consequence thereof, the judge or the legal scholar needed to have recourse to legal analogy. In such situations, the methodological requirement of logico-deductive reasoning was relaxed in favour of a significantly less formal approach to the law.[22] On the European continent, the impressive law codifications in France and Austria and the highly systemic undertakings of the German conceptualists had an impact on the development of the general doctrines of law in any branch of law (*die allgemeine Lehren des Rechts*), especially within the German-speaking legal culture. In legislation, such systemic efforts had their heyday, when the German private law codification *Bürgerliches Gesetzbuch* came into force in 1900.

9.3 The Langdellian Orthodoxy – A Brief Account of Legal Formalism in America

In the United States, the idea of legal formalism is manifested in the *case method* introduced by Christopher Columbus Langdell (1826–1906), Dean of Harvard Law School since 1870. Langdell's model for legal analysis, later somewhat degradingly coined as "Langdellian orthodoxy",[23] quickly gained the dominant position in legal science and legal education in the United States as introduced by Langdell and then elaborated by Langdell's followers James Barr Ames and Joseph Beale.[24] "Mr. Fox, will you state the facts in the case of *Payne v. Cave?*" was the famous kickoff phrase of Langdell's case method in his lecture on contract law at Harvard in 1870. The lecture then continued with: "Mr Rawle, will you give the plaintiff's argument?" The Socratic method of posing questions to students was Langdell's novelty in legal education.

According to Neil Duxbury's concise analysis, the core of Langdell's case method can be stated as follows[25]:

[21]"... die Entfremdung der Rechtswissenschaft von der gesellschaftlichen, politischen und moralischen Wirklichkeit des Rechts ...", Wieacker, *Privatrechtsgeschichte der Neuzeit*, p. 401.

[22]Bydlinski, *Juristische Methodenlehre und Rechtsbegriff*, p. 112.

[23]Grey, "Langdell's Orthodoxy", passim; de Been, *Legal Realism Regained*, pp. 4–6. – Justice O. W. Holmes once sarcastically called Langdell "the greatest living legal theologian". Cited in Horwitz, "The Place of Justice Holmes in American Legal Thought", p. 54. Cf. also Golding, "Jurisprudence and Legal Philosophy in the Twentieth-Century America – Major Themes and Developments", p. 443, where Langdell's approach to the common law is compared to the ideas put forth by the German conceptualists (*Begriffsjurisprudenz*).

[24]Concisely on the case method by C. C. Langdell, James Barr Ames, and Joseph Beale, cf. Duxbury, *Patterns of American Jurisprudence*, pp. 14–25.

[25]Duxbury, *Patterns of American Jurisprudence*, p. 15.

> Langdellian legal science can be seen to consist of four interrelated elements. First, there is the intense respect for *stare decisis*. For Langdell, to be able to discern the precedential status of any case is to have found the key to the science of law. Secondly, anyone gifted with the ability to discern in this fashion will of necessity realize that most reported cases are in fact unhelpful repetitions of extant principles and precedents. Thirdly, anyone who has realized that only a handful of cases are truly relevant to the science of law must also recognize that the number of fundamental legal doctrines is similarly limited. Fourthly, the task of the legal scientist is to classify these fundamental doctrines so as to demonstrate their logical interconnection, as well as to dispel the myth of their formidable number.

The Langdellian approach placed the emphasis of legal analysis on the doctrine of *stare decisis* and the relatively few general legal principles that were effective behind those court decisions. Langdell had been influenced by John Austin's analytical jurisprudence and the nineteenth century positivist ideal of science, and now the American scene of legal science was to be made more "scientific" by adhering to those ideals.[26] The social consequences of law and the set of value premises at the back of law were ruled out from the scope of legal analysis. Instead, the values of formal legal predictability, in line with the general principles of law underlying individual judicial decisions, were given priority in legal analysis under the Langdellian premises.[27]

Dissenting opinions as to the true formality of Langdell's methodology have been voiced, as well. In his articulate treatise *Beyond the Formalist-Realist Divide: The Role of Politics in Judging*, Brian Z. Tamanaha cites Marcia Speciale who characterizes Langdell's version of legal science as "the beginning of anti-formalism".[28] Tamanaha refers to Holmes' unfair critique of Langdell's agenda, which made him the primary target of anti-formalism in the United States. Still, there is no denial of the fact that Langdell did pursue a highly formalist agenda for the legal science, since that was the means of guaranteeing its status as true science in his mind. In that, similarities to the German conceptualists (*Begriffsjurisprudenz*) are striking.

Langdell's, Ames', and Beale's case method provided an easy target for the anti-formalist critique, firstly, by the American school of *sociological jurisprudence* at the end of the nineteenth century and the beginning of the twentieth century, and secondly, by the *American legal realists* in the 1920s and 1930s. For the pragmatism-minded advocates of sociological jurisprudence and legal realism, the effected *law in action* of the actual court decisions, plus the social consequences of law brought into effect, had far more importance than any doctrinal constructions of the *law in the books* of a Langdellian orthodoxy.

Under Langdell's methodology, there was of course no access to Pound's seminal idea of law as a master tool for *social engineering*, nor to Holmes' sarcastic

---

[26] Mendell, "American Jurists, 1860–1960", p. 33.

[27] Cf. also: "... Langdell had argued that law – meaning always private law – should be reduced by legal scientists to a small group of logically categorized founding principles." Duxbury, *Patterns of American Jurisprudence*, p. 21.

[28] Tamanaha, *Beyond the Formalist-Realist Divide: The Role of Politics in Judging*, p. 53.

prediction theory where the *bad man*, only interested in predicting the untoward response of the judges and officials to his conduct, i.e. the sanctions likely to be inflicted upon him, if he decides to break the law.[29] In line with the prediction theory of law, the binding nature of a private law contract was similarly devoid of any moral qualities, i.e. equal to the sanctions that would be inflicted on anyone who failed to satisfy the contractual obligations he had taken to fulfil.[30]

9.4 The Constitutive Elements of Legal Formality by Robert S. Summers

Based on a cross-reading of Ronald Dworkin's conception of legal rules and legal principles, the latter in the wide sense of comprising all kinds of value-laden legal standards,[31] on the one hand, and Robert S. Summers' account of the different facets of *legal formality*, on the other, I argue that *legal rules* (à la Dworkin) are legal decision-making arguments with *high legal formality* (à la Summers), and *legal principles* (à la Dworkin) are legal decision-making arguments with *low legal formality* (à la Summers).[32] According to Summers' analysis, the level of formality of a legal norm may be of the following kind:

(a) *Constitutive* formality: *validity* formality and *rank* formality of a legal norm or argument, i.e.:

   (1) *validity* formality, with reference to the either formal or non-formal source of origin of a legal norm or argument; and
   (2) *rank* formality, with reference to the hierarchical or non-hierarchical status of a legal norm or argument, to the effect that legal rules have gained relative independence from the social values and goals at the back of law and, moreover, exert a normative, binding effect upon the legal discretion of the judge by force of their formal source of origin, whereas legal principles enjoy possibly oblique but still adequate institutional support and content-based

[29] Vilhelm Lundstedt (1882–1955), a Swedish scholar and key representative of the Scandinavian realistic movement, took up the idea of law as a form of social engineering as major ingredient of his philosophy of law.

[30] "The duty to keep a contract at common law means a prediction that you must pay damages if you do not keep it, – and nothing else. If you commit a tort, you are liable to pay a compensatory sum. If you commit a contract, you are liable to pay a compensatory sum unless the promised event comes to pass, and that is all the difference." Holmes, "The Path of the Law", p. 462.

[31] Dworkin, *Taking Rights Seriously*, p. 22: "... in those in hard cases ... [the lawyers] make use of standards that do not function as rules, but operate differently as principles, policies, and other sorts of standards."

[32] Siltala, *A Theory of Precedent*, pp. 41–63; Siltala, *Oikeustieteen tieteenteoria*, pp. 97–102, 756–761.

approval in the community and are, by force of their definition, closely intertwined with social values and/or goals.[33]

(b) *Systemic* formality: static and closed systemic totality of legal rules in the sense of constituting Kelsen's and Merkl's hierarchic norm pyramid, or no more than a loosely defined "system" of legal principles that are, by force of definition, open-ended vis-à-vis certain set of social values and/or goals.
(c) *Mandatory* formality: strong binding force of legal rules vis-à-vis a judge's legal discretion, or the – at least prima facie – weaker, merely persuasive force of legal principles vis-à-vis a judge's legal discretion.[34]
(d) *Structural*, or *norm-logical*, formality: binary logic of the *either/or* kind of applicability in legal rules, or multi-valued logic of the *more-or-less* kind of applicability in legal principles.
(e) *Methodological* formality: semantics-oriented interpretation of legal rules, where recourse to social values and/or goals is at least prima facie ruled out, or the openly value-laden weighing and balancing of legal principles where recourse to social value-laden or goal-oriented elements is required.
(f) *Expressive*, or *logico-linguistic*, formality: semantic characteristics of the legal norm formulation.

= *Deontic formality*: (a) + (b) + (c) + (d) + (e) + (f) above.

The sum total of the various tenets of legal formality (a)–(f) may be called *deontic* formality.

Legal *rules* are legal arguments that are (primarily) based on individual decisions made by institutional decision-making authorities, such as the legislator, courts of justice, and other law-applying officials. Legal rules are or, at the least, may be expressive of *high level of legal formality* in all or most of the categories of legal formality discerned above. Legal *principles* and other value-laden *standards* of law, in turn, are legal arguments that are based on adequate institutional support and sense of approval in the legal community. Legal principles are endowed with *low level of legal formality* in all or most of the categories of legal formality discerned.

A system of legal concepts or institutions defined as a *genealogy* or *pyramid of legal concepts* (*Genealogie der Begriffe*; *Begriffspyramide*), as suggested by

[33] A. J. Merkl's and Hans Kelsen's idea of the *Stufenbau*, or a hierarchical order, of a legal system satisfies the criterion of high rank formality. – It would seem that rank formality, as part of constitutive formality, and systemic formality to some extent overlap in Summers' analysis.

[34] "Only rules dictate results, come what may. When a contrary result has been reached, the rule has been abandoned or changed. Principles do not work that way; they incline a decision one way, though not conclusively, and they survive intact when they do not prevail." Dworkin, *Taking Rights Seriously*, s. 35. – Similarly Dworkin, *Taking Rights Seriously*, p. 26: "A principle like 'No man may profit from his own wrong' does not even purport to set out conditions that make its application necessary. Rather, it states a reason that argues in one direction, but does not necessitate a particular decision."

Georg Friedrich Puchta under the German *Begriffsjurisprudenz*, meets with all the six categories of legal formality discerned, i.e. *constitutive* (i.e. *validity* and *rank*), *systemic*, *mandatory*, *structural*, *methodological*, and *logico-linguistic* formality. The only exception might be methodological formality, since the German conceptualist made room for the use of analogical reasoning in certain cases, as well.

Under high legal formalism, the logical constitution of law is detached from any content-bound tenets of the legal concepts and their systemic totality (= point a). The system of legal concepts is taken as a gapless and internally coherent whole, following the rule-based logic of legal decision-making where individual legal institutions are situated within a logico-conceptual and systemic frame (= point b). Moreover, a systemic totality of such legal concepts is endowed with strong mandatory formality, or normative binding force (= point c). From the point of view of the logic of norms and legal methodology, legal formalism seeks to satisfy the criteria of legal isomorphism (à la Kaarle Makkonen) and the ideology of bound legal decision-making (à la Jerzy Wróblewski) taken to the extreme, since there is no area of free legal discretion left to the judge under such premises (= points d and e). Moreover, the expressive, logico-linguistic qualities of law are deemed to be inherently formal, and not content-bound or intertwined with the prevailing values and goals in society, except in the oblique sense that the basic legal concepts by necessity give effect to certain kinds of social values in an oblique manner (= point f).

Robert S. Summers' idea of the different categories of legal formality and Ronald Dworkin's corresponding idea of legal rules and 'standards that do not function as rules, but operate differently as principles, policies and other sorts of standards',[35] would seem to quite neatly match to one another. A legal norm or legal argument that ranks *high* in all (or most) of Summers' categories of legal formality is a legal *rule* in Dworkin's terminology, valid because of its formal source of origin, or pedigree. A legal norm or legal argument that ranks *low* in all (or most) of Summers' categories of legal formality, by contrast, is a legal *principle*, if it enjoys adequate institutional support and sense of approval in the community.[36]

9.5 *"Der Zweck ist der Schöpfer des ganzen Rechts"* – A Critique of Legal Formalism by Rudolf von Jhering and Lon L. Fuller

From the point of view of legal *methodology* on how to construct and read the law vis-à-vis some actual or merely hypothetical fact-constellation, the borderline between legal formalism and non-formalism is defined by whether *institutional values*, *collective goals*, and *social purposes* of law are allowed to penetrate the judge's or a legal scholar's process of legal discretion or legal decision-making. For the legal formalist, law is an autonomous, self-sufficient phenomenon to the effect that there is no need to look for any concealed premises, policy-agenda, social purpose, or

[35] Dworkin, *Taking Rights Seriously*, p. 22.

[36] Cf. Siltala, *A Theory of Precedent*, pp. 41–63.

institutional values beneath the express manifestations of law in legislation and other official sources of law. For the non-formalist, the notion of law as detached from the underlying edifice of institutional values, collective goals, and social purposes simply makes no sense. For the non-formalist, law is an inherently value-laden, interest-oriented phenomenon that cannot be grasped without having recourse to its purpose-laden social premises.

The most ardent critique of the German conceptualists (*Begriffsjurisprudenz*) was issued by *Interessenjurisprudenz*, i.e. a jurisprudence based on the analysis of social interests and purposes in law founded by Rudolf von Jhering (1818–1892) and Philip Heck (1858–1943).[37] As an antithesis to the highbrow German conceptualism, von Jhering's notion of jurisprudence underscored the inherently *interest-laden* and *purpose-oriented* nature of all law. As a consequence, the law could not be captured in a logical, closed, and gapless system of legal concepts, as had been suggested by Puchta in his idea of the genealogy of legal concepts (*Genealogie der Begriffe*). Rather, law is a thoroughly interest-laden social phenomenon. *Der Zweck ist der Schöpfer des ganzen Rechts* – "the [social] purpose is the creator of all law", as Rudolf von Jhering concisely put it in the motto to his treatise *Der Zweck im Recht* in 1877.[38]

In the 1950s debate with H. L. A. Hart on the premises of legal construction and interpretation, Lon L. Fuller voiced similar ideas on the inherently *interest-laden*, *purpose-oriented*, and *value-bound* nature of law. According to Hart, linguistic concepts, and legal rules that incorporate such concepts, have a *core of certainty*, where the semantic meaning-content of the concept or rule is patently clear, and a *penumbra of doubt*, where several readings of the rule are equally possible.[39] In terms of Makkonen's above classification, Hart's legal semantics matches with the *isomorphic* and semantically *ambiguous* situations of legal decision-making, respectively.

According to Hart, legal interpretation is a *semantic* operation whereby the core/penumbra division is affirmed for the legal rule at hand. Within the core, the meaning-content of the rule is patently clear without further ado; within the penumbra, its meaning-content needs to be elucidated and expounded by legal interpretation. Even then, the original purpose of the rule need not be invoked, but the semantic approach will do. If there are no legal rules with a bearing on the issue, the judge is advised to resolve the case as if he were acting in the role of a "small-scale legislator", free of constraints other than those derived from the constitution and international state treaties with effect on domestic law. According to Fuller, on the other hand, legal argumentation is not even possible without first consulting the community-oriented, purpose-laden background premises of law. It is the inherent

---

[37] On von Jhering's *Interessenjurisprudence*, Wieacker, *Privatrechtsgeschichte der Neuzeit*, pp. 574–578; Larenz, *Methodenlehre der Rechtswissenschaft*, pp. 49–58, 119–125. The key texts of *Interessenjurisprudence* are presented in Ellscheid and Hassemer, eds., *Interessenjurisprudence*.

[38] von Jhering, *Der Zweck im Recht, I*, p. I.

[39] Hart, *The Concept of Law* (1961), pp. 123–124.

purpose of law that defines the semantics of the core and penumbra of a legal rule à la Hart, and not the other way round, as Fuller saw it.[40]

Even earlier in Germany the *Free Law Movement* had attacked the formalist and conceptualist premises of a highly constructivist conception of legal science by the *Begriffsjurisprudenz*. Contrary to Puchta's and other legal formalists' stance on the issue, the legal discretion of the judge could not be captured by deductive syllogisms or logico-conceptual calculi, since the rules of law invariably leave some area of free discretion to the law-applying judge or official. For Hart, that would signify the penumbra of a legal rule. Therefore, the judges not only discover the law in force, but they actively *create* the law in their decisions.[41]

The overt radicalism of the free law movement in underscoring the *sense of social justice* (*Rechtsgefühl*) or *value consciousness* (*Wertfühlen*) prevalent in the community never gained wide ground among the legal profession, even though it in part helped to cut down any excessive formalism in the legal doctrine. The situation with von Jhering's *Interessenjurisprudenz* was rather different. It was far easier for the lawyers to give credit to the idea of the inherently interest-laden nature of law than the excesses of the free law movement.[42] The creative role of the judge under the free law movement bears close similarity to the *sociological jurisprudence* in Europe, and in fact Eugen Ehrlich's writings on the *living law* (*lebendes Recht*) may well be situated under the both intellectual currents.[43] Moreover, according to the French scholar François Gény (1861–1959), the inspired, if somewhat loosely defined idea of the "free scientific research" (*libre recherche scientifique*) was to provide for the basis of legal analysis at the cost of any exercise in legal formalism or system-oriented legal conceptualism.[44]

Parallel to the European schools of legal anti-formalism, such as Rudolf von Jhering's *Interessenjurisprudence*,'s Eugen Ehrlich *Freirechtslehre* and *legal sociology* with the idea of living law (*lebendes Recht*), and François Gény's *libre recherche*

[40]Hart, "Positivism and the Separation of Law from Morals"; Fuller, "Positivism and Fidelity to Law – A Reply to Professor Hart". – Cf. Tamanaha, *Beyond the Formalist-Realist Divide*, pp. 168–170.

[41]On Rudolf von Jhering's "turn to a pragmatist jurisprudence" (*Jherings Wendung zu einer pragmatischen Jurisprudenz*), i.e. jurisprudence of interests, after his years in the formalist school of law, and on the early jurisprudence of interests by Philipp Heck, Heinrich Stoll, and Rudolf Müller-Erzbach, cf. Larenz, *Methodenlehre der Rechtswissenschaft*, pp. 46–58; Wieacker, *Privatrechtsgeschichte der Neuzeit*, pp. 574–579; on the free law movement by Oscar Bülow, Eugen Erhlich, Hermann Kantorowicz (i.e. the pseudonym Gnaeus Flavius), and Hermann Isay, cf. Larenz, *Methodenlehre der Rechtswissenschaft*, pp. 59–62; Wieacker, *Privatrechtsgeschichte der Neuzeit*, pp. 579–581.

[42]Larenz, *Methodenlehre der Rechtswissenschaft*, p. 62. – The key terms *Rechtsgefühl* (*sense of justice*) and *Wertfühlen* (*legal consciousness*) were first adopted by Hermann Isay. Cf. Larenz, *Methodenlehre der Rechtswissenschaft*, p. 61.

[43]Ehrlich, "Freie Rechtsfindung und freie Rechtswissenschaft"; Ehrlich, "Soziologie und Jurisprudenz".

[44]Bergel, *Méthodologie juridique*, pp. 249–253; Bouckaert, Boudwijn, "Gény, François (1861–1959)".

scientifique, the American judges and legal academicians have also showed passion for such legal anti-formalism. What *sociological jurisprudence* and *legal realism* share is a critical stance towards legal formalism in all its manifestations. What all types of legal formalism share is the endeavour to demote the impact of any openly value-laden or purpose-oriented premises on law, unless they can be traced back and locked to the conceptual and systemic edifice of the law. The concession made to analogical reasoning in a situation where no satisfactory legal answer to a legal problem could be derived from the established system of legal concepts patently transgressed the limits of the formalist approach.[45] The intellectual price for such a move was paid in a loss of scientific precision and logical exactitude, if judged in light of the premises acknowledged by the conceptualists themselves.

Like the isomorphic theory of law, legal formalism is aligned with the analysis of semantically clear, routine cases only, leaving the hard cases of legal adjudication quite untouched. In Kaarle Makkonen's terminology, legal conceptualism only covers the situations of legal isomorphism where there exists a picture relation between the two fact-constellations compared. Semantically vague situations of legal decision-making, where recourse to the methodology and canons of legal interpretation is required from the judge, and wholly unregulated situations, where there is no legal norm that could guide the judge's discretion, are out of reach of the formalist approach, strictly defined. It is only in *artificial languages*, like the ones invented in logic and mathematics, that all semantic issues of (legal) interpretation can be avoided, due to the perfection of the logical syntax of language adopted. Yet, it is just because of their fully predetermined character that artificial languages cannot provide a satisfactory ground for legal regulation and judicial decision-making.

There are three unresolved dilemmas in Hart's semantics of the core and the penumbra of legal concepts and legal rules, in Makkonen's isomorphic approach to the law, and in legal formalism in general.

Firstly, the *identification* of an isomorphic situation (à la Makkonen), a bound case of legal decision-making (à la Wróblewski), or the core of settled meanings (à la Hart), and the means of distinguishing them from other legal decision-making situations, is far from self-evident. It seems that the seminal issues of how to construct and read the law logically *precede* the identification of an isomorphic situation (à la Makkonen), the ideology of bound legal decision-making (à la Wróblewski), or the presence of a core of settled meanings (à la Hart), with the effect that interpretation cannot be abolished even under such highly formalist premises.

Secondly, the treatment of *non-isomorphic* situations of legal decision-making or the ones situated on the penumbra of doubt in Hart's legal semantics is left totally uncovered, since the deductive model of logical inference cannot be extended to them. The German formalists suggested having recourse to reasoning by analogy in such cases, but the initial premises of legal formalism are thereby exceedingly compromised.

---

[45] Bydlinski, *Juristische Methodenlehre und Rechtsbegriff*, p. 112.

Thirdly, the formalist approach to the law fails to give an account of how initially isomorphic fact-situations may be *transformed* into non-isomorphic ones of legal ambiguity or legal gap situations, most often due to the changes effected in the institutional value premises of law. For instance, when the European Convention on Human Rights and Fundamental Freedoms was ratified in Finland in 1995, a huge set of former routine cases were transformed into hard cases of legal adjudication overnight, requiring an act of weighing and balancing among the principles of law and social values entailed.

Contrary to what the advocates of legal formalism would have us believe, the legal system is not merely a systemic collection of static legal concepts or fairly immutable general principles that can be arranged into a closed, hierarchical system. Rather, there is a *dynamic* element inherent in all legal systems. When the value premises at the back of law go through profound enough a change, the borderline between the routine cases and hard cases of legal adjudication, and between the typical and non-typical fact-situations, and between the isomorphic and non-isomorphic situations of legal decision-making is affected, as well. Any overly formalist account of law is poorly equipped to cope with such *structural dynamics of change* in law.

The illusion of having logical syllogisms and a genealogy or hierarchy of legal concepts (à la Puchta) resolve the intricacies of law is broken down so soon as the inherently *interest-laden*, *purpose-oriented*, and *value-bound* characteristics of law is openly acknowledged. Moreover, the blindness of legal formalism to the impact and mutual interplay of the institutional and societal value premises at the back of law, on the one hand, and to the economic, moral, and political effects of law in society, on the other, is hard to reconcile with in the era of modern law. If modern law is deemed, as Thomas Morawetz has suggested, as a *deliberative practice*, the identity of which is constantly subject to be defined, questioned, criticized, and possibly redefined anew by those engaged in the legal discourse,[46] any overly formalist notion of law is likely to invite heavy critique and will not survive for long.

---

[46]On law as a *deliberative practice*, Morawetz, "Epistemology of Judging: Wittgenstein and Deliberative Practices", pp. 19–23.

Chapter 10
Natural Law Philosophy: Law as Subordinate to Social Justice and Political Morality in Society

10.1 The Evolvement of Natural Law Philosophy

Analytical legal positivism seeks to maintain a sharp distinction between the formal validity of law and its moral censure or merit and dismerit, as John Austin put it.[1] The legal system consists of formally valid legal rules, as issued by the sovereign ruler in the form of the parliamentary legislation and other institutional sources of law, while it is a task for the legal profession to determine the content of law with respect to different fact-constellations according to the intentions of the sovereign legislator. Any value-laden judgments as to the censure of the law were to be left for those engaged in moral philosophy, religious studies, political philosophy, and natural law philosophy – but not in technical legal analysis – to ponder upon.[2] Similarly, *analytical legal realism* sees the law as the totality of individual decisions reached by the courts of justice and other officials, with reference to the legal rights and legal duties that enjoy effective protection by the courts and other officials. For the positivists and realists alike, the law is accordingly a *social fact*, not a social value or ideal.

Natural law philosophy seeks to distance itself from legal positivism and legal realism alike. It defines the law as subordinate to criteria of (absolute) *religious*, *social*, or *political justice*. With the notion of law so defined, any questions concerning the validity and the moral worth of law are deeply intertwined.

In placing the emphasis on the non-positive, a priori qualities of law that logico-conceptually predate positive law, and on the value-laden, morals-bound qualities of law at the cost of the institutional will-formation of the legislator or courts of justice, natural law philosophy bears affinity to two other schools in modern legal thinking. For the first, the German *Begriffsjurisprudenz* at the late nineteenth and the early twentieth century underscored the inherent logico-conceptual and systemic qualities

[1]"The existence of law is one thing; its merit or demerit is another. Whether it be or be not is one enquiry; whether it be or be not conformable to an assumed standard, is a different enquiry. A law, which actually exists, is a law, though we happen to dislike it, or though it vary from the from the text, by which we regulate our approbation and disapprobation." Austin, *The Province of Jurisprudence Determined*, p. 157.

[2]Kelsen, *Reine Rechtslehre* (1960), p. 1 et seq.

R. Siltala, *Law, Truth, and Reason*, Law and Philosophy Library 97,
DOI 10.1007/978-94-007-1872-2_10,

of the legal phenomena, as argued by Georg Friedrich Puchta in terms of the genealogy of legal concepts (*Genealogie der Begriffe*) and the hierarchical, pyramid-like structure of the system of legal concepts (*Begriffspyramide*). For the second, *legal phenomenology* in the twentieth century equally stresses the a priori, self-evident tenets of law, like the "inherent object-specific structures" of legal phenomena that define the essence and nature of law (*die immanente sachliche Wesensstruktur*),[3] irrespective of any institutional will-formation of the legislator or courts of justice.

Historically, natural law philosophy can be divided into four phases:[4]

(1) *classical* natural law in the Antique Greece and Rome;
(2) *scholastic* natural law in the Middle Ages;
(3) *rationalist* natural law in the seventeenth and eighteenth centuries; and
(4) *modern* natural law since 1950s.

Alternatively, the tradition of natural law philosophy could be divided into two categories of *classical* and *modern*, where the former covers the Antique and the Middle Ages and the latter comprises the time from the mid-seventeenth century to the present times. John Finnis dates the birth of modern natural law in 1660, when Samuel Pufendorf's *Elementorum Jurisprudentiae Universalis Libri Duo* saw daylight.[5]

The idea of an absolutely right normative order for the human community with which all positive law ought to be aligned was known already in the Antique Greece. There, the natural order of things referred to the Aristotelian idea of good life in the Greek *polis*. The conflict between the rights of an individual and the collective interest of the community as a whole that has proven so crucial for modern political theory was not known in Aristotle's times. According to Aristotle, man by his nature is a *zōon polītikon*, a social or political animal for which the preconditions of a good, reasonable life were defined as the virtues of a community-based social ethics and duties owned by each to the Greek *polis*. In consequence, it was the task for the legislator to arrange the social matters in a *polis* so that the citizens could lead their lives virtuously, i.e. taking an active part in the communal matters.

In Aristotle's sharp-eyed insight into the essence of the law and the human nature, general laws are always more or less imprecise and therefore unable to take all the

[3]The term "inherent object-specific structures (of law)", being an approximate equivalent of the German expression *die immanente sachliche Wesensstruktur (des Rechts)*, refers to Hans Welzel's legal phenomenology. Larenz, *Methodenlehre der Rechtswissenschaft*, p. 111. – On legal phenomenology, Pallard and Hudson, "Phenomenology of Law"; Minkkinen, *Thinking without Desire*, chapters "In an Orderly World" (pp. 48–65) and "Right Things to Come" (pp. 66–82).

[4]There can be no post-modern natural law philosophy, due to the denial of any Grand Theory of Law under the distinctively post-modern premises of social analysis, and the idea of (absolute) social justice is of course a prime example of a grand theory in law.

[5]Finnis, "Natural Law: The Classical Tradition", p. 5.

idiosyncratic tenets of an individual case fully into account, necessitating recourse to case-aligned *equity*. Aristotle compares good law to the flexible lead rule adopted by the builders on the Lesbian Island, to the effect that the rule could be bent and moulded so as to fit with the shape of the object measured:[6]

> When the law speaks universally, then, and a case arises on it which is not covered by the universal statement, then it is right, when the legislator fails us and has erred by over-simplicity, to correct the omission – to say what the legislator himself would have said had he been present, and would have put into his law if he had known. Hence the equitable is just, and better than one kind of justice – not better than absolute justice but better than the error that arises from the absoluteness of the statement. And this is the nature of the equitable, a correction of law where it is defective owing to its universality. In fact this is the reason why all things are not determined by law, viz. that about some things it is impossible to lay down a law, so that a decree is needed. For when the thing is indefinite the rule also is indefinite, like the lead rule used in making the Lesbian moulding; the rule adapts itself to the shape of the stone and is not rigid, and so too the decree is adapted to the facts.

In the Middle Ages, Thomas Aquinas (1225–1274) created a remarkable synthesis of *scholastic* natural law philosophy. According to Thomas, there are four normative orders that govern all the creation, viz. (a) *lex aeterna*, or "eternal law", (b) *lex naturalis*, or "natural law", (c) *lex humana*, or "human law", and (d) *lex divina*, or "divine law".[7]

Lex aeterna comprises the great world order by God, the omnipotent Creator, with reference to the all-encompassing "order of things" that is imposed upon all the living creatures and inanimate things alike. Thomas made no essential difference between the inanimate heavenly bodies, the realm of living creatures, and the human kind, all of which were all equally subject to the order of creation. Anachronistically one could say that Thomas failed to distinguish between the *mechanistic*, or *causal*, laws that determine the movement of inanimate heavenly bodies, like the stars and planets, and the *normative*, or *deontic*, laws that seek to steer the conduct of human beings. *Lex naturalis* is that part of the *lex aeterna* that determines the duties of man among the living creation. The commands of the *lex naturalis* are situated higher in Thomas' hierarchy of normative orders than any decrees of the *lex humana*, i.e. positive laws issued by the sovereign ruler for the benefit of the community. The fourth normative order, i.e. *lex divina*, consists of the express revelations and commandments by the omnipotent God for the mankind in Bible and other holy scriptures.

For Thomas Aquinas, the supreme principle of natural law is that of *doing good and avoiding evil*. Moreover, the precepts of natural law are *self-evident*

---

[6] Aristotle, *Nikomachean Ethics*, p. 1796 (Book V, lines 20–32).

[7] Thomas Aquinas, (Extracts from) *The Summa Theologica*, Question 91 ("Of the Various Kinds of Law"), p. 137 et seq.

(*per se nota*) and cannot be validated by reference to any other, still higher principles of religious or social ethics.[8] In all, he defined the concept of law as follows:[9]

> Thus from the four preceding articles, the definition of law may be gathered; and it is nothing else than *an ordinance of reason for the common good, made by him who has care of the community, and promulgated.*

The ordinances of positive law, as issued by the sovereign ruler, are binding only on the condition that they fulfil the criteria of being an ordinance of reason in fostering common good, and having been duly promulgated so as to be publicly known. An *unjust law* is not binding and will not even qualify as a law proper, being no more than a "corruption of law" (*legis corruptio*),[10] i.e. mere violence or brutality by the worldly ruler. What is more, Thomas pointed out that detailed knowledge of the contents of natural law could be gained by human reason. Thereby he significantly paved the way to the breakthrough of a rationalist natural law thinking in the seventeenth and eighteenth centuries.

According to *rationalist* natural law philosophy, the precepts of natural law could be inferred from the immutable nature of man by means of the faculties of human reason. Hugo Grotius (Huig de Groot, 1583–1645), though himself a devout Catholic, placed so much faith in the power of human reason that, as he boldly claimed, the precepts of natural law would be binding even under the "highly unreasonable premise" that almighty God did not exist or that He did not care for the humans. The resulting system of reason-based law culminated in the *ultimate*

---

[8] Thomas Aquinas, (Extracts from) *The Summa Theologica*, Question 91 ("Of the Various Kinds of Law"), Second Article ("Whether the Natural Law Contains Several Precepts, or One Only?"), pp. 156–157: "*I answer that*, As stated above (Q. XCI., A. 3), the precepts of the natural law are to the practical reason, what the first principles of demonstrations are to the speculative reason; because both are self-evident principles. (. . .) Consequently the first principle in the practical reason is one founded on the notion of good, viz., that *good is that which all things seek after*. Hence this is the first precept of law, that *good is to be done and ensued, and evil is to be avoided.* All other precepts of the natural law are based upon this: so that whatever the practical reason naturally apprehends as man's good (or evil) belongs to the precepts of the natural law as something to be done or avoided.' (Italics in original.) – Cf. Finnis, *Natural Law and Natural Rights*, p. 33: ". . . Aquinas asserts as plainly as possible that the first principles of natural law, which specify the basic forms of good and evil and which can be adequately grasped by anyone of the age and reason (and not just by metaphysicians), are *per se nota* (self-evident) and indemonstrable."

[9] Thomas Aquinas, (*Extracts from*) *The Summa Theologica*, Question 90 ("Of the Essence of Law"), Fourth Article ("Whether Promulgation Is Essential to a Law?"), p. 137. (Italics added.)

[10] "*I answer that*, As Augustine says (*De Lib. Arb. i. 5*), *that which is not just seems to be no law at all*: wherefore the force of a law depends on the extent of its justice. Now in human affairs a thing is said to be just, from being right, according to the rule of reason. But the first rule reason is the law of nature, as is clear from what has been stated above (Q. XCI, A. 2 *ad* 2). Consequently every human law has just so much of the nature of law, as it is derived from the law of nature. But if in any point it deflects from the law of nature, it is no longer a law but a perversion of law." Thomas Aquinas, (Extracts from) *The Summa Theologica*, Question 95 ("Of Human Law"), Second Article ("Whether Every Human Law Is Derived from the Natural Law?"), p. 166 (Italics in original.) – Cf. Finnis, *Natural Law and Natural Rights*, pp. 351–368, where the author gives a profound analysis of the issue.

principle or principles of law from which all other rules and principles of natural law could then be inferred.

Since geometry was the leading scientific ideal at the early modern era, the study on law, too, sought to pursue axiomatic scientificity in its methodology and the results attained. The legal system was conceived as an *axiomatic*, *systemic*, and *hierarchical* normative order. By means of logical deduction a detailed set of rules and principles could be derived from the few abstract principles postulated from the nature of man and society. For Grotius, the ultimate principle of natural law was the celebrated maxim *pacta sunt servanda*. Besides Grotius, Samuel Pufendorf (1632–1694) and Christian Wolff (1679–1754) were among the major representatives of rationalist natural law thinking. Such a systemic disposition of law by the reason-based natural law greatly paved the way for the law codifications at the end of the 18th and the beginning of the nineteenth century. Moreover, it provided a source of inspiration for the systemic efforts of the German conceptualists (*Begriffsjurisprudence*) at the latter half of the nineteenth century. The legal systematics by Christian Wolff, in specific, served as the model for Georg Friedrich Puchta's genealogy of legal concepts (*Genealogie der Begriffe*).

The patent predicament with a rationalist conception of natural law, based on the immutable nature of man, has to do with the essential arbitrariness of the ultimate premises of philosophical analysis. Is man by nature a violent creature, inclined to end up in a destructive civil war, if there is no sovereign ruler that could enforce the peace, as Thomas Hobbes (1588–1679) argued? Or is man by nature a peaceful creature, capable of a prolific and fruitful cooperation with others of his kind, if only the rules of contract law and legal means for their due enforcement are provided for, as both Hugo Grotius and John Locke (1632–1704) thought? There is no simple answer to that question, as the true nature of man would seem to lie somewhere in the mid-category "between the angels and the devils".

Modern natural law philosophy refers to a host of post-war intellectual currents that all share the conviction that the force of law cannot be based on its source of origin only, as the legal positivists would have us believe; nor on the effected "law in action" at the courts of justice and other legal officials, as the legal realists see it. Rather, the normative character of law depends on the content of law and the sense of approval it enjoys in the legal community. The impact of modern natural law thinking can most strikingly be seen in the breakthrough of the *human* and *constitutional rights* in the Western legal systems, giving individuals protection against any malpractices by the state officials.

Treaties for the protection of human rights include for instance the International Covenant on Civil and Political Rights; the International Covenant on Economic, Social and Cultural Rights; the Convention on the Rights of the Child; and the European Convention on Human Rights and Fundamental Freedoms, with the annexed authority of the European Court of Human Rights. Such conventions, and the European Convention on Human Rights and Fundamental Freedoms in specific, have greatly strengthened the protection of human rights in the post-war Europe.

Arguments based on human and constitutional rights of the individual have gone through a radical transformation from weak, moral arguments to genuinely legal ones and, perhaps, even ones that often *trump* in the legal deliberation of the judge, in Ronald Dworkin's sense of the term, to the effect that the international or transnational system of human rights protection may effectively curb the infringements of human rights on a national level.[11]

10.2 "*eine wertfreie Beschreibung ihres Gegenstandes*" – The Challenge of Hans Kelsen's *Pure Theory of Law* for Natural Law Philosophy

Hans Kelsen's *Pure Theory of Law* is based on extremely rigorous criteria concerning the *epistemology* and *methodology* of the science of law, to the effect of restraining the legitimate task of legal doctrine and legal analysis to *a value-free description of its subject matter*,[12] with reference to the valid norms of a legal system. A legal scholar, if he wishes to retain his scientific integrity, is not allowed to add any evaluative judgments of his own to the value-free description of the legal norms in force, nor even present any kind of preference order among the semantically possible interpretation outcomes vis-à-vis those norms, since that would have the effect of turning value-free legal *science* into value-laden legal *politics*.

In the preface to the second edition of *Reine Rechtslehre*, Kelsen even boasted of the proven value-neutrality and openness of his conception of law vis-à-vis any feasible social and political ideologies: the very fact that the pure theory of law had received – in Kelsen's mind equally misplaced – critique from a host of mutually exclusive political ideologies was the best proof of the fact that it had accomplished the objectives set for it. Kelsen pointed out that in the various critical reviews the pure theory of law had been labelled as expressive of conflicting ideological positions, to the effect of being a liberal, fascist, social democrat, bolschevist, catholic, protestant, atheist, or even anarchist conception of law, depending on the ideological preferences or aversions of the reviewer.[13] To Kelsen's mind, such labels were all

[11] On the notion of rights as "trumps" in legal argumentation, Dworkin, *Taking Rights Seriously*, pp. 82–84, 364–366.

[12] "Obgleich die Rechtswissenschaft Rechtnormen und sohin die durch sie konstituierten Rechtswerte zum Gegenstand hat, sind doch ihre Rechtssätze – so wie die Naturgesetze der Naturwissenschaft – *eine wertfreie Beschreibung ihres Gegenstandes*." Kelsen, *Reine Rechtslehre* (1960), p. 84. (Italics added.) Cf. Kelsen, *Pure Theory of Law*, p. 79. The translation of Kelsen's main work into English is notoriously less than perfect. Notably, the key term "Rechtssätze" (i.e. legal sentences) is translated as "the rules of law", which is certain to lead the reader astray, unless she knows enough German to be able to consult the original version of the text.

[13] Kelsen, *Reine Rechtslehre* (1960), p. V; Kelsen, *Reine Rechtslehre* (1934), pp. XII–XIII. – Kelsen of course was of a Jewish origin and had to emigrate from Germany first to Austria in 1933 and, then, from Austria to the United States in 1940, following the annexation of Austria to Germany in 1938. In 1945, Kelsen published *General Theory of Law and State*, i.e. an English translation of two of his earlier books *Allgemeine Staatslehre* (1925) and the first edition of *Reine Rechtslehre* (1934). Kelsen died in 1973.

equally misplaced, since the pure theory of law was expressly intended to be – and, so it seems, had succeeded in being – entirely neutral vis-à-vis all social, political, and religious ideologies. The diversified and mutually self-refuting character of the critique collected by the pure theory of law from the critics of the theory proved his conception right, Kelsen concluded.

Patently, Kelsen's open-ended, value-free legal normativism could not fill the legal, moral, and political void that had been left wide open in the havoc of legal positivism and the formal rule of law ideology in the atrocities committed by the *Dritte Reich*. Gustav Radbruch's (1878–1949) intellectual conversion from a neo-Kantian legal philosopher into a full-fledged natural law philosopher in the aftermath of the World War II is illustrative of the intellectual turn of the tide. Now, supra-positive justice (*übergesetzliches Recht*), as advocated by natural law philosophy, would take priority over any "legalized wrongs" (*gesetzliches Unrecht*) that might be committed by the legislator, Radbruch wrote in 1946.[14]

In a sense, Radbruch represents the older layer of natural law philosophy, as he attaches the criteria of law in the traditional, substantive notion of natural law. Since the 1950s, the focus in modern natural law philosophy has to a great extent been laid on the *institutional* or *procedural* means for effectively restraining the discretion of the legislator, courts of justice, and other law-applying officials. The contributions to legal philosophy by Lon L. Fuller, Ronald Dworkin, and partly even H. L. A. Hart are illustrative of such a *non-positivist* approach,[15] evading the patent excesses of older natural law philosophy. Alternatively, the emphasis has been placed on the basic values or basic goods at the back of legislation and legal adjudication, as in John Finnis' legal philosophy. The challenge of Kelsen's analytical and positivist account of law still remains the solid reference against which any non-positivist theories of law are to be judged. Whether the entirely value-free character of Kelsen's pure theory is a blessing or a curse for the legal science depends on the basic choice of legal analysis: is law a social fact, as legal positivism and legal realism both have it, or is a social value, as natural law philosophy has it?

---

[14]Radbruch, "Gesetzliches Unrecht und übergesetzliches Recht"; Radbruch, "Fünf Minuten Rechtsphilosophie". – "There are accordingly grounding legal principles that are stronger than any legal decrees of positive law, so that an enactment that is in conflict with such a principle is void of legal validity. One calls such basic legal principles natural law or law of reason." (Translation by the present author.) Cf. "Es gibt also Rechtsgrundsätze, die stärker sind als jede rechtliche Satzung, so daß ein Gesetz, das ihnen widerspricht, der Geltung bar ist. Man nennt diese Grundsätze das Naturrecht oder das Vernunftrecht." Radbruch, "Fünf Minuten Rechtsphilosophie", p. 328.

[15]Ronald Dworkin's legal philosophy was considered at length above in the context of legal coherence, so I will not re-enter that line of discussion anew. Ronald Dworkin's philosophy of law and the notion of legal principles has been coined the "third theory of law" by J. L. Mackie, since elements drawn from both legal positivism and natural law philosophy are present in it. Thus, the two criteria by means of which Dworkin depicts legal principles, i.e. *institutional support* and *sense of approval* in the community, are linked to the basic ideas of analytical legal positivism and natural law philosophy, respectively.

10.3 The Internal Morality of Law by Lon L. Fuller

Can a criminal law provision be retroactive in effect so that a punishment might be inflicted on someone for committing, or failing to commit, some act, if such conduct had not been formally declared a crime at the time of his committing it? Can the legal system contain secret laws, to the effect that the citizens who are subjected to them have no means of getting to know or becoming acquainted with what it is that is required from them? Can laws require the kind of conduct that, when judged by objective standards, cannot possibly be achieved by the human effort? Can laws require contradictory conduct from its addressees, prohibiting some conduct while at the same time requiring it from the citizens? Can there exist an irresolvable conflict between the "law in the books", as articulated in legislation, on the one hand, and the "law in action", as brought into effect in the actual court practice, on the other? Can the content of law be volatile and in constant flux to such a degree that the laws of yesterday are today completely legal history, and the same goes for the laws of today when looked upon tomorrow?

Lon L. Fuller (1902–1978), an American legal philosopher with a preference for natural law philosophy, answered each of the above questions in the negative in his *The Morality of Law*. To Fuller's mind, law is an inherently *purpose-oriented* and *community-aligned* phenomenon, and not a predominantly linguistic or semantic fact, as H. L. A. Hart and other proponents of legal positivism had argued. As with Thomas Aquinas's naturalist philosophy of law, the origins of Fuller's inherently purposeful, community-based notion of law can be traced back to Aristotle's philosophy. Contrary to what H. L. A. Hart had argued, not even the parliamentary legislator is free in its legal discretion, but any institutional authority endowed with either legislative or judicial powers is bound in its discretion by what Fuller called the *internal morality of law*, or the morality that makes law possible.[16]

Fuller puts forth the argument to the effect that the lawgiver ought to observe no less than eight rules that constitute the internal morality of law and the violation of which would result in a *failure* of the legislative act intended. Fuller's set of criteria is as follows:[17]

(1) *Generality*: legal rules must be general in character, and not drafted on an ad hoc basis for one particular case only, so as to qualify as law.
(2) *Due Promulgation of Laws*: failure to make legal rules publicly known to those affected by them will make it impossible for the norm addressees to obey the law.
(3) *Non-Retroactivity*: retroactive rules cannot guide future action and even undercut the integrity of rules with a proper prospective effect, since it puts them under the constant threat of a retroactive change.

[16] Fuller, *The Morality of Law*, p. 33 et seq.

[17] Fuller, *The Morality of Law*, pp. 33–94, and p. 39 in specific. In Fuller's dense rhetorics of law, these failures are described as "eight distinct routes to disaster". Fuller, *The Morality of Law*, p. 39. – Cf. Hart, "Lon L. Fuller: *The Morality of Law*", pp. 349–353.

(4) *Semantic Clarity*: legal rules must be comprehensible to those affected by them.
(5) *Non-Contradictoriness*: a legal rule cannot require the kind of conduct from its addressees that contradicts what other valid legal rules of the same legal order at the same time require from them.
(6) *Laws Cannot Require What Is Impossible to Fulfil*: legal rules cannot require conduct that is beyond the powers of those affected.
(7) *Constancy of Law Through Time*: introducing frequent, unexpected changes in legal rules will have the effect that those affected cannot orient their action to them.
(8) *Congruence Between Official Action and Declared Rule*: a failure to match legal rules as officially announced with their adjudication by the legal officials will lead to a failure in the legal system.

Fuller coins such criteria as the *internal*, i.e. *institutional* or *procedural*, morality of law,[18] thereby drawing a distinction between his institutional notion of law and Thomas Aquinas's substantive notion of natural law. Fullers writes that "[a] total failure in any of these eight directions does not simply result in a bad system of law; it results in something that is not properly called a legal system at all, except perhaps in the Pickwickian sense in which a void contract can still be said to be one kind of contract."[19] Should the legislator pass a retroactive criminal law; a secret law; a totally incomprehensible law; or some ad hoc laws that would each be enforced only once, for one fact-constellation only, before being derogated; the end result would not be a valid law but an inherent failure in an effort of legislating.

There is one slightly unexpected tenet in Fuller's account of the internal morality of law, however. Though Fuller, being an American legal philosopher, was of course well acquainted with the American case law tradition, the very criteria with which he described the internal morality of law are far better aligned with parliament-issued legislation of the European continental type than with judge-made common law in the United States or the British Commonwealth. In other words, Fuller's scholarly stance is better aligned with the point of view of the European legislator than that of the American judge. Moreover, precedent-based law would seem to rank rather poorly in Fuller's test for the validity of a legal system.[20]

In fact, it is only the requirement of congruence between legislation and official action by the courts and other officials (= Fuller's point 8) plus the rather obvious requirement that laws cannot require conduct that is beyond the powers of those affected (= Fuller's point 6) that concern legislation and legal adjudication with equal concern. Conversely, the criteria dealing with the required generality (= Fuller's point 1), due promulgation (= Fuller's point 2), non-retroactiveness

[18]"In my third chapter [of *The Morality of Law*] I treated what I have called the internal morality of law as itself presenting a variety of natural law. It is, however, a procedural or institutional kind of natural law . . ." Fuller, *The Morality of Law*, p. 184.

[19]Fuller, *The Morality of Law*, p. 39.

[20]Siltala, *A Theory of Precedent*, pp. 165–168, cf. Hart, *The Concept of Law* (1961), pp. 131–132.

(= Fuller's point 3), semantic clarity (= Fuller's point 4), non-contradictoriness (= Fuller's point 5), and relative constancy in time (= Fuller's point 7) of laws would seem to be match rather poorly for judge-made, precedent-based law.

Precedents and other court decisions initially concern the fact-constellation of the case at hand only, and the legal impact of the *ratio decidendi* of a case vis-à-vis the facts of a subsequent case then needs to be considered in separate terms by the subsequent court (= contra Fuller's point 1). It is but rather seldom that the prior court does try to give the *ratio decidendi* of a case some authoritative formulation, to be then acknowledged by the later courts. On the contrary, the *ratio* of a case most often needs to be reconstructed from the outcome of the prior case and the judicial reasons presented by the prior court in its support, while the outline of such reasoning is of course dependent on the particular *precedent-ideology* adopted in the legal systems concerned (= *contra* Fuller's point 2).[21] Precedent-based law is often or even in most cases retroactive in effect, due to the inherent characteristics of case-to-case reasoning (= contra Fuller's point 3). The requirement of linguistic clarity and unambiguity may need to be left rather unattended in the analysis of precedent-based law, since the *ratio decidendi* and obiter dicta elements of a case are frequently closely intertwined in the case, to be then distinguished from each other by the subsequent court only (= contra Fuller's point 4).

The systemic formality of a set of precedents is generally weaker than the respective systemic characteristics of parliamentary enactments,[22] so that the co-existence of several mutually conflicting precedents in a legal system is possible and quite often even a commonplace.[23] In such a situation, the judges need to have recourse to legal analogy and the technique of (fact-based) distinguishing in constructing and reading the law (= contra Fuller's point 5). Finally, the institutional values of relative constancy and predictability of law are far more difficult to attain in precedent-based law than in legislation, since precedents are – by force of their definition – rulings given for an individual case at hand only, to be then possibly extended to cover the facts of the novel case. Therefore, there cannot be any guarantee of the continuity of the evolved court practice or of the stability of the institutional and societal values involved in a system of precedent-based law. Moreover, there is no simple, straightforward technique of overruling the *ratio decidendi* of a case, except by stating so in explicit terms in the reasons given for some later court decision, which sometimes, but not very frequently, does occur. The methods of overruling a precedent are far more uncertain than the use of a derogation law by parliament, by means of which any outdated or otherwise unsatisfactory item of legislation can – once and for all – be made null and void (= contra Fuller's point 7).

---

[21] On the notion of *precedent-ideology* and its manifestations in the Great Britain, the United States, Germany, France, Italy, and Finland, cf. Siltala, *A Theory of Precedent*, pp. 65–148. – The term "precedent-ideology" was suggested to me by Neil MacCormick.

[22] However, if the judges in some legal system were in fact committed to the coherence-seeking premises of Ronald Dworkin's *law as integrity*, that would imply endorsing a strongly systemic notion of precedents, as well.

[23] Cf. the Italian system of precedents where such systemic characteristics would seem to be hard to sustain, Taruffo and La Torre, "Precedent in Italy", passim.

As a consequence, a very different kind of catalogue of the institutional criteria of precedent-based is needed.[24]

Fuller constantly writes of the internal, *institutional*, or procedural morality that is said to structure the law, but he also makes a distinction between the two types of morality, viz. the morality of duty and the morality of aspiration. The *morality of duty* lays down a minimum standard of conduct to be observed by the citizens, officials, and the legislator alike, being of the type of a *command* ('Do this!') or a *prohibition* ('Don't do that!'). The *morality of aspiration*, by contrast, presents (no more than) an ideal that ought to be fulfilled by its addressees to as high a degree as is possible. Such an ideal might concern the strivings of an Aristotelian virtue ethics or, as is the case here, some state of affairs that is specified in legislation or jurisdiction. In line with Robert Alexy's (and Ronald Dworkin's) terminology, one might say that Fuller's morality of duty is aligned with duty-imposing legal *rules*, while the morality of aspiration is aligned with legal *principles* in Alexy's sense of *optimization precepts* or *optimization commands* (*Optimierungsgebote*). In other words, they create an obligation for the judge or other legal official to realize some social values or goals to *as great a degree as is possible.*[25] Such an ideal morality for the legislator lays down a set of precepts for a *supererogatory* morality, or a "morality for the saints", in the sense of establishing an aspiration towards fulfilling to as great an extent as is legally and factually possible the institutional and societal values at the back of the legal system.

Nonetheless, as Fuller himself argues, it is only the requirement of promulgation of laws that exemplifies the morality of duty, while the other seven precepts that make up the internal morality of law give effect to the morality of aspiration only.[26] It is only when the principles of ideal morality of law are followed by the

[24] In my earlier book *A Theory of Precedent*, I argued that the internal morality of law or its equivalent for a system of precedents might entail the following elements: (1) *appositeness* (i.e. expediency) and adequacy of normative and factual information given in a precedent, or a set of precedents; (2) fair *predictability* of outcome of legal adjudication; (3) *systemic balance* (i.e. congruence), with reference to e.g. the judges' collective stance on precedent-following, the prevalent doctrine and tradition of precedents, and the prevalent doctrine of legal sources at larger; (4) *ideological commitment* and *argumentative skills* of those involved; (5) respect for the basic conceptions of *justice* and *fairness* in society; (6) and *integrity in argumentation*. Cf. Siltala, *A Theory of Precedent*, pp. 165–175. – Looking upon the issue now, a few years later, the list seems somewhat over-elaborated. A shorter list, with reference to the two or three first items of the list might do the job, as well.

[25] Alexy, *A Theory of Constitutional Rights*, pp. 47–48: "The decisive point in distinguishing rules from principles is that *principles* are norms which require that something be realized to the greatest extent possible given the legal and factual possibilities. Principles are *optimization requirements*, characterized by the fact that they can be satisfied to varying degrees, and that the appropriate degree of satisfaction depends not only on what is factually possible but also on what is legally possible. The scope of the legally possible is determined by opposing principles and rules." Cf. Alexy, *A Theory of Constitutional Rights*, pp. 67–69, 397.

[26] Fuller, *The Morality of Law*, pp. 43, 44: "All of this adds up to the conclusion that the inner morality of law is condemned to remain largely a morality of aspiration and not of duty. Its primary appeal must be to a sense of trusteeship and to the pride of a craftsman. – To these observations there is one important exception. This relates to the desideratum of making the laws known, or at

lawgiver that – in Fuller's sky-soaring rhetoric – the ideals of *perfection in legality, legal excellence*, and *utopia in legality* may be attained, as the primary appeal of the morality of aspiration must be to *a sense of trusteeship* and *the pride of the craftsman*.[27]

Looking at the issue from the point of view of how to construct and read the law, it is only the requirement of congruence between official action and declared rule (= Fuller's point 8) that explicitly deals with the enforcement of laws by the courts and other officials. Fuller underscores the significance of mutual cooperation and interdependence of the legislator and the courts in the creation and due enforcement of legal rules, but a more profound analysis of such an interaction, and of the other elements of the theory of legal interpretation, is touched upon only in the passing in Fuller's major work, *The Morality of Law*. What is crucial is to identify the "true reason of the remedy", in the terminology of the Heydon case from 1584, and to provide the legal solution accordingly, Fuller writes.[28] Moreover, the judge needs to take into account the inherently *purpose-laden* and *community-aligned* character of law, and therefore – in stark contrast Hart's notion of law in his *The Concept of Law* – legal interpretation should not be seen as a semantic or linguistic operation only. Still, Fuller fails to provide any specific guidelines for the judge or legal scholar as to the right track and course of legal interpretation.[29]

10.4 "The Core of Good Sense in the Doctrine of Natural Law" – The Minimum Content of Natural Law by H. L. A. Hart

H. L. A. Hart passionately criticized Fuller's notion of the internal morality of law in his several writings on the issue. According to Hart, any set of such (meta-level) precepts placed on the legislator and the courts of justice do not concern morality at all. Rather, they deal with the general preconditions of any human undertaking that has a goal-oriented, purposeful character, i.e. being aligned with an effective attainment of some objectives and cut off from any genuinely moral considerations. Just as a kitchen knife is good, if its blade is sharp enough to cut bread, meat, and vegetables well, since that is the function of a kitchen knife; and just as an accurate

---

least making them available to those affected by them. Here we have a demand that lends itself with unusual readiness to formalization. (. . .) With respect to the demands of legality other than promulgation, then, the most we can expect of constitutions and courts is that they save us from the abyss; they cannot be expected to lay out very many compulsory steps towards truly significant accomplishment."

[27] Fuller, *The Morality of Law*, pp. 41, 43.

[28] Fuller, *The Morality of Law*, pp. 82–83.

[29] Perhaps somewhat unexpectedly, Fuller's open-ended idea of legal interpretation even brings into mind the ideological openness of Hans Kelsen's *Pure Theory of Law*, while Fuller's idea of the inherently purpose-laden character of law of course draws his theory of law miles apart from Kelsen's purely formal account of law.

watch is good, since precise time-keeping is the very function of the watch; so legislation and individual court decisions, too, can – and perhaps even ought to be – evaluated from such a technical point of view that is free from moral tint. The law in force is then looked upon from the point of view of a means–ends effectivity, the predictability of the outcomes of adjudication, and the appositeness of the instruments adopted for the goals to be so attained, evading any claims concerning the moral merits, or dismerits, of law in the moral sense.[30]

In Hart's astoundingly sarcastic counter-example Fuller's internal morality of law is likened to the contrived idea of a *morality of poisoning*. Such a misconceived notion of "morality" could similarly be formulated in a set of technical norms, such as: if you wish to effectively poison anyone, you should avoid poisons the shape, colour, or odour of which is apt to raise the attention of the intended victim.[31] Effective means for attaining the desired objective do not necessitate having recourse to any genuinely moral values. Rather, mere reference to a causal means – ends relationship among the states of affairs concerned is enough to establish the intended relation.

Yet, even Hart's own, otherwise expressly positivist and voluntarist conception of law entails a weak element drawn from the natural law tradition, known as the *minimum content of natural law*. According to Hart, a set of self-evident truths of the human nature and the human society constitute the "core of good sense" in the natural law doctrine.[32] Hart's idea of the minimum content of natural law is based on the contingent but nonetheless true presupposition that human society is not a "suicide club" that would exhibit total disinterest to the survival or loss of life of its members. Rather, we are dealing with a (meaningful) social order that aims at providing and guaranteeing the prerequisites of human life by means of legislation and legal adjudication.[33]

If the legislator were to ignore the impact of such contingent but nonetheless true preconditions of human life and human society as the basic vulnerability of human beings, their (no more than) limited altruism towards others, approximate equality of physical strength among them, limited faculties of human understanding, and scarcity of the material resources available, it could not rely on their voluntary norm-conformity and co-operation with respect to any other kind of legal regulation,

[30]On the notions of *instrumental* and *technical* goodness, cf. von Wright, *The Varieties of Goodness*, pp. 19–40. *Instrumental* goodness is related to the judgment of functionality of various kinds of tools and instruments, whereas *technical* goodness is related to a skill or talent. An accurate watch is an example of instrumental goodness, since it is accurate in timekeeping. A skilful watchmaker, on the other hand, is an example of technical goodness, as he is a competent and talented professional in the field.

[31]Hart, "Lon L. Fuller: *The Morality of Law*", pp. 343–363, and p. 350 in specific. Cf. Fuller, *The Morality of Law*, pp. 33–94.

[32]Hart, *The Concept of Law* (1961), p. 194: "The simple truisms we have discussed (...) disclose the core of good sense in the doctrine of Natural Law."

[33]Hart, *The Concept of Law* (1961), p. 188.

either.[34] Still, we are dealing with a *contingent* socio-cultural fact that could be otherwise, and not with a logico-conceptual necessity that would define the human condition. Among fanatic religious and political groups, suicidal behaviour is not all too rare. In non-conventional warfare and acts of terrorism, suicide bombings have been widely used as an effective tool for spreading fear and terror among civilians and military forces.

Since the terrorist plane attack against the twin towers of the WTC (World Trade Center) in New York on September 9th, 2001, and the frequently occurring suicide bombings in the U.S. occupied Iraq and other conflict areas in the world, such incidents have not been as rare as they may have been in the early 1960s, when the first edition of *The Concept of Law* came out. Still, if universalized into a general norm of conduct in any society, such suicidal behaviour would ultimately lead to the vanishing of the whole community, so in general Hart's claim of the non-suicidal character of the human society would seem to hold true.

In accord with Hart's critique of Fuller, I would argue that Hart's own conception of natural law, when read in light of his otherwise expressly positivist theory of law, does not count as a set of genuinely moral norms, either. Rather, Hart's minimum content of natural law, too, is a collection of *technical norms*,[35] to the effect of establishing an effective *means–end relation*, i.e. a causal relation, between certain social goals and the legal means necessary for attaining them.

> An example of a technical norm might be: you are in London and you want to reach Edinburgh before the nightfall. The last train from London to Edinburgh will leave in 10 minutes. If, and only if, you run as fast as you can to the railway station, you will catch the train; otherwise you will miss it. Therefore, you *must* run as fast as you can to the railway station (if you really want to catch the train). There is no moral or legal obligation entailed, but the quasi-normative *must*-clause is attached to a causal, means–end relation between the two states of affairs concerned, the act of running and that of catching the train. Similarly: a will is valid and enjoys legal protection under the Finnish law, if its authenticity is confirmed by the signature of two qualified witnesses who were both present at the occasion of the testator's undersigning the will. Therefore: if you want to make a valid will (that will be legally enforced), you *must* have on the document the signature of two qualified witnesses who were simultaneously present at the occasion and who will thereby confirm the authencity of your signature in the will. In the legal context, technical norms commonly take the form of such norms of competence.

For Hart, the ultimate – and, in fact, only – goal of the social order is the survival of an individual and of the human community. The means for attaining it are in the form of legal rules that have the ultimate effect of protecting the status quo based on the contingent fact of human vulnerability, approximate equality of human strength, limited altruism, and the allocation of scarce resources, and so on. The rules that constitute Hart's minimum content of natural law are therefore devoid of any moral content, and the same goes for Fuller's seminal idea of the internal morality of law according to Hart's vehement critique of Fuller. The minimum content of

[34] Hart, *The Concept of Law* (1961), pp. 189–195.

[35] On the notion of a technical norm, cf. von Wright, *The Varieties of Goodness*, pp. 160–162.

natural law addresses the lawgiver, i.e. the legislator, a court of justice, or other legal official, with a *technical norm* of the following kind: "if you wish to bring about an effectively functioning legal order, you should first provide adequate protection for human life, limb, and property for the members of the community concerned".[36] The only sanction (in a wide sense of the term) attached to such a collection of technical norms, outside of the sphere of morality proper, is the likely collapse of the intended legal and social order, due to a total lack of norm-observation and voluntary co-operation on part of the norm-addressees, if such guidelines are not followed in legislation and legal adjudication.

Fuller coined his notion of natural law as *procedural* or *institutional* in kind.[37] He also made the concession that – with the one exception of due promulgation of laws – the criteria that make up the internal morality of law are expressive of the *morality of aspiration* only, and not the *morality of duty* that would place stricter demands on the lawgiver. Therefore, Fuller's institutional morality of law and Hart's minimum content of natural law may both be read as a collection of technical norms, addressed to the lawgiver *sensu largo*, and the violation of which would render the intended outcome of legislation or legal adjudication more or less defective and ineffective. Therefore, the resulting outcome from a lawgiver's failure to observe the morality of aspiration is not – in contrast to what Fuller himself wrote – "something that is not properly called a legal system at all, except perhaps in the Pickwickian sense in which a void contract can still be said to be one kind of contract".[38] A less than perfect legal system, failing to fully reach some tenet(s) of Fuller's internal morality of law, would still be a *legal* system.

Except for the requirement of due promulgation of laws, a legal system burdened with any other type of institutional failure depicted by Fuller, such as criminal law with retroactive effect, a set of internally contradictory statutes or precedents, or an act of legislation with less than perfect linguistic or semantic qualities, are still perfectly valid law, if only they meet with the specific validity criteria set by the constitution or, in more general terms, the rule of recognition *sensu largo*. In fact, the state of having at least *some* mutually contradictory statutes and precedents is a commonplace situation, rather than a rare anomaly, in any fairly complex legal system, to be then solved by means of legal construction and interpretation.

Hart pointed out that a retroactive criminal law is still perfectly valid law, if it has been enacted according to the criteria specified in the constitution, but in light of criteria that are *external* to law – i.e. the ones entailed in the political morality in society, for instance – it is a prime example of bad, unfit, or corrupt legislation that ought to be avoided because the requirements of the rule of law ideology, on the one hand, and because of the intended effectiveness of law, on the other. Fuller,

---

[36]Hart refers to Fuller's catalogue of the eight criteria that make up the internal morality of law with the term "principles of good craftsmanship [for a conscientious legislator]". Hart, "Lon L. Fuller: *The Morality of Law*", p. 347.

[37]Fuller, *The Morality of Law*, p. 184.

[38]Fuller, *The Morality of Law*, p. 39.

in turn, would argue that such an item of legislation will run short of satisfying the criteria of the internal, institutional, or procedural morality of law and, therefore, does not satisfy the aspirational criteria of attaining the objectives of *perfection in legality*, *legal excellence*, *a utopia in legality*, *a sense of trusteeship*, and *the pride of the craftsman*.[39]

In fact, both Hart and Fuller tackle the issue of craftsmanship in legislation and jurisdiction with more or less similar criteria, while looking at the issue from a very different angle of approach each. In Fuller's terminology, Hart's minimum content of natural law gives effect to the *morality of duty*, where the point of view of the "bad man" of Justice O. W. Holmes' prediction theory of law might well serve as the point of reference. Fuller's idea of an institutional morality of law – with the one exception of the requirement of due promulgation of laws – is rather aligned with the *morality of aspiration* for the virtuous, "saint-like" legislator or judge, establishing a set of *supererogatory* guidelines for the attainment of Fuller's idea of perfection in legality and legal excellence in the pride of the craftsman. Thus, Hart defines the very *minimum* standard of legislation and legal adjudication, while Fuller gives an outline of an *ideal* state of legislation and, to a lesser degree, of legal adjudication.

Both Fuller's institutional morality of law and Hart's minimum content of natural law equally fail to pin down a frame of analysis for the construction and reading of law. Fuller's idea of the inherently purpose-oriented and societal character of law locks the frame of legal construction more strictly than Hart's open-ended model of legal discretion where the relatively unconstrained institutional will-formation of the parliamentary legislator serves as a model for the hard cases of legal adjudication. Despite the general reference to the purpose-oriented and community-aligned essence of law, Fuller, too, leaves the precise criteria for legal interpretation unspecified. Moreover, there is in fact a weakly purpose-laden element in Hart's positivist theory of law, as well. Since human society cannot claim to be a "suicide club", overly self-destructive elements cannot be part of the legal system, either.[40] Yet, despite the naturalist terminology adopted by Hart, he was not willing to make any deeper-reaching commitment to the precepts of a genuinely content-bound natural law, beyond and above positive law.[41]

10.5 The Seven Basic Values by John Finnis

Unlike Lon L. Fuller's institutional, procedural theory of law, John Finnis has defended a *substantive* conception of natural law, based on the *self-evident* tenets of law. Finnis' theory of law is a major contribution to the Thomistic tradition in

[39] Fuller, *The Morality of Law*, pp. 41, 43.

[40] Hart, *The Concept of Law* (1961), p. 188: ". . . for our concern is with social arrangements for continued existence, not with those of a suicide club."

[41] On the critique of the missing purpose-oriented element in Hart's theory of law, cf. Finnis, *Natural Law and Natural Rights*, p. 82.

natural law philosophy. Finnis analyses the issue with help of the seven *basic goods* or *basic values* that constitute the ultimate premises of all law.[42] Like Aristotle, Thomas Aquinas, and Lon L. Fuller before him, Finnis underscores the inherently purpose-laden and community-aligned character of all human action, legislation included. Human society exists for the sake of guaranteeing the attainment of certain objectives necessary for human welfare, and that obvious fact validates the superior position occupied by the seven basic goods above any formally valid acts of legislation and legal adjudication.[43]

According to Finnis, human experience teaches us that there are seven *basic values* or *basic goods* that the legislator, the courts of justice, and other law-applying officials ought to pay due respect to, i.e. *life, knowledge, play, aesthetic experience, sociability (friendship), practical reasonableness*, and "*religion*".[44]

In Finnis' catalogue of the basic values, *life* refers to the factors that enhance human self-preservation and self-determination, inclusive of physical and mental health, freedom from pain, and the procreation of life. *Knowledge* as a basic value refers to the intrinsic, and not only instrumental, value of the true beliefs and theoretical understanding of the man and the world, considered as desirable for their own sake. Finnis refers to the fact that the stance of a sceptic (or a nihilist), to the effect that all human knowledge is claimed to be false and erroneous, is in the last resort self-refuting, if the sceptic (or nihilist) at the same time claims his argument to be true, as usually is the case.[45] *Play*, for Finnis, refers to the significance of various kinds of games with either ritualistic or recreational *raison d'être*, i.e. without any instrumental purpose that would render a game into something else.[46] Man is by nature a *homo ludens*, as Johan Huizinga put it, whose inherent inclination towards play, sports, and games the various forms of art, culture, and societal practices reflect. *Aesthetic experience* refers to the experience of beauty and awe when faced with impressive works of art or the similar phenomena of nature. *Sociability*

---

[42]Finnis, *Natural Law and Natural Rights*, p. 46; cf. MacCormick, "Natural Law Reconsidered".

[43]Juha-Pekka Rentto has written an interesting contribution to Finnis' natural law philosophy in Rentto, *Prudentia Juris: The Art of the Good and the Just*.

[44]Finnis, *Natural Law and Natural Rights*, pp. 85–99. – The exact quantity of basic goods or basic values is a conventional issue, though, devoid of any inherent meaning. A similar catalogue suggested by John Rawls entails four elements, viz. *liberty, opportunity, wealth, self-respect*. Finnis, *Natural Law and Natural Rights*, pp. 82–83. – Finnis also refers to Thomas E. Davitt's essay "The Basic Values in Law: A Study of the Ethicolegal Implications of Psychology and Anthropology" (1968) where the author presents different theories of the basic goods or basic values that loom large in the literature on anthropology, psychology, and philosophy. The range of theories begins from models consisting of only one or two basic values, ending up in a model with no less than 12 basic instincts and 14 basic values. Finnis, *Natural Law and Natural Rights*, p. 97.

[45]Finnis, *Natural Law and Natural Rights*, pp. 73–75. Cf. Wittgenstein, *Űber Gewissheit – On Certainty*, § 115 (pp. 18/18e): "If you tried to doubt everything you would not get as far as doubting anything. The game of doubting itself presupposes certainty."

[46]Games may be one-person games, such as solitaire, or social games for two or more players, such as chess, football, or *quidditch* in J. K. Rowling's Harry Potter books.

(*friendship*) comprises to the various types of social interaction and amity among the humans.

Practical reasonableness means the ability to use one's intellectual faculties to lead a life in accordance with the demands of practical reason, taken in the same sense as Aristotle's *phronesis* and d'Aquina's *prudentia*, in various situations of human life.[47] The notion of practical reasonableness has a central position in Finnis' theory of law. He defines it with the following nine criteria:[48]

(1) a *coherent plan of life* in the same sense as John Rawls' notion of a rational plan of life, i.e. a harmonious set of purposes and orientations;
(2) *no arbitrary preferences* amongst the basic human values in life;
(3) *no arbitrary preferences amongst persons*, as the basic goods can in principle be pursued by any human being;
(4) adequate *detachment* from any specific and limited projects in life, so as to be sufficiently open to all the basic forms of good in the changing circumstances of a lifetime;
(5) adequate *commitment* to any specific and limited projects in life, so as not to abandon any of the basic forms of good lightly or without reason;
(6) the (limited) *relevance of consequences*, as efficiency in pursuing the definite goals in life and that the worth of one's actions should be judged by their effectiveness, fitness for the specific purposes, their utility, and the consequences thereby induced;
(7) *respect for basic values in every act* so that each of the basic values be respected in each and every action taken;
(8) the requirement of pursuing the *common good*; and
(9) the requirement of *following one's conscience* in the value choices taken in life.

Finally, "*religion*" (placed in quotation marks by Finnis) as the seventh basic value refers to the human experiences of the transcendental, the finitude of life, and the justification of moral choices and freedom of will by reference to the afterlife or the like idea. Finnis outlines "religion" in a wide sense, so that it comprises even Cicero's Stoic and Sartre's existential, and rather worldly, reflections of the meaning of life and death, on side with the more traditional forms of a religious ethos.

The basic goods are *self-evident* and, therefore, have no need for demonstration or external justification to add to their patently evident nature. On the self-evident character of knowledge Finnis writes:[49]

---

[47] Finnis, *Natural Law and Natural Rights*, pp. 88–89, 102.

[48] Finnis, *Natural Law and Natural Rights*, pp. 100–133.

[49] Finnis, *Natural Law and Natural Rights*, pp. 64–65. Cf.: "Here each one of us, however extensive his knowledge of the interests of other people and other cultures, is alone with his own intellectual grasp of the *indemonstrable (because self-evident) first principles of his own practical reasoning*." Finnis, *Natural Law and Natural Rights*, p. 85. (Italics added.) – Cf. Wróblewski, *The Judicial Application of Law*, p. 306: "Rationality is a basic value which is not further justifiable in the legal

> The good of knowledge is self-evident, obvious. It cannot be demonstrated, but equally it needs no demonstration.

Finnis' philosophical argumentation constantly verges on the threshold of *logical circularity*, as he seeks to justify the self-evident character of the basic values by their a priori character. From the point of view of logic and philosophy, that is not very satisfactory. Since the contested nature of the basic values is now at stake, one should not make an argument to the effect that the basic values are this-or-that as to their inherent character. Yet Finnis writes:[50]

> More important than the precise number and description of these values is the sense in which each is basic. First, each is equally self-evidently a form of good. Secondly, none can be analytically reduced to being merely an aspect of any of the others, or to being merely instrumental in the pursuit of any of the others. Thirdly, *each one, when we focus on it, can reasonably be regarded as the most important*. Hence *there is no hierarchy amongst them*. (. . .) Each is fundamental. None is more fundamental than any of the others, for each can reasonably be focused upon, and each, when focused upon, claims a priority of value. Hence there is no objective priority of value amongst them.

Similarly, he states concerning the value of knowledge, taken as a basic value:[51]

> It is important to see both how much such sceptics are claiming, and how precise must be their grounds for claiming it. They are claiming much, because their claim, if true, would render mysterious the rational characteristics of the principle that knowledge is a good worth pursuing. These rational characteristics can be summed up as *self-evidence* or obviousness, and *peremptoriness*. As to self-evidence I have said enough already: to someone who fixes his attention on the possibilities of attaining knowledge, and on the character of the open-minded, clear-headed, and wise man, the value of knowledge is obvious. Indeed, the sceptic does not really deny this. How could he? What he does instead is to invite us to shift our attention, away from the relevant subject-matter, to other features of the world and of human understanding.

Finnis' argument is at the strongest in respect to life and knowledge, due to the basic knowledge-oriented tenets of the modern Western culture and way of life. As to the other basic values, i.e. play, aesthetic experience, sociability (friendship), practical reasonableness, and "religion" in the wide sense of the term, his argument is open to critique, as the claimed a priori character of such values is far from self-evident.

---

discourse, and respect for rationality is treated as the strength and weakness of the judicial application of law"; MacCormick, *Legal Reasoning and Legal Theory*, p. 268: "My belief that I ought to strive to be rational is not a belief which I can justify by reasoning." Cf. also Wittgenstein, *On Certainty*; von Wright, "Wittgenstein varmuudesta"; Siltala, *A Theory of Precedent*, pp. 215–216.

[50] Finnis, *Natural Law and Natural Rights*, pp. 92, 93. (Italics added.) – Cf.: "The basic values, and the practical principles expressing them, are the only guides we have. Each is objectively basic, primary, incommensurable with the others in point of objective importance. (. . .) Reason requires that every basic value be at least respected in each and every action." Finnis, *Natural Law and Natural Rights*, pp. 119, 120.

[51] Finnis, *Natural Law and Natural Rights*, p. 71. (Italics added.)

Finnis grounds his thesis of the *universal* character of the basic values on certain empirical, i.e. anthropological and historical, facts which are said to be valid in all human communities.[52] In fact, Finnis' line of reasoning comes rather close to Hart's postulates of the universal character of the minimum content of natural law. For Hart, the self-evident truisms of human physiology and psychology in society, plus the scarcity of material resources available for the humans, grounded the core of good sense in the natural law doctrine.[53] It is only on the condition that such (meta-level) norms of natural law are followed in legislation and in legal adjudication that the general functioning of the legal order can be guaranteed, as Hart argued. Notwithstanding the modest objective of mere human survival on the individual and collective level, Hart's vision does not comprise any positive agenda for the attainment of the common good or the good life, as put forth by the adherents of communitarian and virtue ethics. The outcome of Hart's analysis is, indeed, a *minimum* content of natural law.

Unlike Hart's minimalist theory of natural law, Fuller's concept of natural law carries a truly *utopian* impression on it, since it aims at no less an achievement than the attainment of good life and common good through the satisfaction of the basic values identified. For Fuller, mere survival cannot qualify as the only worthy goal for the human community, to be pursued by legislation and jurisdiction. In all this, Fuller is an intellectual heir of both Aristotle and Thomas Aquinas, and not of Thomas Hobbes, as Hart in his most cynical mode would seem to be. The seven basic values in Finnis' theory of law are based on a set of contingent but – from an anthropological and historical point of view – true claims of man and the human community. Like Thomas Aquinas's scholastic idea of law, Finnis' ultimate premises of law are *self-evident* (*per se nota*) and *peremptory*, placing them firmly out of reach of any criticism that is external to law and the stated goals of the mankind.[54]

---

[52]"These surveys [in anthropological literature] entitle us, indeed, to make some rather confident assertions. All human societies show a concern for the value of human life; in all, self-preservation is generally accepted as a proper motive for action, and in none is the killing of other human beings permitted without some fairly definite justification. All human societies regard the procreation of new human life as in itself a good thing unless there are special circumstances. No human society fails to restrict sexual activity; (. . .) All human societies display a concern for truth, through education of the young in matters not only practical (e.g. avoidance of dangers) but also theoretical or speculative (i.e. religion). (. . .) all societies display a favour for the values of co-operation, of common over individual good, of obligation between individuals, and of justice within groups. All know friendship. All have some conception of *meum* and *tuum*, title or property, and of reciprocity. All value play, serious and formalized, or relaxed and recreational. All treat the bodies of dead members of the group in some traditional and ritual fashion different from their procedures for rubbish disposal. All display a concern for powers or principles which are to be respected as suprahuman; in one form or another, religion is universal." Finnis, *Natural Law and Natural Rights*, pp. 83–84.

[53]Hart, *The Concept of Law* (1961), p. 194.

[54]Finnis, *Natural Law and Natural Rights*, pp. 71–73, where the author defends his position vis-à-vis knowledge as a basic good.

Finnis even puts forth the highly challenging argument that each of the seven basic values is in the last resort of equal worth, making it impossible to establish any kind of fixed priority order among them:[55]

> More important than the precise number and description of these values is the sense in which each is basic. First, each is equally self-evidently a form of good. Secondly, none can be analytically reduced to being merely an aspect of any of the others, or to being merely instrumental in the pursuit of any of the others. Thirdly, each one, when we focus on it, can reasonably be regarded as the most important. Hence there is no objective hierarchy amongst them. (...) Each [of the basic values] is fundamental. None is more fundamental than any of the others, for each can reasonably be focused upon, and each, when focused upon, claims a priority of value. Hence there is no objective priority of value amongst them.

Similarly he wrote:[56]

> The basic values, and the practical principles expressing them, are the only guides we have. Each is objectively basic, primary, incommensurable with the others in point of objective importance. (...) Reason requires that every basic value be at least respected in each and every action.

Finnis writes that the basic values of life, knowledge, play, aesthetic experience, sociability (friendship), practical reasonableness, and "religion" can each, one by one, be placed in the focus of contemplation, and under certain circumstances each individual basic value can be proven to have momentary priority vis-à-vis the other basic values. According to Finnis, the self-evident goodness of theoretical and practical knowledge is indubitable, since the state of understanding the man and the world is always better than the respective ignorance or uncertainty of such issues. Shifting the focus of interest and the context of deliberation will alter the value preferences, too, so that each of the seven basic values may in turn be regarded as the most important.[57]

I do not find Finnis' argument entirely convincing, though. Contrary to what he claims, *life* as a basic value is logically primary to all the other values, basic or any other kind, no matter whether we compare it to the value of theoretical or practical

---

[55] Finnis, *Natural Law and Natural Rights*, pp. 92, 93. – Finnis' line of argumentation of the shifting priority order of the basic values is presented in a concise manner on pages 92–95 of his *Natural Law and Natural Rights*, under the heading "All Equally Fundamental". – Cf.: "Each [basic value] is fundamental. None is more fundamental than any of the others, for each can reasonably be focused upon, and each, when focused upon, claims a priority of value. Hence there is no objective priority of value amongst them." Finnis, *Natural Law and Natural Rights*, p. 93.

[56] Finnis, *Natural Law and Natural Rights*, pp. 119, 120

[57] Finnis, *Natural Law and Natural Rights*, pp. 92–93. – Cf. what Finnis writes on play as a basic value: "But one can shift one's focus, in this way, one-by-one right round the circle of basic values that constitute the horizon of our opportunities. We can focus on play, and reflect that we spend most of our time working simply in order to afford leisure; play is performances enjoyed for their own sake as performances and thus can seem to be the point of everything; knowledge and religion and friendship can seem pointless unless they issue in the playful mastery of wisdom, or participation in the play of the divine puppetmaster (as Plato said), or in the playful intercourse of mind or body that friends can most enjoy." Finnis, *Natural Law and Natural Rights*, p. 93.

knowledge, play in ceremonial rituals or free recreation, aesthetic experience, sociability (i.e. friendship), practical reasonableness, or "religion" in the wide sense of the term. Life as striving for survival, avoidance of needless suffering, and pursuit of individual well-being is shared by all or, at least, most humans, and everything else in human life [sic!] is ultimately conditional upon the preservation of life. For Hart, such a basic instinct inherent in the human nature is the only ground solid enough to provide the condition of possibility for social stability and existence of the legal order: a human society cannot function as a collective suicide club, showing no respect whatever for the life of its members, and still credibly claim to sustain the effectiveness and overall functioning of the legal and social order.

The justification for the present stance vis-à-vis the order of preference of the basic values is relatively simple and, in fact, in full accord with Hart's line of reasoning: without taking the inherent worth of life as the grounding premise of human society, there would be little use for anything else, whether in the form of law or some personal and social commodities. As a consequence, life in the sense of survival of the human kind and society ought to be given the status of the prime basic value, as Hart in effect argues in *The Concept of Law*. Yet, Hart was mistaken in arguing that survival would be the *only* collective value or interest that is worth taking into consideration. In this, Finnis' stance as to the variety of (basic) values in a human society is far more realistic.

Once we abandon the idea of forced deliberative equality among the basic values, Finnis' catalogue of values provides a fecund value-theoretical ground for the analysis of law in line with natural law philosophy. Some basic values are yet missing in Finnis' conception of law, however. Though Aristotle underscored the importance of the social or political values for the good life within the Greek *polis*, even depicting man as a social or political animal (*zōon polītikon*), there is no place for genuinely *political* values in Finnis' catalogue of basic values. Equally, the *procedural* or *institutional* values of law, on which Lon L. Fuller grounded his seminal idea of the internal morality of law, are all absent in Finnis' natural law philosophy.

The two basic values that are closest to Aristotle's *political* philosophy and Fuller's *institutional* tenets of legal philosophy are *sociability* (friendship) and *practical reasonableness* at Finnis' theory of the basic values at the back of law, but they do not really comprise the realm of the social, the institutional, or the political. The same goes for the notion of *human rights* and *constitutional rights* that seem to be lacking in Finnis' account of natural law, such as the right to a fair trial that is guaranteed under Article 6 of the European Convention of Human Rights and Fundamental Freedoms. Though Finnis states that the two terms of natural rights and human rights are equivalent for him,[58] he does not tackle the issue of institutionalized human rights at any depth in *Natural Law and Natural Rights*.

[58] Finnis, *Natural Law and Natural Rights*, p. 198: "Almost everything in this book is about human rights ('human rights' being a contemporary idiom for 'natural rights': I use the terms synonymously)."

Under the prevalent *institutional* premises of modern law, the relative weight accorded to the different kinds of human or constitutional rights does not seem to follow Finnis' open-ended model of situational argumentation, with each basic value possibly claiming relative primacy vis-à-vis the other basic values in some situation in the "twists and turns" of philosophical and legal deliberation. Rather, the relative weight accorded to each type of human rights, constitutional rights, or basic values at the back of such rights is determined by the level of institutional support they enjoy in society along with the sense of appropriateness they have. Some human or constitutional rights have more institutional weight than the others. The line of argument defended here is of course an adaptation of Ronald Dworkin's idea of legal principles and their mode of being in the legal community.

Still, Finnis is right when he points out that value-laden *principles* and *standards* of law cannot be locked in a fixed system or hierarchy of arguments.[59] In this, legal principles are crucially different from legal rules. According to Hans Kelsen's and A. J. Merkl's *Stufenbaulehre*, only legal rules may be part of a *static* system that is locked into a hierarchy of rules and is free from internal conflict. A set of legal principles or other value-laden, contextual standards of law may at the most constitute a *dynamic*, *open-ended* normative system (with the notion of a "system" taken in the weak sense here), always subject to be reconsidered and possibly redefined for each novel case to be judged upon. To the extent that legal principles are locked into a static system of law, they will to a similar extent obtain some of the systemic qualities of formally valid legal rules.[60]

Since the 1950s, human rights have gone through a profound transformation from the immutable, universal, and non-positive values with a religious or moral dint, firmly rooted in the reason-based natural law tradition, into a novel position where they are an integral part of the legal system, in the Western world and elsewhere. The conceptual borderline between natural law and positive law has been shifted, as well. What used to be part and parcel of immutable natural law has now been incorporated into positive law through international human rights conventions and the constitutional rights entailed in national constitutions.

10.6 A Critical Evaluation of Natural Law Theory

The greatest advantage or, depending on the personal preferences and aversions of the observer, the worst failure in natural law philosophy is the intertwinement of law and religious, political, or social morality in it. For the adherents of natural law, the subjugation of positive law to the precepts of political morality is one of the strongholds of the approach, as it is thought to effectively safeguard the public

---

[59] If the right to life is conceived as having primacy vis-à-vis the other basic values, it needs to be defined as a rule and not as a principle.

[60] I refer to the notion of systemic formality and other tenets of legal formality à la Robert S. Summers, as touched upon above in the context of legal formalism.

against any legal wrongs committed by the legislator or the courts of justice. For the critics of the approach, such as H. L. A. Hart, the intertwinement of law and morality is a source of conceptual confusion and has the unfortunate side effect of collapsing the distinction between the formal validity of law and its moral merit or demerit.

Natural law philosophy downplays the *institutional* virtues of legal predictability and uniformity in legal adjudication, stressing the content-bound issues of law and equity instead. Yet, there are no theoretical obstructions to combining the two issues in legal analysis, if the premises of how to construct and read the law are defined in precise enough a manner. The collection of basic values in Finnis' philosophy of law cannot provide a fixed reference ground for such combined reasoning, unless the relative weight of each basic value is locked up for good, which according to Finnis is not possible. The resulting outcome will be a free-floating system (in the weak sense of the term) of the basic values and legal principles, necessitating recourse to the act of *weighing and balancing* among them. At the same time, the objective of legal predictability is lost. Also, the justification of the *ultimate* premises of such philosophical or legal reasoning may prove to be problematic, if the self-evident character of the basic values is not taken at the face value.

Instead of locking the ultimate premises of law and legal deliberation in the self-evident, pre-given *basic values* of the type advocated by John Finnis, Lon L. Fuller's *internal morality of law*, with reference to the *institutional* or *procedural* values involved, would seem to a far better match with the value premises at the back of legislation and legal adjudication. H. L. A. Hart's idea of the minimum content of natural law, on the other hand, will not provide for any positive agenda for the construction of welfare in society. Mere survival hardly qualifies as the only worthy goal for the human community. Both Fuller and Finnis are able to provide something more productive for legal analysis, Fuller for the procedural and Finnis for the substantive sense of legal deliberation.

Chapter 11
Radical Decisionism: Social Justice on a Strictly Contextualist Basis

11.1 The Significance of the Institutional Meta-Theory of Law

Legal literature is a cumulative fabric of at least partially overlapping texts all of which assert something about the law and society. Some texts are mutually concurrent, while others are mutually conflicting. Some texts are freestanding and self-supporting, while others lean on other texts for their argumentive force. Still, all legal texts make the claim of contributing *something* to the prevailing or critical concept of law, providing either support or critique for some ideological stance on the law and legal phenomena.

What gives a linguistic assertion on how to construct and read the law its *legal* quality is its relation to the (primarily) institutional and (supplementarily) societal *meta-theory* or *meta-narrative* or *meta-context* of the law. The meta-theory of law lays down a certain kind of *frame of analysis* for the construction and interpretation of law, with coverage of the set of logico-conceptual, ontological, epistemological, methodological, and axiological premises involved. It in other words pins down the *constitutive* criteria of law, resulting in e.g. the concept and definition of law; the internal logic adopted in legislation and legal adjudication, i.e. the binary logic of legal rules or the multi-valued, fuzzy logic of legal principles; the sum total of the institutional and non-institutional sources of law, along with the value premises entailed in them; and the models of legal reasoning acknowledged in a legal system.

Above, the array of feasible meta-narratives of law were outlined with the following kinds of criteria:

(a) The presence or absence of an isomorphic picture relation between the two fact-constellations, or states of affairs, compared, the one as given in the fact-description of a legal rule and the other as possibly existent in the world, under the *isomorphic theory* of law.
(b) The prevalence of mutual match, reciprocal support, common alignment, absence of dissonance, and/or shared congruence of arguments derived from the institutional and non-institutional, i.e. societal, sources of law under the *coherence theory* of law.

R. Siltala, *Law, Truth, and Reason*, Law and Philosophy Library 97,
DOI 10.1007/978-94-007-1872-2_11, © Springer Science+Business Media B.V. 2011

(c) The approval or disapproval of the method and outcomes of legal reasoning in the universal audience, taken as a subjective thought construct of the speaker, under the *new rhetoric*.
(d) The external consequences of law in society under *philosophical pragmatism* and *social consequentialism*.
(e) Retracing the original intentions of the legislator or a precedent-issuing court of justice under *legal exegesis* and *analytical legal positivism*.
(f) The effected law in action in the sense of the totality of the legal rights and legal duties effectively enforced by the courts of justice and other legal officials under *analytical legal realism*.
(g) Common acceptance or recognition of certain phenomena as legal, or the set of mutual expectations and cooperative dispositions to the said effect in a legal community, under *legal conventionalism*.
(h) The logico-conceptual and systemic qualities of law under *legal formalism*.
(i) Recourse to the precepts of absolute religious, social, or political justice under *natural law philosophy*.

Other feasible frames of legal analysis could be added to the list, as well. The meta-theory or meta-context of legal analysis might entail a reference to law as a surface-structure level ideological phenomenon that passively reflects the more foundational, deeper-structure level economic phenomena in society (*Marxist theory of law and society*); the self-evident, a priori characteristics of the phenomena as "things-in-themselves" (*phenomenology of law*); or the claimed gender-related bias in the predominant, patriarchal view on the law and society (*feminist philosophy of law*), to name but three feasible alternatives to the nine divergent meta-theories of law discerned above. Any meta-theory of law seeks to present a relatively balanced notion of the constitutive premises of the law and society by attaching the premises of legal analysis to some fixed reference ground. It is only under a *radically decisionist* account of law that the grip of any feasible *meta-theory* (or *meta-narrative*, or *meta-context*) of law can be evaded.

11.2 Denial of All Feasible Meta-Theories of Law: Kadi-Justice, the German Free Law Movement, and Carl Schmitt on the Law

A radically decisionist and contextual notion of law refuses to acknowledge the bearing of any *meta-theory* (or meta-narrative, meta-context) of law. Under fully consistent contextualism, the same goes for all kinds of non-legal meta-theories, as well. According to a decisionist approach, legal decisions ought to be made on the merits of an individual case only, without recourse to any external reference that could frame and structure the decision-making situation. As a consequence, arguments of an ad hoc or even ad hominem kind, adjusted for the individual case at hand only, will have priority over arguments derived from the traditional institutional and societal sources of law. The goal to be pursued in such discretion is strictly case-bound justice, tailored for the facts of the case at hand only.

What Max Weber wrote about the traditional *Kadi*-justice goes for the radically situationist conception of law in general: as "informal judgments rendered in terms of concrete ethical or other practical valuations. (...) *Kadi*-justice knows no rational 'rules of decision' (*Urteilsgründe*) whatever".[1] In contrast to Kant's *categorical imperative*, the outcome of such purely ad hoc based discretion cannot be extended to a universally binding norm, as that would require having recourse to *some* meta-theory of law and society.

The *Free Law Movement* (*Freirechtsschule*, *Freirechtsbewebung*) had its short-lived heyday in Germany, Austria, and partly even France at the first quarter of the twentieth century. Of modern schools of law, it best illustrates a strictly decisionist approach to the law, free from all meta-level constraints. Its methodological agenda was advocated by e.g. Eugen Erhlich (1862–1922), Hermann Kantorowicz (a.k.a. Gnaeus Flavius, a pseudonym, 1877–1940), Ernst Fuchs (1859–1929), Johann Georg Gmelin, and Hermann Isay (1873–1938). Oscar Bülow (1837–1907) is often named as a precursor of the free law movement.[2] In France, the idiosyncratic approach of François Gény (1861–1938), to the effect that the judge is to have recourse to a free scientific, socially oriented investigation (*libre recherche scientifique*) in the construction and interpretation of law,[3] has close resemblance to the ideas defended by the free law movement.

The free law movement was born out of the critique of the excesses of legal formalism that had been committed by Puchta and other German conceptualists. The formalists had looked upon the judge's act of legal discretion as a purely logical operation, i.e. a *logical syllogism* in which legal consequences could be logically drawn from the combination of the *norm premise*, derived from the sources of law, and the *fact premise* that consists of the material facts of the case. There was no room left for a genuine legal discretion by the judge in the act of applying the legal norms to the facts of the case. Rejecting any such futile exercises in formal logic, the proponents of the free law movement put forth the argument that the judge ought to adjust the decision to the prevailing *notion of justice* (*Rechtsgefühl*) or *value consciousness* (*Wertfühlen*) in the legal community. Echoes of Aristotle's notion of case-bound equity as an essential part of the law can perhaps be heard here.[4]

The free law movement insisted that the existence of free judicial discretion in various occasions of judicial decision-making be acknowledged, in stark contrast to

---

[1] Weber, *Economy and Society*, p. 976.

[2] Larenz, *Methodenlehre der Rechtswissenschaft*, pp. 59–62; Wieacker, *Privatrechtsgeschichte der Neuzeit*, pp. 579–581; Lind, "Free Law Movement", pp. 314–318. – In the essay, Lind gives a good and concise introduction in English of the main thoughts by Ernst Fuchs, Johann Georg Gmelin, Eugen Ehrlich, and François Gény, with Oskar Bülow (1837–1907) presented as a forerunner of the movement at the end of the nineteenth century.

[3] On François Gény as a legal thinker, Bouckaert, "Gény, François (1861–1959)"; Bergel, *Méthodologie juridique*, pp. 249–253.

[4] Aristotle, *Nicomachean Ethics*, p. 1796 (Book V, lines 20–32).

the position held by the more formal approaches to the law. To put it concisely, the free law movement defended the following three theses on legal analysis[5]:

(a) judicial adjudication is a free and creative act, with a significant amount of discretionary lawmaking granted to the judges;
(b) all written law, no matter whether it be in the form of codes, statutes, or precedents, is by necessity incomplete and incapable of providing answers to all pertinent legal issues; and
(c) all rules of legal construction, including those aimed at restricting free judicial discretion, entail implicit value judgments and the application of formally extra-legal principles.

Such a notion of a highly judge-centred law is not far from the idea of a *virtuous judge* whose duty it is to enforce what is just for the fact-constellation at hand, in line with the ideas advocated by natural law philosophy. As the *Rules for the Judge* put it in Sweden in the sixteenth century[6]:

> A good and clever judge is better than good law, since he may settle the issue to match with what is equitable; but if the judge is evil and wicked, there is no use of even good law, since he will bend and twist it as he likes.

In the German Weimar Republic, a radically contextualist notion of law and sovereignty was put forth by the constitutional lawyer and one of the top-ranking legal advisors of the *Dritte Reich* in the 1930s, Carl Schmitt (1888–1985). Schmitt's notion of law is a prime example of decisionist stance vis-à-vis the seminal issues of legal and political philosophy.[7] In the heated debate with Hans Kelsen, Schmitt argued for the *Führerprinzip* or *Führerbefehl* ideology with reference to the ultimate power to declare the state of emergency. Kelsen, on the other hand, defended the sovereignty of the parliament under the traditional rule of law ideology.[8] According to Schmitt and the legal positivists alike, ultimate power in society is derived from

---

[5]Lind, "Free Law Movement", p. 315.

[6]Cf.: "What is not right and equitable cannot be the law either; it is due to its equitableness that the law is acknowledged" (# 9); "All laws need to be applied with good reason, since the greatest [i.e. most severe] justice is the greatest injustice, and there must be an element of charity in law, as well." (# 10); "The benefit of the common people is the best law; and therefore, what proves to be for common benefit shall be law even, if written law would seem to order otherwise" (# 13). (Translations by the present author.) – Olaus Petri (1493–1552), a Swedish scholar and clergyman, drafted the *Rules for the Judge* (*Domarregler*) in the early sixteenth century. Even today, Olaus Petri's rules for the judge are printed at the beginning of the law book in Finland. Of course, they do not have the force of law but only denote the moral and social context of judging.

[7]Schmitt, *Über die drei Arten des rechtswissenschaftlichen Denkens*, pp. 20–24; Schmitt, *Political Theology: Four Chapters on the Concept of Sovereignty*; Medina, "Decisionist Philosophy of Law". – The best commentary in English to Schmitt's legal and social thinking is David Dyzenhaus' *Legality and Legitimacy: Carl Schmitt, Hans Kelsen and Hermann Heller in Weimar*, where the three legal philosophers are concisely compared.

[8]Schmitt, *Der Hüter der Verfassung*; Kelsen, "Wer Soll der Hüter der Verfassung Sein?". Cf. Dyzenhaus, *Legality and Legitimacy: Carl Schmitt, Hans Kelsen and Hermann Heller in Weimar*.

the will of the sovereign ruler, but the notion of the *sovereign* is defined in different terms within the two intellectual traditions. For Schmitt, the sovereign was not necessarily the national Parliament, as the legal positivists would have it. Rather, the sovereign is the one institution that is endowed with the power to proclaim the *state of emergency*: "Sovereign is he who decides on the exception."[9]

Schmitt sought to distance his notion of the law and state from the traditional positivist theory where the ideas of a social contract, sovereignty under the rule of law, and parliamentary legislation have a key position.[10] Though Schmitt may have evaded the impact of *legal* meta-theories in his decisionist notion of law and society, he could not unshackle his political philosophy from the various kinds of social, political, or ideological meta-theories. Working in the service of the *Dritte Reich* since 1933, Schmitt placed his faith in the ultimate success of the National Socialist ideology, which can hardly be claimed to be free from the impact of ideological metanarratives on law, society, and politics. As it stands, the National Socialist ideology was based on an array of quasi-scientific metanarratives of the social order, such as the *Blot und Boden* ("blood and soil") ideology, the *Führerprinzip* or *Führerbefehl* ideology under which the will of the *Führer* had the force of law, and the absolute *Herrschaft* of the Aryan race in respect to the other races, plus other dogmas of National Socialism.[11]

Before Schmitt, a radically decisionist account of the law and human society had been defended by Jean Bodin (1530–1596) and Thomas Hobbes (1588–1679).[12] The impact of Friedrich Nietzsche's philosophy, too, can be seen at the back of Schmitt's notion of law.[13] The focus of Schmitt's philosophy of law was on the questions of constitutive law and the concept of the sovereign, not on issues on how to construct and read the law or the limits placed on the judge's legal discretion. Therefore, I will not enter Schmitt's conception of law in more detail. Instead, I will consider two candidates for a decisionist view on the law and society, viz. Thomas Wilhelmsson and Martti Koskenniemi.

---

[9]Schmitt, *Political Theology*, p. 5. Cf. also: "All law is 'situational law'. The sovereign produces and guarantees the situation in its totality. He has the monopoly over this last decision. Therein resides the essence of the state's sovereignty, which must be juristically defined correctly, not as the monopoly to coerce or to rule, but as the monopoly to decide. The exception reveals most clearly the essence of the state's authority. The decision parts here from the legal norm, and (to formulate it paradoxically) authority proves that to produce law it need not be based on law." Schmitt, *Political Theology*, p. 15.

[10]According to article 48 of the Weimar constitution, the President of the Republic was bestowed the right to proclaim the state of emergency to restore general order and security if the state had fallen into social unrest. The state of emergency was proclaimed twice during the Weimar republic, i.e. in 1919–1924 and 1930–1932, and then again after the fire of the *Reichstag* building in Berlin in February 1933. Tuori, "Carl Schmitt ja vastavallankumouksen teoria", pp. 15–16; Medina, "Decisionist Philosophy of Law", p. 185.

[11]After 1936, Schmitt fell from grace within the National Socialist movement, but thanks to his connections he retained his chair as a law professor in Berlin.

[12]Schmitt, *Über die drei Arten des rechtswissenschaftlichen Denkens*, pp. 22–24; Medina, "Decisionist Philosophy of Law", p. 184.

[13]Medina, "Decisionist Philosophy of Law", p. 184.

11.3 Decisionism in Jurisprudence, I: Thomas Wilhelmsson on the Small-Scale, Good Narratives on Legal Responsibility

In the recent Nordic literature, Thomas Wilhelmsson has defended the agenda of a *social civil law*, i.e. private law that is adapted so as to be highly responsive to the need for enhanced protection of the weaker party to a private law contract or other arrangement.[14] As a means to attaining the said goal, Wilhelmsson, firstly, advocates the adoption of *concrete*, *situational concepts* in legal analysis, like e.g. a debtor or an employee who has been affected by some grave, unexpected economic misfortune, such as serious illness or unemployment, while the outcome is not mainly due to his own fault; at the cost of the traditional, *abstract role concepts*, such as the debtor/creditor or the employer/employee taken in the abstract sense, i.e. without reference to the economic or other "extra-legal" circumstances of the case. With a few exceptions mainly in the field of consumer law, the latter types of legal concepts are yet commonly adopted in legislation and in judicial decisions.[15]

Secondly, Wilhelmsson is committed to the idea of observing *goal-rationality* in legislation and judicial decision-making, paving the way for the protection of the weaker party to a private law agreement "writ large" and serving as a common model for all types of private law transactions. And thirdly, Wilhelmsson has defended the idea of radically transforming the mainstream conception of legal systematics and legal interpretation into a more dynamic, socially more responsive conception of the law, to the effect of turning some individual legislative provision or precedent-based rule that is generally taken as an *exception* to the main rule into a *main rule* to be followed in the subsequent legal adjudication, if the ideological goals related to the interests of the weaker party to a private law transaction or the like arrangement are thereby advanced.

The idea of turning the settled *main rule/exceptions to the main rule* categories in some branch of law upside down will make it possible to present "alternative", critical interpretations of law, with reference to the *l'uso alternativo del diritto* ideology that was envisioned by a group of left-wing Italian judges after World War II. Wilhelmsson's agenda of social civil law, with its idea of seeing the law as a catalyst of welfare-oriented social reform, is based on the notion of *l'uso alternativo del diritto*, as now modified for the needs of the protection of the weaker

---

[14] Wilhelmsson, *Social civilrätt*; Wilhelmsson, "Sosiaalisen siviilioikeuden metodiset lähtökohdat"; Wilhelmsson, "Sosiaalinen siviilioikeus"; Wilhelmsson, "Sosiaalinen suorituseste"; Wilhelmsson, *Social Contra ct Law and European Integration*.

[15] Wilhelmsson, *Social civilrätt*, p. 139; Pöyhönen, *Sopimusoikeuden järjestelmä ja sopimusten sovittelu*, p. 274. – Article 11 of the Finnish Interest Act makes it possible to alleviate the legal interest of an overdue payment, if grave economic difficulties have fallen upon the debtor because of illness, unemployment, or similar reason, said state of affairs has not been induced mainly by fault of the debtor himself, and there are weighty reasons present for alleviating the interest.

party to a private law contract.[16] As a consequence, Wilhelmsson downgrades the role of traditional legal systematics, due to the emergence of a new kind of non-systematicity in law that can be most clearly detected in the law of the European Union. According to Wilhelmsson, the rules and principles of EU law from time to time behave like a "jack-in-the-box" vis-à-vis the national law, to the effect of emerging out of the box when you least expect it to happen.[17]

In addition, Wilhelmsson introduces the idea of the *small-scale, good narratives on legal responsibility*, to be duly recognized and enforced by the courts and other officials. According to Wilhelmsson, the social context of law and legal analysis have gone through a profound change, to the effect of having deprived the traditional meta-narratives of modern law of their initial appeal, and having left the lawyers in a world of *fragmented* legal doctrines and disbelief in any all-encompassing theory or systematics of law. Under the *postmodern condition* of law, the idea of an all-encompassing system of law or grand-scale narratives of legal responsibility have to be renounced as no longer valid, giving way to a loose set of small-scale, good narratives on legal responsibility only.[18]

Still, to the extent that the *goodness* of such small-scale, good narratives on legal responsibility in Thomas Wilhelmsson's novel narratology of law is judged in light of the values entailed in, and fostered by, the Nordic *welfare state* ideology, i.e. the rule of law ideology as twisted by the protection of the weaker party to a private law contract or other arrangements that deviate from the maxim of *pacta sunt servanda*, there is no escape from the reach of a large-scale meta-context or meta-narrative of law. We are firmly back on the legal ground defined by the Nordic welfare state ideology, once the inherent *goodness* of such "small-scale, good narratives on legal responsibility" is to be judged by the circumstances of the weaker party to a contract. In other words, we are back in square one where the Grand Narratives of Modernity loom large.

In his later essay "The Ethical Pluralism of Late Modern Europe and Codification of European Contract Law", Wilhelmsson puts forth the bold but patently self-refuting claim that the *constitutional rights* may now be taken as a promising candidate for a "grand legal narrative" for the postmodern law.[19] The claim is self-refuting, since there cannot be a legitimate reference to any meta-theory or meta-narrative of law, if the allegedly post-modern condition of law is taken seriously. Thus, the key question remains unanswered: on what account do Wilhelmsson's "small-scale, good narratives on legal responsibility" qualify as *good*, if the impact of any meta-theories or meta-narratives of law is denied?

---

[16] In Finland, the Marxist ideology of the *l'uso alternativo del diritto* gained popularity among radical legal academics and scholars in the political turmoil of the 1970s, with Lars D. Eriksson as one of the intellectual pathfinders of the leftist movement in the academic world.

[17] Wilhelmsson, "Jack-in-the-Box Theory of European Community Law".

[18] Wilhelmsson, *Senmodern ansvarsrätt*, p. 193 et seq.

[19] Wilhelmsson, "The Ethical Pluralism of Late Modern Europe and Codification of European Contract Law", pp. 141–146.

11.4 Decisionism in Jurisprudence, II: Martti Koskenniemi on the International Lawyer's Radically Situational Ethics

Martti Koskenniemi is an author in international law, known for his inclination towards critical legal studies. In his breakthrough treatise *From Apology to Utopia: The Structure of International Legal Argument*, he drew inspiration from and leaned heavily on the methodological tools provided by the *Critical Legal Studies* movement. In the book, Koskenniemi ruthlessly subjected the patterns of argumentation in international law to a methodological *deconstruction* à la the Critical Legal Studies movement, leaving behind a shattered collection of "ruins and ashes" there where the shiny doctrines of international law – such as the doctrines of state sovereignty, customary law, the doctrine of legal sources in international law, and so on – had once been raised with great ambition.[20]

In the CLS-spirited discourse on law since the 1970s, Jacques Derrida's idea of philosophical deconstruction has been welcome as a quick *methodological* tool for revealing and turning around the prevailing ranking order of the conceptual dichotomies within the law. That, however, is hardly what the French philosopher and main architect of deconstruction, Jacques Derrida (1930–2004), had in mind when he wrote the key texts of deconstruction. In fact, Derrida expressly rejected the idea that deconstruction might be turned into a straightforward method or tool for philosophical analysis: "Deconstruction is not a method and cannot be transformed into one."[21] Instead, deconstruction as envisioned by Jacques Derrida deals with the enigmatic *ultimate premises* and extreme boundaries of any philosophical idea or conception within the Western metaphysics, concerning for instance the ultimate prerequisites of language and human knowledge.

In Koskenniemi's shrewd analysis, the structure or pattern of international legal argumentation is proven highly volatile and inherently unstable in the face of competing, mutually exclusive claims as presented by the parties to an international legal dispute. In a hard case of international law, all traditional legal arguments, like the one based on *state sovereignty*, can equally well – and equally poorly – be employed by both of the parties to a legal dispute. The use of such arguments may lead either to the ultimate success or total failure for either of the two parties involved, depending on the ideological preferences of the court, arbitrator, or tribunal concerned,[22] and the same goes for any other type of legal argument analysed by Koskenniemi. As a consequence, any legal argument that might be brought up by the disputants to a case will ultimately fail, ultimately having the effect of cancelling each other

[20]The apt phrase of the "ruins and ashes" of international law was coined by Jarna Petman, who so depicted the outcome of Koskenniemi's methodological deconstruction in the post-graduate seminar conducted by me on September 28th, 1998. Prof. Koskenniemi was present at the seminar as well.

[21]Derrida, "Letter to a Japanese Friend", p. 3.

[22]Koskenniemi, *From Apology to Utopia*, pp. 208–209 (*Right of Passage* Case (1960) between India and Portugal), pp. 212–213 (*Nuclear Tests* Case (1974) between Australia & New Zealand and France).

out and leaving the judge, arbitrator, or other international tribunal with no *legal* arguments to lean on in his decision-making.

An intellectual surprise awaits the reader of Koskenniemi's lucid prose at the end of the book, when the so far constant, and unproductive, interplay of the two lines of argumentation, the one *apologetic* and the other *utopian*, is suddenly given up, and a novel shift in philosophical argumentation is adopted.[23] Having carefully "deconstructed" the shiny edifice of international law, Koskenniemi cannot leave the matter as it is, with international law turned into a shack of ruins and ashes, or a shattered body of conflicting theories, misfiring conceptual dichotomies, and failing doctrines of international law. Rather than letting the story end in such a nihilistic vision reserved for international law by the *Crits*-inspired methodological deconstruction, the agenda of critical social theory is "saved" by having recourse to a set of novel premises of analysis that are not *legal* in any viable sense of the term. In the enigmatic end chapter of the book, i.e. "Beyond Objectivism",[24] Koskenniemi rejects the Critical Legal Studies ideology and outlines a *radically decisionist* stance towards legal argumentation in international law.

Thus, a lawyer engaged in international law is advised to be "normative in the small";[25] to make room for interdisciplinary and discursive openness in his discretion, in disregard of any conventional borderlines erected between the different branches of enquiry; to adopt an ad hoc notion of justice,[26] in the sense of having an authentic ethical commitment to the values of critical social or political morality and giving effect to the idea of integrity as a lawyer. In effect, the lawyer engaged in issues of international law is required to reject all the common tools of legal analysis, along with his professional self-conception of what it means to "think like a lawyer".[27]

---

[23]Here, I refer to the end of the first edition of the book, and not to the Epilogue in its second printing.

[24]Koskenniemi, *From Apology to Utopia*, pp. 458–501.

[25]"Rather than be normative in the whole (and be vulnerable to the objections of apologism-utopianism) he [i.e. the international lawyer] should be *normative in the small*. He can attempt, to the best of his capability, to isolate the issues which are significant in conflict, assess them with an impartial mind and offer a solution which seems best to fulfil the demands of the critical programme, as outlined in the previous section. In this way, he can fulfil his *authentic commitment*, his *integrity as a lawyer*." Koskenniemi, *From Apology to Utopia*, pp. 496–497. (Italics added.)

[26]"For issues of *ad hoc* justice are both difficult to solve and can never be solved with the kind of certainty lawyers once hoped to attain. Their solution in a justifiable way requires entering intellectual realms formerly held prohibited from the lawyer. (...) this involves venturing into history, economics and sociology, on the one hand, and politics on the other. It involves the isolation and appreciation of what is significant in the particular case – in other words, realizing whatever authentic commitment there might exist for the parties in conflict. This is a task of practical reason. If my formulation of it seems question-begging and *leaves open the 'method'* whereby it should be conducted, this is only because *no such given 'method' can be outlined in the abstract* which would fulfil what is reasonable in some particular circumstance." Koskenniemi, *From Apology to Utopia*, p. 497. (Italics added.)

[27]"Engaging in practical reasoning, the lawyer shall have to recognize that solving normative problems in a justifiable way requires, besides impartiality and commitment, also wide knowledge of

Koskenniemi's novel intellectual stance is like the perfect counter-image of Kelsen's pure theory of law, i.e. an *impure theory of law* under which all traditional concepts, sources, doctrines, models, and arguments of international law, such as international legal conventions, customary law, legal principles, and state sovereignty, and legal opinions presented in the legal doctrine, will all have to go, leaving the field of discourse open for arguments derived from the realm of international politics and personal moral commitments of the lawyer concerned. In a discourse on international law so carefully "purged" from anything even remotely legal, it is arguments derived from critical political morality and the corresponding practices of international law that are now given effect. In his later writings Koskenniemi has not returned to or revived the idea of the lawyer's authentic ethical commitment, and – so it seems – he has silently dropped the notion.

But how could Koskenniemi's novel situational approach with its emphasis on a loose combination of contextual justice, methodological and interdisciplinary openness, the lawyer's authentic ethical commitment to some subject-bound moral ideals, and the (no more than) small-scale normativity evade the philosophical pitfalls of a methodological deconstruction that proved so fatal for the mainstream conception of international law? As I see it, Koskenniemi's novel situationist, contextualist, and decisionist notion of international law is as vulnerable to the ever-present threat of CLS-inspired methodological deconstruction as Thomas Wilhelmsson's idea of the small-scale, good narratives on legal responsibility proved to be. There simply is no escape from the pervasive, all-encompassing "logic of deconstruction", once reference is made to some Grand Theory of Law, such as the theory of social justice and allocation of social risk in a welfare state (à la Wilhelmsson) or the critical theory of law (à la Koskenniemi). A genuinely decisionist, ad hoc based ethics of law would be a different issue, but then one could not make any claims as to the attainment of the set of more or less leftist values fostered by the American *Crits* or the proponents of the Scandinavian welfare state ideology. The grand meta-narratives of modernity, with the CLS-inspired idea of methodological deconstruction being one of them, cannot be avoided, if the claim of the somehow reason-based quality of the outcome of decision-making is put forth.

Having successfully deconstructed the shiny edifice of modern international law, Koskenniemi's ultimately futile effort of "saving the phenomena" with the help of critical theory is like the forced ending of a stage play in the Antique Greece, where the *deus ex machina* was finally lowered down on the stage in a basket in the final act of the play, providing all the answers to the complexities and open endings

---

social causality and of political value and, above all, capacity to imagine alternative forms of social organization to cope with conflict. It shall lead him to overstep the boundaries between practice and doctrine, doctrine and theory. The construction of *contextual justice* will demand an imaginative effort *to rethink the contexts* in which traditional roles have been formulated and in which their social effects have remained so unsatisfactory. The rethinking of contexts, again, makes it possible to imagine alternative social routines both for the lawyer and his "clients" while the very dynamism of the process *excludes claims of objectivity and universal normative truth*." Koskenniemi, *From Apology to Utopia*, p. 498. (Italics added.)

of the drama. But why should critical social theory be any less vulnerable to the demolishing touch of deconstruction than the more mainstream-spirited theories of international law, both enladen with a metaphysical dint of its own? The impact of CLS-spirited deconstruction is like the mirror image of *King Midas' touch*: it turns everything it touches, not into gold was the case with King Midas' touch, but into a heap of ruins and ashes. The grip of the meta-narratives of modernity, with CLS-inspired methodological deconstruction included among them, cannot be avoided, if the claim of the *acceptable* or *reasonable* quality of the outcome of such decision-making is voiced, as it is made in Koskenniemi's analysis.

In the *Epilogue* to the second printing of *From Apology to Utopia*, published in 2005, Koskenniemi in effect restates his original position vis-à-vis the inherent tension of the argumentation patterns in international law.[28] The radically decisionist CLS stance on law as no more than "politics all the way down" is even now echoed in the Epilogue to Koskenniemi's *From Apology to Utopia*,[29] and so is the resolute recourse to case-bound situationality.[30]

Koskenniemi's shrewd analysis of international law is continued in his second major work, *The Gentle Civilizer of Nations: The Rise and Fall of International Law 1870–1960*, published in 2002. At the end of the book, Koskenniemi envisions an optimistic return to a *cultural formalism* that would not seem to differ much from the plain formalism of Kelsen's *Pure Theory of Law*, except for the (postmodern) *irony* entailed in the former.[31] In Kelsen's theory of law, on the other hand, there is no trace of irony to be found in his scientific and philosophical reflections. So, how could Koskenniemi's novel doctrinal position of cultural formalism evade the reach of deconstruction, the devastating outcomes of which were so skilfully unfolded in Koskenniemi's earlier treatise?

Read side by side, Koskenniemi's two books on international law make up a vicious circle of argumentation, where the CLS-spirited reading of international law in *From Apology to Utopia* relentlessly deconstructs, dissolves, and breaks down the reconstructive cultural formalism that *The Gentle Civilizer of Nations* so hopefully leans on and seeks to enforce; while *The Gentle Civilizer of Nations*, in turn, promises an eternal return to the bliss of a legal and cultural formalism that

---

[28] Koskenniemi, "Epilogue", pp. 562–617.

[29] Koskenniemi, "Epilogue", p. 596: "There is no space in international law that would be "free" from decisionism, no aspect of the legal craft that would not involve a "choice" – that would not be, in this sense, a *politics of international law*." Cf.: "*False Necessity* (...) carries to extremes the thesis that everything in society is politics, mere politics, and then draws out of this seemingly negativistic and paradoxical idea a detailed understanding of social life." Unger, *False Necessity*, p. 1.

[30] Koskenniemi, "Epilogue", p. 616.

[31] Koskenniemi, *The Gentle Civilizer of Nations*, pp. 494–509, and 503–504, 508–509 in specific. – Koskenniemi was the visiting lecturer at my seminar for post-graduate students on 6th November 2002, answering to a set of questions prepared in advance by three (then) post-graduate students of international law, Päivi Leino, Anja Lindroos, and Jarna Petman. The question posited by Petman – and Koskenniemi's answer – as to the relation between cultural formalism and Kelsen's formal theory of law were brought up in that context.

the "deconstructive turn" of the *From Apology to Utopia* turned down and proved unfounded. The interplay of the nihilistic *deconstruction* in the *From Apology to Utopia* and the formalism-reaffirming *reconstruction* in *The Gentle Civilizer of Nations* leaves the reader puzzled in the midst of a philosophical whirlwind, without any solid philosophical ground to lean on.[32] Only the strained and ultimately unconvincing final chapter of *From Apology to Utopia*, "Beyond Objectivism", breaks out from the never-ending circle of deconstruction and reconstruction.[33] That, however, is as vulnerable to the *deconstructive* critique of the other parts of the said book as it is defenceless against the *reconstructive* critique entailed in *The Gentle Civilizer of Nations*. There is no escape from the logic of deconstruction.

11.5 A Critical Comment of Radical Decisionism

Legal decisionism, strictly defined, is fully detached from any meta-theories or meta-narratives of law that would reach for the institutional and non-institutional, or societal, sources of law. Still, once the institutional and societal sources of law are bypassed in legal argumentation, there is nothing left that could possibly warrant the *legality* of the outcome of such deliberation. As Aleksander Peczenik pointed out, the criteria of the legality of decision-making in any Western type of legal system are intertwined with the concept of the (mainly) institutional sources of law[34]:

> The sources of law are, moreover, related to the *concept* of "legal argumentation". One cannot reject all or almost all of them and still be involved in *legal* argumentation.

Moreover, it seems that extreme contextualism or situationism in law is not so easy a stance to sustain after all. Above, Carl Schmitt's situationist social and political thinking still made a commitment to the ideological tenets of National Socialism in the 1930s. Preference for *small-scale, good narratives on legal responsibility* in Thomas Wilhelmsson's would-be contextualist legal thinking proved to be conditional on the grand meta-theory of human rights in a Nordic welfare state. Similarly, the idea of the lawyer's radically *situational ethics* or *authentic ethical commitment* in the field of international law at the end of Martti Koskenniemi's *From Apology to Utopia*, with reference to a combination of contextual justice, methodological and interdisciplinary openness, and no more than small-scale normativity, could not

---

[32] If the (meta)narrative of international law is read chronologically, with *The Gentle Civilizer of Nations* providing for the "rise and fall" of international law in 1870–1960 and *From Apology to Utopia* providing for the end of the story ever after, the question still remains: why should the (meta)narrative of international law remain immune to the touch of deconstruction in its heyday 1870–1960?

[33] Recourse to situationality is repeated in Koskenniemi, "Epilogue", p. 616.

[34] "Rättskällorna är dessutom relaterade till *begreppet* 'juridisk argumentation'. Det går inte att på en och samma gång förkasta alla eller nästan alla av dem och ändå argumentera *juridiskt*." Peczenik, *Vad är rätt?*, p. 226. (Italics in original; translation by the present author.)

provide effective protection against the dissolving forces of methodological deconstruction. It is only on the condition that *all* the feasible premises of analysis that lean on *any* meta-theory, or meta-narrative, of law are discarded that a truly situationist conception of law can be attained. The price for such an argumentative move is paid in the loss of any *legal* qualities of decisions reached under such premises.

Chapter 12
Intermission

12.1 The Ten Frames of Legal Analysis, as Contrasted with Jerzy Wróblewski's Three Ideologies of Judicial Decision-Making and Kaarle Makkonen's Three Situations of Legal Decision-Making

The nine plus one *frames of legal analysis* on how to construct and read the law discerned above give a concise outline on the issues of legal argumentation.[1] Each frame locks up a criterion, or a set of more-or-less converging criteria, for judging the semantic qualities of a legal sentence, defined as its *truth-value* (reference) and *meaning-content* (sense) in Frege's conception of semantics. Following Carnap's model of semantics, we may speak of the *extension* and *intension* of the sentence, respectively. The frames of legal analysis and the corresponding criteria of legal semantics are as follows:

(a) *An Isomorphic Theory of Law*: a picture relation of structural similarity is thought to prevail between the two states of affairs compared, the one as given in the fact-description of a legal rule and the other as existing in the world.
(b) *Coherence Theory of Law*: mutual convergence of arguments derived from the institutional and non-institutional (i.e. societal) premises of law, as defined in terms of *mutual match*, *reciprocal support*, *common alignment*, *absence of dissonance*, and/or *shared congruence vis-à-vis* one another when inserted into, and read as part of, the same narrative pattern.
(c) *The New Rhetoric/Societal Approval*: approval or disapproval of the outcome and methods of legal argumentation in the intended universal audience, defined as a *subjective thought construct of the speaker*.
(d) *Philosophical Pragmatism/Social Consequentialism*: economic or other external effects of law in society, as suggested by e.g. the economic analysis of law.

[1] Nine plus one, and not ten, frames of legal analysis, because radical, ad hoc based decisionism denies the impact of any legally qualified criteria in the construction and interpretation of law.

R. Siltala, *Law, Truth, and Reason*, Law and Philosophy Library 97,
DOI 10.1007/978-94-007-1872-2_12, © Springer Science+Business Media B.V. 2011

(e) *Subjective Interpretation/Legal Exegesis*: retracing the *original intentions* of the legislator or a court of justice, as reconstructed from the law text and the *travaux préparatoires* at the back of it or the justificatory reasons given in support of a precedent.
(f) *Objective Interpretation/Analytical Legal Realism*: law as the (in past) effected and the (in future) enforceable judicial decisions, with reference to the totality of legal rights and duties that enjoy effective legal protection by courts and other legal officials.
(g) *Legal Conventionalism*: law as expressive of collective intentionality in the well-established legal practices and usages in the community, defined with reference to the common *acceptance* or *recognition* of certain social phenomena as having legal significance or as a set of *mutual expectations* and *cooperative dispositions* to the said effect among the members of the legal community.
(h) *Legal Formalism*: law as a closed, hierarchical, and internally consistent system of the basic legal concepts and their hierarchical relations, along with the accompanying mode of logico-deductive reasoning, as outlined in Germany by Georg Friedrich Puchta's *genealogy* or *pyramid of legal concepts* (*Genealogie der Begriffe*, *Begriffspyramide*) and in America by Christopher Columbus Langdell's case method, later known as the "Langdellian orthodoxy".
(i) *Natural Law Philosophy*: the law as a subordinate part of absolute social, religious, or political morality, defined as the internal morality of law (Lon L. Fuller); the seven basic values at the back of law (John Finnis); the minimum content of natural law (H. L. A. Hart); or the human and constitutional rights acknowledged in the legal system.[2]
(j) *Radical Decisionism*: justice on a purely ad hoc basis, as detached from all feasible meta-theories, or meta-narratives, of the law, society, or politics.

It is only with reference to *some* frame of legal analysis that a consistent and adequately justifiable account of the process and the outcome legal argumentation can be given.

Above, Jerzy Wróblewski introduced the distinction between the three ideologies of *bound*, *free*, and *legal and rational* judicial decision-making.[3] The bound and the free ideologies are at the two opposite ends of the line, while the ideology of legal and rational judicial decision-making is situated in the middle. Kaarle Makkonen presented a similar typology of the judge's legal decision-making situations in terms of, firstly, the *isomorphic* situation where a picture relation prevails between the two fact-constellations compared and where no act of legal interpretation in the strict

---

[2]Ronald Dworkin's seminal idea of the role of legal principles with possibly oblique but still legally adequate institutional support and a sense of approval in the community is a "third theory of law" (as coined by J. L. Mackie), since there are elements drawn from legal positivism and natural law philosophy in it.

[3]Wróblewski, *The Judicial Application of Law*, pp. 265–314.

sense of the term is required from the judge[4]; secondly, the *semantically ambiguous* situation where recourse to the methods of legal interpretation is required from the judge; and thirdly, the legally *unregulated* situation where there is no legal norm whatever in the legal system that would have bearing on the fact-constellation to be ruled upon.[5]

Wróblewski's three ideologies of judicial decision-making and Makkonen's three situations of a judge's legal decision-making would seem to correspond to one another so that Wróblewski's *bound* judicial ideology more or less matches with Makkonen's *isomorphic* situation of legal decision-making, since the outcome of legal construction is determined by purely logico-conceptual and systemic criteria in both. Similarly, Wróblewski's *free* judicial ideology would seem to match with Makkonen's *unregulated* situation of legal decision-making, since the judge is not bound by the institutional or societal sources of law in either alternative. Finally, Wróblewski's *legal and rational* judicial ideology would seem to match with Makkonen's *semantically vague*, ambiguous situation of legal decision-making where recourse to the methodology of legal interpretation is required.

Though both Wróblewski and Makkonen were committed to the constitutive premises of *analytical jurisprudence*, there are some key differences in the two approaches. Wróblewski's three ideologies of judicial decision-making are each defined as a self-standing position vis-à-vis the two other alternatives. In Makkonen's typology of the three situations of legal decision-making, on the other hand, the *isomorphic* situation is defined as logically primary vis-à-vis the two other models, since the semantically ambiguous and the unregulated situation of legal decision-making are defined by the *absence* of an isomorphic relation between the two fact-constellations compared. Moreover, Wróblewski's classification is aligned with the various *sources of law*, while Makkonen's typology has more to do with the *semantics* of a judge's legal decision-making.

Makkonen's *unregulated* situation of legal decision-making refers to a situation where there is no valid legal rule that would stand in an isomorphic picture relation to the facts of the case. Makkonen's semantically *vague* situation, in turn, refers to a situation where a particular legal norm, as duly identified by the judge as having relevance for the present fact-situation, needs to be semantically elucidated before it can be applied to the facts of the case. Wróblewski's ideology of *free* judicial decision-making refers to a case where the judge or other legal official may reach a particular decision in disregard of the pertinent sources of law, envisioned by

[4]Makkonen, *Zur Problematik der juridischen Entscheidung*, pp. 78–79: "... kann es sich um einen so klaren und allseitig deutlich gestalteten Fall handeln, dass die anzuwendende Rechtsnorm der entscheidenden Instanz ohne weiteres sofort bekannt ist. Zwischen den gegebenen Tatsachen und den im Rechtsnormsatz dargestellten Tatsachen herrscht dann das Verhältnis des Abzubildenden zum Bilde. Wir gebrauchen für eine derartige Lage die Benennung *Isomorphiesituation*." (Italics in original.)

[5]Makkonen, *Zur Problematik der juridischen Entscheidung*, p. 78 et seq. In German: *Isomorphiesituation, Auslegungssituation, ungeregelte Situation.*

the German free law movement as a *sense of justice* (*Rechtsgefühl*) or *collectively sustained values* (*Wertfühlen*) in the legal community. Finally, Wróblewski's ideology of *legal and rational* judicial decision-making underscores the impact of the institutional and societal sources of law.

The *isomorphic theory of law* seeks to analyse the judge's legal discretion as the presence or absence of an isomorphic relation between the two states of affairs compared, the one as given in the fact-description of a legal rule and the other as existing in the world. *Legal formalism*, in turn, puts emphasis on the logico-conceptual and systemic tenets of legal construction and interpretation. They both give effect to the ideas entailed in Wróblewski's ideology of bound judicial decision-making and Makkonen's isomorphic situation of legal decision-making. The ontological commitments entailed in them comprise a set of states of affairs with a legal tint under the isomorphic theory and a set of basic legal concepts under legal formalism.

The *coherence theory of law* attaches the criteria of how to construct and read the law to the relations that prevail among the *institutional* and *societal* sources of law. The new rhetoric by Chaïm Perelman and its correlative phenomena in the field of legal argumentation take the approval of the methodology and outcome of interpretation in the ideal, universal audience as decisive in legal construction and interpretation. *Legal exegesis* and *legal positivism* in so far as the latter, too, comprises a theory of legal interpretation seek to retrace the original intentions at the back of legislation or a precedent. Alf Ross' *analytical legal realism* is aligned with the effected law in action of the actual court practice, with coverage of the effectively protected legal rights and duties of individuals, judged in light of the collective normative ideology commonly adopted by the judiciary. Finally, *legal conventionalism* defines the law as commonly accepted or at least commonly recognized societal practices that might as well be defined as *mutual expectations* and *cooperative dispositions* of the members of a legal community.

The five approaches mentioned last – legal coherence, the new rhetoric, legal exegesis with either legislative or judicial bent, the effected law in action under analytical legal realism, and legal conventionalism – comprise the *institutional* or *societal* sources of law (or both) as the criteria of legal argumentation. Thus, they satisfy the criteria of Wróblewski's *legal and rational* judicial decision-making and Makkonen's semantically unclear situation of legal decision-making.

In fact, even the isomorphic theory of law could be situated under the legal and rational ideology of law, as well, though it is a borderline case. From the point of view of the *legal source doctrine*, the isomorphic theory of law is aligned with the institutional sources of law since it is from such material that the valid legal rules are to be inferred. From the point of view of legal *methodology*, on the other hand, the isomorphic theory has no use for the canons of legal interpretation proper, except in the sense of identifying and enforcing the existence of the required relation of structural similarity between the two fact-constellations compared. Therefore, the isomorphic model has more affinity with Wróblewski's ideology of bound judicial decision-making and under Makkonen's isomorphic situation of legal decision-making.

Social consequentialism under the premises of philosophical pragmatism stresses the economic and other external effects of law in society, to be judged in terms of economic efficiency, effected transaction costs, and the allocation of various risks in society. *Natural law philosophy* stresses the inherent relation that the law has to the vital criteria of (absolute) religious or communal justice. The *teleological* element in social consequentialism and the *axiological* dimension in natural law philosophy have the effect of cutting legal interpretation off from the *institutional* premises of law, by subjecting legal interpretation to a set of criteria that are external to such institutional premises of legal decision-making. Thus, both approaches would seem to satisfy the criteria of Wróblewski's ideology of free judicial decision-making and Makkonen's unregulated situation of legal decision-making, when viewed from the *internal* point of view of the institutional facets of law.

Finally, *radical decisionism* is difficult to classify vis-à-vis Wróblewski's and Makkonen's theories of law, because of its total rejection of all legal, social, political, religious, and ethical meta-context of law. Yet, as such it is closest to Wróblewski's ideology of free judicial decision-making and Makkonen's unregulated situation of legal decision-making.

Summarizingly, the ten frames of legal analysis may be presented in the form of Diagram 12.1 vis-à-vis Jerzy Wróblewski's three ideologies of bound, free, and legal and rational judicial decision-making and Kaarle Makkonen's three situations of a judge's legal discretion in terms of legal isomorphism, semantic ambiguity, and total absence of a legal rule.

Taken together, the ten frames of legal interpretation present a fairly comprehensive catalogue of the philosophically defensible approaches to legal interpretation. The *meta-context* of legal argumentation and the related criteria of *how to construct and read the law* to a great extent vary from one frame of legal analysis to another. It is only in radical, ad hoc based decisionism that the pertinence of any meta-context of law and legal analysis is categorically denied.

12.2 Jerzy Wróblewski's Ideology of Legal and Rational Judicial Decision-Making Law as a Compound of the Legislative Ideology, Judicial Ideology, and a Societal Conception of Law and Justice

Wróblewski speaks of the ideology of *bound* judicial decision-making with reference to the idea of legal formalism and the "mechanistic" judge denied of any genuine powers of legal interpretation. The role of the judge is reduced to that of "a mouth that reads the letter of the law", as Baron de Montesquieu put it.[6] That,

[6]"Mais, si les tribunaux ne doivent pas être fixes, les jugements doivent l'être à une telle point, qu'ils ne soient jamais qu'un texte précis de la loi. (...) Mais les juges de la nation ne sont, comme nous avont dit, que la bouche qui prononce les paroles de la loi; des êtres inanimés qui n'en peuvent modérer ni la force ni la rigueur." Montesquieu, *L'esprit des lois*, pp. 399–404.

Ideologies of Judicial Decision-Making (Jerzy Wróblewski) & **Situations of Legal Decision-Making** (Kaarle Makkonen)	**Frame of Analysis: Criteria on How to Construct and Read the Law in a Well-Reasoned Manner**
– Ideology of ***Bound*** Judicial Decision-Making (Wróblewski) – ***Isomorphic*** Situation of Legal Decision-Making (Makkonen)	(1) ***Isomorphic Theory of Law***: a picture relation between the two states of affairs (2) ***Legal Formalism***: logico-conceptual & systemic elements of law
– Ideology of ***Legal & Rational*** Judicial Decision-Making (Wróblewski) – ***Semantically Ambiguous*** Situation of Legal Decision-Making (Makkonen)	(3) ***Coherence Theory of Law***: mutual congruence and reciprocal support among the institutional & societal sources of law (4) ***The New Rhetoric***: approval of the method & outcome(s) of legal reasoning at the intended ideal, universal audience (5) ***Legal Exegesis***: retracing the original intentions of the legislator/court of justice (6) ***Analytical Legal Realism***: the effected law in action at the courts and officials (7) ***Legal Conventionalism***: acceptance or recognition of social phenomena as legal or mutual expectations to the said effect in the community
– Ideology of ***Free*** Judicial Decision-Making (Wróblewski) – ***Unregulated*** Situation of Legal Decision-Making (Makkonen)	(8) ***Social Consequentialism***: economic or other external effects of law in society (9) ***Natural Law Philosophy***: attainment of social or religious justice through law (10) ***Radical Decisionism***: *ad hoc* justice in disregard of any meta-theories of law

Diagram 12.1 The frames of legal analysis vis-à-vis Jerzy Wróblewski's three ideologies of judicial decision-making and Kaarle Makkonen's three situations of legal decision-making

of course, is an extreme situation for the judge of being bound by the law. Yet, even Wróblewski's ideology of legal and rational decision-making is a "bound" ideology, since the judge is bound by arguments that can be derived from the institutional and non-institutional sources of law acknowledged in the legal community. As Aleksander Peczenik pointed out, the criteria of legality are intertwined with the use of such sources of law in legal argumentation[7]:

> The sources of law are, moreover, related to the *concept* of "legal argumentation". One cannot reject all, or almost all, of them, and still be engaged in *legal* argumentation.

[7] "Rättskällorna är dessutom relaterade till *begreppet* 'juridisk argumentation'. Det går inte att på en och samma gång förkasta alla eller nästan alla av dem och ändå argumentera *juridiskt*." Peczenik, *Vad är rätt?*, p. 226. (Italics in original; translation by the present author.)

Therefore, Wróblewski's ideology of *legal and rational* judicial decision-making looms large in any analysis that seeks to outline the constitutive premises of *legal* decision-making, strictly defined. Finally, under the ideology of free judicial decision-making, the judge, though not bound by any legal sources or logico-conceptual and systemic premises, may still be constrained by the constitutive elements of the *political morality* in society.

Wróblewski's ideology of legal and rational judicial decision-making can be further divided into the following subcategories:

(a) *Legislative ideology*, as given effect in the constitution, parliamentary enactments, the *travaux préparatoires* (if any), administrative decrees, and the regulations, directives, and decisions with general applicability by the European Union vis-à-vis the EU Member States, and duly signed and ratified international legal conventions.
(b) *Judicial ideology* as collectively and (presumably) more or less uniformly internalized by the judges and other legal officials, as given effect in precedents and other judicial decisions, inclusive of the decisions given by the Court of the European Union and the European Court of Human Rights with respect to the EU Member States and the states that have signed and ratified the European Convention on Human Rights and Fundamental Freedoms, respectively.
(c) *A societal conception of law and justice*, as given effect in the established usages of customary law, settled practices on the allocation of contractual liability among the parties to a private law contract, decisions and resolution recommendations given by private and semi-official arbitration boards, and standards of professional ethics and well-esteemed professional practices acknowledged by the legal profession.

The *legislative ideology* comprises the idea of seeing the law as a result of the official will-formation of the state in abstract laws. The *judicial ideology* comprises the judges' and other legal officials' conception of law, as manifested in the effected law in action of individual court decisions and the premises they are based on. Finally, a *societal conception of law and justice* comprises the legal community's point of view to the law, as the view of the majority or in some other sense of the democratic rule.

The relative weight accorded to the different kind of legal source material to a great extent varies in different legal systems, depending on the cultural, linguistic, and historical characteristics entailed. In the Continental and Nordic legal systems, parliamentary legislation and other elements of the legislative ideology usually gain priority over precedents and the like elements of the collective judicial ideology, and over customary law and the like elements of a societal conception of law and justice. In Sweden, in specific, the *travaux préparatoires* have occupied a weighty position as a source of law. In the English and American common law, on the other hand, the part of judicial ideology that is embodied in the construction of the *ratio decidendi* of a precedent generally gains priority over any legislative intentions and over any purely societal accounts of law and justice as well.[8] The role of a societal conception of law and society, and of the accompanying community-based sources of law, has been in constant decline in the Western world since the emergence of the great law codifications at the late eighteenth and the early nineteenth century. Today, such community-oriented arguments usually have the status of supplementary sources of law only in most, if not all, Western legal systems.

Recent global changes in law and society have to some extent altered the picture, resulting in the emergence of *international*, *multinational*, and *transnational* law on side with the more traditional national law in legal analysis[9]; the impact of the old and new kind of *lex mercatoria*; the creation of a novel *ius commune* in Europe, with reference to the border-crossing EU law and the protection of human rights on a European or global scale; the law of the *cyberspace* of the internet; and so on. Such changes have to some extent levelled down the differences between the two, or three, legal traditions in the Western world, i.e. the common law tradition, the civil law tradition of the Continental Europe, and the law of the Nordic countries.

The relation between the various *sources of law* and *frames of legal analysis* under Jerzy Wróblewski's *legal and rational* ideology of law can be summarizingly depicted with Diagram 12.2.

Legislative ideology gives effect to the will-formation of the state, as expressed in the constitution, parliamentary legislation, and the official *travaux préparatoires*, if any, and administrative regulations. The impact of such an ideological stance vis-à-vis law can best be seen articulated in legal positivism and legal exegesis, with emphasis on the original intentions of the parliament; the coherence theory of law, on the condition that legislation and possibly even the *travaux préparatoires* are acknowledged as sources of law; analytical legal realism, if the impact of legislation and the legislative intentions entailed in the *travaux préparatoires* are acknowledged as having a normative impact on the judge's legal discretion; and the new rhetoric and legal argumentation theory, if such legislative documents are to be duly taken into account by the judges and other officials as is commonplace in all Western legal systems.

Judicial ideology, as collectively and, presumably, more-or-less uniformly internalized by the judiciary and other law-applying officials, looks upon the law from the point of view of the judge and other officials, as the effected "law in action" in the court practice. In specific, the judicial ideology comprises the judges' *precedent-ideology*, i.e. the methods adopted by the judiciary in constructing the *ratio decidendi* of an individual court case and distinguishing it from the *obiter dicta* elements of that decision. Analogically, the notion of such precedent-ideology may be extended to cover other judicial decisions, as well. Judicial ideology will find

[8] The part of judicial ideology that deals with the definition and separation of the *ratio decidendi* of a case from the *obiter dicta* elements in that case may be called a *precedent-ideology*. Cf. Siltala, *A Theory of Precedent*.

[9] A concise account of the concept of *transnational* law is given in Glenn, "A Transnational Concept of Law", passim.

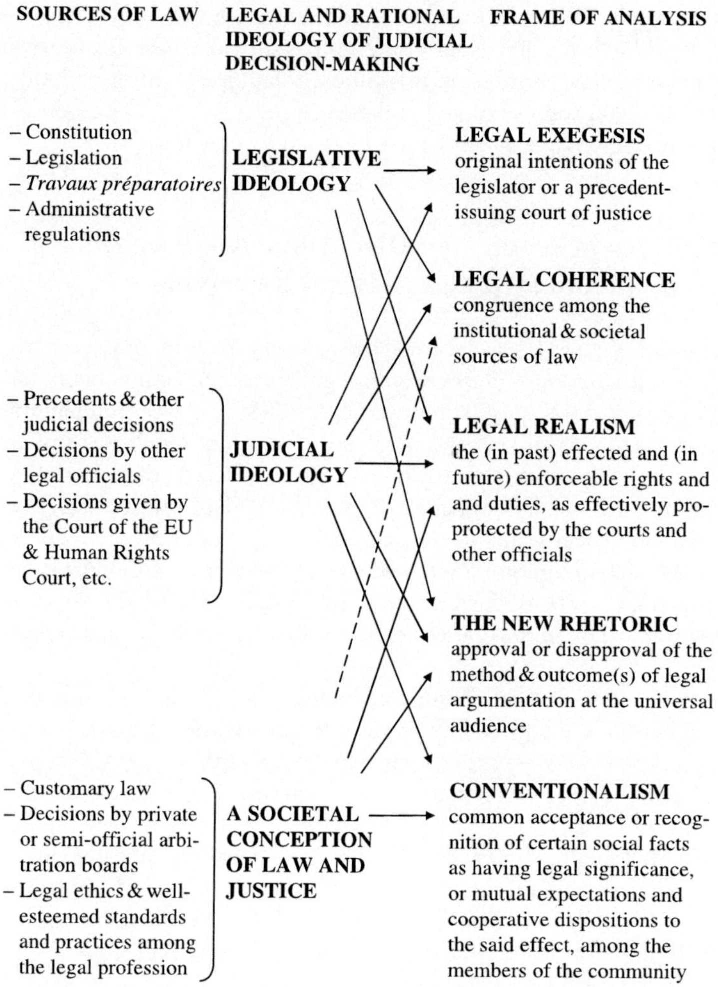

Diagram 12.2 The institutional and societal sources of law, the three constitutive elements of the legal and rational ideology of judicial decision-making, and the five frames of legal analysis entailed

support in the five distinct frames of legal analysis, i.e. legal positivism and legal exegesis, the coherence theory of law, analytical legal realism, the new rhetoric and legal argumentation theory, and legal conventionalism.

A *societal conception of law and justice* gives primary effect to the different kinds of non-institutional, societal sources of law, such as *lex mercatoria* and other manifestations of customary law; well-settled conventions, usages, and practices on the allocation of liability among the parties to a private law contract; decisions given by private and semi-official arbitration boards; and professional standards of esteem and professional ethics among the legal profession of some branch of law. Such arguments may gain importance under the coherence theory of law, the new rhetoric, analytical legal realism, and legal conventionalism. In addition, the requirement of coherence may have impact on the mutual relations of different kinds of non-institutional, societal sources of law, if there are several societal elements involved. In the diagram, the broken arrow depicts such a phenomenon.

12.3 From a Synchronic to a Diachronic Approach: Two Sequential Models of Legal Reasoning

So far, the focus of analysis has been on a *synchronic* account of the criteria of legal construction and interpretation. However, legal reasoning as it actually takes place at a court of justice or other official most often follows a *sequential* pattern, justifying a switch to a *diachronic* mode of analysis in which different types of arguments may follow one another in a chronological order. In recent literature, two sequential models of legal reasoning stand out, viz. Neil MacCormick's theory of legal reasoning as defined in terms of the three C's of the *consistency*, *coherence*, and *consequences* of legal interpretation; and the model of legal argumentation adopted by the *Bielefelder Kreis*, defined in terms of the *linguistic*, *systemic*, *teleological-axiological*, and *intentional* arguments, to be utilized in that chronological order.[10]

In fact, sequential models are quite a commonplace in the legal source doctrine. Aleksander Peczenik's and Aulis Aarnio's three-part model of the *must*-sources, *should*-sources, and *may*-sources of law may be read in a sequential manner, where the one category of legal source material needs to be exhausted before turning to the following one.[11]

Thus, Kaarle Makkonen's catalogue of the three legal decision-making situations in terms of the isomorphic, semantically ambiguous, and unregulated cases of legal discretion could be read in a diachronic manner, to the effect that the judge's process of legal interpretation starts with a search for an isomorphic relation in the two fact-constellations at hand. If the search for isomorphism fails, the judge will then have recourse to the methodology of legal semantics at the presence of linguistic ambiguity. Finally, if that effort equally fails to settle the issue, reasoning based on analogy will then be adopted at the absence of any legal rule with normative bearing on the case at hand, according to Makkonen. Wróblewski's three-partite classification of the judicial ideologies could naturally be read in a similar manner, though neither Makkonen nor Wróblewski suggests such an interpretation.

---

[10] Similar models of argumentation can of course be found in the American literature on jurisprudence, as well. For instance, in Wilson Huhn's lucid presentation of the topic, *Five Types of Legal Argument*, the five categories of *text*, *intent*, *precedent*, *tradition*, and *policy* are analysed in light of the American experience. Cf. Huhn, *Five Types of Legal Argument*.

[11] Cf. Peczenik, *On Law and Reason*, pp. 319–371; Aarnio, *The Rational as Reasonable*, pp. 89–101.

12.3.1 Neil MacCormick's Theory of the Three C's in Legal Reasoning: From Consistency and Coherence to the Consequences of Law

Ota Weinberger (1919–2009) and D. Neil MacCormick (1941–2009) are the two founders of the *institutional* approach to legal theory, based on insights into "how to do things with words",[12] as now applied in the legal context. Austin's notion of the trilogy of *locutionary*, *illocutionary*, and *perlocutionary* speech-acts was loosely based on Ludwig Wittgenstein's late philosophy after his "linguistic turn" in the early 1930's. Now, the scope of legitimate uses of language was extended beyond the strict limits of the picture theory of language, making room for a great variety of *language-games* in society. Wittgenstein's ideas were taken up and further elaborated by the *Oxford school of linguistic philosophy*, i.e. *ordinary language philosophy*, in the 1950s and 1960s.

Neil MacCormick's and Ota Weinberger's institutional approach provides a credible account of how legal *institutions* (*in abstracto*) and their individual *instances* (*in concreto*), such as marriages, wills, contracts, mortgages, the legislative power of the Parliament, or the jurisdictional power of the Supreme Court of Justice, can initially be *created*, subsequently *altered* in content, *enforced* as to their legal effects, and ultimately *derogated* by means of certain linguistic expressions.[13]

In *Legal Reasoning and Legal Theory* and in his other writings on the issue Neil MacCormick has argued for a *sequential* theory of legal reasoning.[14]

According to MacCormick, legal reasoning at a court of justice or other law-applying official commonly takes place in the following order: from deductive *consistency* among the linguistic arguments to the attainment of legal *coherence* among the pertinent set of legal principles, if the deductive approach fails to resolve the issue, and ultimately to *consequentialist* arguments of the external social effects of legal adjudication and the values entailed therein, if the search for legal coherence

---

[12]Austin, *How to Do Things with Words*, passim.

[13]The *institutions/instances* dichotomy in institutional theory of law is parallel to the *type/token* dichotomy in linguistic philosophy.

[14]The late Neil MacCormick's main works in jurisprudence include *Legal Reasoning and Legal Theory* (1978), *Questioning Sovereignty: Law, State, and Nation in the European Commonwealth* (1999), *Rhetoric and the Rule of Law: A Theory of Legal Reasoning* (2005), *Institutions of Law: An Essay in Legal Theory* (2007), and *Practical Reason in Law and Morality* (2008). The four books mentioned last make up the series *Law, State, and Practical Reason*. In addition, MacCormick was a member of the research group *Bielefelder Kreis* that produced two first-rate contributions to the topics of comparative legal argumentation theory: *Interpreting Statutes: A Comparative Study* and *Interpreting Precedents: A Comparative Study*. I have very warm personal recollections of Sir Neil from October 1998, when he acted as the official opponent at the public defence of my doctoral dissertation, *A Theory of Precedent*, and from August 2006, when he was the honorary guest at my post-graduate seminar, devoted to his legal philosophy under the title *Post-Sovereign Nations, Rhetorics, and the Rule of Law – A Seminar on Neil MacCormick's Institutional Philosophy of Law*.

equally fails to resolve the issue.[15] MacCormick's theory might be (re)labelled the *Theory of the Three C's in Legal Reasoning*: from linguistic *consistency* to the pursuit of principled, analogy-aligned *coherence* among legal principles and, ultimately, to the value-laden social *consequences* of law.

In outlining the final premises of law in analogy to Hans Kelsen's basic norm (*Grundnorm*) or H. L. A. Hart's rule of recognition, MacCormick introduces the notion of *underpinning reasons*. They are "reasons for accepting the [legal] system's criteria of validity", with reference to "*consequentialist* arguments which are essentially *evaluative* and therefore in some degree *subjective*."[16] MacCormick further argues that the two categories of *rightness reasons* and *goal reasons* in Robert S. Summers' typology of the two types of substantive reasons are essentially the "two sides of the same coin".[17] As is well known, Ronald Dworkin has put forth the argument to the effect that the *rights* of an individual, based on *legal principles*, ought to be recognized as legal *trumps* over social policies, based on *collective goals*. According to MacCormick, teleological or consequentialist reasons can always be transformed into value-laden rightness reasons, and vice versa. An institutional theory of law would seem to be more open to value-laden arguments than Kelsen's or Hart's analytical legal positivism.[18]

MacCormick's three-partite approach to legal reasoning would seem to match well with the isomorphism-oriented *isomorphic* theory of law at its first stage of striving for deductive linguistic consistency; with the *coherence* theory of law at its second stage of seeking to attain legal coherence among a set of legal principles; and with the pragmatism-oriented approach of social *consequentialism* under pragmatist terms at its third, final stage of analysis, where the external social consequences of law are deemed significant, even if the three successive alternatives are now defined in a somewhat less strict manner than above. Still, the main tenets of the three approaches are present even now: the inherent link to legal linguistics and formal deductive logic at the first phase[19]; the idea of legal coherence among a set

[15] A concise summary of MacCormick's early account of legal reasoning is in MacCormick, *Legal Reasoning and Legal Theory*, pp. 250–251. Cf. his later summary: "The conclusive or clinching point of argument when a case still stands open after such testing for *consistency* and *coherence* is an argument about *consequences* . . ." MacCormick, *Rhetoric and the Rule of Law*, p. 104. (Italics added.)

[16] MacCormick, *Legal Reasoning and Legal Theory*, pp. 64, 106.

[17] MacCormick, *Legal Reasoning and Legal Theory*, pp. 117–120 (with the coin metaphor is on p. 120); cf. Summers, "Two Types of Substantive Reasons: The Core of a Theory of Common-Law Justification", passim.

[18] In *Institutions of Law*, MacCormick takes a critical stance vis-à-vis legal positivism à la Kelsen and Hart, and labels his own thinking as a *post-positivist* philosophy of law. MacCormick, *Institutions of Law*, p. 279: "It is perhaps most sensible to say that this book presents an institutional theory of law, and that this theory draws inspiration both from some strands of thought previously advanced by self-proclaimed 'legal positivists' and from others derived from 'natural law' theorizing. It is post-positivist, if not anti-positivist."

[19] In *Rhetoric and the Rule of Law*, pp. 49–77 ("Defending Deductivism"), MacCormick defends the challenging idea that the deductive, syllogistic model of reasoning defines the inherent structure

of value-laden legal principles or standards at the second phase; and an eye on the social effects of law at the third phase of argumentation.

Summarizingly, Neil MacCormick's theory of legal reasoning would seem to match fairly well with the above outline of legal analysis, if analysis is restricted to the frames of law that focus on linguistic *consistency* under the *isomorphic* theory of law, *coherence* among legal principles under the *coherence* theory of law, and the external *consequences* of law in society under *philosophical pragmatism.*

12.3.2 The Bielefelder Kreis*: A Sequential Order of the Linguistic, Systemic, Teleological-Axiological, and Transcategorical Arguments in Legal Reasoning*

The research group *Bielefelder Kreis* consists of first-class legal philosophers in the field of analytical jurisprudence, such as Jerzy Wróblewski, Neil MacCormick, Robert S. Summers, Robert Alexy, Aleksander Peczenik, Aulis Aarnio, Svein Eng, and the Italian comparatist Michele Taruffo.[20] The *Bielefelder Kreis* focused on a comparative and theoretical analysis of legal reasoning, drawing its methodological inspiration mostly from analytical jurisprudence and legal argumentation theory. The group was active from the mid-1980s to the late 1990s. It published two books: *Interpreting Statutes: A Comparative Study* (in 1991) *and Interpreting Precedents: A Comparative Study* (in 1997).[21]

The mode of reasoning in most of the highest national courts included in the analysis by the *Bielefelder Kreis* was seen to follow a *sequential* logic of legal argumentation; being reminiscent of the one adopted by Neil MacCormick, himself

---

of law, even if the express justification of the decision were given in less formal terms. As a consequence, a legal decision can always be transformed into an instance of syllogistic reasoning, if the relation between the norm and fact premises and the outcome of such reasoning is questioned, which defines the "deeper" logic of reasoning in the Western legal systems.

[20] I had the privilege of acting as the secretary of the *Bielefelder Kreis* in two of its meetings, first in Bologna and Florence, Italy, and then in Tampere, Finland, in the mid-1990s, when the book *Interpreting Precedent* was being drafted. The standard of legal scholarship was exceptionally high in the group, with Jerzy Wróblewski (in sessions during the 1980s) usually acting as the "master of legal analytics", summarizing the discussion so far conducted from time to time, and Neil MacCormick and Robert S. Summers, as the two chairmen of the group, keeping the discussion on the right track, i.e. the current point of issue. Legal comparative issues were mainly taken care of by Michele Taruffo, the Italian legal comparatist, while all the other members of the *Bielefelder Kreis* were professionals in analytical jurisprudence and legal argumentation theory. – The description of the role held by Jerzy Wróblewski in the meetings of the *Bielefelder Kreis* in the 1980s is based on what Aulis Aarnio, himself a member of the group, once told me.

[21] Since over 10 years have passed since the publication of the latest work of the group and since some of the key members of group are now deceased, i.e. Jerzy Wróblewski (†1990), Aleksander Peczenik (†2005) and Neil MacCormick (†2009), and since the group has not been called in for the preparation of some new project, we may – regrettably – have to look upon the *Bielefelder Kreis* as a historical phenomenon nowadays.

a member of the group.[22] Even the naming of the categories of argument are quite similar, viz. logical and linguistic consistency at the first stage, coherence among principles of law at the second stage, and the value-laden consequences of law in society at the third stage in MacCormick's analysis; and the categories of *linguistic*, *systemic*, and *teleological-axiological* arguments in the analysis by the *Bielefelder Kreis*. It is only the fourth category added to the list by the *Bielefelder Kreis*, viz. the *transcategorical* argument, or the intentions of the lawgiver, that is a novelty here and fails to find a match in MacCormick's respective analysis.[23] Due to the ambivalent character of the transcategorical argument, one might perhaps do better without it.

According to the *Bielefelder Kreis*, the methodology utilized in the context of statutory law commonly makes use of four types of argument, each with several subcategories, with the following sequence of arguments:

A. Linguistic arguments:

(1) the argument from *ordinary* meaning;
(2) the argument from *technical* meaning.

B. Systemic arguments:

(3) the argument from *contextual-harmonization*, with reference to the legal systemic context of a statute or a set of statutes, as found in the same branch of law or the legal system in totality;
(4) the argument from *precedent*, with reference to the observance of the doctrine of stare decisis (sensu largo) and the idea of a *jurisprudence constante* in jurisdiction;
(5) the argument from *analogy*, with reference to the prior interpretation of some other statutory provisions in the same branch of law as the one now under consideration;
(6) *logico-conceptual* argument, with reference to a consistent interpretation of general legal concepts in a branch of law;
(7) the argument from the *general principles of law*, with reference to the weighing of such legal principles as have impact on the legal issue,
(8) the argument from *history*, with reference to historically evolving interpretation of a statute,

---

[22]The division of legal source material, and of arguments derived from them, in the two books by the *Bielefelder Kreis* is adopted from Aleksander Peczenik's model where such material is divided into the three categories of *must*-sources, *should*-sources, and *may*-sources.

[23]MacCormick and Summers, eds., *Interpreting Statutes*, pp. 512–525. – In his summary account of the results attained by the *Bielefelder Kreis*, MacCormick, though he briefly mentions it (on p. 125), yet bypasses the transcategorical argument in the further elaboration of the thematics. Cf. MacCormick, *Rhetoric and the Rule of Law*, p. 124 et seq. Summarizingly on the prima facie sequence of arguments, MacCormick and Summers, *Interpreting Statutes*, pp. 530–532.

C. Teleological-Axiological Arguments:

(9) the argument from *purpose*, with reference to the postulated "point and purpose", or purposes, of a statutory provision, as found in e.g. the *travaux préparatoires* of the enactment;

(10) the argument from *substantive* reasons, with reference to the such values entailed in a statutory provision as are deemed fundamental for the legal order.

D. The Argument from Intention:

(11) the *transcategorical* argument, with reference to the legislative *intention* at the back of legislation, by means of which the prior categories of argument may be "transcended" and priority be given to some specific linguistic, systemic, or teleological-axiological reading of law, due to its having the best match with the authentic intentions of the lawgiver.

The meta-level notion of a *transcategorical* argument that closes the sequence of putting forth of arguments in the *Bielefelder Kreis* catalogue is by far the most problematic of the four main types of argument discerned. *Linguistic* arguments either follow the ordinary use of linguistic concepts or some technical subcategory, such as the linguistic usage adopted in the field of engineering, statistics, medicine, or physics. The wide array of argument types under *systemic* arguments are relatively easy to identify in any legal system, and so is reference to the social purposes and values at the back of an item of legislation in all but excessively formalist modes of legal reasoning. The category of systemic arguments perhaps should be broken down into smaller units, as all the *legal*, i.e. institutional arguments, are entailed therein. *Teleological-axiological* arguments correspond to Neil MacCormick's idea of consequentialist arguments in legal reasoning, and that is where MacCormick ended the issue.

But *why* will some specific linguistic, systemic, or axiological-teleological interpretation be chosen among the various alternatives, each backed by some institutional or other kinds of arguments? The *Bielefelder Kreis* seeks to provide an answer with the *transcategorical* argument, or the intentions of the lawmaker. It is left for such a transcategorical, *meta-level* argument to determine the ranking order for the case at hand between the *first-level* arguments of linguistic, systemic, and teleological-axiological kind. Recourse to the transcategorical argument is open to critique, since there is no way of finding out whether the proposed content of such a closing argument in fact corresponds to the original intentions of the parliamentary at the time of issuing the enactment or those of a court of justice at the time of its giving out a precedent.[24] If the linguistic, systemic, and teleological-axiological

[24] On the argument from intention, MacCormick and Summers, eds., *Interpreting Statutes*, pp. 522–525.

arguments cannot settle the issue, some kind of meta-level criterion is of course needed to resolve the argumentative deadlock. Still, it would be fairer to present the constitutive premises of any meta-level arguments in as open terms as is possible, without invoking a reference to any postulated entity that escapes scientific control, as the use of a transcategorical argument in effect does.

Chapter 13
Law and Metaphysics

13.1 The Truth of a Legal Sentence As Determined by the Frame of Analysis Adopted

As mentioned in the Introduction above, the truth of a linguistic proposition or sentence is commonly defined with reference to one of the following three alternatives in the traditional philosophical literature:

(a) the *correspondence* theory of truth: there is an *isomorphic*, picture relation between a linguistic assertion and the corresponding fact or state of affairs in the world;
(b) the *coherence* theory of truth: there is a mutual match and reciprocal congruence among a set of linguistic propositions or arguments under;
(c) the *pragmatic* theory of truth: *warranted assertability* can be applied to certain beliefs or conceptions, defined in terms of the empirically observable consequences of a belief, its approval or disapproval at the intended audience of argumentation, or its being commonly accepted or recognized as having certain kind of qualities in the community.

In the legal context, the required link to a philosophically sound and solid theory of truth may need to be softened and weakened a bit, so as to make room for the *institutional* characteristics of law.

Though neither of the two founders of modern semantics, Gottlob Frege and Rudolf Carnap, focused on the semantics of law in specific, Frege's idea of the *reference* (*Bedeutung*, *nominatum*) and *sense* (*Sinn*) of a linguistic sign or expression may well be extended to the domain of law. Naturally, the same goes for Carnap's method of *extension* and *intension*. Since the semantic reference (Frege) or extension (Carnap) of an assertion is equal to its *truth-value*, such a conception of language by necessity entails a commitment to *some* internally consistent conception of truth.

Modern law is a *constructive*, inherently interpretation-bound phenomenon (Ronald Dworkin); an *essentially contested concept* that is open to a host of divergent readings and interpretations (W. B. Gallie); or a *deliberative practice* (Thomas

R. Siltala, *Law, Truth, and Reason*, Law and Philosophy Library 97,
DOI 10.1007/978-94-007-1872-2_13, © Springer Science+Business Media B.V. 2011

Morawetz) whose identity is always open to be challenged and possibly redefined by those engaged in the legal discourse. Therefore, there is no one right definition of the concept of law, nor of the constitutive criteria that determine the semantic qualities of a legal assertion on how to construct and read the law.[1] In other words, there is no absolute, a priori, or self-justified point of view to the law that could oust other alternatives out from legal deliberation and legal discretion. But nor can there be a totally non-committed, self-sustaining *view from nowhere* to the law that would be free from all the philosophical and ideological premises that define the very subject matter and methodology of legal analysis. The analysis of law will need to incorporate some stance on "what there is" in the sphere of law, in the sense of the constitutive elements of a legal ontology; the inclusion and exclusion of different kind of legal source material and types of argument under legal epistemology; the commonly approved models of legal reasoning under legal methodology; the logico-linguistic commitments of the law; axiological premises concerning the relation of the law to social values and ideologies; and so on.

Without an express or tacit entailment of such philosophical prerequisites in legal analysis, the notion of law could not be configured in the first place, or at least not in a fairly consistent manner. In the domain of law and legal analysis, the epistemic and semantic concepts of *truth* and *knowledge* can only give effect to *qualified*, *conditional*, or *provisional* knowledge that is by necessity relative to, and determined by, a set of theory-laden premises that define the constitution of law with reference to the *ontological*, *epistemological*, *methodological*, *logico-conceptual*, *axiological*, and possibly other commitments involved.

The frame of legal analysis adopted determines the semantic qualities of a legal assertion on how to construct and read the law in terms of the *reference/extension* and *sense/intension*, or the *truth-value* and *meaning-content*, of the said assertion. The truth of a legal assertion to the effect that "the content of law vis-à-vis fact-constellation F_N is x" is conditional on a set of *truth-constituting* premises, defined by the ideologies of *bound*, *legal and rational*, and *free* judicial decision-making by Jerzy Wróblewski and the frames of legal analysis discerned under them. Due to the essentially contested character of law, none of the frames of analysis discerned may claim absolute authority or priority position vis-à-vis the other alternatives, even if the frames of analysis situated under the legal and rational ideology do gain more weight than the bound and free alternatives in the modern law.

To put it concisely, the semantic qualities of an assertion on how to construct and read the law can be depicted as follows[2]:

The *reference* (Frege) or *extension* (Carnap) of a legal assertion is equal to one of the following alternatives:

[1]The same goes for any feasible definition of post-modern law with at least as good a reason, no matter what specific reading is attached to the fuzzy, problematic attribute *post-modern*.

[2]In the text, the sub-index "L" refers to the *legal* elements in the sense of the institutional (and partly societal) tenets, the sub-index "F" to the *formal* elements, and the sub-index "S" to the *substantive* or axiological-teleological elements involved.

(a) The *institutional* truth-value "true$_L$" or "false$_L$", if the constitutive premises of the ideology of *legal and rational* judicial decision-making have been adopted, specified as:

(a/1) a relation of mutual match, reciprocal support, common alignment, absence of dissonance, and/or shared congruence vis-à-vis one another of arguments drawn from the institutional and non-institutional sources of law, according to the *coherence theory of law*;
(a/2) approval or disapproval of the methods and outcome of legal argumentation at the intended universal audience, defined as a subjective thought construct of the speaker, according to the Perelmanian *new rhetoric*;
(a/3) retracing, as authentically as is possible, the original intentions of the legislator or court of justice, as reconstructed in light of the official *travaux préparatoires* at the back of an item of legislation or the express reasons given in support of a precedent, according to *legal exegesis*;
(a/4) the evolvement of such legal rights and duties that enjoy effective protection at the courts of justice and other officials, as judged in light of the normative ideology collectively internalized by the judiciary *sensu largo*, according to *analytical legal realism*;
(a/5) the acceptance or recognition of certain social phenomena as having legal significance or the prevalence of mutual expectations and cooperative dispositions to the said effect in the legal community, according to *legal conventionalism*.

(b) The *formal* truth-value "true$_F$" or "false$_F$", if the constitutive premises of the ideology of *bound* judicial decision-making have been adopted, specified as:

(b/1) an isomorphic, picture relation of structural similarity prevails between the two states of affairs compared, the one as given in the fact-constellation of a legal rule and the other as existing in the world, according to the *isomorphic theory of law*;
(b/2) the logico-conceptual and systemic criteria of law, according to *legal formalism*.

(c) The *substantive* truth-value "true$_S$" or "false$_S$", if the constitutive premises of the ideology of *free* judicial decision-making have been adopted, specified as:

(c/1) the external consequences of law in society, as judged in light of the (other) human or social sciences, according to *social consequentialism*;
(c/2) absolute social or religious justice or political morality under which all legislation and judicial decisions must yield, according to *natural law philosophy*;
(c/3) social justice taken on a strictly ad hoc basis, in denial of any meta-level theory, or meta-narrative, of law and society, according to *radical decisionism*.

The *sense* (Frege) or *intension* (Carnap) of a legal sentence, in turn, is equal to the specific *meaning-content* of law, as determined by the bound (formal), legal and rational (institutional), or free (substantive) frame of legal analysis.

13.2 The Logico-Conceptual Constitution, Normative Ontology, and Structural Axiology of Law

Legal rules and principles regulate society, or "something" in society, but what is it that the law seeks to regulate? What is the *ontological constitution* of law or the "things", objects, entities, or artefacts that form the "furniture of the world" within the realm of law? The law entails a set of commitments that constitute the alleged *reality structure* of law with reference to "on what there is" in the law. The metaphysical commitments of law may comprise three types of elements: the *logico-linguistic constitution*, *normative ontology*, and *structural axiology* of law. Taken together, they provide the "nuts and bolts" of the legal universe, i.e. the ontological edifice of the law and legal phenomena as conceived by the "order of things" in the legal community.

For the first, the *logico-conceptual constitution* of law comprises the various ways of conceptualizing legal phenomena with the conceptual categories and legal doctrinal constructions based on such linguistic devices. For instance, the conceptual domain of the law can be defined with a set of mutually correlative legal rights and duties, as notably outlined by Wesley Newcomb Hohfeld for the concept of legal ownership. The legal doctrine of ownership and the legal position of the owner of certain object of property can be defined with the four *right-concepts* (right, privilege, power, and immunity) and the correlative *duty-concepts* (duty, "no-right", liability, and disability). Hohfeld's conceptual scheme can be presented in the form of the set of legal correlatives and legal opposites.[3] The legal position of A, the owner of property item *x*, has no semantic reference except for the system of rights and duties as laid down by the law so that the right-positions occupied by A are matched with a corresponding duty-positions occupied by another person B, as defined by the valid legal rules of the legal system concerned.

Alternatively, Georg Friedrich Puchta's idea of the genealogy, or pyramid, of legal concepts (*Genealogie der Begriffe*, *Begriffspyramide*) might be adopted to the effect of establishing a highly systemic conception of the mutual relations of law, logic, and language. Finally, as a third example of how to outline the logico-conceptual edifice of law is Thomas Wilhelmsson's idea of switching over to *concrete*, *person-related*, and *situational* concepts in the legal doctrine, such as the concept of a debtor who has been affected by some grave, unexpected economic misfortune, like serious illness or unemployment, which outcome is not due to his own fault. Wilhelmsson downgrades the role of traditional abstract and relational

[3] Hohfeld, *Fundamental Legal Conceptions as Applied in Judicial Reasoning*, p. 35 et seq., and summarizingly p. 36.

role concepts (à la Hohfeld and Puchta) in legal analysis, in the image of the debtor/creditor or employer/employee cut off from the economic or other non-legal circumstances that might affect the social position of the legal subject concerned.[4]

There is no one right way of conceptualizing the legal phenomena, even if Hohfeld's model of mutually interlocking, relational concepts would seem to be predominant at present.

The ontological commitments of law and legal analysis comprise two categories, the one aligned with legal *norms* or the like entities under the *normative ontology* of law, and the other aligned with the inherent *value* element in law under the *structural axiology* of law. The issues of normative ontology and structural axiology of law are intertwined in the domain of law.

For the second, the *normative ontology* of law comprises the ontological commitments of law, with reference to the "things", phenomena, states of affairs, or entities that dwell in the domain of law. The normative ontology of law may be defined e.g. with the following entities, if the Hohfeldian approach, as modified by legal principles, is acknowledged:

(a) a system of correlative *legal rights* and *legal duties* as allocated to individual legal subjects, as envisioned by W. N. Hohfeld;
(b) a set of *legal rules*, as laid down by the law-making and law-applying authorities, and *legal principles*, as endowed with possibly no more than oblique but still legally adequate institutional support and a sense of approval in the community;
(c) subsequently retraceable individual decisions made by the law-making and law-applying authorities and well-settled societal practices and usages in the legal community, as manifested in the institutional and non-institutional, i.e. societal, *sources of law*;
(d) *social values & collective goals* at the back of legal rules and legal principles, as acknowledged in the institutional and non-institutional sources of law.

Legal rules are formally valid arguments for legal decision-making that are primarily based on individual, subsequently retraceable decisions made by the law-making and law-applying authorities, i.e. the parliamentary legislator, the courts of justice, and other officials. *Legal principles*, in turn, are valid arguments for legal decision-making that are primarily based on the well-settled practices and usages of customary law in the community, such as decisions given by various kinds of private or semi-official arbitration boards or the code of professional ethics and well-esteemed legal standards adopted by the legal profession or some fraction of it.

An argument is *valid* in the present sense of the term, if it can be derived from, and traced back to, the institutional or non-institutional sources of law and if it is given some legal value in the community. Different frames of analysis on how to construct and read the law give different weights to different combinations of legal

[4] Wilhelmsson, *Social civilrätt*.

rules and legal principles, and to the various institutional and societal premises, plus the social values and collective goals, at the back of such rules and principles.

Finally, the *structural axiology* of law looks upon the law from the point of view of the *social values* and *goals* entailed in the sources of law. It also comprises the inherent potential of such values and goals of being transformed into value-laden legal principles, if they come to satisfy the twin criterion of enjoying institutional support and a sense of approval in the community, or possibly further into legal rules, if they become incorporated in, and acknowledged by, individual decisions given by the institutional law-making or law-applying authorities in the legal community.

Of the various facets of law and metaphysics, the *logico-conceptual constitution* of law looks upon the issue from the point of view of logic and linguistics. The *normative ontology* of law is aligned with on what there is in the realm of law, i.e. the "nuts and bolts" of the legal universe. Finally, the *structural axiology* of law places the focus on the inherently value-laden characteristics of the law. To put it concisely, the bound, legal and rational, and free ideologies of judicial decision-making, as outlined by Jerzy Wróblewski, along with the elements of the logico-linguistic constitution, normative ontology, and structural axiology of law can be presented with Diagram 13.1.

The diagram above depicts the *bound*, *legal and rational*, and *free* ideologies of judicial decision-making by Jerzy Wróblewski, with approximate match with the isomorphic, semantically ambiguous, and totally unregulated legal decision-making situations by Kaarle Makkonen. Each of the three ideologies of judicial decision-making entails several sub-categories that, due to lack of space, are not depicted here. Thus, the ideology of legal and rational judicial decision-making would comprise the coherence theory of law, the new rhetoric, analytical legal positivism and legal exegesis with either legislative or judicial bent, analytical legal realism, and philosophical conventionalism in the field of law. The ideology of bound judicial decision-making would comprise an isomorphic theory of law and legal formalism. The ideology of free judicial decision-making would entail social consequentialism, natural law philosophy, and radical ad hoc based decisionism.

The ideology of *bound* judicial decision-making occupies the upper left-hand side corner of the diagram, with reference to the logico-formal and systemic criteria of how to construct and read the law. The ideology of *free* judicial decision-making occupies the lower right-hand side corner of the diagram, with reference to the openly axiological and teleological criteria in the construction and interpretation of the law. Finally, the mid-area in-between the bound (formal) and the free (substantive) alternatives is occupied by the ideology of *legal and rational* judicial decision-making, with reference to the (predominantly) institutional and (supplementarily) societal criteria of legal argumentation.

The formal tenets of law predominate at the left-hand side of the diagram, and their impact is intensified towards the left-hand side upper corner of the diagram. The substantive characteristics of law predominate at the right-hand side of the diagram, and their impact is intensified towards the right lower corner of the diagram. The legal and rational ideology of law, in turn, is a combination

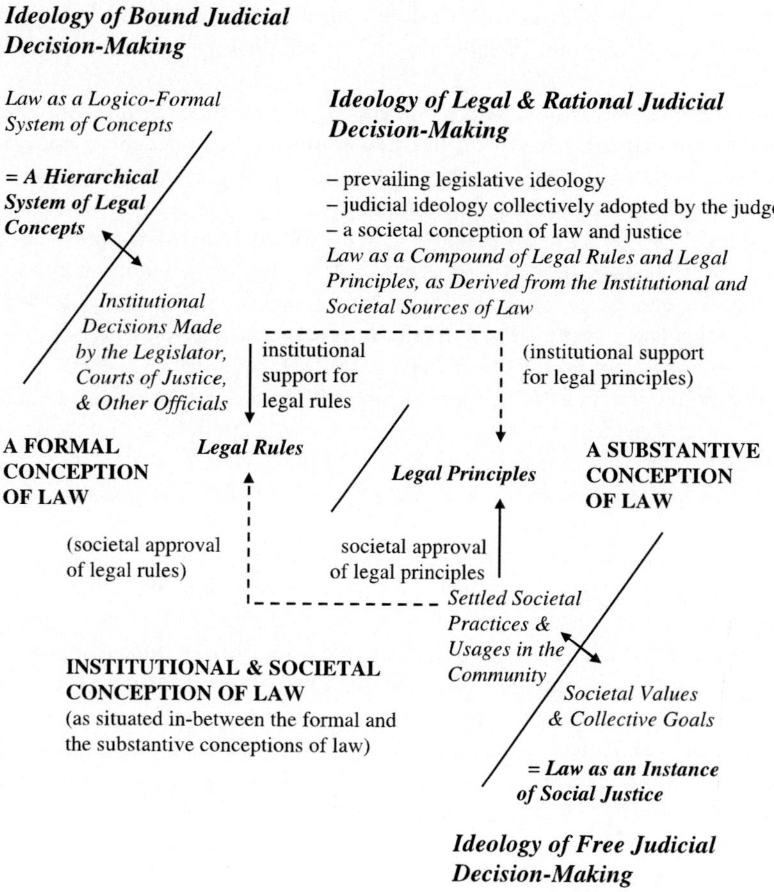

Diagram 13.1 The ideologies of bound, legal and rational, and free judicial decision-making, along with the logico-linguistic constitution, normative ontology, and structural axiology of law, and with coverage of the legal concepts, legal rules and legal principles, and societal values and collective goals entailed

of moderately formal and moderately substantive tenets of law. The institutional sources of law and rule-bound arguments drawn from them are the more formal, or source-oriented, constitutive elements of law; whereas the non-institutional sources of law and principle-aligned arguments drawn from them are the more substantive, or content-oriented, constitutive elements of the law.

Legal *rules* are formally valid arguments in legal decision-making, primarily based on decisions made by the law-making and law-applying authorities. According to H. L. A. Hart, they can be identified by their formal source of origin, as captured in the rule of recognition of the legal system concerned. Nevertheless, even legal rules need to enjoy some degree of content-based approval in the legal community, since a rule that is deemed grossly unjust would fall into disuse by the officials and citizens alike, despite having perfectly formal validity ground in legislation or judicial decision-making. In such a case, we are dealing with an instance of a *desuetudo*.

Legal *principles* are value-laden, context-sensitive arguments in legal decision-making that are primarily based on the well-settled societal practices and usages that are commonly approved in the legal community of legal professionals, some other professional group, or the legal community at large. As pointed out by Ronald Dworkin, legal principles need to enjoy a sense of content-based approval in the legal community. Since they are inherently intertwined with value-laden criteria, legal principles cannot be identified by their formal source of origin only. What is more, they must enjoy some kind of institutional support so as to qualify as properly *legal* principles and not principles of, say, morality or religion.

The distinctive manner of "being-in-the-world" of the legal phenomena may be collected under the three headings of the logico-conceptual constitution, normative ontology, and structural axiology of law. Taken together, they account for the distinctive metaphysics of law under the *épistémè*, or *order of things*, in Michel Foucault's sense of the term.[5]

The *logical constitution* or, in wider terms, the *logico-conceptual constitution* of law naturally comprises the logical and linguistic commitments of law and legal analysis, with reference to the *logical syntax* of a legal language, as suggested by Rudolf Carnap for the language in general.[6] The *normative ontology* of law entails the "nuts and bolts" or elementary "building blocks" of the law, such as legal rights and duties; legal rules and principles; institutional and societal sources of law; or social values and collective goals entailed in the former. Finally, the *structural axiology* of law comprises the axiological commitments of law in the form of social values and collective goals acknowledged in law.

Different characteristics of legal metaphysics gain weight under the different ideologies or situations of judicial decision-making.

The logical syntax of law is aligned with the *formal* tenets of law, as manifested in Wróblewski's *bound* judicial ideology and Makkonen's *isomorphic* situation of legal decision-making. The normative ontology of law underscores the *institutional* tenets of law, as manifested in Wróblewski's *legal and rational* judicial ideology and Makkonen's *semantically ambiguous* situation of legal decision-making. Finally, the structural axiology of law is aligned with the *substantive* tenets of law, as manifested in Wróblewski's *free* judicial ideology and Makkonen's *unregulated* situation of legal decision-making.

Still, also the logico-linguistic tenets and the axiological premises of law require some ontological frame to pin down the legal concepts and social values of law into "something" in the reality. Similarly, the axiological value commitments and the institutional prerequisites of law require some logico-linguistic formulation to be taken into account in the legal analysis. Finally, the conceptual frame and the

[5] Foucault, *Les mots et les choses*.

[6] Carnap, *The Logical Syntax of Language*.

ontological entities of law need to sustain some kind of relation to the value premises at the back of the law so as to reach the axiological element inherent in law.

13.3 A Systemic Order of Things Among the Rules and Principles of Law

As Oliver Wendell Holmes once sardonically noted, the traditional idea of the American common law is "a chaos with a full index".[7] If, however, the legal system is deemed to be something else than a mere chaotic heap of haphazard, overlapping, and zigzagging legal rules, principles, standards, precepts, or whatever "things" are thought to inhabit the legal universe, we need to somehow account for the phenomenon of *legal systematics* as a systemic "order of things" among such rules, principles, and standards of law. In fact, to successfully carry out the task of legal interpretation requires first having *some* working conception of legal systematics.

It is a task for *theoretical* legal doctrine to analyse the systemic order of things among the rules and principles of law, while it is a task for *practical* legal doctrine to provide arguments for the interpretation of law vis-à-vis particular fact-constellations of either actual or merely hypothetical kind.[8] Taken together, the theoretical and practical aspects of the legal doctrine account for the task of how to construct and read the law vis-à-vis various feasible fact-constellations, as either come into existence in the world or as merely configured in the legal imagination of a legal scholar. Yet, a judge or other official engaged in the application of law rarely, if ever, seeks to enforce some specific notion of legal systematics as a goal to be attained as such. His passion for legal knowledge is far more concrete, having to do with the facts of the case at hand and the legal consequences to be attached to them by force of law.

According to the two Argentinian scholars, Carlos Alchourrón (1931–1996) and Eugenio Bulygin, legal systematization can be defined as the *reformulation* of the original normative system, or the "basis", that was initially laid down by the legislator[9]:

---

[7]The phrase is commonly attributed to Thomas Erskine Holland. Cf. Holland, *Essays on the Form of the Law* (London, 1870), as cited in Reimann, "Holmes's *Common Law* and German Legal Science", p. 114.

[8]On the two notions of theoretical and practical legal doctrine (or legal dogmatics), cf. Aarnio, *The Rational as Reasonable*, pp. 14–15, and the reference entailed.

[9]Alchourrón and Bulygin, *Normative Systems*, p. 79. (Italics added.) – Cf.: "*Reformulation of the system*: consisting in the substitution for the original basis of another one. This usually occurs when the number of sentences in the basis is very large. The replacement of a very extensive basis by another that is more restricted but deontically equivalent is considered by jurists to be an advantage, since applying the system thereby becomes simpler. On the other hand, this operation does not modify the system itself but only its representation. Frequently when jurists speak about the systematization of the law, they mean precisely what we call reformulation of the basis." Alchourrón and Bulygin, *Normative Systems*, p. 71 (italics in the original). – Cf.: "We have characterized a legal system as a normative system whose basis is composed of legal sentences. The fact that jurists reformulate the basis of a system, substituting some sentences for others, does not

> Generally speaking, the reformulation of a system consists in the replacement of the basis by a new one, that is *less extensive*, *more general* and *normatively equivalent*.

Alchourrón and Bulygin define legal systematization with the requirement of *normative equivalence* of the two normative systems, the "basis", or the basic, *original* system, as initially produced by the legislator, and the novel, *reformulated* system, as subsequently (re)produced by the legal science.[10] The novel, reformulated system is deemed to be *normatively equivalent* to the basic, original system, in the sense that the normative consequences entailed in it are equivalent to those entailed in the basic system, while the concepts utilized in the reformulated system are *less extensive* and *more general* than the ones utilized in the basic, original system. The requirement of *normative equivalence* of the two normative systems thus boils down to the requirement that the same normative consequences be attached to the same fact-constellations, or states of affairs, under the both.

As I see it, (the process of) legal systematization and (the outcome of) legal systematics can be defined in two distinct ways, the one *formal* and the other *substantive* in kind.

A *formal* notion of the process of legal systematization and the outcome of legal systematics legal systematics and systematization can be outlined in terms of Carnap's *method of extension and intension*, as now applied to Alchourrón's and Bulygin's requirement of the relation of *normative equivalence* between the two normative systems concerned. The extension of a sentence denotes its *truth-value*, and the intension of a sentence is equal to its specific *meaning-content*. A legal system S_n that consists of a set of legal rules and (possibly) legal principles can be depicted by a set of legal sentences to the said effect. As a consequence, the notion of *equivalence* of two normative systems, the basic, original system (S_{orig}) and the reformulated system (S_{refor}) can be defined as follows:

> The two normative systems (S_{orig}) and (S_{refor}) are *equivalent*, if and only if they are equivalent in extension and equivalent in intension. They are *equivalent in extension*, if and only if they obtain the same truth-value on the same values of variables; and they are *equivalent in intension*, if and only if they produce the same set of meaning-contents on the same values of variables.[11]

The requirement of such normative equivalence, though valid from the point of view of logic, will not exhaust the epistemic needs and expectations of the legal

affect the identity of the system, provided that the new basis is *normatively equivalent* to the original. There is no change in that system, in the sense that its normative consequences remain the same." (Italics added.) – A solid account of Alchourrón's and Bulygin's conception of a normative system is in Aarnio, *Reason and Authority*, pp. 237–240.

[10] Alchourrón and Bulygin, *Normative Systems*, p. 80: "The requirement of *normative equivalence* is most important: only if the new basis has the same normative consequences as the original can we regard the result as the same system reformulated. If the new basis lacks some of the normative consequences of the original, or has new consequences, we are confronted not by the same system, but by a different one." (Italics in original.)

[11] The terms S_{orig} and S_{refor} of course refer to the *original* and the *reformulated* normative system, respectively.

profession, however. As a consequence, a *substantive* notion of (the process of) legal systematization and (the outcome of) legal systematics is needed, as well. It deals with the formation and internal structure of the legal doctrine, defined in terms of the *systemic weights* that are attached to the various legal rules and legal principles in a legal system. Enforcing a systemic *order of things* within a set of rules and principles signifies the act of determining the relative weight of each vis-à-vis all the other rules or principles that belong to the same normative system or some branch or sub-class of it.

Legal systematics in the substantive sense concerns the decision which legal rule (or rules) is given the status of the *predominant*, *leading*, or *main* rule (or rules) in some branch of law, to be applied frequently and in the vast majority of cases; and, conversely, which (other) rules are deemed as *exceptions* to the main rule, i.e. *supplementary* rules that are to be interpreted more strictly and applied in some less frequent or exceptional cases. Moreover, if defined in a wide sense of the term, legal systematics comprises even the decision which legal principle (or principles) is given the status of the *leading*, *major*, or *predominant* principle (or principles) in some branch of law and, respectively, which (other) principles are taken as no more than *receding*, *weak*, or *supplementary* principles of law, endowed with less argumentative force, an inclination to yield when contested by some predominant principle, and applied in a more constrained manner than the leading principle.

The term *systemic intensity* may be adopted to describe the inherent propensity of legal norms to satisfy such systemic qualities. In a set of legal principles, the level of systemic intensity is significantly lower than in a set of legal rules, due to the inherently less formal qualities of principles. Because of the weaker systemic intensity that may be attained in a set of legal principles, the very notion of a *legal system* would need to be weakened so as to cover legal principles, too. If so (re)defined, the concept of a legal system will be very different from the one adopted above by Alchourrón and Bulygin. At the same time, it would have better coverage vis-à-vis the contents of a legal system taken as a compound of both legal rules, valid due to their formal source of origin, and legal principles, endowed with legal weight because of the institutional support and sense of approval they enjoy in the community.

A legal system signifies the act of locking up a complex *priority order* for the *rule/rule*, *principle/principle*, and *rule/principle* combinations that may emerge within it, as captured in the *main rule/exceptions to the main rule* and the *leading principle/supplementary principles of law* categorizations in the legal system as a whole or in some specific branch of it.

Legal doctrine need not, and most often does not, aim at only satisfying the idea of legal systematization as a *reformulation* of the basic legislative system in another system that is "less extensive, more general and normatively equivalent" vis-à-vis the basic system, as argued above by Carlos Alchourrón and Eugenio Bulygin.[12] If

[12] Alchourrón and Bulygin, *Normative Systems*, p. 79. Cf. Aarnio, *Reason and Authority*, pp. 243–244.

that were the case, no novel normative results could ever be achieved through legal systematization, as the requirement of normative equivalence of the two normative systems, defined as the *equality in extension* and *equality in intension*, would effectively block any progress or alteration in legal analysis. Still, far more often lawyers aim at some *alteration*, *modification*, *refinement*, or *adaptation* of the basic system, so as to bring about some novel normative outcomes so as to have a better match with the changes in society. Such an act of systematization signifies a *redefinition* or *modification* of the basic system, and the novel normative system that is thereby brought into effect may be called a *redefined*, *revised*, or *modified* system, instead of the *reformulated* system à la Alchourón and Bulygin.

13.4 Textual Coherence, Institutional Authorities, and the Legal Community

In his essay "American Jurisprudence through English Eyes: The Nightmare and the Noble Dream", H. L. A. Hart situated American legal philosophy in the late 1970s between the two extremes of a *nightmare* vision of law, as represented by the legal realists, and the *noble dream*, as represented by Ronald Dworkin's idea of the law as a "seamless web of reasons", or a coherent collection of value-laden rules and principles of law.[13] Adopting one or the other of the extreme options for legal studies will have the effect of eradicating traditional legal doctrine and analytical jurisprudence from among the legal and social sciences, reducing it to an instance of politics (à la realists) or morality (à la Dworkin). Hart's own idea of the place for jurisprudence was safely in the middle, avoiding both the bleak cynicism of the realists and – in Hart's opinion – the unfounded idealism manifested by Dworkin.

Despite the claimed weaknesses of Hart's own methodological stance,[14] his impact on subsequent jurisprudence has been nothing short of tremendous.[15] Reminiscent of Hart's analysis, Brian Z. Tamanaha has looked upon the law in light of *legal formalism* and *social consequentialism* or a *non-instrumentalist* and

[13] Hart's poetic depiction of Dworkin as the "noblest dreamer" of them all, i.e. the prime idealist among the legal philosophers, is of course an allusion to Shakespeare's play *Julius Caesar*. Hart, "American Jurisprudence through English Eyes: The Nightmare and the Noble Dream", p. 137. Hart refers to the sarcastic speech given by Marc Anthony, a friend of Caesar's, after Caesar's cruel murder by the conspirators, with Brutus among them: "This was the noblest Roman of them all:/All the conspirators, save only he,/Did that they did in envy of great Caesar;/He, only in a general honest thought/And common good to all, made one of them." (William Shakespeare: *Julius Caesar*, Act 5, scene 5, 68–72.)

[14] Hart own depiction of his methodology as *descriptive sociology* in the preface of *The Concept of Law* in specific has invited criticism from the scholars acquainted with the social sciences and the sociological approach to law in general. Hart, *The Concept of Law* (1961), p. V.

[15] For instance, a recent anthology on the methodology of legal theory focuses solely on Hart's influence on jurisprudence and the responses to it by other scholars. Cf. Giudice, Waluchow, and Del Mar, *The Methodology of Legal Theory, Vol. 1*.

an *instrumentalist* conception of law.[16] Other authors, too, have voiced similar thoughts. Indeed, it seems that the fate of the modern or postmodern law is to be trapped in-between the two alternatives of bleak *cynicism* and naïve *idealism* (Hart), or text-oriented legal *formalism* and socially oriented legal *realism* (Tamanaha), or all-inclusive *apology* and unfounded *utopia* in argumentation in the field of international law (Koskenniemi).[17] Above, a similar sounding dichotomy was given in terms of the *bound* and the *free* ideologies of judicial decision-making (Wróblewski) and the *isomorphic* and the *unregulated* situations of legal discretion (Makkonen).

Rejecting the two extremes of barren formalism and excessive social realism in neglect of the institutional tenets of law, I prefer to configure the prerequisites of modern law, legal analysis, and legal argumentation in terms of Wróblewski's ideology of legal and rational judicial decision-making and the three constitutive elements involved: (a) the *institutional authorities* engaged in the task of legislation and legal adjudication, i.e. the parliamentary legislator, courts of justice, and other legal officials; (b) the set of institutional and non-institutional *sources of law*, as produced by the official state authorities vis-à-vis the institutional sources and by the legal professionals and legal community at large vis-à-vis the societal sources; and finally (c) the *legal community* that has the last word on the merits and shortcomings of any proposed method and outcomes of legal argumentation. Different combinations of the five frames of legal analysis discerned yield different outcomes as to how to construct and read the law, but the aimed satisfaction of the twin requirement of *legality* and *rationality* in legal discretion guarantees that the impact of at least some of such tenets be acknowledged.

As was argued above, the *coherence theory of law* is focused on the mutually converging relations that are thought to prevail among the institutional and non-institutional, or societal, sources of law, placing the emphasis on the textual and coherence-enhancing tenets of law in legal reasoning. Institutional authorities and the legal source material produced by them gain the most significance under such premises of legal reasoning. *Legal exegesis*, in association with *analytical legal positivism*, and *analytical legal realism* both underscore the role of institutional authorities in shaping the law, with reference to the role of the parliamentary legislator in legal exegesis and the courts of justice and other legal officials in analytical legal realism. In the *new rhetoric* and *legal conventionalism*, the role of the legal community is given prime importance.

---

[16]On the two notions of legal formalism and social consequentialism, Tamanaha, *Beyond the Formalist-Realist Debate: The Role of Politics in Judging*; on instrumentalist and non-instrumentalist conceptions of law, Tamanaha, *Law as a Means to an End: Threat to the Rule of Law*. – Interestingly, Brian Z. Tamanaha seeks to combine traditional analytical legal positivism (à la Hart) with the social and realistic tenets of modern law under "a socio-legal positivist approach to the law" or "realistic socio-legal theory". Tamanaha, *A General Jurisprudence of Law and Society*, p. 133 et seq; Tamanaha, *Realistic Socio-Legal Theory: Pragmatism and a Social Theory of Law*, p. 129 et seq.

[17]Koskenniemi, *From Apology to Utopia: The Structure of International Legal Argument.*

In all, legal argumentation is a form of *deliberative practice* that takes place under three different types of constraints:

(a) the *textual* constraints provided by the text-based sources of law and the canons of methodology applied to them;
(b) the *institutional* constraints provided by the institutional authorities, such as the legislator and the courts of justice, involved in the task of creating, altering, and derogating the legal norms in force;
(c) the *community-aligned* constraints provided by the legal community on the legitimacy of the outcome of legal construction and interpretation.

The issues of textual coherence, the decision-making power of the institutional authorities, and the role accorded to the legal community each have a (shifting) position under Jerzy Wróblewski's ideology of legal and rational judicial decision-making. The weight given to each element depends on the particular frame of legal analysis adopted.

13.5 (Is There) A Future for Analytical Jurisprudence?

Several profound changes have taken place in the conception of modern law and society, when viewed on a global scale, affecting the mode of legal analysis.

For the first, the role of various kinds of legal instruments with only loose connection to the will of the parliamentary legislator have to a great extent been enhanced in society. The role of *judge-made, precedent-based* law has increased and the role of traditional legislation has slightly declined even in the Continental and Nordic legal systems that have traditionally been based on the primacy of parliamentary legislation. That development is mostly due to the impact of *multinational* and *transnational* law that is manifested in the precedents given by the two European courts, viz. the Court of the European Union and the European Court of Human Rights.

The effected change in the relative weight given to national legislation and to multinational precedents with cross-border legal effects has induced a similar change in the concept of law as well. The effected law in action at the courts, as proffered by *legal realism*, has gained more weight, while the positivist notion of law has been in parallel decline, no matter whether the law has been defined as sanction-based orders as issued by the sovereign ruler (Austin); a hierarchical system of norms whose legal validity is based on the transcendental-logical *Grundnorm* (Kelsen); or a set of rules that can be identified with the rule of recognition for the legislative norms, being of the type "what the Queen in Parliament enacts is (valid) law in England" (Hart).

For the second, the role of the *non-institutional*, i.e. societal or community-based law has been strengthened by the recent technological changes. The breakthrough of novel digital communication technology, data copying and transfer with no loss of data in the process, global network systems like the Internet and the platforms of social media incorporated in it, and the administration of global net site domain addresses and protocols have more with the non-institutional than the institutional law to do. As a consequence, legal *conventionalism* that is based on common acceptance or recognition of certain social phenomena as having legal significance has gained ground at the cost of the institutional facets of law that the positivist and the realist approaches underscore. There are other tenets, too, that lay the emphasis on the societal, community-aligned, and non-institutional tenets in law at the cost of the state-bound, institutional law with either legislative or judicial bent.

In business law transactions, recourse to litigation in ordinary courts is frequently ruled out by arbitration clauses to the said effect. Such manifestations of a discretionary, *negotiable* law clearly belong to the sphere of community-aligned, societal law even though the very possibility of dispositive law is based on the express or tacit will of the legislator. In a similar manner, semi-autonomous *self-regulation* by some profession in society, like the attorneys-at-law, bookkeepers, or auditors, gives effect to a societal, community-based notion of law. *Soft law*, in turn, refers to the recommendations, guidelines, and qualification standards that are issued by the officials or professionals of a certain field. Soft law standards may still have a great de facto bearing on the issues covered by them, despite the fact that they do not have formal mandatory force or authorized standing.

The attainment of all-inclusive *cohesion* or *coherence* in a collection of norms derived from the fields of transnational or multinational law, judge-made law, negotiable law, legal self-regulation, and soft law is harder than in the officially promulgated, institutional law, due to the weaker systemic characteristics of the former category of legal norms, or "proto-norms" if taken as raw material for the legal norms proper. Constructing the subject-related intended *universal* audience vis-à-vis such norms is not easy either, if the thought construct of a universal audience is defined with the shared form of life and the possibility of reasoned value-consensus or, at the least, reasoned majority stance on values among those concerned, as Aulis Aarnio's theory of legal argumentation would require.[18] In all, the future of modern law would seem to have more to do with a fragmented dissensus than an overarching consensus as to the basic values and other facets of the common form of life.

For the third, the highly unexpected rise of *religion* and religious values in the world is bound to induce some thorny issues for the future law. Religion may or may not be anchored in the premises of traditional natural law philosophy, depending on what kind of religious values and convictions we are dealing with. Islamic values will not match well with classic natural law philosophy by Thomas Aquinas or the more modern one proffered by John Finnis. The impact of religion will seek to provide religious answers to social issues, no matter whether we are dealing with the freedom of speech and press, the neutrality or commitment of public education vis-à-vis the religious and other convictions, or the regulation of public space in society in general.

---

[18] Aarnio, *The Rational as Reasonable*, p. 221 et seq.

Fourthly, the impact of both backward-looking textual formalism and future-oriented social consequentialism can be felt within modern law, putting pressure upon the judges on how to construct and read the law from the point of view of textual authenticity and the rule of law ideology, on the one hand, and sensitivity to the entirely novel issues that may quite unexpectedly surface in society, on the other.[19] Here, the *instrumentalist* tenets of law seem to be gaining ground at the cost of the inherent logic of the law, as manifested in the variety of legal formalism and also in the Marxist conception of law and society.[20]

The modern law is certainly not in the midst of "withering away" by force of the irrevocable progress of class-consciousness and the dismantling of the forces of economic production in society, as the Marxists would have it. Quite on the contrary, the place of law in the Western world is stronger and safer than ever, due to the multi-faceted process of European legal integration, the effected state treaties on the protection of the human rights and the procedures for their enforcement in national courts and the European Court of Human Rights in specific, provisions to a similar effect incorporated in the national constitutions, and the enhanced progression of globalization where the need for legal rules and principles is badly felt. Though to a great extent economic in its hue, the current situation with the law in society will not easily yield to the categories and models of a Marxist analysis. Rather, an openly Marxist approach has been bracketed with the fall of the leftist option in politics in all the Western societies and to a great extent in the former Eastern Europe, as well. The winner of this round is not to be found among the ideological heirs of Karl Marx and Georg Lukács, but among "the men of statistics and the masters of economics", as Oliver Wendell Holmes put it at the end of the nineteenth century.

Finally, to judge the value of some fresh approach, methodology, or stance in law and legal analysis one will need to have recourse to a non-biased, ideologically neutral platform for the judgment. It is still one of the strengths of *analytical jurisprudence* that it can easily incorporate a great variety of different models, approaches, or ideologies of law for an impartial judgment. What Kelsen so confidently wrote of the essentially value-free, ideologically open character of the pure theory of law, turning the critique it had received from various directions into its profit, is a valid methodological *credo* for legal analysis, today and in future.[21] Though analytical jurisprudence has been declared dead and buried for long by some of its most passionate critics, its future looks safe enough as long as the need survives in society to find a reasoned answer to the core issue of the legal doctrine: *from the point of view of the law, how is the state of affairs* x *to be judged?*

---

[19]On the notion of rational acceptability in legal argumentation, Aarnio, *The Rational as Reasonable*, passim; on the unpredictable element in the EU law, Wilhelmsson, "Jack-in-the-Box Theory of European Community Law".

[20]The Marxist ideology of law and society was not considered above, except briefly in Section 5.4. "'Why Efficiency?' – A Critical Evaluation of the Economic Analysis of Law, with Brief Comments on the Marxist Theory of Law", since the Marxist approach does not entail a consistent theory of legal argumentation.

[21]Kelsen, *Reine Rechtslehre* (1960), p. V; Kelsen, *Reine Rechtslehre* (1934), pp. XII–XIII.

References

Aarnio, Aulis. *The Rational as Reasonable: A Treatise on Legal Justification*. Dordrecht: D. Reidel Publishing Company, 1987.

Aarnio, Aulis. *Laintulkinnan teoria*. Helsinki: Werner Söderström Osakeyhtiö, 1988.

Aarnio, Aulis. *Reason and Authority: A Treatise on the Dynamic Paradigm of Legal Dogmatics*. Aldershot: Ashgate/Dartmouth, 1997.

Alchourrón, Carlos E., and Eugenio Bulygin. *Normative Systems*, Library of Exact Philosophy, 5. Wien and New York, NY: Springer, 1971.

Alexy, Robert. *A Theory of Constitutional Rights*. Translated by Julian Rivers. Second edition. Oxford: Oxford University Press, 2002.

Alexy, Robert. *A Theory of Legal Argumentation: The Theory of Rational Discourse as Theory of Legal Argumentation*. Translated by Ruth Adler and Neil MacCormick. Oxford: Clarendon Press, 1989.

Alexy, Robert, and Aleksander Peczenik. "The Concept of Coherence and Its Significance for Discursive Rationality." *Ratio Juris* 3 (1990): 130–47.

Anderson, C. Anthony. "Alfred Tarski (1901–1983), Alonzo Church (1903–1995), and Kurt Gödel (1906–1978)." In *A Companion to Analytic Philosophy*, edited by A. P. Martinich, and Ernest Sosa, pp. 124–38. Blackwell Companions to Philosophy Series. Oxford: Blackwell, 2001.

Anscombe, Elizabeth. "On Brute Facts." *Analysis* 18 (1958): 69–72.

Anscombe, Elizabeth. *Intention*. Second edition. Oxford: Basis Blackwell, 1963.

Aquinas, St. Thomas. "(Extracts from) The Summa Theologica". In *Jurisprudence: Texts and Readings on the Philosophy of Law*, edited by George C. Christie, and Patrick H. Martin, pp. 132–84. Second edition. American Casebook Series. Denver, CO: West Publishing Co, 1995.

Aristotle. "*Nicomachean Ethics*." In *The Complete Works of Aristotle Vol. II*, edited by Jonathan Barnes, 1729–1867. Bollinger Series LXXI:2 Sixth Printing, with Corrections. The United States of America. The Revised Oxford Translation. Princeton, NJ: Princeton University Press, 1995.

Austin, John Langshaw. *How to Do Things with Words*. The William James Lectures, delivered in Harvard University in 1955, Second edition, edited by J. O. Urmson, and Marina Sbisà. Oxford, New York, NY: Oxford University Press, 1986.

Austin, John. *The Province of Jurisprudence Determined*. Edited by Wilfrid E. Rumble. Cambridge: Cambridge University Press, 1995.

Ayer, A. J., ed. *Logical Positivism*. New York, NY: The Free Press, 1959.

Bankowski, Zenon, White, Ian, and Hahn, Ulrike, eds. *Informatics and the Foudantions of Legal Reasoning*. Dordrecht: Kluwer, 1995.

Been, Wouter de. *Legal Realism Regained: Saving Realism from Critical Acclaim*. Jurists: Profiles in Legal Theory. Stanford, CA: Stanford University Press, 2008.

Bergel, Jean-Louis. *Méthodologie juridique*. Paris: Presses Universitaires de France, 2001.

Bergholtz, Gunnar. *Ratio et auctoritas. Ett komparativrättsligt bidrag till frågan om domsmotiveringens betydelse främst i tvistemål*. Lund: Juridiska Föreningen i Lund, 1987.

R. Siltala, *Law, Truth, and Reason*, Law and Philosophy Library 97,
DOI 10.1007/978-94-007-1872-2, © Springer Science+Business Media B.V. 2011

Bobbio, Norberto. *Il Positivismo Giuridico. Lezioni de Filosofia del diritto, raccolte dal Dott. Nello Morra*. Torino: G. Giappichelli Editore, 1979.

Bouckaert, Boudewijn. *De exegetische school. Een kritische studie van de rechtsbronnen- en interpretatieleer bij de 19de eeuwse commentatoren van de Code Civil*. Antwerpen: Kluwer rechtswetenschappen, 1981.

Bouckaert, Boudewijn. "Gény, François (1861–1959)." In *The Philosophy of Law: An Encyclopedia, Vol. I*, edited by Christopher B. Gray, pp. 328–29. New York, NY and London: Garland Publishing, 1999.

Bouckaert, Boudewijn. "Exegetical School". In *The Philosophy of Law: An Encyclopedia, Vol. I*, edited by Christopher B. Gray, pp. 276–78. New York, NY and London: Garland Publishing, 1999.

Brusiin, Otto. *Tuomarin harkinta normin puuttuessa*. Helsinki: Suomalainen lakimiesyhdistys, 1938.

Bydlinski, Franz. *Juristische Methodenlehre und Rechtsbegriff*. Zweite, ergänzte Auflage. Wien and New York: Springer, 1991.

Calabresi, Guido. "Some Thoughts on Risk Distribution and the Law of Torts". *Yale Law Journal* 70 (1961): 499–553.

Carnap, Rudolf. "The Elimination of Metaphysics Through Logical Analysis of Language." In *Logical Positivism*, edited by A. J. Ayer. Translated by Arthur Pap. New York, NY: The Free Press, 1959. Originally published in "Überwindung der Metaphysik durch Logische Analyse der Sprache." In *Erkenntnis* 1932.

Carnap, Rudolf. *Meaning and Necessity: A Study in Semantics and Modal Logic*. Second edition. Chicago, IL and London: The University of Chicago Press, 1988.

Carnap, Rudolf. *The Logical Syntax of Language*. Translated by Amethe Smeaton (Countess von Zeppelin). Chicago and La Salle, IL: Open Court, 2002.

Coase, R. H. "The Problem of Social Cost." *The Journal of Law and Economics* III(1960): 1–44. Reprinted in: Coleman, Jules and Jeffrey Lange, eds. *Law and Economics, Vol. 1*. The International Library of Essays in Law and Legal Theory. Aldershot: Dartmouth, 1992, pp. 3–46.

Coffa, J. Alberto. *The Semantic Tradition from Kant to Carnap: To the Vienna Station*. Edited by Linda Wessels. Cambridge: Cambridge University Press, 2003.

Cooter, Robert. "Prices and Sanctions." *Columbia Law Review* 84(1984): 1523–60. Reprinted in: Coleman, Jules and Jeffrey Lange, eds. *Law and Economics, Vol. 1*. The International Library of Essays in Law and Legal Theory. Aldershot: Dartmouth, 1992, pp. 87–124.

Costa, Pietro, and Danilo Zolo, eds. *The Rule of Law: History, Theory and Criticism*. With the cooperation of Emilio Santoro. The Netherlands: Springer, 2007.

Derrida, Jacques. "Letter to a Japanese Friend." In *Derrida and Différance*, edited by David Wood, and Robert Bernasconi, pp. 1–5. Evanston, IL: Northwestern University Press, 1988.

Dickstein, Morris. "Introduction: Pragmatism Then and Now" In *The Revival of Pragmatism: New Essays on Social Thought, Law, and Culture*, edited by Morris Dickstein, pp. 1–18. Durham, NC: Duke University Press, 1998.

Dickstein, Morris, ed. *The Revival of Pragmatism: New Essays on Social Thought, Law, and Culture*. Durham, NC: Duke University Press, 1998.

Duxbury, Neil. *Patterns of American Jurisprudence*. Oxford: Clarendon Press, 1995.

Dworkin, Ronald. "Can Rights Be Controversial?" In *Taking Rights Seriously: With a New Appendix, a Response to Critics*, edited by Ronald Dworkin, pp. 279–90. Cambridge, MA: Harvard University Press, 1978.

Dworkin, Ronald. "Hard Cases." In *Taking Rights Seriously: With a New Appendix, a Response to Critics*, edited by Ronald Dworkin, pp. 81–130. Cambridge, MA: Harvard University Press, 1978.

Dworkin, Ronald. "The Model of Rules, I." In *Taking Rights Seriously: With a New Appendix, a Response to Critics*, edited by Ronald Dworkin, pp. 14–45. Cambridge, MA: Harvard University Press, 1978.

Dworkin, Ronald. "The Model of Rules, II." In *Taking Rights Seriously: With a New Appendix, a Response to Critics*, edited by Ronald Dworkin, pp. 46–80. Cambridge, MA: Harvard University Press, 1978.

Dworkin, Ronald. *Taking Rights Seriously: With a New Appendix, a Response to Critics*. Cambridge, MA: Harvard University Press, 1978.

Dworkin, Ronald. "Taking Rights Seriously." In *Taking Rights Seriously: With a New Appendix, a Response to Critics*, edited by Ronald Dworkin, pp. 184–205. Cambridge, MA: Harvard University Press, 1978.

Dworkin, Ronald. "Appendix: A Reply to Critics". In *Taking Rights Seriously. With a New Appendix, a Response to Critics*, edited by Ronald Dworkin, pp. 291–368. Cambridge, MA: Harvard University Press, 1978.

Dworkin, Ronald. *A Matter of Principle*. Oxford: Oxford University Press, 1985.

Dworkin, Ronald. "How Law Is Like Literature." In *A Matter of Principle*, edited by Ronald Dworkin, pp. 146–66. Oxford: Oxford University Press, 1985.

Dworkin, Ronald. "Is There Really No Right Answer in Hard Cases?" In *A Matter of Principle*, edited by Ronald Dworkin, pp. 119–45. Oxford: Oxford University Press, 1985.

Dworkin, Ronald. *Law's Empire*. London: Fontana Masterguides, 1986.

Dworkin, Ronald. *Is Democracy Possible Here? Principles for a New Political Debate*. Princeton, NJ: Princeton University Press, 2006.

Dworkin, Ronald. *Justice in Robes*. Cambridge, MA and London: The Belknap Press of Harvard University Press, 2006.

Dworkin, Ronald. "Pragmatism, Right Answers, and True Banality." In *Pragmatism in Law and Society*, edited by Michael Brint, and William Weaver, pp. 359–88. New Perspectives on Law, Culture, and Society. Boulder, CO: Westview Press, 1991.

Dyzenhaus, David. *Legality and Legitimacy: Carl Schmitt, Hans Kelsen and Hermann Heller in Weimar*. Oxford: Oxford University Press, 1997.

Ehrlich, Eugen. "Frei Rechtsfindung und freie Rechtswissenschaft." In *Frei Rechtsfindung und freie Rechtswissenschaft (Leipzig 1903) & Soziologie und Jurisprudenz (Czernowitz 1906) 2*, edited by Eugen Erhlich. Neudrucksausgabe in einem Band. Aalen: Scientia Verlag, 1987.

Ehrlich, Eugen. "Soziologie und Jurisprudenz." In *Frei Rechtsfindung und freie Rechtswissenschaft (Leipzig 1903) & Soziologie und Jurisprudenz (Czernowitz 1906) 2*, edited by Eugen Erhlich. Neudrucksausgabe in einem Band. Aalen: Scientia Verlag, 1987.

Ellscheid, Günter , and Winfried Hassemer, eds. *Interessenjurisprudenz*. Darmstadt: Wissenschaftliche Buchgesellschaft, 1974.

Finnis, John. *Natural Law and Natural Rights*. Oxford: Oxford University Press, 1988.

Finnis, John. "Natural Law: The Classical Tradition." In *The Oxford Handbook of Jurisprudence and Philosophy of Law*, edited by Jules Coleman, and Scott Shapiro, with Himma, Kenneth Einar, associate editor, pp. 1–60. Oxford: Oxford University Press, 2002.

Fish, Stanley. *Doing What Comes Naturally. Change, Rhetoric, and the Practice of Theory in Literary and Legal Studies*. Durham and London: Duke University Press, 1989.

Foucault, Michel. *Les Mots et les choses. Une Archéologie des sciences humaines*. Bibliothèque des sciences humaines. Paris: Éditions Gallimard, 1966.

Foucault, Michel. *L'Archéologie du savoir*. Bibliothèque des sciences humaines. Paris: Éditions Gallimard, 1969.

Foucault, Michel. *L'Ordre du discours. Leçon inaugurale au Collège de France prononcée le 2 décembre 1970*. Paris: Éditions Gallimard, 1971.

Foucault, Michel. *The Order of Things: An Archaeology of the Human Sciences*. London: Tavistock, 1974.

Frank, Jerome. *Law and the Modern Mind*. Gloucester, MA: Peter Smith, 1970.

Frege. "On Sense and Reference." In *Analytic Philosophy: An Anthology*, edited by A. P. Martinich, and David Sosa, pp. 7–18. Blackwell Philosophy Anthologies. Oxford: Blackwell, 2001.

Fuller, Lon L. "Positivism and Fidelity to Law – A Reply to Professor Hart." *Harvard Law Review* 71(1958): 630–72. Reprinted in: Finnis, John, ed. *Natural Law, Vol. II*. The International Library of Essays in Law and Legal Theory. Aldershot: Dartmouth, 1991, pp. 309–51.

Fuller, Lon L. *The Morality of Law*. Revised edition. New Haven, CT and London: Yale University Press, 1969.

Gallie, W. B. "Essentially Contested Concepts." *Proceedings of the Aristotelian Society* 56 (1955–1956): 167–98.

Geiger, Theodor. *Vorstudien zu einer Soziologie des Rechts*. København: Universitetsforlaget i Aarhus Ejnar Muksgaard, 1947.

Giudice, Michael, Wil Waluchow, and Maksymilian Del Mar. *The Methodology of Legal Theory. Vol. 1*. Aldershot and Burlington, VT: Ashgate, 2010.

Golding, Martin P. "Jurisprudence and Legal Philosophy in the Twentieth-Century America – Major Themes and Developments." *Journal of Legal Education* 36(1986): 441–80. Reprinted in: Golding, Martin P. *Legal Reasoning, Legal Theory and Rights*. Collected Essays in Law. Aldershot: Dartmouth; Burlington, VT: Ashgate, 2007, pp. 141–180.

Gray, John Chipman. *The Nature and Sources of the Law*. Second Edition, from the author's notes, by Ronald Gray. Gloucester, MA: Peter Smith, 1972. First Edition by Columbia University Press, 1909; New and Revised Edition in 1921 by The MacMillan Company.

Greimas, Algirdas Julien, and Joseph Courtés. *Sémiotique. Dictionnaire raisonné de la théorie du langage*. Paris: Hachette Supérieur, 1993.

Grey, Thomas C. "Langdell's Orthodoxy." *University of Pittsburgh Law Review* 45 (1983): 1–53.

Hallberg, Pekka. *The Rule of Law*. Helsinki: Edita Publishing, 2004.

Hallberg, Pekka. *Prospects of the Rule of Law*. Helsinki: Edita Publishing, 2005.

Hänninen, Sakari. *Aika, paikka, politiikka. Marxilaisen valtioteorian konstituutiosta ja metodista*. Oulu: Tutkijaliiton julkaisusarja 17, 1981.

Hart, H. L. A. *The Concept of Law*. Oxford: Clarendon Press, 1961.

Hart, H. L. A. *Essays in Jurisprudence and Philosophy*. Oxford: Clarendon Press, 1983.

Hart, H. L. A. "Lon L. Fuller: *The Morality of Law*." In *Essays in Jurisprudence and Philosophy*, edited by H. L. A. Hart, pp. 343–63. Oxford: Clarendon Press, 1983.

Hart, H. L. A. "Positivism and the Separation of Law from Morals." In *Essays in Jurisprudence and Philosophy*, edited by H. L. A. Hart, pp. 49–87. Oxford: Clarendon Press, 1983.

Hart, H. L. A. *The Concept of Law*. Second edition, with a Postscript by Hart, edited by Penelope A. Bulloch, and Joseph Raz. Oxford: Clarendon Press, 1994.

den Hartogh, Govert. *Mutual Expectations: A Conventionalist Theory of Law*. Law and Philosophy Library. The Hague: Kluwer Law International, 2002.

Heil, John. "Analytic Philosophy". In *The Cambridge Dictionary of Philosophy*, edited by Robert Audi, pp. 22–3. Cambridge: Cambridge University Press, 1995.

Helin, Markku. *Lainoppi ja metafysiikka. Tutkimus skandinaavisen oikeusrealismin tieteenkuvasta ja sen vaikutuksesta Suomen siviilioikeuden tutkimuksessa vuosina 1920–1960*. Helsinki: Suomalainen lakimiesyhdistys, 1988.

Himma, Kenneth Einar. "Inclusive Legal Positivism." In *The Oxford Handbook of Jurisprudence and Philosophy of Law*, edited by Jules Coleman, and Scott Shapiro, with Himma, Kenneth Einar, associate editor, pp. 125–65. Oxford: Oxford University Press, 2002.

Hohfeld, Wesley Newcomb. *Fundamental Legal Conceptions as Applied in Judicial Reasoning*. New Haven, CT and London: Yale University Press, 1964.

Holmes, Oliver Wendell, Jr. "The Path of the Law." *Harvard Law Review* 10(1897): 457–78. Reprinted in: Summers, Robert S., ed. *American Legal Theory*. The International Library of Essays in Law and Legal Theory. Aldershot: Dartmouth, 1992, pp. 3–24.

Horwitz, Morton J. "The Place of Justice Holmes in American Legal Thought." In *The Legacy of Oliver Wendell Holmes, Jr*, edited by Robert W. Gordon, pp. 31–71. Stanford, CA: Stanford University Press, 1992.

Horwitz, Morton, J. *The Transformation of American Law 1870–1960: The Crisis of Legal Orthodoxy*. New York, NY and Oxford: Oxford University Press, 1994.

Horwitz, Paul, ed. *Theories of Truth*. The International Research Library of Philosophy. Aldershot, Brookfield, EI: Dartmouth, 1994.

Huhn, Wilson. *Five Types of Legal Argument*. Second edition. Durham, NC: Carolina Academic Press, 2008.

Jakobson, Roman. "Linguistics and Poetics." Reprinted in: Thomas A. Sebeok, ed. *Style in Language*. Cambridge, MA: The MIT Press, 1960, pp. 350–77.

James, William. "Pragmatism's Conception of Truth." *The Journal of Philosophy Phychology and Scientific Methods* IV(6) (1907): 141–155. Reprinted in: Horwich, Paul, ed. *Theories of Truth*. Aldershot and Brookfield, WI: Dartmouth, 1994, pp. 17–31.

Jhering, Rudolf von. *Der Zweck im Recht, I*. Hildesheim, New York, NY: Georg Olms Verlag, 1970. Herausgegeben mit einem Vorwort und mit zwei bisher unveröffentlichen Ergänzungen aus dem Nachlass Jherings versehen von Christian Helfer. Reprografischer Nachdruck der 4. – Auflage Leipzig 1904.

Jonkka, Jaakko. "A Model for the Weighing and Balancing of Interest in the Prosecutor's Legal Discretion." *Scandinavian Studies in Law* 51 (2007): 229–62.

Kairys, David, ed. *The Politics of Law: A Progressive Critique*. Third edition. New York, NY: Basic Books, 1998.

Kalela, Jorma. *Historiantutkimus ja historia*. Helsinki: Hanki ja jää & Gaudeamus, 2000.

Kelsen, Hans. *Der Soziologische und der juristische Staatsbegriff. Kritische Untersuchung des Verhältnisses von Staat und Recht*. 2. Neudruck der 2. Auflage Tübingen 1928. Aalen: Scientia Verlag, 1981.

Kelsen, Hans. "Wer Soll der Hüter der Verfassung Sein?" *Die Justiz* 6. Band (1931): 5–56. Reprinted in: Hans Klecatsky, René Marci,ć and Herbert Schambeck, eds. *Die Wiener rechtstheoretische Schule. Ausgewählte Schriften von Hans Kelsen, Adolf Julius Merkl und Alfred Verdross*. Tome 2. Wien – Frankfurt – Zürich: Europa Verlag; Salzburg – München: Universitätsverlag Anton Pustet; 1968, pp. 1873–922.

Kelsen, Hans. *General Theory of Law and State*. Translated by Anders Wedberg. Cambridge, MA: Harvard University Press, 1949.

Kelsen, Hans. *Reine Rechtslehre. Mit einem Anhang: Das Problem der Gerechtigkeit*. Zweite, vollständig neu bearbeitete und erweiterte Auflage. Wien: Verlag Franz Deuticke, 1960.

Kelsen, Hans. *Pure Theory of Law*. Translation from the Second (Revised and Enlarged) German Edition by Max Knight. Gloucester, MA: Peter Smith, 1989.

Kelsen, Hans. *Allgemeine Staatslehre*. Wien: Österreichische Staatsdruckerei, 1993. First edition in 1925.

Kennedy, Duncan. "Freedom and Constraint in Adjudication: A Critical Phenomenology." *Journal of Legal Education* 36: 518–562. Reprinted in: Boyle, James, ed. *Critical Legal Studies*. The International Library of Essays in Law and Legal Theory. Aldershot: Dartmouth, 1992, pp. 45–89.

Kelsen, Hans. *Reine Rechtslehre. Einleitung in die rechtswissenschaftliche Problematik*. 1. Auflage. 2. Neudruck der 1. Auflage Leipzig und Wien 1934. Mit Vorwort zum Neudruck von Stanley L. Paulson und Vorrede zum 2. Neudruck von Robert Walter. Aalen: Scientia Verlag, 1994.

Kennedy, Duncan. *A Critique of Adjudication {fin de siècle}*. Cambridge, MA: Harvard University Press, 1997.

Klami, Hannu T. "Tapaoikeus." In *Encyclopædia Iuridica Fennica – Suomalainen oikeustietosanakirja, osa VII: Oikeuden yleistieteet*, edited by Heikki E. S. Mattila et al., pp. 1135–37. Jyväskylä: Suomalainen Lakimiesyhdistys, 1999.

Koskenniemi, Martti. *From Apology to Utopia: The Structure of International Legal Argument*. Helsinki: Lakimiesliiton Kustannus, 1989.

Koskenniemi, Martti. *The Gentle Civilizer of Nations. The Rise and Fall of International Law 1870–1960*. Cambridge: Cambridge University Press, 2002.

Koskenniemi, Martti. "Epilogue." *From Apology to Utopia: The Structure of International Legal Argument*. Reissue with New Epilogue. Cambridge: Cambridge University Press, 2005, pp. 562–617.

Kuhn, Thomas S. *The Structure of Scientific Revolutions*. Second edition, enlarged. International Encyclopedia of Unified Science. Chicago, IL: The University of Chicago Press, 1970.

Lacey, Nicola. *A Life of H. L. A. Hart: The Nightmare and the Noble Dream*. Oxford: Oxford University Press, 2004.

Lagerspetz, Eerik. *A Conventionalist Theory of Institutions*, Acta Philosophica Fennica. Helsinki: Societas Philosophica Fennica, 1989.

Lagerspetz, Eerik. *The Opposite Mirrors: An Essay on the Conventionalist Theory of Institutions*. Law and Philosophy Library. Dordrecht: Kluwer, 1995.

Larenz, Karl. *Methodenlehre der Rechtswissenschaft*. Sechste, neu bearbeitete Auflage. Heidelberg: Springer, 1991.

Lasser, Mitchel de S.-O.-L'E. *Judicial Deliberations: A Comparative Study of Judicial Transparency and Legitimacy*. Oxford: Oxford University Press, 2004.

Lasswell, Harold D., and Myres S. McDougal. *Jurisprudence for a Free Society: Studies in Law, Science and Policy, Vols I–II*. The Netherlands: Kluwer Law International and New Haven, CT: New Haven Press, 1992.

Levi, Edward H. *An Introduction to Legal Reasoning*. Chicago, IL and London: The University of Chicago Press, 1949.

Lewis, David. *Convention: A Philosophical Study*. Great Britain: Blackwell, 2002. First published by Harvard University Press in 1969.

Lind, Douglas. "Free Law Movement." In *The Philosophy of Law: An Encyclopedia, Vol. II*, edited by Christopher B. Gray, pp. 314–18. New York, NY and London: Garland Publishing, 1999.

Lind, Douglas. "Pragmatist Philosophy of Law". In *The Philosophy of Law. An Encyclopedia, Vol. II*, edited by Christopher B. Gray, pp. 678–81. New York and London: Garland Publishing, 1999.

Llewellyn, Karl. *The Bramble Bush. On Our Law and Its Study*. New York: Oceana Publications, Inc., 1991.

Luhmann, Niklas. *Das Recht der Gesellschaft*. Frankfurt am Main: Suhrkamp Verlag, 1993.

MacCormick, Neil. *Legal Reasoning and Legal Theory*. Oxford: Oxford University Press, 1978.

MacCormick, Neil. "Natural Law Reconsidered." *Oxford Journal of Legal Studies* 1(1981): 99–109. Reprinted in: Finnis, John, ed. *Natural Law, Vol. I*. The International Library of Essays in Law and Legal Theory. Aldershot: Dartmouth, 1991, pp. 225–235.

MacCormick, Neil. *Questioning Sovereignty. Law, State, and Nation in the European Commonwealth*. Oxford: Oxford University Press, 1999.

MacCormick, Neil. "Dworkin as Pre-Benthamite." In *Ronald Dworkin and Contemporary Jurisprudence*, edited by Marshall Cohen, Edited and with a Preface by Marshall Cohen, pp. 182–201. London: Duckworth, 2001. Original edition in 1984.

MacCormick, Neil. *Rhetoric and the Rule of Law: A Theory of Legal Reasoning*. Oxford: Oxford University Press, 2005.

MacCormick, Neil. *Institutions of Law: An Essay in Legal Theory*. Oxford: Oxford University Press, 2007.

MacCormick, Neil, and Robert S. Summers, eds. *Interpreting Statutes: A Comparative Study*. Aldershot: Dartmouth, 1991.

MacCormick, Neil, and Robert S. Summers. eds. *Interpreting Precedents: A Comparative Study*. Aldershot: Ashgate/Dartmout, 1997.

MacCormick, Neil, and Ota Weinberger. *An Institutional Theory of Law: New Approaches to Legal Positivism*. Law and Philosophy Library. Dordrecht: D. Reidel Publishing Company, 1986.

Makkonen, Kaarle. *Zur Problematik der juridischen Entscheidung. Eine strukturanalytische Studie*. Turku: Annales Universitatis Turkuensis, 1965.

Malcolm, Norman. *Ludwig Wittgenstein: A Memoir*. With a Biographical Sketch by Georg Henrik von Wright. Second Edition, with Wittgenstein's Letters to Malcolm. Oxford: Oxford University Press, 2001.

Manninen, Juha. "Uuden filosofisen liikkeen ja sen manifesti synty". In *Wienin piiri*, edited by Ilkka Niiniluoto and Heikki Koskinen, pp. 27–128. Helsinki: Gaudeamus, 2002.

Marmor, Andrei. "Exclusive Legal Positivism." In *The Oxford Handbook of Jurisprudence and Philosophy of Law*, edited by Jules Coleman, and Scott Shapiro, with Himma, Kenneth Einar, associate editor, pp. 104–24.Oxford: Oxford University Press, 2002.

Martinich, A. P., and David Sosa, eds. *Analytic Philosophy: An Anthology*. Blackwell Philosophy Anthologies. Oxford: Blackwell, 2001.

Mattei, Ugo. *Comparative Law and Economics*. U.S.A.: The University of Michigan Press, 1997.

Medina, Vincente. "Decisionist Philosophy of Law." In *The Philosophy of Law: An Encyclopedia, Vol. I*, edited by Christopher B. Gray, pp. 186–88. New York and London: Garland Publishing, 1999.

Mendell, Mark. "American Jurists, 1860–1960." In *The Philosophy of Law: An Encyclopedia, Vol. I*, edited by Christopher B. Gray, pp. 32–35. New York and London: Garland Publishing, 1999.

Merkl, Adolf Julius. "Das Recht im Lichte seiner Anwendung." In *Gesammelte Schriften. Erster Band. Grundlagen des Rechts*, edited by Adolf Julius Merkl, pp. 85–146. Erster Teilband. Herausgegeben von Mayer-Maly, Dorothea – Schambeck, Herbert and Grussman, Wolf-Dietrich. Berlin: Duncker and Humblot, 1993.

Merkl, Adolf Julius. "Das doppelte Rechtsanlitz. Eine Betrachtung aus der Erkenntnistheorie des Rechtes." In *Gesammelte Schriften. Erster Band. Grundlagen des Rechts*, edited by Adolf Julius Merkl, pp. 227–52. Erster Teilband. Herausgegeben von Mayer-Maly, Dorothea – Schambeck, Herbert and Grussman, Wolf-Dietrich. Berlin: Duncker and Humblot, 1993.

Merkl, Adolf Julius. *Gesammelte Schriften. Erster Band. Grundlagen des Rechts*. Erster Teilband. Herausgegeben von Mayer-Maly, Dorothea – Schambeck, Herbert and Grussman, Wolf-Dietrich. Berlin: Duncker and Humblot, 1993.

Merkl, Adolf Julius. "Prolegomena einer Theorie des rechtlichen Stufenbaues." In *Gesammelte Schriften. Erster Band. Grundlagen des Rechts*, edited by Adolf Julius Merkl, pp. 437–92. Erster Teilband. Herausgegeben von Mayer-Maly, Dorothea – Schambeck, Herbert and Grussman, Wolf-Dietrich. Berlin: Duncker and Humblot, 1993.

Miettinen, Seppo K. *Logiikka – Perusteet*. Helsinki: Gaudeamus, 2002.

Minkkinen, Panu. *Thinking without Desire: A First Philosophy of Law*. Oxford and Portland, OR: Hart Publishing, 1999.

Montesquieu, Baron de. *L'esprit des lois, Oeuvres Complètes, II*. Texte présenté et annoté par Roger Callois. Bibliothèque de Pléiade., pp. 227–995. Paris: Gallimard, 1951.

Moore, G. E. *Principia Ethica*. With the Preface to the Second Edition and Other Papers Edited and with an Introduction by Thomas Baldwin. Cambridge: Cambridge University Press, 1993.

Morawetz, Thomas. "Epistemology of Judging. Wittgenstein and Deliberative Practices." In *Wittgenstein and Legal Theory*, edited by Dennis M. Patterson, pp. 3–27. Boulder, CO, San Francisco, CA, Oxford: Westview Press, 1992.

Morawetz, Thomas. "Law as Experience: The Internal Aspect of Law." In *Law's Premises, Law's Promise. Jurisprudence after Wittgenstein*, edited by Thomas Morawetz, pp. 195–234, The Collected Essays in Law Series. Aldershot: Ashgate/Dartmouth, 2000.

Nagan, Winston P., and Andrew R. Willard. "Lasswell/McDougal Collaboration: Configurative Philosophy of Law." In *The Philosophy of Law: An Encyclopedia, Vol. II*, edited by Christopher B. Gray., pp. 481–83. New York, NY and London: Garland Publishing, 1999.

Nagel, Thomas. *The View from Nowhere*. New York and Oxford: Oxford University Press, 1986.

Neurath, Otto. "Protocol Sentences." *Logical Positivism*, edited by George Schick, and Ayer, A. J., pp. 199–208 New York: The Free Press, 1959. Originally published in III *Erkenntnis 1932/33*.

Niiniluoto, Ilkka. *Johdatus tieteenfilosofiaan. Käsitteen- ja teorianmuodostus*. Helsinki: Otava, 1984.

Niiniluoto, Ilkka. *Critical Scientific Realism*. Oxford: Oxford University Press, 1999.

Niiniluoto, Ilkka, and Koskinen, Heikki, eds. *Wienin piiri*. Helsinki: Gaudeamus, 2002.

O'Connor, D. J., ed. *A Critical History of Western Philosophy*. Hampshire and London: MacMillan Publishing, 1964.

Ogorek, Regina. *Richterkönig oder Subsumtionsautomat? Zur Justiztheorie im 19. Jahrhundert*. Frankfurt am Main: Vittorio Klostermann, 1986.

Pallard, Henri R., and Richard Hudson. "Phenomenology of Law." In *The Philosophy of Law: An Encyclopedia, Vol. II*, edited by Christopher B. Gray, s. 645–47. New York, NY and London: Garland Publishing, 1999.

Patrick, Glenn, H. "A Transnational Concept of Law." In *The Oxford Handbook of Legal Studies*, edited by Peter Cane, and Mark Tushnet, pp. 839–62. Oxford: Oxford University Press, 2003.

Pears, Davis. *The False Prison: A Study of the Development of Wittgenstein's Philosophy, Vols I–II*. Oxford: Clarendon Press, 1987.

Peczenik, Aleksander. *The Basis of Legal Justification*. Sverige: Lund, 1983.

Peczenik, Aleksander. *On Law and Reason*. Law and Philosophy Library. Dordrecht: Kluwer, 1989.

Peczenik, Aleksander. *Vad är rätt? Om demokrati, rättssäkerhet, etik och juridisk argumentation*. Stockholm: Fritzes Förlag AB, 1995.

Peczenik, Aleksander. "Coherence." In *The Philosophy of Law: An Encyclopedia, Vol. I*, edited by Christopher B. Gray, pp. 124–25. New York and London: Garland Publishing, 1999.

Peirce, Charles Sanders. *Pragmatism and Pragmaticism: Collected Papers of Charles Sanders Peirce, Vol. V*. Edited by Charles Hartshorne and Paul Weiss. Cambridge, MA: Harvard University Press, 1934.

Peirce, Charles Sanders. *Johdatus tieteen logiikkaan ja muita kirjoituksia*. Valinnut ja suomentanut Markus Lång. Tampere: Vastapaino, 2001.

Perelman, Chaïm. *The Realm of Rhetoric*. Notre Dame, IN and London: University of Notre Dame Press, 1982. Original edition in French, William Kluback, trans., *L'Empire rhétorique: rhétorique et argumentation*. Introduction by Carroll C. Arnold.

Perelman, Chaïm. *Rhétoriques*. Bruxelles: Éditions de l'Université de Bruxelles, 1989.

Perelman, Chaïm. "Une théorie philosophique de l'argumentation." In *Rhétoriques*, edited by Chaïm Perelman, pp. 243–56. Bruxelles: Éditions de l'Université de Bruxelles, 1989.

Perelman, Chaïm , and Lucie Olbrechts-Tyteca. *Traité de l'Argumentation. La nouvelle Rhétorique*. Paris: Presses universitaires de France, 1958. 5e édition. Bruxelles: Éditions de l'Université de Bruxelles, 1988.

Pihlström, Sami. *Tutkiiko tiede todellisuutta? Realismi ja pragmatismi nykyisessä tieteenfilosofiassa*. Helsinki: Helsingin yliopiston filosofian laitoksen julkaisuja, 1997.

Pintore, Anna. *Law Without Truth*. United Kingdom: Deborah Charles Publications, 2000.

Popper, Karl. *Objective Knowledge: An Evolutionary Approach*. Revised edition. Oxford: Oxford University Press, 1979.

Posner, Richard A., ed. *The Essential Holmes: Selections from the Letters, Speeches, Judicial Opinions, and Other Writings of Oliver Wendell Holmes, Jr*. Edited and with an Introduction by Richard A. Posner. Chicago, IL: The University of Chicago Press, 1992.

Posner, Richard A. *Economic Analysis of Law*, 6th edition. New York: Aspen Publishers, 2003.

Pound, Roscoe. "Law in Books and Law in Action." *American Law Review* 44 (1910): 12–36.

Pound, Roscoe. *Social Control Through Law*. With a New Introduction by A. Javier Trevino. New Brunswick, NJ and London: Transaction Publishers, Second Printing, 2002.

Pöyhönen, Juha. *Sopimusoikeuden järjestelmä ja sopimusten sovittelu*. Helsinki: Suomalaisen lakimiesyhdistyksen julkaisuja, 1988.

Quine, Willard Van Orman. "Two Dogmas of Empiricism." In *From a Logical Point of View: Nine Logico-Philosophical Essays*. Second edition, edited by Willard Van Orman Quine, pp. 20–46. Cambridge, MA and London, England: Harvard University Press, Reprinted in: Curd, Martin and A.J. Cover. *Philosophy of Science: The Central Issues*. New York and London: W.W. Norton & Company, 1998, pp. 280–301. Revised, with a New Foreword by the Author, 14th Printing.

Quinton, A. M. "Contemporary British Philosophy. In *A Critical History of Western Philosophy*, edited by D. J. O'Connor (pp. 530–55). Hampshire and London: MacMillan Publishing, 1964.

Radbruch, Gustav. "Fünf Minuten Rechtsphilosophie." In *Rechtsphilosophie*, edited by Gustav Radbruch, 327–29. Stuttgart: K.F. Koehler Verlag, 1945, 1973Achte Auflage. Herausgegeben von Erik Wolf und Hans-Petter Schneider

Radbruch, Gustav. "Gesetzliches Unrecht und übergesetzliches Recht" (1946). In *Rechtsphilosophie*, edited by Gustav Radbruch, pp. 339–50, Achte Auflage. Herausgegeben von Erik Wolf und Hans-Petter Schneider. Stuttgart: K.F. Koehler Verlag, 1973.

Radbruch, Gustav. *Rechtsphilosophie*. Achte Auflage. Herausgegeben von Erik Wolf und Hans-Petter Schneider. Stuttgart: K.F. Koehler Verlag, 1973.

Raunio, Kyösti. *Positivismi ja ihmistiede. Sosiaalitutkimuksen perustat ja käytännöt.* Helsinki: Gaudeamus, 1999.

Rawls, John. *A Theory of Justice*. Oxford: Oxford University Press, 1980.

Rawls, John. *Collected Papers*. Edited by Samuel Freeman. Cambridge, MA, and London: Harvard University Press, 1999.

Rawls, John. "Two Concepts of Rules." Reprinted in: Rawls, John. *Collected Papers*, edited by Samuel Freeman, pp. 20–46. Cambridge, MA and London: Harvard University Press, 1999. Originally published in: LXIV *The Philosophical Review*, 1955, pp. 2–32.

Reimann, Mathias W. "Holmes's *Common Law* and German Legal Science." In *The Legacy of Oliver Wendell Holmes, Jr*, edited by Robert W. Gordon, pp. 72–114. Stanford, CA: Stanford University Press, 1992.

Reimann, Mathias. 1999. "Savigny, Friedrich Carl von (1779–1861)." In *The Philosophy of Law: An Encyclopedia, Vols. II*, edited by Christopher B. Gray, pp. 772–73. New York and London: Garland Publishing.

Rentto, Juha-Pekka. *Prudentia Juris: The Art of the Good and the Just*. Turku: Turun yliopiston julkaisuja, 1988.

Rescher, Nicholas. "Pragmatism". In *The Oxford Companion to Philosophy*, edited by Ted Honderich, pp. 710–13. Oxford: Oxford University Press, 1995.

Reynolds, Noel B., and Thomas J. Lowery. "Convention and Custom." In *The Philosophy of Law: An Encyclopedia, Vol. I*, edited by Christopher B. Gray, pp. 161–63. New York, NY and London: Garland Publishing, 1999.

Rorty, Richard. *Consequences of Pragmatism. (Essays: 1972–1980)*. Brighton, Sussex: The Harvester Press, 1982.

Ross, Alf. *On Law and Justice*. Berkeley, CA: University of California Press, 1958.

Ross, Alf. *Theorie der Rechtsquellen. Ein Beitrag zur Theorie des Positiven Rechts auf Grundlage dogmenhistorischer Untersuchungen*. Neudruch der Ausgabe Leipzig und Wien, 1929. Aalen: Scientia Verlag, 1989.

Ross, Alf. *Towards a Realistic Jurisprudence: A Criticism of the Dualism in Law*. Translated from the Danish by Annie I. Fausbøll. Reprint of the Edition Copenhagen, 1946. Aalen: Scientia Verlag, 1989.

Ross, Alf. *Om ret og retfærdighed. En indførelse i den analytiske retsfilosofi*. København: Nyt nordisk forslag, 1953.

Ross, Alf. "Validity and the Conflict between Positivism and Natural Law". In *Normativity and Norms. Critical Perspectives on Kelsenian Themes*, edited by Stanley L. Paulson, and Bonnie Litschewski Paulson, pp. 147–63. Oxford: Clarendon Press, 1998.

Ruiter, Dick W. P. *Legal Institutions*. Law and Philosophy Library. Dordrecht: Kluwer, 2001.

Ryle, Gilbert. *The Concept of Mind*. Middlesex: Penguin/Peregrine Books, 1963.

Salmon, Wesley C. "Logical Empiricism". In *A Companion to the Philosophy of Science*, edited by W. H. Newton-Smith, pp. 233–42. Oxford: Blackwell Publishers Ltd., 2000.

Sampaio Ferraz, Tercio. "Topique". In *Dictionnaire encyclopédique de théorie et de sociologie du droit*, Deuxième edition entièrement refondue, corrigée et augmentée sous la direction de André-Jean Arnaud et de, J.-G. Belley, J. A. Carty, M. Chiba, J. Commaille, A. Devillé, E. Landowski, F. Ost, J.-F. Perrin, M. van de Kerchove, and J. Wróblewski, pp. 615–17. Paris: LDGJ, 1993.

Savigny, Friedrich Carl von. "Vom Beruf unserer Zeit für Gesetzgebung und Rechtswissenschaft." In *Thibaut und Savigny. Ihre Programmatische Schriften*, pp. 95–192. Herausgegeben und Mit einer Einführung von Prof. Dr. Hans Hattenhauer. München: Verlag Franz Vahlen, 1973.

Scheffler, Israel. *Four Pragmatists. A Critical Introduction to Peirce, James, Mead, and Dewey*. London: Routledge and Kegan Paul and New York: Humanities Press, 1974.

Schlegel, John Henry. *American Legal Realism and Empirical Social Science*. Chapel Hill, NC and London: University of North Carolina Press, 1995.

Schmitt, Carl. *Political Theology: Four Chapters on the Concept of Sovereignty*. Translated by George Schwab. Cambridge, MA and London: The MIT Press, 1985.

Schmitt, Carl. *Über die drei Arten des rechtswissenschaftlichen Denkens*. Zweite Auflage Unveränd. Ausg. Der 1934 in der Hanseatischen Verl.-Anst, Hamburg erschienenen 1. Auflage. Berlin: Duncker and Humblot, 1993.

Schmitt, Carl. *Der Hüter der Verfassung*. Berlin: Duncker and Humblot; 4. Auflage, 1996.

Searle, John R. *Speech Acts: An Essay in the Philosophy of Language*. New York, NY: Cambridge University Press, 1992.

Searle, John R. *The Construction of Social Reality*. England: The Penguin Press, 1995.

Searle, John R. *Making the Social World: The Structure of Human Civilization*. Oxford: Oxford University Press, 2010.

Siltala, Raimo. *A Theory of Precedent: From Analytical Positivism to a Post-Analytical Philosophy of Law*. Oxford and Portland, OR: Hart Publishing, 2000.

Siltala, Raimo. *Oikeustieteen tieteenteoria*. Helsinki: Suomalainen lakimiesyhdistys, 2003.

Smith, C. S. "The Redundancy of Reasoning". In *Informatics and the Foudantions of Legal Reasoning*, edited by Zenon Bankowski, and Ian White, and Ulrike Hahn, pp. 191–204. Dordrecht: Kluwer, 1995.

Soames, Scott. *Philosophical Analysis in the Twentieth Century, 1: The Dawn of Analysis*. Princeton, NJ and Oxford: Princeton University Press, 2005.

Soames, Scott. *Philosophical Analysis in the Twentieth Century, 2: The Age of Meaning*. Princeton, NJ and Oxford: Princeton University Press, 2005.

Spaak, Torben. *Guidance and Constraint: The Action-Guiding Capacity of Theories of Legal Reasoning*. Uppsala: Iustus Förlag, 2007.

Stenius, Erik. *Wittgenstein's Tractatus: A Critical Exposition of the Main Lines of Thought*. England: Thoemmes Press, 1996. First edition: Basil Blackwell, 1960.

Summers, Robert S. "Two Types of Substantive Reasons: The Core of a Theory of Common-Law Justification." *Cornell Law Review* 63(1978): 707–88. Reprinted in: Summers, Robert S. *The Jurisprudence of Law's Form and Substance*. Aldershot: Ashgate/Dartmout, 2000, pp. 155–236.

Summers, Robert S. *Instrumentalism and American Legal Theory*. Ithaca, NY and London: Cornell University Press, 1982.

Summers, Robert S. "Theory, Formality and Practical Legal Criticism." *Law Quarterly Review* 106 (1990): 407 et seq. Reprinted in Summers, Robert S. *Essays on the Nature of Law and Legal Reasoning*. Berlin: Duncker and Humblot, Schriften zur Rechtstheorie, Heft 151, 1992, pp. 154–76.

Summers, Robert S., ed. *American Legal Theory*. The International Library of Essays in Law and Legal Theory. Aldershot: Dartmouth, 1992.

Summers, Robert S. *Essays on the Nature of Law and Legal Reasoning*. Berlin: Duncker and Humblot, Schriften zur Rechtstheorie, Heft 151, 1992.

Summers, Robert S. "Form and Substance in Legal Reasoning." In *Essays on the Nature of Law and Legal Reasoning*, edited by Robert S. Summers, pp. 138–53. Berlin: Duncker and Humblot, Schriften zur Rechtstheorie, Heft 151, 1992.

Summers, Robert S. "The Formal Character of Law." *Cambridge Law Journal* 51 (1992): 242–62.

Summers, Robert S. "How Law is Formal and Why it Matters." *Cornell Law Review* 82(1997): 1165–229. Reprinted in Summers, Robert S. *The Jurisprudence of Law's Form and Substance*. The Collected Essays in Law Series. Aldershot: Ashgate/Dartmouth, 2000.

Summers, Robert S. *The Jurisprudence of Law's Form and Substance*. The Collected Essays in Law Series. Aldershot: Ashgate/Dartmouth, 2000.

Tamanaha, Brian Z. *Realistic Socio-Legal Theory: Pragmatism and a Social Theory of Law*. Oxford: Oxford University Press, 1997.

Tamanaha, Brian Z. *A General Jurisprudence of Law and Society*. Oxford: Oxford University Press, 2001.

Tamanaha, Brian Z. *Law as a Means to an End: Threat to the Rule of Law*. New York, NY: Cambridge University Press, 2006.

Tamanaha, Brian Z. *Beyond the Formalist-Realist Divide: The Role of Politics in Judging*. Princeton, NJ: Princeton University Press, 2010.

Tarski, Alfred. "The Concept of Truth in Formalized Languages." In *Logic, Semantics, Metamathematics: Papers from 1923 to 1938*, edited by Alfred Tarski, pp. 152–78. Translated by J. H. Woodger. Second edition, edited and introduced by John Corcoran. Indianapolis, IN: Hackett Hackett, 1983.

Taruffo, Michele, and Massimo La Torre. "Precedent in Italy." In *Interpreting Precedents: A Comparative Study*, edited by Neil MacCormick, and , Robert S. Summers, pp. 141–88. Aldershot: Ashgate/Dartmout, 1997.

Teubner, Gunther. "How the Law Thinks: Towards a Constructivist Epistemology in Law." *Law and Society Review* 23 (1989): 727–57.

Teubner, Gunther. *Law as an Autopoietic System*. Translated by Anne Bankowska and Ruth Adler. Edited by Zenon Bankowski. Oxford: Blackwell, 1993.

Thibaut, Anton Friedrich Justus. "Über die Nothwendigkeit eines allgemeinen Bürgerlichen Rechts für Deutschland." In *Thibaut und Savigny. Ihre Programmatische Schriften*, pp. 61–94. Herausgegeben und Mit einer Einführung von Prof. Dr. Hans Hattenhauer. München: Verlag Franz Vahlen, 1973.

Thibaut, Anton Friedrich Justus, and Friedrich Carl von Savigny. *Thibaut und Savigny. Ihre Programmatische Schriften*. Mit einer Einführung von Prof. Dr. Hans Hattenhauer. München: Verlag Franz Vahlen, 1973.

Tuomela, Raimo. "Collective Acceptance, Social Institutions, and Social Reality". *The American Journal of Economics and Sociology* 62(1) (2003 January): pp. 123–65.

Tuomela, Raimo. *The Philosophy of Social Practices: A Collective Acceptance View*. New York, NY: Cambridge University Press, 2002.

Tuomela, Raimo. *The Philosophy of Sociality: The Shared Point of View*. Oxford: Oxford University Press, 2007.

Tuomela, Raimo. "Collective Intentionality and Social Agents." Paper presented in the AI conference *IMF*, Toulouse, May 21–23, 2001; Accessed February 2, 2011. http://www.valt.helsinki.fi/staff/tuomela/papers/toulouse.htm

Tuori, Kaarlo. "Carl Schmitt ja vastavallankumouksen teoria." In *Poliittinen teologia. Neljä lukua suvereenisuusopista*, edited by Carl Schmitt, pp. 7–24. Suomentanut Tapani Hietaniemi. Esipuheet: Kaarlo Tuori, Markku Koivusalo ja Mika Ojutkangas. Paradeigma-sarja. Helsinki: Tutkijaliitto, 1997.

Tuori, Kaarlo. *Critical Legal Positivism*. Aldershot: Ashgate, 2002.

Unger, Robeto Mangabeira. *The Critical Legal Studies Movement*. Cambridge, MA and London: Harvard University Press, 1983.

Unger, Robeto Mangabeira. *False Necessity: Anti-Necessitarian Social Theory in the Service of Radical Democracy. Part I of Politics: A Work in Constructive Social Theory*. Cambridge: Cambridge University Press, 1987.

Waismann, Friedrich. *The Principles of Linguistic Philosophy*. Second Edition. Edited by Rom Harré. Preface by Gordon Baker. Basingstoke: MacMillan, 1997.

Walker, Ralph C. S. *The Coherence Theory of Truth: Realism, Anti-Realism, Idealism*. London and New York, NY: Routledge, 1989.

Walker, Ralph C. S. "Theories of Truth." In *A Companion to the Philosophy of Language*, edited by Bob Hale, and Crispin Wright, pp. 309–30. Blackwell Companions to Language. Oxford: Blackwell, 1999.

Weber, Max. *Wirtschaft und Gesellschaft*. Tübingen: J.C.B. Mohr, 1972.

Weber, Max Weber. *Economy and Society: An Outline of Interpretive Sociology*. Edited by Guenther Roth and Claus Wittich. Berkeley, CA: University of California Press, 1978.

Wieacker, Franz. *Privatrechtsgeschichte der Neuzeit, unter besonderer Berücksichtigung der deutschen Entwicklung.2*. neuarbeitete Auflage. Göttingen: Vandenhoeck and Ruprecht, 1967.

Wihuri, Antti-Juhani. "Auditorion käsitteestä ja auditoriosidonnaisesta argumentaatiosta." *Oikeustiede – Jurisprudentia* XXIII (1990): 339–403.

Wilhelmsson, Thomas. *Social civilrätt*. Helsinki: Lakimiesliiton kustannus, 1987.

Wilhelmsson, Thomas. "Sosiaalinen siviilioikeus." In *Encyclopædia Iuridica Fennica. Suomalainen oikeustietosanakirja, I: Varallisuus- ja yritysoikeus*, edited by Heikki E. S. Mattila et al., pp. 782–85. Helsinki: Suomalainen lakimiesyhdistys, 1994, with two-column lay-out.

Wilhelmsson, Thomas. "Sosiaalinen suorituseste." In *Encyclopædia Iuridica Fennica. Suomalainen oikeustietosanakirja, I: Varallisuus- ja yritysoikeus*, edited by Heikki E. S. Mattila et al., pp. 785–87. Helsinki: Suomalainen lakimiesyhdistys, 1994, with two-column lay-out.

Wilhelmsson, Thomas. *Social Contract Law and European Integration*. Aldershot: Dartmouth, 1995.

Wilhelmsson, Thomas. "Theory of European Community Law." In *Law and Diffuse Interests in the European Legal Order – Recht und diffuse Intressen in der Europäischen Rechtsordnung. Liber amicorum Norbert Reich*, edited by Ludwig Krämer, Hans-W. Micklitz, and Klaus Tonner, pp. 177–93. Baden-Baden: Nomos Verlagsgesellschaft, 1997.

Wilhelmsson, Thomas. *Senmodern ansvarsrätt. Privaträtt som redskap för mikropolitik*. Helsinki: Lakimiesliiton kustannus, 2001.

Wilhelmsson, Thomas. "The Ethical Pluralism of Late Modern Europe and Codification of European Contract Law." In *The Need for a European Contract Law: Empirical and Legal Perspectives*, edited by Jan Smits, pp. 121–52. Groningen: Europa Law Publishing, 2005.

Wittgenstein, Ludwig. *The Blue and Brown Books: Preliminary Studies for the 'Philosophical Investigations'*. London: Basil Blackwell; New York, NY: Harper & Row, 1958.

Wittgenstein, Ludwig. *ÜberGewissheit – On Certainty*. Edited by G. E. M. Anscombe and G. H. von Wright. Translated by Denis Paul and G. E. M. Anscombe. Oxford: Basil Blackwell, 1969.

Wittgenstein, Ludwig. *Notebooks 1914–1916*. Second edition. Edited by G. H. von Wright and G. E. M. Anscombe, with an English translation by G. E. M. Anscombe. Index prepared by E. D. Klemke. Oxford: Basil Blackwell, 1961, 1979; Chicago, IL: The University of Chicago Press, 1984.

Wittgenstein, Ludwig. *Tractatus Logico-Philosophicus*. London and New York: Routledge & Kegan Paul, 1986. First edition in 1922. Translated by C. K. Ogden, with an Introduction by Bertrand Russell. International Library of Psychology, Philosophy and Scientific Method.

Wittgenstein, Ludwig. *Philosophical Investigations – Philosophische Untersuchungen*. Zweite Auflage/Second Edition. Translated by G. E. M. Anscombe. Oxford and Malden, MA: Blackwell, 1997.

Wood, David, and Robert Bernasconi, eds. *Derrida and Différance*. Evanston, IL: Northwestern University Press, 1988.

Wright, Georg Henrik von. *The Varieties of Goodness*. London and Henley: Routledge and Kegan Paul, 1963.

Wright, Georg Henrik von. *Explanation and Understanding*. International Library of Philosophy and Scientific Method. Lontoo: Routledge and Kegan Paul, 1971.

Wright, Georg Henrik von. "A Biographical Sketch." In *Ludwig Wittgenstein: A Memoir*, With a Biographical Sketch by Georg Henrik von Wright. Second Edition, with Wittgenstein's Letters to Malcolm, edited by Norman Malcolm, pp. 3–20. Oxford: Oxford University Press, 2001.

Wróblewski, Jerzy. *Contemporary Models of the Legal Sciences*. Łodź: Polish Academy of Sciences, 1989.

Wróblewski, Jerzy. *The Judicial Application of Law*. Law and Philosophy Library. Dordrecht: Kluwer, 1992.

Name Index

Subject Index

Note: The letter 'n' following the locators refer to notes cited in the text.